包容·健康·负责任

INCLUSIVE · HEALTHY · RESPONSIBLE FINANCE

中国普惠金融发展报告（2019）

THE REPORT OF FINANCIAL INCLUSION DEVELOPMENT IN CHINA (2019)

主　　编　贝多广
执行主编　莫秀根

责任编辑：贾　真
责任校对：张志文
责任印制：程　颖

图书在版编目（CIP）数据

包容·健康·负责任：中国普惠金融发展报告．2019/贝多广主编．—北京：中国金融出版社，2019.10

ISBN 978—7—5220—0274—3

Ⅰ.①包…　Ⅱ.①贝…　Ⅲ.①金融事业—研究报告—中国—2019　Ⅳ.①F832

中国版本图书馆 CIP 数据核字（2019）第 196661 号

包容·健康·负责任：中国普惠金融发展报告．2019
Baorong·Jiankang·Fuzeren：Zhongguo Puhui Jinrong Fazhan Baogao. 2019
出版发行　中国金融出版社
社址　北京市丰台区益泽路 2 号
市场开发部　(010)63266347，63805472，63439533（传真）
网 上 书 店　http：//www.chinafph.com
　　(010)63286832，63365686（传真）
读者服务部　(010)66070833，62568380
邮编　100071
经销　新华书店
印刷　北京侨友印刷有限公司
尺寸　185 毫米×260 毫米
印张　17.5
字数　340 千
版次　2019 年 10 月第 1 版
印次　2019 年 10 月第 1 次印刷
定价　148.00 元
ISBN 978—7—5220—0274—3
如出现印装错误本社负责调换　联系电话（010）63263947

2019 中国普惠金融国际论坛
中国·北京

发　布

主　　编：贝多广
执行主编：莫秀根

课题主要成员（按姓氏首字母拼音顺序排列）：
贝多广　邓　鹏　顾　雷　黄媚媚
赖丹妮　刘　琰　陆俊宇　莫秀根
王　硕　汪雯羽　张晓峰　张亦辰

课题参与人员（按姓氏首字母拼音顺序排列）：
陈兆东　林　好　刘澄清　鲁　梅
孙　毅　吴敬茨　吴跃华　朱　琦

鸣　　谢

资助单位及机构：

Visa 公司

民生银行

宜信普惠

平安普惠

浙江省农村信用社联合社

前言

近几年流行一句话“重要的事情说三遍”。在普惠金融中重要的事情是什么?

包容，包容，包容。

普惠金融就是包容性金融。它的宗旨就是将传统金融体系排斥的或服务不够的企业和人群都包容进来，为它们提供金融服务，最终形成一个包容性的普惠金融生态体系。

哪些企业和人群被传统金融体系排斥或服务不够?众所周知，就是中小微企业和弱势人群（以下简称“中小微弱”）。传统金融体系之所以排斥或服务不够是有许多原因的，如信息缺失、成本高昂及“中小微弱”金融素养匮乏等。当金融体系，包括传统金融机构和新型金融服务机构，开始覆盖“中小微弱”这部分客户时，原有的问题依然存在，同时，又出现诸多新的问题。一段时间实践下来，让人感到一地鸡毛。

拨云开雾，我们透过现象看到普惠金融与传统金融最大的不同之处在于：第一，服务对象有很大不同，“中小微弱”具有自身的特征，他们的行为在很大程度上取决于他们对金融健康的认知。第二，正因为这批客户的特殊性，包容性金融，即普惠金融要求服务机构相应调整自己的服务方式，要以一种负责任金融的心态提供服务，其中的核心就是要高度重视客户保护。

讲到金融健康，这是一个颇新的概念。我们把它解读为：消费者个人发挥其金融知识、利用金融工具、采取合理金融行为，以达到的个人财务状态。

我们都知道，人的身体有健康、亚健康和不健康等状况，财务状况也同样如此。国际上将健康概念引入金融领域，用来描述消费者获得金融服务后所引发的财务状况。这里包含消费者对金融常识的认识和掌握，涉及金融教育和金融素养的提高。根据我们在农村开展的调研，农村居民通常在这些指标上得分偏低，这也是农村金融难以开展、农民不太愿意接受信贷和保险服务的一个重要原因。当使用金融产品和金融服务时，消费者如何才能既充分获得金融服务的利益，又能防范金融服务中可能存在的风险，都是可以用金融健康的概念去考察的。至于个人因金融服务而形成的财务状况，更是每个消费者都应该心知肚明的基本信息，就像人们应该知道自己的血压、血脂、血糖指标一样。我们知道一个人大量食用垃圾食品会导致血脂高、血糖高等后果，在金融服务中，消费者过度配置风险资产或过度负债都属于不健康的行为，会带来负面的经济后果。

金融健康是从金融消费者角度观察问题，而“负责任金融”这个概念主要从金融服务供应方角度观察。因为普惠金融服务供应商面对的是金融素养尚待提高的人群，供应商应该怀抱负责任的态度，以客户保护作为基本服务准则，以客户为中心来设计产品、营销产品并提供售后服务，以确保普惠金融业务实现商业价值和社会价值的双重目标。

客户保护是普惠金融事业中一项非常重要的内容。正如二十多年前当我们开始建设中国资本市场的时候，我们知道，如果没有对投资者的保护机制，资本市场将成为割韭菜的场地。可以说，投资者保护机制是资本市场的必要条件。同样，在建设普惠金融的新时代里，客户保护也是推进普惠金融的必要条件。没有有效的客户保护机制，就不会有健康的普惠金融。监管部门格外重视金融消费者保护，就像资本市场特别重视投资者保护一样。在资本市场中有分类合格投资者的制度安排，强调信息披露透明、公开、公正、公平。当务之急是要回答，在普惠金融体系中应强调什么？

有一些学术研究表明，收入越低的人越容易冒险，存在金融不健康倾向。当服务于这些人群时，服务机构更应以负责任的态度来提供服务。这应当是包容性金融的特征之一。

此外，普惠金融建设中还有一个重要议题是，如何引导社会资金关注普惠金融？只有社会资金主动进入作为中介机构的普惠金融服务机构，普惠金融才可能持续、有效地成长和壮大。这里我们要考虑资本市场的作用，证券化无疑是一条很好的途径，建立金融机构间的小额贷款二级市场也是一条可以探索的途径，市场上已经有一些这方面的实践，政策上亟须鼓励和支持。

我们在过去几年的实践中深刻认识到，普惠金融绝不仅仅是向“中小微弱”提供信贷或其他各类金融服务。解决“融资难、融资贵”问题只是建设普惠金融生态体系的结果，从长远价值来说，建设这样一个生态体系、确立这样一个目标更为重要。就像人得了糖尿病，只是一味地吃降糖药而不改变生活方式，如不调整饮食、不加强运动，吃药也只是治标不治本。在国家推进普惠金融发展的进程中，建设普惠金融生态体系才是至高的目标。

普惠金融的本质是全面提高“中小微弱”的生存能力、发展能力，甚至是创新能力。从这个意义上讲，在建设普惠金融的进程中，我们特别强调金融教育、金融素养及金融能力。每一家普惠金融服务供应商在提供金融服务产品的同时还应具备客户赋能的功能。大家都知道“授之以鱼”和“授之以渔”的区别，这也是负责任金融的要义所在。

过去几年的普惠金融实践给了我们很多启示。其中有一点对我们来说印象深刻，就是普惠金融的规范发展，不仅仅依赖监管部门的监管和法律法规的完善，更依赖整个行业的自律和合规。作为普惠金融的吹鼓手和观察者，我们更期待市场的实践者能够真正自律，以客户为中心，并且负责任地开展各项业务。一个社会的和谐发展取决于法治和道德的完美结合，同样，在推进普惠金融的进程中，监管和自律的紧密结合也是整个行业健康发展的基本要求。

国家颁布《推进普惠金融发展规划（2016—2020 年）》已进入第四个年头，作为这一进程的观察者，我们可以看到不少经验和教训。其中一项重要的体会是，普惠金融确实是说易行难的事业。换而言之，每往前推进一步，都会出现一些新的问题。比如，在鼓励以数据分析为基础的金融科技时，发现隐私保护问题变得十分突出，甚至数字化本身还带来数字鸿沟问题。由此可见，普惠金融事业可能不是一蹴而就、毕其功于一役的事情，而是一项需要耐力、具有技术含量、更加依赖市场机制的事业。中国花了近二十年才建立起现代银行体系，差不多也花了二十年建立起资本市场体系，目前这个金融体系仍然是初步的和需要不断完善的。由此推断，在中国建立普惠金融生态体系至少还需要二十年的历程。从这一意义上来说，这是一项任重而道远的目标。

如果把建立现代银行体系和建立资本市场视作中国金融发展进程中的前两个阶段，目前中国已经正式迈入了金融发展的第三阶段，即建立普惠金融生态体系的阶段。从眼下无数论坛讨论的热点就可以看出，普惠金融已经成为最热点，就像二十多年前，大小论坛都在讨论资本市场一样。在这样如火如荼的热闹之中，作为学者当然要冷静和清醒。好在我们有过去将近四十年金融发展的经验和教训，这次应该会比较成熟。

中国普惠金融研究院也进入第五个年头。可喜地看到，我们的影响力正在行业、监管、社会及国际上逐步扩大。2019 年的绿皮书完全由我们自己的研究团队独立完成，而且质量也有明显提高，这是我们成长过程中一个小小的却值得庆贺的里程碑。在此，要向主持这项工作的莫秀根博士及他所率领的团队全体同仁表示由衷的敬佩。藉此机会，也向长期支持我们的战略合作伙伴、资助本年度绿皮书项目的合作伙伴及其他合作伙伴表示衷心的感谢。

贝多广

2019 年 7 月 20 日

于北京宣武门

Preface

In recent years, there has been a popular stating that "Important Thing Needs to be Said Thrice." What is that important thing in inclusive finance?

It is right there in the name: Inclusion, Inclusion, Inclusion.

It is important to emphasize that inclusive finance needs to live up to its name. Its purpose is to include the enterprises and people who have been excluded from the traditional financial system. Eventually, through providing financial services to them, it will form an inclusive finance ecosystem.

Which enterprises and people have been excluded or inadequately served by the traditional financial system? As we know, they are the micro, small and medium-sized enterprises (MSMEs) and disadvantaged individuals. There are many reasons for the exclusion or lack of services in the traditional financial system, such as information asymmetry, high cost, and lack of financial literacy, etc.. When the financial system, including traditional financial institutions and new financial service providers, began to include those previously excluded, many old and new problems started to appear, hampering the effectiveness of financial inclusion and leading to more confusion.

At the core, there are two major differences between inclusive finance and traditional finance. The first difference lies in the target audiences. As main the target audience for inclusive finance, MSMEs and the disadvantaged individuals have unique characteristics and their behaviors depend largely on their perceptions of financial health. The second difference lies in the service models of financial institutions. Due to the unique characteristics of these customers, financial inclusion requires financial service providers to adjust their service methods accordingly. It is necessary to provide financial services in a responsible manner with a focus on customer protection.

Financial health is a relatively new concept. We interpret it as the personal financial status of consumers based on their level of financial literacy, their use of financial tools, and as a result of their financial actions.

Just like people's health status can be classified as healthy, sub-healthy, and sick, so is their financial status. The concept of health has been introduced into the financial sector internationally to describe the financial situation as a result of consumers' access to financial services. This includes consumers' understanding and mastery of financial knowledges, and it involves financial education and financial literacy. According to our research conducted in rural areas, rural residents usually score low on the financial health indicators, which is also an important reason why rural finance is difficult to be carried out and farmers are less willing to accept credit and insurance services. The concept of Financial health can guide consumers to enjoy financial services while avoiding potential risks. People should regularly observe and monitor their financial health status caused by their use of financial services, just like monitoring their health conditions. We know that consuming a large amount of junk food could lead to high blood pressure and high blood sugar level. In financial services, over-allocation of risky assets or excessive debt by consumers is also unhealthy and has negative economic consequences.

Financial health is a concept from the perspective of financial consumers while the concept of responsible finance is mainly viewed from the perspective of financial service providers. Since inclusive financial service providers serve people with low financial literacy levels, they should adopt a responsible attitude, take customer protection as the fundamental principle, and provide services with a customer-centric design. This will ensure that the inclusive financial business achieves the double bottom-lines of commercial value and social value.

Customer protection is a very important part of inclusive finance. Just like the development of China's capital market since over 20 years ago when investor protection mechanism prevented retail investors from losing large amount of money caused by market manipulation. It could be said that an investor protection mechanism is a necessity for the capital market. Similarly, in this new era of inclusive finance, customer protection is also a necessity for the existence of inclusive finance. Without effective customer protection mechanisms, there will be no healthy inclusive finance.

Regulatory agencies pay special attention to financial consumer protection, just like how the capital market has focused on investor protection. In capital market, there are institutional arrangements for classifying qualified investors, emphasizing transparency, openness, impartiality, and fairness in information disclosure. The big question now is that what should be emphasized in the inclusive finance system?

Some academic studies have shown that people with lower incomes are more likely to take risks and display unhealthy financial tendency. When serving these people, service providers should treat them in a responsible manner. This should be one of the characteristics of financial inclusion.

Another important issue in the construction of inclusive finance is how to channel social capitals into the inclusive finance business. Inclusive finance could grow effectively only when social capitals actively flow into inclusive financial service providers who serve the role of intermediaries. Here we need to consider the role of capital market. Securitization is undoubtedly a good way to raise capital. Establishing a secondary market for microfinance among financial institutions would also be a good idea to explore. There are already some practices in the market, but the government needs to create policy to ensure proper practice.

In the past few years of implementation, we have realized that inclusive finance is more than just providing credit and other types of financial services to MSMEs and the disadvantaged individuals. Solving the problem of costly and difficult financing should be the outcome of building an inclusive finance ecosystem. We realized that this goal of building an inclusive finance ecosystem is more important when considering its long-term benefits. Just as people get diabetes, they could just take hypoglycemic drugs without changing their lifestyles. But then it only accounts for the symptom but not the disease itself. In the process of promoting the development of inclusive finance throughout the nation, the goal should be the establishment of an inclusive finance ecosystem as an ultimate cure to the imbalanced growth and development.

Inclusive finance in its essence is the improvement of the MSMEs and disadvantaged individuals in terms of survivability, development, and even creativity. In this sense, in the process of building inclusive finance, we place special emphasis on financial education, financial literacy and financial capabilities. Each inclusive financial services provider should have the ability of customer education while providing financial services and products. Everyone knows the difference between "giving a man fish" versus "teaching a man how to fish" . This is the essence of a responsible financial system.

The financial inclusion practices in the past few years have given us many insights. The one impressed me most is that, the normative development of inclusive finance depends not only on the supervision of the regulatory agencies and the improvement of laws and regulations, but also on the self-regulation of the entire industry. As proponents and observers of inclusive finance, we expect the practitioners to be truly self-regulated, customer-centric, and responsible in their business. The harmonious development of society depends on the perfect combination of law and morality. Similarly, in the process of promoting inclusive finance, the close integration between supervision and self-discipline is also the basic prerequisite for the healthy development of the entire industry.

We have entered the fourth year since the announcement of the *Plan for Advancing Inclusive Finance Development* (*2016—2020*). As observers of the implementation process, we saw many lessons and experiences. We realize that inclusive finance is easier said than done. There will be new obstacles following every step we take. For example, when we encourage data-based financial technology, it is found that the issue of privacy protection has become very crucial and even digitalization itself has brought about the problem of digital gap. It could be seen that realizing inclusive finance will not be a race but a marathon that requires endurance, technical skills, and market mechanisms. It took China nearly 20 years to establish a modern banking system and it took almost 20 years to establish a capital market system. At present, this inclusive financial system is still in its preliminary stage and needs to be continuously improved. Based on previous experience, we expect that it will take at least another 20 years to establish an inclusive finance ecosystem in China. In this sense, this will be a long but worthwhile journey.

If the establishment of a modern banking system and the establishment of a capital market are considered to be the first two stages in China's financial development process, then China has now officially entered into the third stage-the establishment of an inclusive finance ecosystem. Based on discussions from countless conferences, it could be seen that inclusive finance has presently become the hottest topic, just like how they discussed the establishment of capital markets more than 20

years ago. As scholars, we must be calm during the discussion fervor. Fortunately, we have the experiences and lessons of financial development for nearly forty years in the past. This time, we could learn from past lessons and avoid the same pitfalls.

As the Chinese Academy of Financial Inclusion (CAFI) enters its fifth year, we are thrilled to see that our influences are expanding across different fields, industries, agencies, and societies both nationally and internationally. Report 2019 was completely written independently by our own in-house research team and the quality has improved significantly. This is a small but noteworthy milestone in our development. Here, I would like to express my sincere admiration to Dr. Mo Xiugen, who presided over this work, and all the colleagues he led. We also take this opportunity to express our sincere gratitude to our long-term strategic partners, our sponsors, and other cooperative organizations.

Bei Duoguang
Written in Xuanwumen, Beijing
20th July, 2019

目录

第二部分　金融健康

第三部分　负责任金融

第四部分　普惠金融与社会发展

Contents

Part Ⅳ Inclusive Finance and Social Development

概要

一、中国普惠金融发展现状

普惠金融在中国经过多年发展，其发展程度在世界范围内已经处于较为领先的水平。目前，我国普惠金融发展势头良好，不仅政府部门出台了很多政策支持普惠金融的发展，市场也在不断创新和发展，普惠金融的数量和形式都更加丰富，但是在发展过程中仍然存在一些问题亟须解决。

我国政府部门在推动普惠金融的发展中主要采取的措施：一是2015年12月31日国务院印发《推进普惠金融发展规划（2016—2020年）》（国发〔2015〕74号），以总体思路、健全多元化广覆盖的机构体系、创新金融产品和服务手段、加快推进金融基础设施建设、完善普惠金融法律法规体系、发挥政策引导和激励作用、加强普惠金融教育与金融消费者权益保护、组织保障和推进实施共八部分，提出了推动普惠金融发展的建议，为我国普惠金融的发展指明了方向。二是2017年5月中国银监会等11部委联合印发了《大中型商业银行设立普惠金融事业部实施方案》，要求商业银行从当前实际出发，设立普惠金融事业部。通过建立适应普惠金融服务需要的事业部管理体制，构建科学的治理机制和组织架构，健全专业化服务体系，提高普惠金融服务能力，缓解小微企业、“三农”、创业创新、脱贫攻坚等领域的“融资难、融资贵”问题，提高金融服务可得性、使用率和质量，为实体经济提供有效支持，防止“脱实向虚”。三是制定有利于普惠金融发展的货币政策和财政政策，例如，为了加大对小微企业、“三农”的支持力度，中国人民银行下调农村信用社、村镇银行等农村金融机构的存款准备金，财政部对金融机构的小微企业贷款利息收入免征增值税。四是对银行发展普惠金融提出明确要求，2019年4月25日中国人民银行副行长刘国强指出，确保2019年实现五家国有大型商业银行小微企业贷款余额同比增长30%以上、小微企业信贷综合融资成本降低1个百分点的目标。五是加强对普惠金融新形式的监管，2017年4月10

月，中国银监会正式发布《中国银监会关于银行业风险防控工作的指导意见》（银监发〔2017〕6号），明确P2P的整改重点在校园贷和现金贷。

普惠金融在市场发展中主要有以下几个新变化：一是机构发展差异较大。其中，小额信贷机构发展趋于稳定，2008—2015年，小额信贷机构数量迅速增长，2015年底达到最高点为8910家，随后出现下降趋势，2018年底全国共有小额贷款公司8133家；P2P平台经历大洗牌，2007—2018年，P2P平台激增至6430家，但是其中停业及问题平台达到5409家，正常运营平台数量为1021家，较2017年底减少了1219家，截至2019年6月底，P2P网贷行业正常运营平台数量下降至864家；互联网小额信贷机构规范发展，2010—2018年，全国共有超过280家互联网小额贷款公司，其中93家平台注册资本金在5亿元以上（含5亿元），在监管暂停批设互联网小额贷款后，针对地方金融监管部门批设并监管的200多家互联网小额贷款公司，将出台统一的管理办法；互联网私人银行作用凸显，微众银行（WeBank）、网商银行（Mybank）等互联网私人银行成为普惠金融的排头兵。二是商业模式不断创新，越来越多的金融科技公司与金融机构探索助贷、联合贷款业务。三是金融科技公司为传统金融机构赋能，帮助解决了传统金融业效率低、费用高等问题。

在普惠金融发展过程中，也出现了一些引发思考的问题：一是金融机构存在“使命飘移”的风险。农村信用合作社是我国普惠金融的主要参与者，近年来农村信用合作社经历了商业化改革变为农村商业银行，部分农村商业银行已经在资本市场上市，上市后股东对其盈利性的要求和政府对其发展普惠金融的要求存在冲突，与其服务“三农”的初始目标是否会发生冲突还有待观察。二是征信系统公共物品属性与商业化的关系仍然不明朗。一方面，我国官方征信系统即中国人民银行征信系统目前有征信记录的自然人占总人口的比重不足30%；另一方面，私营征信系统逐渐发展起来，如芝麻信用通过数字技术积累了海量的信用数据，征信系统一直被视为公共物品，而现在私营部门纷纷建立信用系统以谋求商业价值。它们之间既互补又竞争的关系值得进一步观察，因此征信系统的管理与规范成为关注点。三是金融机构在政策要求下开展普惠金融业务，可能承受商业可持续性的压力。政府为了扶持普惠金融的发展，对金融机构相关贷款的利率上限作出要求，而机构资金成本缺乏降低的空间，金融机构开展普惠金融业务的盈利性难以保证，其是否能够实现商业可持续性有待观察。四是金融创新与合规性的权衡，联合贷款和助贷等商业模式的创新为普惠金融发展带来了新的活力，但由于监管的滞后无法对其合规性进行监督，容易引发金融风险，不利于普惠金融的健康发展。五是在数字金融的条件下，消费者保护问题更加复杂，消费者的金融健康已经成为普惠金融发展中必须考虑的问题。随着金融科技的发展，消费者隐私泄露问题也更加严重，随之大大提高了金融纠纷发生的概率，如何防范消费者隐私信息泄露、减少金融纠纷的发生值得思考。如何保证金融服务给消费者带来健康的结果，如何引导消费者健康地使用金融服务，已经成为当今政府、金融机构和社会必须探讨的问题。六是金融机构应负的责任。金融机构在提供服务的过程中是强势一方，需掌握更多的产品信息及了解金融产品的风险。增加服务的透明度、公平性和包容性，可以提高金融服务的社会效益。

针对以上提到的我国普惠金融的最新发展情况及其遇到的问题，中国普惠金融研究院课题组成员经过实地调研、重点访谈及内部讨论，最终确定《中国普惠金融发展报告（2019）》从“包容、健康、负责任”的角度来解读普惠金融，并讨论普惠金融与社会发展之间的关系。本报告根据研究主题，采用问卷调查、典型案例分析和文献研究等方法，进行规范分析和实证分析。本报告中用于实证分析的基础数据主要来源：一是国家统计局、中国人民银行、中国银保监会、各级政府及公开发表或出版的国内外论文和著作中的相关统计数据；二是中国普惠金融研究院在浙江、甘肃、北京等地开展的家庭和小微企业调研问卷数据；三是中国普惠金融研究院在全国开展的小额贷款公司的调查问卷数据。

二、包容性金融

包容性金融是普惠金融的另一种提法，在这里特别提出来是让读者了解两者同体异名的关系。在过去四年的报告中，我们分别讨论了“好金融、好社会”“普惠金融的国家发展战略”“普惠金融能力建设”“攻坚最后一公里”等主题。本报告沿袭过去的讨论，继续分析监管、数字技术和传统银行在普惠金融发展中的作用。更值得强调的是，本报告首次论述普惠金融与宏观经济发展的关系。

普惠金融具有宏观经济的目标和微观层面的具体结果。发展普惠金融不但要在微观层面将被排斥的群体纳入金融服务体系，而且在宏观层面也能通过发展普惠金融来促进经济增长（第一章）。普惠金融作为一种发展理念与包容性增长具有天然的联系，两者都是通过增加中小微企业和弱势群体的包容性来改善其处境，缓解贫富差距。由于金融排斥性也是社会排斥性的重要组成部分，因此发展普惠金融、解决金融的排斥问题也是实现经济包容性增长的重要途径。普惠金融促进经济增长的途径，从微观方面看，可以改善家庭生活福利，增加经济收入；从宏观方面看，普惠金融加速了商品流通、提高了经济效率，有利于经济稳定，可以促进社会诚信环境建设，提高政府效率，增加就业。因此，有必要采取措施推动普惠金融的发展，以实现促进包容性增长的目标。第一，加强数字信息的基础设施建设，整合分散在不同机构和部门的数据资源。第二，加强数字化信用体系建设，促进社会诚信发展。第三，建立数字化的监管体系，保障经济的稳定和安全。第四，加强金融能力建设，提高弱势群体的生产效率。同时，应强调政府在发展普惠金融、促进包容性增长方面的作用，集体行动的协调和集中力量的需要，都意味着政府必须在普惠金融建设中发挥重要作用。

普惠金融要取得上述宏观结果，需要有微观上具体措施的支持。要提升金融服务的包容性，需要普遍采用数字技术、实施包容性监管，也需要金融机构的战略转型。

数字技术的应用可以提供低成本的金融服务，大幅度地增加金融服务的边界，提升金融服务的包容性（第二章）。在提升金融服务的包容性方面，数字技术最显著的作用：一是降低运营成本、风险管理成本和金融服务的交易成本；二是通过提升风险识别效率和风险处置效率，提供多样的小额分散金融产品以分散风险，提升风险控制的有效性；三是通过提供个性化、多元化的金融产品供给，结合传统金融与新兴金融的优势，促进竞争性供给的增长。值得注意的是，数字金融有其局限性，它的交易成本、能力等构成了数字金融的服务边界，数字鸿沟限制它无限地将服务送达至所有的人群。

包容性金融需要包容性监管保驾护航，为其提供宽松的监管环境（第三章）。包容性监管应包含三层含义：一是柔性监管，对互联网金融市场复杂的经营行为，不能简单地将所有不符合现行规定的市场行为认定为金融犯罪；二是适度监管，在守住不发生系统性风险底线的同时，对互联网金融的监督管理留有余地，在保障消费者资金安全、信息安全和人身安全的前提下进行监管；三是差异化监管，监管者强调金融环境的多变性、参与主体的多元性、经营方式的多样性，在监管目标、监管手段等方面具体业务具体对待。我国目前的监管环境让普惠金融从业者和互联网金融平台处于尴尬境地，暧昧的管制政策可能会使普惠金融陷入刑事陷阱，失调的法律体系会让普惠金融平台处于泛刑罚化边缘，而淡薄的风险意识会使普惠金融从业者面临刑事风险。为了防范普惠金融从业者和互联网金融平台的法律风险，首先，应构建普惠金融违法防控综合法律体系，加快制定关于普惠金融的规章制度，协调传统法律与互联网金融法规，在现有的法律框架基础上增加新的罪名，以适应互联网时代新型金融违法犯罪行为的认定。其次，提高分析研判能力，建立健全风险预警防范机制，开发监测风险预警系统，观察普惠金融违规犯罪的发展趋势，从源头上减少风险隐患。再次，加大部门间协作力度，建立信息甄别和共享机制。最后，建立法律援助，引入风险防控机制，转事后被动补救为事前积极防控，事前对互联网金融参与者设置严格的审核程序避免风险。

作为金融体系中“百业之母”的传统银行，应当从意愿和能力两个方面着手，提供普惠金融服务，推动经济包容性增长（第四章）。普惠金融具有“双重目标”，一方面要投资于社会影响力；另一方面更要有商业竞争能力，后者是前者的基础。目前，银行在普惠金融服务转型过程中存在着一系列困境。随着利率市场化的不断推进，新型机构逐步进入金融服务市场，竞争不断加剧，造成了银行的总资产收益率、净资产收益率、净利差等盈利指标逐年下降。在这种背景下，实施普惠金融战略、扩大新的客户群体，是其提升盈利的重要途径与趋势之一。研究发现，作为普惠金融重要的服务对象，小微企业或小微经济体的融资需求与目前银行的供给存在不小的缺口。这种缺口的存在会带来潜在的利润，因此银行有意愿提供更多的服务。但在服务能力方面，银行需要根据小微群体的需求特征，运用数字技术改造机构，提供以客户为中心的产品，构建综合化金融服务生态圈。同时，在运用技术及与其他机构合作的基础上降低服务价格，获得更广泛的客户群体，提升盈利水平，成功完成普惠金融服务转型。我们建议适当提高利率弹性以增加市场资金供给，构建多层次的市场体系以促进机构的互补与合作，重视客户保护以促进金融机构以客户为中心设计产品，构建信用与法律基础设施，并实施以科技投入和小微企业能力建设为主的财政补贴。

三、金融健康

在普惠金融的初级阶段，人们聚焦于如何解决可得性和使用率的问题。由于金融自身带有风险的特性，使用金融服务同样也可能导致正、负两面的效果。普惠金融的内容不能局限于服务的使用，更重要的是要产生良好的结果，尤其是在中国普惠金融迅速发展时期，金融健康应该成为人们关注的焦点之一。在这部分，我们介绍了金融健康的概念，也讨论了一些被认为有潜在风险的业务（包括“P2P”“现金贷”）与金融健康的关系。

符合包容性发展的金融服务会产生金融健康的结果（第五章）。金融健康是指消费者可以通过金融知识、利用金融工具、采取合理的金融行为，以达到的个人财务状态。金融健康的客观方面衡量消费者的收支、资产、借贷、保险四个方面。收支方面衡量消费者是否有稳定、合理的收入和支出结构；资产方面衡量消费者是否有足够的应急资金和固定资产；借贷方面衡量消费者是否有合理的债务结构及可供获得的贷款渠道；保险方面衡量消费者是否有充足、合适的保险。主观方面，金融健康衡量消费者对目前财务状况的满意度及对未来财务状况的信心。CAFI 开展的一个数字金融客户研究项目显示，在测算我国消费者金融健康水平时，计算得出受访者的金融健康平均分为 67.79 分。从金融健康的五个指标看，得分最高的为收支指标和主观指标，说明我国消费者较重视收入和支出的平衡性和可持续性，且对自身金融状况大体较为满意，其他各项指标的平均分在 65.2～68.5 分，较为均衡。进一步研究影响我国居民金融健康的因素得到：消费者的个人收入和支出数额越高，金融健康程度越高；房地产资产与金融资产越多，金融健康程度越高；消费者年龄越大，金融健康程度越高，女性消费者的金融健康状况低于男性，消费者的身体健康状况显著高于其金融健康水平。已婚者的金融健康水平普遍高于未婚者，农村户籍的消费者金融健康显著低于城镇户籍的消费者。与金融知识相比，金融行为对提升消费者个人金融健康的作用更为显著。

部分金融消费者不健康的金融投资行为有可能激发 P2P 风险事件（第六章）。在 P2P 的借款人方面，P2P 行业的平均借款期限有逐年递增的趋势；借款人总数先上升，2017 年 11 月达到峰值，之后随着行业风险暴露事件开始出现下滑；男性的借款需求远大于女性；借款人主要以 22～38 岁年龄段群体为主；超过 50% 的借款人主要是用于生活消费；大多数借款人借款在 3 家 P2P 平台以内。在 P2P 的出借人方面，每月投资 P2P 的人数在 2017 年 11 月达到最高峰，2018 年 P2P 平台暴雷事件集中爆发后出借人数已出现大幅下滑；出借人更多地选择了上市公司系；出借人中超过 55% 为男性；出借人平均年龄为 37 岁；专科及以上学历的客户占比超过 82%，接近 70% 的出借人年收入在 10 万元以内（包含 10 万元）；接近 75% 的出借人表示选择 P2P 平台的收益率为 8%～12%；出借人更加青睐短期产品。P2P 行业相对收益较高，操作方便，再加上低投资门槛、相对比较灵活的投资期限、可刚性兑付等优势，使 P2P 获得了大量出借人的青睐。在 P2P 行业多次暴雷事件和严监管驱使下，出借人选择 P2P 平台更加趋于理性，但仍然有大部分人将 P2P 作为主要的理财投资产品。针对 P2P 平台的风险，建议不要将个人和家庭而用于养老、教育和满足基本生活所需的资金投在 P2P 项目。同时，也需要进一步加强对大众 P2P 出借人能力建设的培养。

现金贷具备完善的金融供给体系、丰富金融市场层次的普惠性，对消费者金融健康有积极作用，是大量低收入人群重要的融资渠道（第七章）。无场景依托、无指定用途、无客户群体设定、无抵押的现金贷具有方便、快捷的特点，是长尾客户信贷的重要来源，弥补了长尾客户的贷款需求。现金贷可以帮助借款人平滑现金流，使借款人从财务冲击中恢复，也有助于借款人抓住机遇改善生活状态。但是金融消费者需要将债务和利息负担保持在一个可控的范围内，否则将面临过度负债的问题。现金贷还具有完善社会信贷体系、丰富社会信贷服务层级的作用。受监管、良性发展的现金贷行业有助于从侧面打压地下高利贷、维护社会稳定。同时，随着互联网大数据征信的发展，现金贷还具有补全社会个人征信数据的功能。由于监管政策的收紧，配套的法律法规建设仍不完善，以及现金贷消费者网络游戏、赌博等不良生活方式和盲目创业行为，导致我国部分现金贷的产品出现“714”（7 天或 14 天的超短期高利率借贷）、产业链“作坊化”、形态“地下化”的特征。本报告的分析表明，中国消费者的储蓄习惯和借贷习惯依旧比较保守，贷款申请者对利率变动相当敏感，所谓的现金贷引发社会过度借贷等问题并不广泛存在。但是我国普罗大众特别是长尾客户的金融能力尚弱，若金融服务供应商不负责任地恶意骗贷，很容易将这些客户带入债务深渊，因此，需要个人的金融能力建设和提高普惠金融服务供应商的负责任态度。

四、负责任金融

消费者的金融健康，一方面与消费者的金融能力和行为有关；另一方面也与金融机构的服务有关。保证金融服务给消费者带来健康的结果是金融机构义不容辞的责任。负责任金融以透明、公平和包容为内涵，在实践中体现出以客户服务为中心的服务理念。

负责任金融是实现金融健康的重要保证（第八章）。负责任金融是指以透明、公平的方式提供金融服务，促进负责任金融发展的策略包括行业行为准则和标准、消费者保护法律法规与监管、提高消费者金融能力三大支柱，其本质是以客户为中心和客户保护。在行业自律方面，我国金融行业协会数量增加、规模扩大。中国银行业协会等行业自律组织积极制定本行业的自律规则，以规范行业发展。在法律法规与监管方面，《中华人民共和国消费者权益保护法》《中华人民共和国商业银行法》是法律基础，《中国人民银行金融消费权益保护工作管理办法（试行）》《中国人民银行金融消费者权益保护实施办法》等是相关的政策条文。中国人民银行内设金融消费权益保护局，是承担和履行金融消费者保护职责的监管主体。在消费者金融能力建设方面，2013 年中国人民银行、中国证监会、中国银监会和中国保监会制定了《中国金融教育国家战略》。在数字经济时代，各方都需要正视金融责任，共同建设透明、公平、包容的行业环境。第一，倡导行业自律，作为数字金融服务供应商的互联网平台应当清醒地认识到平台应肩负的责任。除传统金融服务供应商的基本责任之外，互联网平台还承担更新的金融责任。第二，鉴于互联网金融创新的超前性，监管部门需要更好的“平衡术”。一方面，能更有效地识别并监控风险；另一方面，又能包容合法合规的互联网金融创新。第三，金融消费者需要以开放的心态学习互联网与数字金融知识，提升金融资产保护与配置能力。

金融消费者隐私信息保护及纠纷解决是负责任金融的应有之义（第九章）。数字技术在金融领域的应用促进了金融的包容性，但是数字技术的普及也带来了消费者隐私信息泄露的问题，甚至产生金融纠纷，给消费者带来损失。消费者隐私信息泄露主要是由数据收集和使用不当造成的，无论消费者年龄长幼或学历高低都无法避免隐私信息泄露的风险，消费者不具备保护自身隐私信息的能力。因此，保护消费者隐私信息需要企业承担更多，也是其负责任的体现。企业在保护消费者隐私信息安全中负有告知义务、安全保障义务、合理使用义务、限期持有和妥善销毁义务。为了更好地保护消费者的隐私信息，应提升保护技术，互联网企业应随时根据行业发展的新变化做好隐私信息保护技术的升级与创新，确保对消费者信息负责任。应建立统一法律，明确在消费者信息保护过程中各方的责任，监督行业规范发展。同时，也要规范行业自律，建议设立行业自律组织作为保护主体保护消费者的信息。为了更好地解决金融纠纷，首先，金融机构应提高重视程度，赋予内部纠纷解决部门更高的权限，可将消费者金融纠纷解决效果作为绩效考核的内容，同时加强外部机构对其监管；其次，应打通诉讼通道，简化诉讼程序，建立有利于消费者维权的诉讼费用制度；最后，引导消费者增强自我保护意识，加强对消费者的宣传力度，让消费者提高警惕性。

负责任金融本质是以客户为中心，在普惠金融领域讨论以客户为中心的理念有着重要的意义（第十章）。首先，传统金融机构要提供普惠金融服务，必须改变现有的服务方式，以中小微客户需求为导向和出发点，重新设计产品架构和服务体系。其次，数字普惠金融的发展中要求服务提供商能够以客户为中心进行产品设计，尽量减少数字鸿沟，在便捷性、易用性、安全性上均以客户为核心。此外，以客户为中心的产品设计更加强调针对不同的客户，根据客户群体的特点，提供不同的金融服务。最后，普惠金融服务的群体具有可变性，这也就要求提供普惠金融服务的产品能随着客户群体范围的变化而作出相应调整，时刻明确服务的客户群体范围，了解客户群体行为特征，才能让产品保持旺盛持久的生命力。企业在经营过程中应设计以客户为中心的产品。以客户为中心的产品设计原则就是企业在能力范围内最大限度地满足客户的需求，并且针对普惠金融客户的特点，在产品设计时充分考虑用户的理解能力、使用习惯等因素，针对特定客户群体开发出符合其特点的产品。企业以客户为中心的管理理念，其主要核心就是打破传统企业中各个部分单线工作的业务模式，强调为了满足客户的需求，多个部门之间通过跨部门合作给客户提供一套全方位的服务体系。

以客户为中心要求对金融服务制定合理的价格，利用市场机制定价才能真正提供对供应方和需求方都合适的金融服务（第十一章）。合理的金融服务价格主要由客户的需求和金融机构的供给能力决定。客户的需求可以从个人特征、金融行为、金融能力等维度的变量来判断。通过对浙江省丽水市的案例分析可知，金融服务消费者的个人特征、金融行为及金融能力等都会对其金融服务需求产生不同程度的影响。若不考虑特定客户群的特定特征，很容易错误预测金融服务消费者的需求，进而导致不合理的市场定价。同时我们也发现，一些理论上会对消费者可接受最高贷款利率造成影响的因子，如储蓄和理财的习惯，实际上并无显著影响。因此，金融机构应对不同金融产品的目标客户群进行精准画像，从而更好地对金融服务消费者的需求作出判断。而金融机构的供给能力则应充分考虑资金成本、运营成本及风险成本。自由市场竞争能发挥推动产业优化升级的作用，自动淘汰回报低的投资。当政府规定一个低于市场均衡利率的价格上限，会导致一些资本被分配到生产率较低的投资项目上，造成低效资源配置及无谓损失，而偏离均衡的价格管制会造成贷款难、过度贷、民间融资盛行等问题，违反了普惠金融包容性的原则。

五、普惠金融与社会发展

普惠金融以服务的可得性和使用性为基本内涵，与金融机构的责任、消费者金融健康、宏观经济的增长和发展都有紧密联系。在实践中，小微金融机构是普惠金融发展的重要参与方，并在其中发挥着重要作用，当前小微金融机构主要通过信贷服务帮助小微企业获得融资服务、提高生产效率，而小微企业是中国农村最重要的经济模式。中国政府提出了乡村振兴的战略规划，普惠金融可以在其中发挥极为重要的作用。

乡村产业的发展是包容性经济发展的重要部分，需要普惠金融服务的支持，同时乡村小微经济的金融健康水平较高也会对其金融能力产生正面影响（第十二章）。通过对北京及其周边地区企业的调研发现，企业规模普遍偏小，管理水平不高、创新能力不够，导致融资较为困难。虽然新型农村金融机构的普惠金融服务在不断加强，数字金融技术普及也为乡村的包容性发展带来新机会，但是企业现金流管理、财务记账等问题亟待解决，金融机构也需要进一步创新产品，提升利用科技服务乡村产业的能力。通过调研结果发现，在支付与融资方面，普惠金融服务可以起到非常大的作用。首先，新型机构的加入增强了包容性。新型金融机构的加入丰富了市场主体层次，带来支付方式的数字化和融资渠道的多元化，增强了金融体系的包容性。其次，非现金支付的广泛应用可降低企业成本，积累信用数据。目前，乡村中非现金支付方式占比大于现金支付。一方面，交易与支付的线上化，可以节省费用；另一方面，通过线上交易积累交易行为等数据可为企业积累一定的信用数据，增加小微企业融资可获得性的概率。再次，数字金融技术可部分缓解融资难的问题。新型数字金融技术从行为数据出发，对信用评分比较高的潜在客户进行“预授信”，在很大程度上解决了无抵押、无担保的问题，促进了融资需求的满足。最后，融资服务可以补充企业的流动资金及扩大企业规模。

通过调查发现，小额贷款公司已经在普惠金融发展中发挥了先锋作用，其中最为突出的成绩就是促进了金融科技的发展和金融服务的普及应用（第十三章）。小额贷款公司在经济发展中的作用还包括服务“中小微弱”，弥补了金融服务的不足；促进金融科技的普及应用和创新；激活民间资本，打通经济体系的毛细管道；维持生计，稳定就业；缓冲风险，将民间借贷纳入监督体系。小额贷款属于风险业务，对小额贷款公司的风险分析发现，其流动性风险差别大、利率风险温和、资本风险不高、信贷风险两极分化。影响小额贷款公司的风险因素：地域差异会形成公司不同的生存环境；公司成熟度可提高其生产能力；融资是企业生存发展的关键；高素质人才至关重要；信用贷款和担保抵押一样稳妥；分期等额本息有利于还款；贷款期限影响公司生存；绝大多数小额贷款公司综合利率合规；小额度客户的信用较好；农林牧渔业很讲信用，而互联网贷款是未来的希望。在对小额贷款公司进行监管时有以下建议：将小额贷款公司的服务纳入普惠金融服务体系中；在中央统一政策和加强监督的前提下按属地进行监管；建立健全全国监测网，促进监管科技的应用；适当放松对杠杆率的限制，拓宽融资渠道；丰富金融产品，适度对现金贷进行监管；由市场决定利率，通过竞争降低贷款价格；将信息安全和客户保护作为监管的核心；加强对小额贷款公司的能力建设。

普惠金融可以促进小微企业增信并降低其违约风险（第十四章）。常用的信用评价指标能够反映企业的可贷性，但是不能有效地反映小微企业的贷款需求，信用和实际贷款的转化率低。更值得警惕的是，有些指标在增信的同时也增加了违约风险。人们普遍认为，与信用和信贷需求都有关系的指标，如利率，其实与一些信用和需求指标没有显著的关系。这些问题可能是由数据可得性造成的。数字化信用评价为解决这些问题提供了有效的方法，从多维度给企业细致画像，使信用评价同时反映其可贷性和信贷需求。小微企业资金不足的问题可从以下几个方面解决：首先，加快培育良好的诚信文化和信用环境。通过宣传提高社会对小微企业信用体系建设的认识，引导小微企业主动提高信用意识。其次，小微企业积极完善内部信用制度建设。再次，利用金融科技手段实现信用服务数字化。充分利用金融科技，构建开放的信息共享平台，强化多方合作，将各类数据转化成信贷数据，还原小微企业信用水平与风险画像。同时，加速建立科学规范的信用服务指标体系。根据企业规模、企业家素质、所在行业、财务状况、无形资产等方面的差异及信用评价和信贷需求的共同因子构建全面的信用指标体系。最后，加速构建小微企业担保服务体系及增信措施。设立国家层面和地方政府层面的信贷风险专项基金，成立专门为小微企业融资提供担保的政府性担保公司，帮助小微企业融资增信。

Summary

1. Overview of the Development of Inclusive Finance in China

After years of development, Chinese initiatives in inclusive finance have reached the forefront of the field. Currently, inclusive finance in China continues to grow with rapid pace. The government has been issuing many policies in support, the market has been constantly innovating and developing, and inclusive finance has been increasing in variety and form. But there are still challenges that need to be addressed.

The main measures taken by Chinese government in promoting the development of inclusive finance are as follows: First, on December 31, 2015, the State Department issued the *Plan for Advancing Inclusive Finance Development (2016－2020)*. This plan is divided into 8 sections: the general idea, institutional system with multi-faceted coverage, innovation in financial products and service means, acceleration in the construction of basic financial infrastructure, improvement in the regulations and laws regarding inclusive finance, guidance and stimulation through policies, enhancement in the education of inclusive finance and consumer rights protection, and organizational guarantees and implementations. These sections shed a guiding light on the future development of inclusive finance in China. Second, in May 2017, the China Banking Regulatory Commission, along with eleven other departments, jointly issued the *Implementation Plan for the Establishment of Inclusive Financial Business Units for Large and Medium-sized Commercial Banks*. With an eye on real market circumstances, the plan requires commercial banks to set up an inclusive finance department within their organizational structure. By establishing a management system for business units that meet the needs of inclusive financial services, building a scientific governance mechanism and organizational structure, improving the professional service system and the inclusive financial services capabilities, alleviating the problems of "costly and difficult financing" of microenterprises, "Three Rural Issues", entrepreneurial innovation, and poverty alleviation, and improving the availability, usage, and quality of financial services, the banks then could provide effective support for the real economy and prevent the tendency to the fictitious economy. Third, the government has formulated monetary and fiscal policies that are conducive to the development of inclusive finance. For example, in order to increase support for microenterprises and the "Three Rural Issues", the central bank has lowered the deposit reserve ratio of rural financial institutions such as the rural credit cooperatives and rural banks. The Ministry of Finance will exempt the VAT on the interest income of microenterprise loans of financial institutions. Fourth, the government will make clear the requirements to the banks regarding the development of inclusive finance. On April 25, 2019, Liu Guoqiang, deputy governor of the People's Bank of China, laid out a goal of an increase of 30% in microenterprise loans from the five state-owned large commercial banks in 2019 and a reduction of 1% in microenterprise credit financing cost. Fifth, the government will strengthen the supervision on new forms of inclusive finance. On April 10, 2017, the website of the China Banking Regulatory Commission officially issued the *Guiding Opinions of the China Banking Regulatory Commission on Banking Risk Prevention and Control*, which clarified that the focus of P2P reforms will be on the campus loans and cash loans.

There exist several changes in inclusive finance when the market is continuously developing: First, financial institutions vary significantly. Among them, the growth of microfinance institutions tends to be stable. From 2008 to 2015, the number of microfinance institutions increased rapidly, reaching a peak of 8910 at the end of 2015 before heading in a downward trend to 8133 by the end of 2018. P2P platforms experienced several major ups and downs. They surged to 6430 in the 2007—2018 period. But the number of foreclosed and problematic platforms reached 5409 and the number of normally operating platforms was only 1021, which was 1219 fewer than the number at end of 2017. By the end of June 2019, the number of normal operating platforms in the P2P online lending industry has dropped to only 864. The Internet microfinance industry developed in a regulated manner. In 2010—2018, there were more than 280 Internet microfinance companies in the country, of which 93 were with registered capital of more than 500 million yuan (inclusive). After the suspension of establishing new Internet small loans companies, a unified management process will be created to oversee these 280 Internet Microfinances Institutions. The role of Internet private banking is becoming prominent. WeBank and Mybank have become the vanguard of inclusive finance. Second, there are continuous innovation in inclusive finance business model. More and more fintech companies are partnering up with financial institutions in exploring co-lending and agency lending programs. Third, fintech companies have empowered traditional financial institutions by helping and solving the problems of low efficiency and high costs in the traditional financial industry.

During the developing process of inclusive finance, several interesting issues arose: First, there is the potential risk of "Mission Drifting" in financial institutions. Rural credit cooperatives are the main participants of China's inclusive finance. In recent years, some rural credit cooperatives have experienced commercial reforms and became rural commercial banks. Some of these rural commercial banks have been listed on the capital market. After the listing, conflict might exist between the shareholders' desire for profitability and the government's requirement for the development of inclusive finance and it remains to be seen whether this will be a major problem with the initial objective of serving the "Three Rural Issues" . Second, the relationship between the public good property of the credit referencing system and commercialization remains unclear. On one hand, the public credit referenceing system of the central bank currently has record of less than 30% of the total population. On the other hand, the private companies have created their own credit referencing system from the accumulation of a large amount credit information from commercial activities. For example, Zhima Credit has accumulated a large amount of credit data through digital technology. The credit information system has always been regarded as a public good. But now the private sector wants to seek commercial value from the system. Further observations need to be made regarding the competing and complementary nature of the credit referencing systems. Therefore, focus need to be placed on the management and regulation of the credit information system. Third, financial institutions may face pressure when achieving financial sustainability under certain policy requirements. In order to support the development of inclusive finance, the government has imposed interest rate ceiling on relevant loans of financial institutions, but the institutions lack rooms to ensure the profitability and sustainability of inclusive financial activities. Further follow-ups are needed to see whether profitability can be sustained. Fourth, there exists a trade-off between financial innovation and compliance. The innovation of business models such as co-lending and agency lending has brought new vitality to the development of inclusive finance. However, due to the lag of supervision, it is impossible to supervise the compliance for the new business model, which could lead on unsupervised financial risk and not conducive to the healthy development of inclusive finance. Fifth, the situation of financial health and consumer protection under the conditions of digital finance has become a complicated issue that must be addressed in the development of inclusive finance. With the development of financial technology, the problem of consumer privacy has become more severe, which has greatly increased the probability of financial disputes. It is important to consider how to prevent consumer privacy information from leaking and reducing the occurrence of financial disputes. In addition, the government, financial institutions, and society must ensure that financial services do not lead to financial ruin for the consumers. Sixth, it is important to clarify the responsibility of financial institutions. Financial institutions are relatively more powerful relative to consumers when providing financial service due to their expertise on product details and risks. So, by increasing the transparency, fairness and inclusiveness of services, the financial institutions could improve the social benefits of financial services.

In response to the latest development and problems mentioned above, the research team of Chinese Academy of Financial Inclusion (CAFI) has conducted field research, key interviews and internal meetings, and decided to interpret the *Report of Financial Inclusion Development in China* (*2019*) from prospective of Inclusion, Health and Responsibility. The report will also discuss the relationship between financial inclusion and social development. According to the research topics, the report conducts empirical and normative analysis using surveys, case studies, and literature review. The data for the empirical analysis mainly comes from the following: First, works and paper published by the National Bureau of Statistics, the People's Bank of China, the China Banking Regulatory Commission, and various levels of central and local government. Second, the survey data o f households and microenterprises from surveys conducted by CAFI in Zhejiang, Gansu and Beijing. Third, the survey data from the national small loan companies survey conducted by CAFI.

2. Inclusive Finance

In previous reports, we discussed inclusive finance with the themes of "Good Finance, Good Society" "National Development Strategy of Financial Inclusion" "Capacity Building in Financial Inclusion" and "Conquering the Last Mile" respectively. This report follows in a similar vein and continues to analyze the role of regulation, digital technology and traditional banks in the development of inclusive finance.

More importantly, this is the first time that the report will discuss the relationship between inclusive finance and macroeconomic development.

Inclusive finance has goals on the macro level and concrete results shown at the micro level. The development of inclusive finance will not only bring the excluded societal members back into the financial system at the micro level, but also promote economic growth on the macro level (Chapter 1). As a concept, inclusive finance has a natural connection with inclusive growth. Both alleviate the gap between the rich and the poor by increasing the inclusivity of small and medium-sized enterprises and vulnerable groups. Since financial exclusion is also an important part of social exclusion, the development of inclusive finance and the reduction in financial exclusion are also important ways to achieve economically inclusive growth. From the micro perspective, inclusive finance can improve the welfare of family life and increase households' economic income. From a macro perspective, inclusive finance could accelerate circulation of goods, improve economic efficiency, create economic stability, construct a social credit system, improve government efficiency, and increase employment. Therefore, it is necessary to take measures to promote the development of inclusive finance in order to further promote inclusive growth. We should strengthen the construction of data infrastructure and integrate data resources dispersed in different institutions and departments, strengthen the construction of the digital credit system and promote the development of social integrity, establish a digital regulatory system to ensure economic stability and security, and strengthen financial capacity building and improve the production efficiency of vulnerable groups. At the same time, it is important to emphasize the role of the government in developing inclusive finance and promoting inclusive growth. The amount of effort and coordination required for such a task means that the government must play a vital role in the development of inclusive finance.

The macro results of inclusive finance need to be supported by specific measures at the micro level. Improvements in the inclusiveness of financial services will require the widespread implementation of new digital technologies, inclusive regulation, and the strategic transformation of financial institutions.

The application of digital technology can reduce costs in financial services, greatly increase the reach of financial services, and enhance the inclusiveness of financial services (Chapter 2). In terms of improving financial inclusiveness, the significant roles of digital technologies are: First, technologies lowers operating costs, risk management costs and transaction costs. Second, through improving the efficiency of risk identification and risk resolution efficiency and providing risk diversifying products, technologies improve risk control effectiveness. Third, technologies promote a healthy growth of competitive supply by providing personalized and multi-faceted financial products and combining the advantages of traditional finance and digital finance. It is worth noting that digital finance has its limitations. Though small, cost and capability required for the digital financial services are still limiting its further reach. Digital gap limits the ability of technologies from providing service to everyone.

Inclusive finance requires inclusive supervision to provide an effective regulatory environment (Chapter 3). Inclusive supervision has three pillars. The first pillar is flexible regulation. Due to the complexity of the online financial market, one could not simply identify all market behaviors that do not comply with the current regulations as financial crimes. The second pillar is moderate supervision. While maintaining a red line of systemic risks, one should leave room for the development of Internet finance and supervise under the premise of ensuring consumers' fund security, information security and personal security. The third pillar is differentiated supervision. Regulators should accept the diversity of the financial environment, participating entities business methods, regulatory objectives, and regulatory measures and treat different businesses and entities accordingly. China's current regulatory environment puts inclusive financial practitioners and Internet financial platform in a compromising position. The ambiguous regulatory policy may lead inclusive finance into legal danger. The ambiguous legal system will hand down penalty upon inclusive financial platforms. Practitioners of inclusive finance might even face criminal convictions. In order to prevent the legal risks of inclusive financial practitioners and Internet financial platforms, we should build a comprehensive legal system concerning inclusive finance. First, we need to form a comprehensive legal system, speed up the formulation of rules and regulations regarding inclusive finance, and coordinate laws and regulations regarding traditional finance and Internet finance. Definition for new crimes should be added under the structure of established law to combat the inundation of new types of Internet crime. Second, we need to establish risk prevention and monitoring mechanism. This could lower risk and follow the trends in illegal financial crimes involved with inclusive finance, thereby nipping the problem in the bud. Third, it is important to increase inter-departmental collaboration and establish information filtering and sharing mechanisms. Finally, it is important to establish legal aid, introduce risk prevention and control mechanisms, transform the attitude from passive remediation to active prevention. One realistic step in that attitude transformation could be entrance restriction in Internet finance to reduce risk.

As the "mother of all industry", traditional banks should improve their wiliness and ability to provide inclusive finance services to promote economic inclusive growth (Chapter 4). Inclusive finance has "double bottom-line": social impact and financial sustainability. The latter is the foundation of the former. Presently, banks face a series of difficulties while providing inclusive financial services. With the continuing development of interest rate liberalization, new types of institutions are entering into the financial services market stimulating competition. As of a result, traditional banks' total return on assets, return on net assets, net profit spread and other profit indicators are declining year by year. In this context, implementing inclusive financial strategy and expanding new customer groups are potential solutions for improved profitability. It is found that as important target clients of inclusive finance, microenterprises and micro economic entities have huge unmet demand in bank financing. Such a demand gap can bring potential profits, so banks are willing to provide more services. To enhance banks' capabilities, banks can use digital technology to find the demand characteristics of the micro economic entities, provide customer-centric products, and build an integrated financial service ecosystem. Banks can also strengthen cooperation with other institutions, gain access to a wider customer base, improve profitability, and successful complete its transition to the inclusive finance model. We recommend increasing the interest rate at a suitable and flexible amount to increase capital market supply, building a multi-level market system in order to promote complementarity and cooperation between institutions, creating a credit and legal infrastructure, and implementing financial subsidies focused on technological investment capacity building of SMEs.

3. Financial Health

In the early stages of inclusive finance, people focused on how to solve the problem of availability and usage of financial services. Due to the inherent risk within finance, the use of financial services could lead to positive and negative effects. The content of inclusive finance should go beyond the use of services, to the achievement of satisfying results. Especially when inclusive finance is developing rapidly in China, people should value financial health as one of the key focus points. In this part, we introduce the concept of financial health and discuss the relationship between some businesses that are considered to be potentially risky, including "P2P" and "cash loans", and their relationship with financial health.

Financial services that aligns with inclusive development will produce beneficial outcomes in financial health (Chapter 5). Financial health refers to the personal financial status that consumers can achieve through financial knowledge, use of financial instruments, and reasonable financial behavior. The objective aspects of financial health measure consumers' cash flow, assets, loans, and insurance. The aspect of cash flow measures whether the consumers have a stable and reasonable income and expenditure structure; the aspect of assets measures whether the consumers have sufficient emergency funds and fixed assets; the aspect of loans measures whether consumers have a reasonable debt structure and available loan channels; the aspect of insurance measures whether consumers have adequate and appropriate insurance. Subjective measures include consumer satisfaction with the consumer's current and future financial conditions. When analyzing the financial health level of Chinese consumers in a survey by CAFI, we discovered that the average financial health score of respondents was 67.79 points. From the five indicators of financial health, the highest scores are in the categories of revenue and expenditure indicators and subjective indicators, indicating that Chinese consumers pay more attention to the balance and sustainability of their income and expenditure, and are generally satisfied with their financial situation. The average scores of other indicators are between 65.2～68.5. Further research on the factors affecting the financial health of Chinese residents indicats: Personal income and expenditure of the consumer has a positive correlation with financial health. The amount of real estate assets and financial assets are also positively correlated with financial health. Age of the consumer also has a significantly positive coefficient. Female consumers on average have lower financial health than male consumers. Better physical health is associated with higher financial health score. Married consumers on average have higher financial health than unmarried/divorced consumers. The financial health of rural consumers is significantly lower than that of urban ones. Compared with financial knowledge, financial behavior has a more significant effect on the improvement of the consumers' personal financial health.

Some financial consumers' unhealthy financial investment may trigger risks in the P2P industry (Chapter 6). Here are some findings on P2P borrowers: The average borrowing period of the P2P industry has been increasing year by year. The total number of borrowers reached a peak in November 2017, and then declined with the collapse of several P2P platforms in 2018. Demand is much higher for male borrowers than for female borrowers. Borrowers are mainly between 22 to 38 years old. More than 50% of borrowers use their loans for living expenses. Most borrowers borrow from 0 to 3 P2P platforms. Findings on P2P lenders include: The number of investors in P2P per month reached its peak in November 2017. After the outbreak of collapses in many P2P platforms in 2018, the number fell sharply. Lenders are choosing to lend to more reputable platforms. More than 55% of the lenders are male. The average age of the lenders is 37 years. The rate of college degree or above among the lender is over 82% and more than 70% of lenders have annual income lower than 100000 yuan (inclusive). Around 75% of the lenders choose P2P platform with a required rate of return of 8%~12%. The lenders prefer short-term financial products. P2P products are characterized by relatively high return, easy operation, low investment threshold, flexible investment period which increases the attractiveness of P2Plending. After the massive closures in 2018 and strict regulations, lenders have become more rational in choosing P2P platforms. However, there are still a large number of people who use P2P as their main financial investment product. Taking risks into consideration, we suggest that individuals should keep funds for pension, education, and basic living away from P2P investments. At the same time, it is necessary to further the capacity building of P2P lenders.

Cash loan enriches the financial supply system, improves the inclusiveness of the financial market, helps to enhance consumer financial health and is an important way of financing for low income individuals (Chapter 7). Cash loans have the characteristics of no scenarios, no requirement of proceeds usage verification, no borrower restriction, and no collateral. It is an important source of credit for long-tail consumers. Cash loans can help borrowers smooth cash flow, enable borrowers to recover from financial shocks, and seize opportunities for improvements. But financial consumers need to keep their debt and interest burdens within a manageable range, or they will face the problem of excessive debt. Cash loans have the function of improving the social credit system. The properly regulated development of the cash loan industry helps to suppress the "underground borrowing" and maintain social stability. At the same time, with the development of big data, cash loans also have the function of supplementing social credit information. Sudden tightening up of regulatory policies, lack of sufficient laws and regulations, and consumers' unhealthy lifestyles and lack of financial capacity led to the illegal "714" (7 days or 14 days ultra-short-term high-interest) loans with disastrous consequences for borrowers involved. However, due to relatively conservative consumption and borrowing habits of Chinese consumers, borrowers' sensitivity to changes in interest rates, we believe that properly regulated cash loans will not lead to wide-spread social problems. However, the financial ability of the general public in China, especially among the long-tail consumers, is still weak. Financial service providers need to keep consumers' welfare in heart and be responsible in their business to keep customers away from overindebtedness.

4. Responsible Finance

The financial health of the consumers is on one hand related to the financial ability and behavior of the consumers and on the other related to services of the financial institutions. It is the responsibility of financial institutions to ensure that their financial services bring beneficial results to the consumers. Financial responsibility is based on transparency, fairness, and inclusiveness, and relies on the "Consumer Centricity" mentality.

Responsible finance is an important basis for consumers' financial health (Chapter 8). Responsible finance means that financial institutions should provide financial services in a transparent and fair way. The pillars for promoting responsible financial development include industry codes of conduct, consumer protection laws and regulations and supervision, and improvements in consumer financial capabilities. In essence it is "Consumer Centricity" and "Consumer Protection" . In terms of industry self-regulation, the number of financial industry associations in China has increased in number and magnitude. Self-regulatory organizations such as the China Banking Association actively develop relevant industry self-regulatory rules to regulate the development of the industry in a responsible way. In terms of law, the *Law of the People's Republic of China on the Protection of Consumer Rights and Interests* and the *Law of the People's Republic of China on Commercial Banks* form the backbone. The *Measures for the Administration of the Protection of Financial Consumption Rights of the People's Bank of China* (*Trial*) and the *Implementation of the Protection of Financial Consumer Rights of the People's Bank of China Measures* are related policy provisions. The Financial Consumer Rights Protection Bureau of the People's Bank of China is the main body of supervision and responsible for financial consumer protection. In terms of consumer financial capacity building, in 2013, the People's Bank of China, the China Securities Regulatory Commission, the China Banking Regulatory Commission, and the China Insurance Regulatory Commission formulated the *National Strategy for China's Financial Education*. In the digital age, all parties need to jointly build a transparent, fair, and inclusive industry environment. First, it is important to advocate industry self-discipline, the Internet platform as a digital financial service provider should clearly understand the importance of platform responsibility. The Internet platform assumes more financial responsibilities compared to traditional financial institutions. Second, given the advancement in Internet financing, regulators need to "balance" their ability in identifying and monitoring risks more effectively with their ability in accommodating legal compliant Internet finance innovations. Third, financial consumers need to learn about the Internet and digital finance with an open mind and improve their ability to manage their financial assets.

Financial consumer privacy protection and dispute resolution are especially important in a responsible financial system (Chapter 9). Digital technology in finance has greatly promoted the development of financial inclusion. But the spread of digital technology has also led to many breaches of private consumer information and even caused financial disputes which caused severe losses to consumers. Breaches in private data is mainly caused by improper data collection and usage. No matter the demographic of the consumer, the risk of data breach cannot be avoided. Consumers do not have the capacity to protect their private data. Therefore, that responsibility must be on the shoulder of financial services providers. Financial service providers have the oblitigation to inform, protect, manage, limit, and destroy user data. In order to better protect consumer privacy, protection technologies should be upgraded to the latest version. Internet companies should always upgrade and innovate privacy protection technologies based on the innovation and development of their industry in order to safeguard their consumers. At the same time, the government should establish a unified law, clarify the responsibilities of all parties in the process of consumer information protection, and supervise the development of industry norms. It is also necessary to encourage industry self-regulation, and it is recommended to set up an industry self-regulatory organization as a way to protect consumers. In order to better resolve financial disputes, financial institutions should prioritize their importance give internal dispute resolution departments higher authority. Perhaps the results of resolved financial dispute could be used in the institutions' evaluation. Another way to resolve financial dispute is to open a litigation channel, simplify its process, and lower the cost for the consumer in seeking litigation. Finally, it is important to enhance consumer education to increase their awareness of financial risks.

The nature of responsible finance is "Customer Centricity" (Chapter 10). First, in order to provide inclusive financial services, traditional financial institutions must change their existing service model and redesign their products and service system based on the needs of small and medium customers. Second, the development of digital inclusive finance requires service providers to design products with customers at the center, with the intent to minimize the digital gap and focus on customers in terms of convenience, ease of use and security. Third, customer-centric product design emphasizes the importance of providing financial services according to the characteristics of customers. Finally, the groups served by inclusive financial service is fluid, which requires that the products that provide inclusive financial services to be adjusted accordingly. By adapting with clear definition and flexibility, the products could weather through highs and lows. Enterprises should design "Customer Centricity" products when conducting their business. The customer-centered product design principle is that the company should meet the customer's needs to the greatest extent possible. In addition, the company should consider the understanding, habits and other characteristics of consumers in order to develop products that meet user characteristics. To accomplish this customer-centric thinking in enterprises, the enterprises need to break the traditional isolated working culture but incorporate an inter-departmental cooperation model to provide complete and comprehensive service packages to consumers.

"Customer Centricity" requires fair pricing defined by market mechanism, and we believe fair pricing is the premise of long term development of financial inclusion (Chapter 11). Fairprices are mainly determined by the demands of customers and the supply capacity of financial institutions. Customers' demands determined by personal characteristics, financial behavior, and financial capabilities. Through the case analysis of Lishui County, Zhejiang Province, the personal characteristics, financial behavior, and financial capabilities of consumers have different degrees of impact on financial service needs. Without considering the specific characteristics of customer groups, it is easy to mischaracterize them, which in turn leads to unreasonable pricing. At the same time, it is also found that some factors that theoretically should affect consumers' interest rate ceiling, such as savings and wealth management practices, have virtually no significant impact. Therefore, financial institutions should conduct accurate analysis of the target demographic of their products, so as to better judge the needs of the consumers on financial services. The financial institutions' supply capacity should factor in the cost of capital, operating costs, and risk. Free market competition can play a role in promoting industrial optimization and automatically eliminate investment with low returns. When the government stipulates a price ceiling below the market equilibrium interest rate, some capital is allocated to less productive investment projects, resulting in inefficient resource allocation and deadweight losses. Deviation from the equilibrium price control will lead to problems such as large unmet demands, excessive loans, and emergence of "underground" market, which violates the principles of inclusive finance.

5. Inclusive Finance and Social Development

The core of inclusive finance is the accessibility and usability of services. In addition, it is closely related to financial institutions' responsibilities, consumer financial health, and even macroeconomic growth and development. In practice, small and micro financial institutions are important participants in the development of inclusive finance. The core services provided by small and micro financial institutions are credit services, which small and micro enterprises could use to improve their production efficiency. Small and micro enterprises are the most important economic entities in rural China. The Chinese government has proposed a strategic plan for rural revitalization, in which inclusive finance can play an important role.

The development of rural industries is an important part of inclusive economic development and requires the support of inclusive financial services. At the same time, the level of financial health of rural micro-economics might have a positive impact on its financial capabilities (Chapter 12). Through the survey of enterprises in Beijing and its surrounding areas, we discovered that most small enterprises lack management skills and innovation ability, making financing difficult. Although there is constant improvement in the inclusive financial services by the newer rural financial institutions and there is a constant proliferation of digital technology which brings forth new opportunities of development, issues such as corporate cash flow management and accurate financial accounting still need to be improved. Financial institutions need to create more innovative financial products and improve their technological service to rural industry. According to our survey results, inclusive financial services can play a very important role in payment and financing. First, the inclusion of new institutions has increased inclusiveness. The new financial institutions have enriched the market structure, brought digitization of payment methods, diversified financing channels, and enhanced the inclusiveness of the financial system. Second, the widespread use of non-cash payments can reduce business costs and accumulate credit data. Presently, non-cash payment in rural areas is more prevalent than cash payment. On one hand, with the transformation of offline transactions and payments to online methods, costs could be saved. On the other hand, by accumulating transaction behaviors data such as online transactions, financial institutions could gain data for the basis of credit for small and micro enterprises. Third, digital financial technology can partially alleviate the difficulty of financing. Starting with behavioral data, the new digital financial technology could identify and "pre-lease" potential customers with high predicted credit score, which largely solves the problem of financing customers due to lack of collaterals and guarantees. Finally, financing services could improve liquidity and help business expansion.

Based on our survey data, it is found that microfinance companies are playing a pioneering role in the development of inclusive finance (Chapter 13). The role of microfinance companies in economic development includes serving the disadvantaged, promoting the popularization and innovation of financial technology, stimulating private capital, and bringing liquidity to every nooks and crannies in society. Some effects are that livelihoods are maintained, risks stabilized, and private lending is brought under the system of supervision. Microfinance is a risky business. It is found that the liquidity risk of microfinance companies is fluctuating, the interest rate risk is moderate, the capital risk is relatively low, and the credit risk is polarizing. Geographic location and the quality of the employees are some of the key factors that influence microfinancing company risks. Here are some more findings: Credit loans are as safe as collateralized loans. Equal instalment payment helps repayment. The loan maturity offered affects the company's survival. Most microcredit companies offer interest rate in compliance, and small-value customers often have good credit. The "farming, forestry, animal husbandry and fishery" industries are also very creditworthy. And it is believed that online borrowing is the future. It is suggested that the government include microfinance companies in the inclusive financial service regulation system. Supervision should be carried out based on geographic terms with a unified central policy. A national monitoring network should be established to promote the usage of regulatory technologies. The government should also appropriately relax the restrictions on leverage, broaden financing channels, enrich financial product types, moderately regulate cash loans, further encourage interest rates liberalization, reduce loan prices through competition, regard information security and consumer protection as the founding principle of regulatory agencies, and strengthen the capacity building for microfinancing companies.

Inclusive finance could promote microenterprises to increase their credit and reduce their default risk (Chapter 14). Commonly used indicators could reflect the loanability of enterprises, but they cannot effectively reflect the loan demand of microenterprises. In reality, the conversion rate of credit and actual loans is low. What is more alarming is that some indicators are actually positively correlated with default risk. Indicators such as interest rates that are commonly believed to be related to credit and credit demand are actually not significantly related to some credit and credit demand indicators. These findings might be limited to our sample. Digital credit evaluation provides an effective way to solve these problems. A multidimension profile creation, can create a credit evaluation that reflects both loanability and credit demand of enterprises. To solve the problem of insufficient funds for microenterprises, we came up with several proposals. First, it is crucial to cultivate a culture of integrity and credit. We should promote the importance of a social credit system for microenterprises, and guide microenterprises to take the initiative in educating their own credit awareness. Second, microenterprises should actively take charge in the construction of their own internal credit mechanisms. Third, microenterprise should make full use of financial technology. Building an open information sharing platform, strengthening multi-party cooperation, and converting various types of data into credit data all help to form correct risk portrait of small and micro enterprises. At the same time, we should establish a proper credit service indicator system. A comprehensive credit indicator system should be constructed based on different enterprise size, management quality, industry, financial status, intangible assets, and other common factors. Fourth, we should establish proper credit enhancement program and guarantee service system to better assist the microenterprises. The government should establish special funds at the national and local levels, which could provide guarantees and credit enhancement services for microenterprises.

绪　论

在普惠金融理念框架内，可持续发展、包容性增长、包容性金融、金融健康、负责任金融等概念之间具有非常密切的内在联系。普惠金融宏观上通过促进包容性增长，肩负着推动经济可持续发展的重任；微观上通过满足低收入人群的金融需要，为他们提供透明、包容和公平的负责任的金融服务，确保金融健康，加速生活水平的改善。可见，普惠金融发展在国计民生中具有重要意义。

也许有读者要问，作为《中国普惠金融发展报告》系列文献之一，本期报告为什么要聚焦在“包容、健康和负责任”？为什么要将看似不相关的概念放在一起讨论？部分读者可能对这三个概念有所了解，但是要在普惠金融的框架下讨论，仍会觉得有些新鲜，也可能有些困惑，其中可能有语言翻译的原因，例如，普惠金融的英文原意实际上是包容性金融；也可能是惯用表达的原因，例如，人们比较熟悉的是身体健康，没有意识到金融也有健康和不健康的说法；又如，负责任是大家熟悉的概念，尽管我们知道任何个人和机构都有自己需要承担的责任，对金融机构而言也是如此，但大部分读者或许仍然不清楚什么是负责任金融。

将普惠金融还原为包容性金融，是为了帮助读者从包容性增长和可持续发展的角度来理解普惠金融。增长和发展是人们普遍关心的概念，它们和普惠金融具有本质上的内在联系。普惠金融之所以得到广泛关注，不仅仅是因为它能解决普罗大众基本的金融需求问题，更重要的是它关系到经济的增长模式，关系到人类的发展前景。普惠金融是否能够健康发展，不仅影响当代人的公平发展，也影响未来的公平发展。

从包容性增长和可持续发展的大视野来审视普惠金融，我们会发现，金融服务的可得性、使用性和质量等基本的包容性指标未能满足人们更高的期待。贝多广和莫秀根（2017）在《超越普惠金融》一书中试图打破包容性概念的局限，论述能力建设在普惠金融中的重要性。许多实践和研究发现，达到包容性的基本要求并不能保证金融服务使用者的生活福利水平得到提升。例如，过度贷款对部分金融服务用户造成了伤害。因此，为了确保金融服务能够产生“好社会”的效果，金融健康（Financial Health）成为普惠金融发展中需要考虑的问题。这也许能够解释普惠金融比包容性金融概念更受青睐的原因，因为普惠强调了金融服务必须有益。这也是我们提出金融健康概念的原因。

保证金融服务的可得性、使用性和质量，是金融体系中利益相关者必须担负的责任。同样地，保证金融服务健康有益也是他们的责任，或许是更重要的责任。例如，在过度贷款问题上，金融服务使用者负有责任，监管者负有责任，但是，我们要强调金融机构的责任，因为它们是金融供求关系中强势的一方，掌握金融服务更多的信息，了解各种金融服务的风险，掌握风险防范的手段。负责任金融要求金融机构提供的服务，不但要可得、可用、质量要可靠，更要对使用者有益。

我们要在普惠金融的框架下，诠释从微观层面的负责任金融、金融健康，到宏观层面的包容性增长和可持续发展的内在逻辑关系。首先，我们将回顾可持续发展的含义，揭示包容性增长在可持续发展中的前提作用及普惠金融是包容性增长的支柱，阐述金融健康是符合包容性发展要求的金融服务应该产生的结果，最后讨论如何通过发展负责任金融确保金融健康，乃至实现包容性增长和可持续发展。

一、可持续发展

可持续发展已经成为当今社会的重要议题，联合国于2016年发布的《2030年可持续发展议程》提出的17项目标中，有7项目标与普惠金融有紧密关系。可见，普惠金融是实现可持续发展的重要手段。

可持续发展包含多方面含义。简单地说，可持续发展是代际间和群体之间的公平发展问题。很多文献把可持续发展定义为每一代人在改善生活的过程中都不要妨碍往后各代人改善他们的生活，以及在同一代人中任何一个群体的发展都不要阻碍其他群体的发展。在可持续发展的概念中，将任何一代人、任何一个群体排斥在外都是不公平的。因此，消除排斥、提高发展的包容性，是可持续发展的重要含义。

可持续发展包含经济、社会和环境等方面的内容。

首先，可持续发展最直接、最根本的目的是应对自然资源枯竭问题。自然资源可以划分为可再生资源和不可再生资源（比如生物资源是可再生资源，土地是不可再生资源），也可以划分为可枯竭资源和不可枯竭资源（比如生物和水从整体上是不可枯竭资源，石油资源是可枯竭资源）。如果开发过度，不仅可枯竭资源将被耗尽，可再生资源也可能失去再生的能力。

其次，资源是经济增长和人类发展的基础，只有合理利用资源才能使可持续发展成为可能。任何经济活动都离不开自然资源。人力资源和资本必须与自然资源结合才能够进行生产活动。不可移动、不能再生的可枯竭资源在很大程度上决定了经济的增长和发展，它们的枯竭意味着某些经济活动的终结。虽然随着技术的发展，可枯竭资源的利用率得到了提高，也可能出现可代替的资源，但是不可持续的本质并未改变。

再次，在过去的300多年里，以利益最大化为核心的西方经济理论的盛行，造就了许多经济增长的奇迹，大幅提高了人们的生活水平。近20多年来，人们开始对这种理论指导下的经济增长模式进行反思，认为此种模式有两个主要缺陷：一是部分人的生活水平仍然停留在较低水平，长时间没有得到改善；二是部分自然资源面临枯竭的危险。也就是说，这种增长模式没有给当代人带来公平的利益，同时也威胁到了未来人类的生活水平，这对未来人类是不公平的。这种增长模式将部分当代人和未来人类排除在发展之外，既没有包容性也没有可持续性。

最后，当我们从社会发展的角度审视可持续发展的时候，可以发现它不仅关乎自然资源，还涉及其他资源的问题。如果包括教育、卫生健康和文化在内的各种社会资源被某一社会阶层长期占用，其他阶层就很难利用社会资源来改善自己的生活和社会地位，转而过度依赖自然资源，造成自然资源的局部枯竭甚至全部枯竭，乃至造成社会混乱。在经济层面，金融资源的过度集中和就业机会的不平等，都将危害经济的增长和可持续发展。

由此可见，实现可持续发展必须以包容性增长为前提。可持续发展是一个动态的概念，只有在经济增长的前提下，公平发展才会成为可能。历史经验已经证明，简单的增长模式由于缺乏包容性而不可持续，因此包容性增长已经成为可持续发展必要的经济条件。

二、普惠金融是包容性增长的重要支柱

包容性增长是一种有利于可持续发展的经济模式，实现包容性增长需要社会各方面的共同努力及各种要素的共同发力。本报告第一章将对包容性增长进行更加深入的讨论。这里简要分析普惠金融与包容性增长的关系。

包容性增长的主要障碍是社会排斥，由于各种原因，一部分人在社会经济活动中或主动或被动受到排斥。主动排斥是因为个人的原因，如个人由于不愉快的经历不愿意参加社会经济活动。被动排斥的原因包括地理位置偏远、个人能力不足、资源缺乏、社会制度缺陷、种族和性别歧视等。我国存在的诸多社会排斥中，最典型、影响最深远的是对农村居民的排斥，这是造成城乡差别的根本原因。

首先，我国长期以来实行的城乡差别对待政策，将很多农村居民排斥在城市就业、

医疗卫生、教育及基础设施服务之外。改革开放以来，这种情况虽然有所好转，但是没有本质的改变。在市场经济条件下，虽然农村劳动力可以相对比较自由地流动，有机会到城市就业，收入大幅提高，但是由于户籍的限制，在城市就业的农村劳动力不能享受城市的福利待遇，其家庭成员也不能随之移居城市享受城市生活的便利，就形成了大批的留守人员，主要是儿童、妇女和老人。改革开放带来的有限经济收入增长，弥补不了对家庭照顾的缺失和对社会福利的缺位，形成了巨大的社会隐患。

其次，城乡不同的财产制度造成农村资产流动性差、变现难。其典型例子为房屋和土地产权不明确，农村家庭无法通过金融杠杆增加投入，不能通过资产的流动扩大经济规模进行扩大生产。生产规模和家庭劳动能力不匹配，劳动报酬低。

最后，我国改革开放以后建立的金融体系，照搬了西方工业革命以后形成的金融制度，重在服务产业化发展，忽略了民生服务。例如，大型银行没有将消费金融列为其服务内容，中小微企业的金融服务体系长期没有建立起来。中华人民共和国成立初期成立的信用合作社，初衷是服务农村居民消费和生产经营，在市场经济的诱惑和产业经济思想的主导下，放弃原来的使命，转型为产业服务的金融机构，最后成为农村金融资源的“抽水机”，抽取农村资金输送到城市，导致农村资金外流、农村金融资源短缺。农村家庭经营活动呈递减态势，收入来源越来越依赖于城市就业，收入差距扩大。农村经济和社会迅速凋敝。

促进全社会的包容性增长，现阶段应该从乡村振兴抓起，而普惠金融是乡村振兴的重要抓手。在现代经济中，农村不再局限于农业产业，农村居民也不是纯粹意义上的小农。农村是一个多元化社会，是多种民族、多种文化、多种产业、多种生计、多种生活方式的综合体。包容性增长是农村经济发展最合适的模式，能够满足农村多元化、复杂化的金融需要非普惠金融莫属。

三、金融健康是普惠金融的必然结果

普惠金融的核心价值是将金融服务的商业目标与社会目标有机结合，忽略任何一个目标都不能算是成功的普惠金融模式。正如包容性增长一样，普惠金融也要给“中小微弱”提供商业性金融服务，促使其生活改善的速度超过富裕阶层，只有这样，普惠金融才有可能实现社会协调发展的目标。因此，普惠金融发展必须要导向健康的金融结果。

贝多广等（2016）提出“好金融，好社会”的概念，要求金融服务的结果一定是健康的、正面的。2010 年印度发生的小额贷款风波，除政治、风险控制不当、盲目扩张等原因之外，过度商业化也是其主要原因之一。它提醒我们，只有兼顾社会目标和商业目标，普惠金融才可能实现健康持续发展。

（一）以满足需求为基本原则

在市场经济条件下，金融产品已经成为个人、家庭、企业和其他任何实体日常不可或缺的必需品。无论是农村居民还是城市居民，要提高生活质量进一步改善生活，都离不开金融服务。企业要生存和发展，更离不开金融服务，改善金融服务是企业发展必要的条件。

对于个人和家庭来说，普惠金融不能只是金融供给，也不能只停留在金融服务的可得性和服务质量上，更重要的是家庭实际使用金融服务。要使金融服务得到使用，它必须能够满足使用者的需要。而使用者的需要是多方面的，存在个体之间的差异。

一是存储的需要。除小部分个人和家庭以外，大多数个人和家庭的收入常常是不稳定的。出于跨时空生活水平优化的需要，需要平滑消费，避免生活水平的变化过于剧烈。人们需要将一部分收入存储，以备未来不时之需。另外，为了购买大件耐用品，人们同样需要将收入存储。存储的意义还在于为将来的教育、投资、疾病和灾害风险等做好准备。因此，存储是每一个人和家庭的一项基本需要。

二是转账支付的需要。无论是消费、经营还是家庭成员之间的收入转移，转账支付都是一项基本的需要。一方面，在城镇化过程中，大量劳动力从农村向城市转移，他们需要将部分劳动收入向生活在农村的父母子女等转移，以保证家庭成员的生活需要；另一方面，在数字经济时代，网店经营成为重要的谋生手段，与此同时，人们也越来越习惯于网上购物，因此无论是收入水平的提高还是生活质量的提高，对数字支付的依赖性都越来越高。

三是信贷需要。人们可以通过储蓄来平滑消费，也可以通过信贷来平滑消费。更重要的是，信贷作为一种生产资本，可以帮助个人增加投资、扩大经营规模、提高劳动生产效率、增加收入，尤其是对于存在剩余劳动力而资本又短缺的家庭，信贷给他们提供了将劳动力投入生产的机会。

四是抵御风险的需要。个人在家庭生活和生产中可能遇到各种各样的风险，包括疾病、市场风险、社会动荡、自然灾害等，有的可能会对生产、生活产生较大的冲击，导致消费和收入发生激烈的震荡。除了储蓄和信贷，保险也是抵御风险的有效办法。

五是资产管理需要。个人和家庭长期积累形成的资产，需要进行有效的管理才能避免折旧和通货膨胀等造成的资产价值流失，用积累的资产扩大收入提高生活水平。

六是投资需要。投资是提高未来收入的重要途径，其形式可以包括人力资源投资，如教育和健康，也可以是生产经营投资。投资对个人的金融能力要求更高，投资不当也可能导致生活水平急剧下降。

金融服务要满足上述六种最基本的服务需要，也要意识到每个人的需求是不同的。影响个人金融服务需求的决定因素包括收入水平、性别、年龄、教育水平、经历、社会环境等，金融产品的多样性是普惠金融需要提倡的重要内容。只有市场上存在不同利率、不同额度和不同期限的丰富多样的金融产品，才能满足各种人群的不同需求。

（二）以提高生活水平为最终目标

金融满足人们的各种需求，其最终目标是实现生活的改善。生活的改善包括两个方面：一方面是数量的增加，另一方面是质量的提高。

生活水平在数量上的提高包括收入的增加和物质的丰富程度。由于普惠金融能够满足人们的基本需求特别是生产上的需求，因此可以增加劳动机会，提高生产效率，从而提高人们的收入水平。正如我们在讨论包容性增长时提出的，要使低收入人群的收入增长率高于富裕人群的增长率。

生活质量的提高可以理解为在同等收入的条件下提升人们的满足感。普惠金融服务为低收入人群提高家庭内转移支付的便捷程度，使家庭内个体之间的生活水平相对均衡，提高了家庭整体的满足感。数字化的消费支付使人们节约了大量的时间，也可以提升人们的满足感。储蓄和消费信贷让人们生活水平处于比较平稳的状态，增强了生活的幸福感。

（三）以金融健康为必然结果

普惠金融在保持自身商业可持续的前提条件下，不断满足所有服务对象特别是低收入消费者的基本需要，持续改善消费者的生活水平，这就要求普惠金融服务对金融消费者产生健康的结果。

金融健康是对普惠金融提出的更高要求。它要求金融服务能够帮助消费者实现他们的经济生活目标，其具体包括改进储蓄消费习惯，提升信用意识与金融能力，提高缓冲经济波动的能力，提升生活质量并达到一个可持续的健康的金融状态的目标。金融健康体现在收支是否平衡、债务是否得到良好的管理、是否具有财务储备、是否具有财务计划、是否具有应对经济冲击的计划、是否能够有效利用各种金融工具等。金融健康事关广大金融消费者，不仅涉及没有获得金融服务或者金融服务不足的人群，也涉及中等收入人群。

比较常见的不健康的金融行为包括过度借贷、非理性投资和理财。最近一两年出现的 P2P 金融风险事件究其原因，除了部分 P2P 金融平台自身存在问题，部分是由于金融消费者不健康的金融投资行为激发引起的。如果仅仅加强对 P2P 金融平台的管控，而不提高金融消费者的金融素养，则很难从根本上消除金融风险。同时，植根于不健康金融行为的金融风险有可能在其他平台以其他形式出现，如股市、小额信贷、民间借贷等都可能成为金融风险的爆发点。

消费者的金融健康可以促进金融稳定和可持续发展。特别是对于信贷服务来说，消费者健康的金融行为，可以降低银行信贷风险，增加国家金融系统的稳定，尤其是在数字时代，金融服务普遍使用网络交易，对客户的直接观察被数字画像代替。在没有业务人员直接接触的情况下，客户的金融健康尤为重要。不健康的金融行为容易通过网络传递给金融机构，感染其他客户，迅速引发金融风险。

四、负责任金融是金融服务的基本要求

负责任金融对金融服务供应商提出了更高的要求。除了提供高质有益的金融服务，更高的道德水准要求金融机构必须具有较高水平的使命感和责任感，要为消费者的金融健康负责，提供更加透明、包容和公平的金融产品和服务（Stein、Randhawa 和 Bilandzic，2011）。

（一）负责任金融的内涵

提高金融服务的透明度，就是要将金融服务的主要信息提供给金融消费者，尤其是利率、风险和可能产生的效果。其目的是要增加金融消费者的信心，减少信息不对称，提高金融服务的效率、透明度和稳定性，让金融消费者根据自己的需要来选择金融服务。出于竞争和营销的需要，有些金融机构采用虚报利率、隐瞒风险、夸大效果等欺骗方式误导客户进行消费，导致消费者过度贷款、遭受风险的危害。这些行为都是不负责任的表现。

中国普惠金融研究院此前的调研表明，手续烦琐、缺乏担保抵押、没有合适的金融产品等是造成金融排斥的主要原因。这些损害金融包容性因素的存在，主要是因为金融机构对高端客户和低收入客户采用相同的风控标准。低收入客户因为很难达到这样的标准而被排除在外。提高金融的包容性，金融机构需要简化手续、减少对低收入人群的排斥。

实行同样的标准表面上看似公平，实际上提高了低收入人群获得金融服务的难度，剥夺了他们获得金融服务的机会。只有根据不同人群的需要，设计和提供满足不同人群需要的产品，使不同阶层都有获得金融服务的机会，才是公平的金融服务。出于对低收入人群的不信任而设置的旨在将其排斥在外的贷款条件和手续，是一种不负责任的表现。

（二）以客户为中心

金融机构以客户为中心开展负责任金融业务，也是实现普惠金融商业可持续和社会目标的重要办法。它是“以人为本”理念在金融服务中的具体应用，是普惠金融商业模式成功的关键。普惠金融的客户是一个复杂多样的群体，具有多样的需求，不能从单一维度去理解，否则将导致设计的服务产品单一，无法满足复杂多样的需求。只有围绕客户的特点和需求，才能设计出低收入客户既可以获得又能使用得上的金融产品和服务。客户使用了金融产品和服务才能受益，供应方才有利润以维持商业活动。金融机构将以客户为中心的理念引入商业活动，可以产生以下五个方面的良好效果：

一是提高客户的采纳率和使用率。只有客户采纳并经常使用金融产品和服务，金融服务才能给客户创造价值。从客户的需求出发设计产品和服务，能满足客户的差异化需求，从而提高采纳率和使用率，同时也可增加金融机构的利润，使其可持续发展。

二是改善市场地位。在激烈的市场竞争中，以客户为中心的商业模式是一种“区分器”，将不同的客户区分开来，满足其不同的要求，并对新的需求作出及时的反应，因此能维持现有客户，吸引新的客户，增加市场份额。

三是降低成本以满足特定细分客户群体的需要。在技术进步的基础上，金融机构与客户的沟通得到加强，并降低个性化产品和服务的成本。特别是采用金融科技的手段和数字化的配送渠道，为客户提供更加便利的服务，提高商业模式的适用性。

四是满足客户保护和监管的要求。除了上述提到的合适的产品设计和服务，以客户为中心的商业模式从根本上遵循公平和尊重的客户原则。由于增加了与客户的互动，加深了对客户的了解，从而增加了透明度，使定价更加合理，投诉机制更加有效，能更好地保护客户隐私。

五是履行社会责任的义务。普惠金融的最终目的是要平衡商业利益和社会效益。增加金融服务的包容性是金融机构的社会责任。“中小微弱”群体有机会以金融服务为杠杆享受社会福利，提高生活水平。

（三）可持续的金融服务

跨越时间的生活水平的提高，需要普惠金融提供持续性的服务，这绝非一朝一夕之功。可持续的金融服务以财务可持续性为基础，要达到商业可持续性的目标，不仅需要采用适当的利率，也要对金融风险进行有效的控制。

适当的利率是一种理想的状况，通往此目标的过程中往往存在操作性障碍，最主要的原因是信息不对称，无论是金融消费者、政府还是其他第三方，都无法获得确切的成本信息判断怎样才是适当的定价。只有金融机构自身掌握其成本信息，出于利润最大化的目的，金融机构往往就高定价。适当利率最有效的确定方法是由市场定价。

人们很容易将市场定价与高利率联系在一起，这其实是一种错误的认识。高利率是由市场竞争不充分、供给不足造成的。充分竞争才是降低利率的有效途径。充分竞争可以提升金融科技的应用、降低成本、提高服务质量等。消费者是竞争的最终受益者。

市场竞争可能有利于风控，也可能导致风险的爆发。金融机构为了获得稳定的回报，需要对风险进行有效的控制。

（四）从三个维度实现负责任金融

实现负责任金融需要政府、金融机构和消费者通力合作。消费者保护原则、行业自律、金融能力建设构成确保落实负责任金融的三个主要层面。

综上所述，普惠金融宏观上通过促进包容性增长肩负着可持续发展的重任，微观上通过满足低收入人群的金融需要，帮助其改善生活并实现金融健康。可见，普惠金融发展在国计民生中具有重要意义。发展普惠金融需要政府、金融机构和金融消费者的共同努力，这样才能最终实现商业绩效和社会绩效的双重目标。

第一部分

包容性金融

宏观上，普惠金融可以促进包容性增长，推动可持续发展；微观上，普惠金融可以满足普罗大众的金融服务需求，提高生活水平。

第一章 普惠金融与包容性增长

【摘要】本章帮助读者理解社会排斥和金融排斥与收入差距之间的关系，解释包容性增长的内涵、意义和挑战，分析我国改革开放以来经济增长的包容性，讨论普惠金融在包容性增长中发挥的作用，提出促进包容性增长的普惠金融措施。

普惠金融是最近几年一直备受关注的议题，但总体而言，国内各界基本上仍然就金融讲金融，尚未将它当作促进经济增长和社会发展的重要手段。因此，有必要从国家整体经济发展的角度，探讨普惠金融与经济包容性增长的关系，以及金融排斥和社会排斥将导致的社会后果。这方面的文献虽然较多，但是仍然需要具有说服力的研究成果作为讨论的基础。

在“2017年中国普惠金融国际论坛”上，中国人民银行行长易纲曾经专题论述了普惠金融与宏观经济增长的关系，认为普惠金融的发展可以促进宏观经济增长。贝多广等（2016）提出的“好金融，好社会”概念也隐含了普惠金融与社会发展的必然联系。King和Levine（1993）认为，金融体系对经济增长和发展极其重要。良好的金融体系有利于创新科技、降低成本、增加储蓄、积累资本和发展生产力，优化资源配置、提高生产效率，促进经济增长，改善发展水平。

当然，普惠金融的概念最初并不是为了促进经济增长，而是为了解决增长中的不平等现象和扶贫等发展问题提出来的。大量研究证明，不平等问题产生于增长过程中，也必须要在增长中才能解决。增长是解决包容性问题和不平等问题的基础。因此，厘清普惠金融、经济增长和公平发展三者之间的关系，是本报告开篇就需要讨论清楚的问题。

普惠金融的本意是包容性金融，其相对应的概念是包容性增长，与它们相对的两个概念是金融排斥和社会排斥。有文献认为它们之间是因果关系，也有文献认为是包含关系，即金融排斥是社会排斥的一部分。包容性金融和包容性增长都是将被排斥的群体包含到金融服务和经济增长中来，让他们得以分享经济成果从而消除社会不平等现象，因此，它们的目标和服务对象是相同的。

经济增长常常被认为与技术、资本和人力资本三个要素有关，其深层次的根源在于科技、金融、贸易、教育、医疗、公共卫生和政府等因素。联合国增长与发展委员会根据十三个长期高速增长的经济体的经验指出，只有包容性增长模式才可以保持经济长期的高速增长。这些经济体具备以下共同点：战略性地融入世界经济，充分利用世界分工和资源；保持宏观经济的稳定，有利于动员国内尤其是劳动力资源；保持高储蓄率和高投入率；具有专注、可信赖、有能力的政府。

本报告从社会排斥和它所引起的社会后果的角度讨论为什么经济要有包容性，并从统计学角度论证我国改革开放以来的经济增长是否具备包容性，再用国际相关研究文献讨论普惠金融能在包容性增长中发挥什么样的作用，最后提出可以采取什么样的普惠金融措施来促进经济的包容性增长。

一、为什么增长要有包容性

改革开放以来，中国的经济增长举世瞩目，国民的生活及福利水平都得到了大幅提高。根据《中国统计年鉴》数据，2000—2017 年，我国人均国民收入年均增长率为 12.54%（未除去物价因素）。人均国民收入长期的高速增长在给国民带来巨大福利的同时，也带来一些我们不愿意看到的结果。从我国基尼系数变化情况来看（见图 1-1），虽然 2009 年以后有明显的下降趋势，但是自 2003 年以来一直处于收入差距超过警戒区间（0.4～0.5）。根据国家统计局（2001）的报告，1999 年以前我国的基尼系数均低于 0.4。华中师范大学中国农村问题研究中心（2007）研究认为，我国的基

资料来源：中华人民共和国统计局网。

图 1-1 全国居民人均可支配收入基尼系数

尼系数于2000年前后突破了0.4的警戒线。这些数据引发了人们对社会不平等问题的担忧和对经济增长模式的思考。

（一）不平等的增长模式

经济增长与收入不平等之间的关系长期受到关注，Kuznets（1955）曾经提出一个假说，即经济增长会在一定时间内拉大收入差距，但随着经济增长收入差距会出现一个拐点，之后收入差距会缩小。总体而言，在一定的增长阶段内收入差距加大是不可避免的。Kuznets的假说是基于城镇化过程提出来的，城镇化会吸引一部分农村劳动力到城市就业，在拉动经济增长的同时提高这部分人的收入，于是出现收入差距。随着城镇化进程的进一步发展，其他农村劳动力逐步得到就业，收入差距逐步缩小。从图1－2可以看出，我国城乡差距确实有先升后降的现象，似乎和Kuznets的假说有些契合。但是，当我们同时观察城乡收入差距和增长率变化时，发现两者似乎具有线性关系，城乡收入差距随着经济增长速度的加快而上升，随着经济增长的放缓而下降。随着国民收入水平的提高，城乡收入差距不断扩大，而不是人们希望的那样先升后降。也就是说，如果未来经济增长加快，城乡收入差距还会再次拉大。

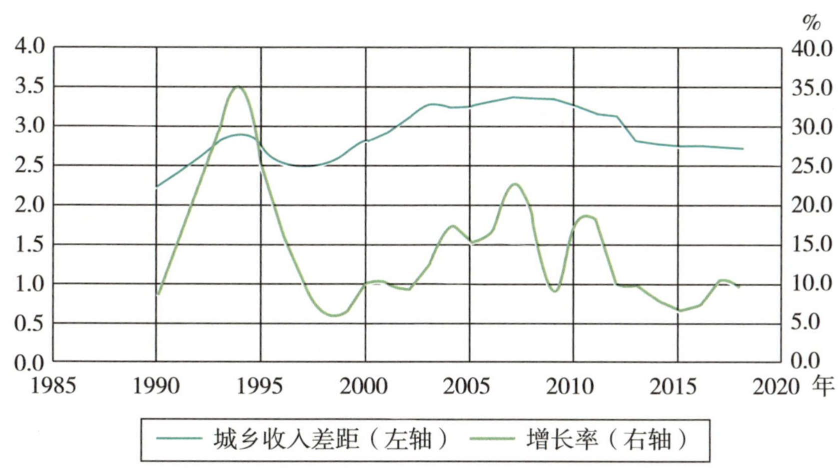

资料来源：《中国统计年鉴》。

图1－2 历年城乡收入差距

深入分析地区内的收入差距发现，经济增长带来的红利并没有被均匀分配给不同人群。随着经济增长和收入水平的提高，分配不平等的现象不仅没有得到缓解，反而进一步恶化。根据统计资料（见表1－1），无论是城市还是农村，低收入户（收入最低的20%家庭）的收入增长率都低于高收入户（收入最高的20%家庭）的收入增长率。这种趋势的必然结果就是收入差距加大。城镇高收入家庭与低收入家庭的收入差距从 2000 年的 3.6 倍上升到 2017 年的 5.6 倍；同时期农村的收入差距从 6.5 倍上升到 9.5 倍。全国范围的收入差距更大，2017 年已经达到 10.9 倍，而且在不断扩大。如果任由这种趋势发展，经济的高速增长可能会导致社会的分裂和动荡。

表 1-1　可支配收入差距变化情况

按收入分组	全国			城镇			农村		
	2013 年	2017 年	增长率（%）	2000 年	2017 年	增长率（%）	2000 年	2017 年	增长率（%）
低收入户（20%）	4402.4	5958.4	7.86	3132.0	13723.1	9.08	802.0	3301.9	8.68
中等偏下户（20%）	9653.7	13842.8	9.43	4623.5	24550.1	10.32	1440.0	8348.6	10.89
中等收入户（20%）	15698.0	22495.3	9.41	5897.9	33781.3	10.81	2004.0	11978.0	11.09
中等偏上户（20%）	24361.2	34546.8	9.13	7487.4	45163.4	11.15	2767.0	16943.6	11.25
高收入户（20%）	47456.6	64934.0	8.15	11299.0	77097.2	11.96	5190.0	31299.3	11.15

资料来源：《中国统计年鉴》。

（二）缺乏包容性是收入差距的主要根源

在经济高速增长和高基尼系数长期并存的社会中，低收入人群的生活也在不断地改善，只不过是改善的速度明显低于高收入人群。生活改善的速度不平衡背后的原因是机会的不平等，其最终表现为部分人被排斥在经济增长之外，即经济增长缺乏包容性。

社会排斥有多方面的原因。在主观因素方面，弱势人群在教育、健康、年龄、能力、地位等方面处于不利地位，是其遭受社会排斥的主要原因；个人不恰当的意识和心态也会造成自我排斥。在客观条件方面，地理位置、交通、经济、基础设施、通信等不利因素会将某些人群排斥在社会经济活动之外；此外，社会安全、制度、政策和法制等也可能引起社会排斥。

在市场经济条件下，社会排斥表现为缺乏参与经济活动的机会。人们缺乏金融资本和自然资源就无法生产出足够的产品参与市场交易，因而不能分享市场交换的红利，而低收入又造成人们无法参与某些本该参加的社会活动（如消费）；缺乏人力资本就无法进入劳力市场，丧失就业机会，而失业又导致人们被排斥在某些社会关系和制度之外，因此失业和贫困常常成为衡量社会排斥的主要指标。社会排斥越严重，收入不平等现象越严重。

（三）金融排斥加剧收入差距

收入差距是在经济增长中形成的，人力资源、自然资源、资本和制度等要素驱动经济增长，也决定了收入差距的变化方向。在自然资源和制度相对稳定的条件下，人力资源和资本在不同人群中的分配决定了收入分配，在我国尤为如此。如表 1－2 所示，工资性收入是我国居民最重要的收入来源，占 56%以上；经营性收入和转移性收入加起来超过 35%，成为第二大收入来源；财产收入在收入中占据比例较小。这种收入结构在 2013 年后有微小变化，工资性收入和经营性收入有减少的趋势，而财产性收入和转移性收入有所增加。

表 1－2　不同阶层的收入结构　　单位：%

收入结构	工资性收入	经营性收入	财产性收入	转移性收入
全国居民				
2017 年	56.3	17.3	8.1	18.3
2013 年	56.9	18.8	7.8	16.6
城镇居民				
2017 年	61.0	11.2	9.9	17.9
2000 年	71.2	3.9	2.0	22.9
农村居民				
2017 年	40.9	37.4	2.3	19.4
2000 年	30.8	62.5	2.0	3.5
2012 年按收入等级划分				
农村全部居民	41.1	42.1	3.0	8.2
低收入户	42.9	40.5	2.3	14.4
中等偏下户	42.7	46.1	1.8	9.4
中等收入户	45.4	44.4	2.0	8.2
中等偏上户	47.2	42.7	2.3	7.7
高收入户	42.7	44.7	4.7	8.0
2002 年按收入等级划分				
农村全部居民	34.1	57.3	2.4	3.6
低收入户	26.9	68.2	1.7	3.2
中等偏下户	30.1	65.8	1.4	2.7
中等收入户	35.0	60.7	1.5	2.8
中等偏上户	38.0	57.2	1.7	3.1
高收入户	40.6	51.0	3.9	4.5

资料来源：《中国统计年鉴》。

收入结构在城乡之间有比较大的差别，如表 1－2 所示，城镇居民更加依赖于工资性收入，财产性收入也明显比农村居民高。农村居民同时依赖于工资性收入和经营性收入，财产性收入总体不超过 3%。从绝对值看，2017 年城镇居民工资性收入达 22201 元，农村居民工资性收入只有 5498 元，二者间相差 16703 元，经营性收入、财产性收入和转移性收入之间的城乡差异分别为−963 元、3304 元和 3921 元。城乡差别背后的原因可以追溯到就业机会对农村劳动力的排斥、金融服务对农村居民更为严重的排斥、市场对农村财产的排斥、城乡社会保障的差异。这些因素综合起来形成了对农村居民更加严重的社会排斥。金融服务排斥不但直接影响农村地区居民的经营活动和财产性收入，而且可以通过产业结构影响农村居民的就业机会，加剧城乡收入差距。

金融排斥同样会导致农村居民内部的收入差距。如表 1－3 所示，2002—2012 年，经营性收入增长随着家庭收入的增加而加快，低收入户和高收入户的年均增长率相差约 6 个百分点。这种增长速度的差异使低收入户经营性收入的比重从 68.2%下降到 40.5%（见表 1－2），下降了约 28 个百分点，相比之下，高收入户的比重只下降了 6 个百分点。即便低收入户的工资性收入、财产性收入和转移性收入的年均增长率都比高收入户高，也抵消不了经营性收入增长的差别带来的差距，农村内部的收入差距进一步扩大。

表 1－3　农村居民不同收入水平家庭纯收入增长情况　　单位：%

年均增长率	家庭人均收入	工资性收入	经营性收入	财产性收入	转移性收入
低收入户	10.45	15.94	4.57	22.02	30.22
中等偏下户	12.00	16.29	7.93	19.07	25.97
中等收入户	12.52	16.13	8.68	19.21	24.61
中等偏上户	12.84	15.87	9.23	19.43	22.72
高收入户	12.41	12.98	10.93	16.44	17.69

资料来源：《中国统计年鉴》（2002—2012 年）。

显然，金融服务排斥对我国居民收入结构产生了重要的影响。一方面，我国的传统金融体制对产业发展优先支持，尤其是城镇大型的产业项目给城镇居民带来巨大的就业机会，有利于城镇工资水平的提高，扩大城乡收入差距；另一方面，缺乏直接金融服务，特别是金融资本从农村逃离，使农村产业凋敝，农村家庭不能有效利用其拥有的资源进行生产经营，尤其是农村低收入家庭经营性收入的增长跟不上其他收入来源的增长速度，农村内部收入分化更加严重。

（四）包容性增长

国际社会和国内社会已经逐渐认识到社会排斥特别是金融排斥的危害，意识到解决排斥问题刻不容缓。包容性增长作为一种比较理想的增长模式被人们接受。

首先，包容性增长是一种基于机会平等的增长模式，而不是过去简单的增长模式。简单的增长模式是通过提高任何生产要素的生产率以获得经济增长，包容性增长允许社会各个阶层，特别是弱势群体有平等的机会来提高他们的生产率。因此，包容性增长既强调经济的增长速度，也强调增长模式（Ianchovichina 和 Lundstrom，2009）。

其次，包容性增长是一种跨行业的广泛参与的增长模式。不同阶层的广泛参与有利于经济增长的平等分配，也有利于可持续性发展。因此，包容性增长具有公平、机会平等和利益受到保护的含义，要求所有参与者（包括商家和个人）都具有同等的入市、获取资源和在公正的监管环境中开展活动的机会。包容性增长通过促进机会平等而不是通过再分配促进收入平等分配，由此提高那些被排除在外的群体的收入水平。

最后，包容性增长具有利贫（pro-poor）的意义，不是单纯的扶贫模式。单纯的扶贫模式是一种局部的增长模式，只要求贫困群体获得实实在在的收入增长；而包容性增长是一种全面的增长模式，要求贫困人群的增长率高于富裕群体。联合国开发计划署国际包容性增长政策中心（Ranieri 和 Ramos，2013）认为，中国近期的经济增长虽然大幅降低了贫困发生率，但同时扩大了收入差距，所以不能算是利贫的增长模式。

二、我国经济增长驱动力及其包容性

中国经济的高速增长对消除极端贫困起到了非常重要的作用，只有在经济增长的前提下，才有可能将新增经济收入分配给贫困群体，并进一步解决分配不平等的问题。大量事实证明，我国经济持续高速增长主要得益于以下五个方面的因素：改革开放、宏观经济稳定、高储蓄率和投资率、市场主导、政府效率高。从统计学角度分析这些驱动因素包含的经济指标与收入差距的相关性，可以从一定程度上论证我国经济增长是否具有包容性。

（一）改革开放

我国经济驶上高速发展的轨道是以改革开放为前提的。改革开放以来，我国利用国际消费市场扩大出口，拉动国内市场，扩大经济总量。进出口的增长成为我国扩大开放的重要标志。分析自 2000 年以来各省（自治区、直辖市）人均进出口与人均

GDP 的关系，发现两者的相关系数为 0.55，说明它们之间具有相当强的正相关关系，或者说，进出口的增长率可以解释很大一部分经济的增长。

进一步分析发现，各地人均进出口增长率具有很大的变化。如图 1-3 所示，自 2000 年以来，各省（自治区、直辖市）的进出口增长率是不一样的，最高的为重庆，年均增长 23.2%；最低的为青海，年均增长 7.7%。总体来看，西南方向进出口增长率偏高，东北方向进出口增长率偏低。这种长期的进出口增长差异，可能是改革开放给每个地方、每个家庭带来的机遇不平等的重要根源之一。对于家庭来说，开放政策给他们带来的最重要的红利就是就业机会。

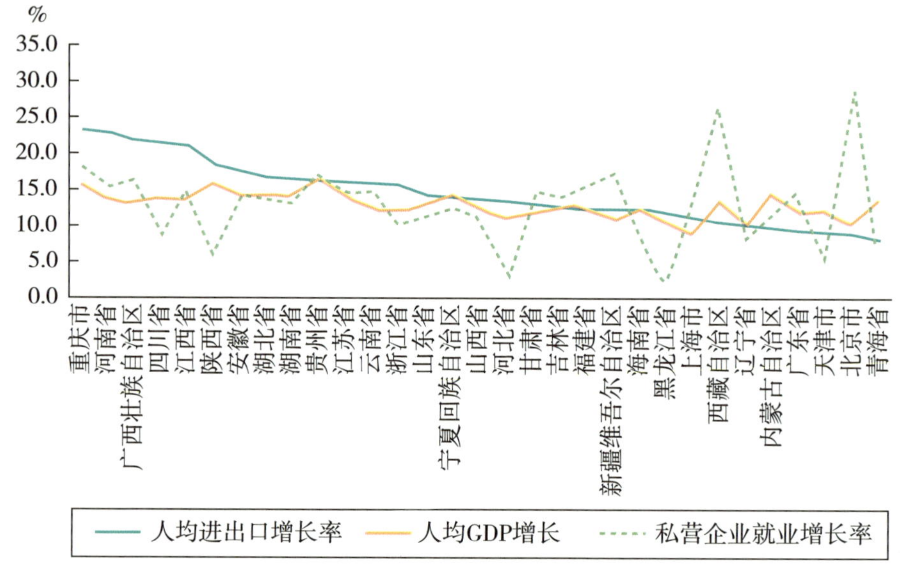

资料来源：《中国统计年鉴》。

图 1-3　2000—2017 年经济增长与进出口、就业的关系

改革开放通过进出口创造了大量的就业，为城市特别是农村富余劳动力提供了大量的就业机会，最直观的变化就是私营企业的兴起，可以推断，进出口增长促进了私营企业就业机会的增加。我们分析了 31 个省（自治区、直辖市）2000—2017 年进出口增长率与私营企业就业人数，发现两者之间的关系系数很小，只有 0.06，这个结果似乎否定了我们的推断。进一步观察图 1-3 发现，北京和西藏是两个例外，其私营企业的就业增长率极高，而进出口增长率不高。北京是大企业包括私营企业的总部所在地，提供的工作岗位比较集中，所以就业增长率是个例外。西藏由于地处内陆高原，其私营企业的产品主要销往国内其他省（自治区、直辖市），所以进出口增长率不高。除此之外，其他地区的进出口增长率和私营企业的就业增长率似乎存在比较明显的关系。

将两个地区去除后分析其他 29 个省（自治区、直辖市）两个指标的相关性，其系数为 0.40，因此，我们确信进出口的增长可以带动私营企业的增长从而增加就业。地区间进出口增长的差异同样可以解释城镇就业增长率的差异，其相关系数达 0.33。

地区间的进出口差异影响到就业机会的差异，其必然导致收入的差异。如表 1－4 所示，进出口增长率与城镇单位职工工资、城镇居民和农村居民收入的增长都呈正相关关系，其中与农村居民的收入增长关系最密切，相关系数约为 0.63，而与城镇居民的收入相关较小。

表 1－4　进出口增长与收入增长的相关系数

	人均进出口增长率	人均 GDP 增长率	城镇单位职工工资增长率	城镇居民收入增长率	农村居民收入增长率
人均 GDP 增长率	0.4438				
城镇单位职工工资增长率	0.4512	0.3406			
城镇居民收入增长率	0.1837	0.1030	0.0811		
农村居民收入增长率	0.6254	0.2880	0.5564	0.0879	
城乡差距变化	－0.3572	－0.0686	－0.3717	0.5460	－0.7512

资料来源：《中国统计年鉴》。

人均进出口的增长不仅带来经济总量的增长，而且具有非常明显的缩小城乡收入差距的效果。如表 1－4 所示，两者的关系呈负相关关系，系数为－0.3572。城镇单位职工平均工资与进出口的增长率呈正相关关系，相关系数为 0.4512。城镇单位职工包含非私营法人单位和私营法人单位的职工，特别是私营单位的职工大多数来自附近的农村地区，就业机会和平均工资的增加都有利于缩小城乡收入差距。

通过对我国经济增长的分析发现，改革开放带来了进出口增长，增加了就业机会，能够对农村劳动力具有较好的包容性。在这种包容性的前提下，进出口带来城镇职工平均工资的增长，而城镇职工大多数实际上是农村劳动力，因此进出口带动了农村居民收入的增长。进出口拉动的增长具有明显的“利贫性”，是一种包容性增长。

（二）宏观经济稳定

宏观经济的稳定除了需要一个稳定的政治环境，金融货币政策的稳定也起到了非常重要的作用，汇率、通货膨胀和利率都要维持在可控的范围内。我国在这方面的表现相当出色，改革开放以来没有出现大的经济波动，成功地抵御了 1997 年亚洲金融危机和 2008 年国际金融危机的冲击，增强了投资者的信心，稳定了就业。

宏观经济的波动与货币供应有密切的关系，如表1-5所示，为货币供应、人均GDP、价格、城乡差别及基尼系数之间的关系。很显然，无论是M_0、M_1还是M_2，其供应量的适当增长，都与剔除物价因素后的人均GDP增长有密切关系。不同的是，M_0供应的增长同时带动物价上涨，而M_1和M_2的增长与物价上涨率呈负相关关系，表现为对物价上涨的抑制作用。货币供应、物价和GDP增长与城乡收入差距及基尼系数都有非常密切的正相关关系。单纯以货币政策来刺激经济增长很难直接增加经济的包容性。

表1-5　2000年以后宏观经济主要指标相关系数

	货币和准货币（M_2）供应量增长率	货币（M_1）供应量增长率	流通中现金（M_0）供应量增长率	人均GDP（99价）增长率	居民消费价格增长率	城镇居民消费价格增长率	农村居民消费价格增长率	城乡收入差距
货币和准货币（M_2）供应量增长率	1							
货币（M_1）供应量增长率	0.6769	1						
流通中现金（M_0）供应量增长率	0.7119	0.5138	1					
人均GDP（99价）增长率	0.4369	0.3263	0.7515	1				
居民消费价格增长率	−0.1125	−0.3642	0.2639	0.3559	1			
城镇居民消费价格增长率	−0.1779	−0.4060	0.2160	0.2997	0.9932	1		
农村居民消费价格增长率	−0.0022	−0.2891	0.3411	0.4288	0.9874	0.9630	1	
城乡收入差距	0.7767	0.4421	0.8378	0.7988	0.2738	0.1959	0.3814	1
基尼系数	0.4725	0.0625	0.3261	0.3488	0.5135	0.4743	0.5528	0.5931

金融政策经常被当成稳定经济增长的一种重要手段。分析 2002 年以来人均社会融资规模的增长率（见表 1-6）发现，宏观层面的融资增长和 GDP 增长呈正相关关系，也和城乡收入差距、基尼系数呈正相关关系。人均人民币贷款社会融资规模增长率则与 GDP 增长呈微弱的负相关关系，但是具有扩大收入差距的效果。简单地增加社会融资并不能有效地解决发展不平衡问题。

表 1-6　2000 年以后主要金融指标相关系数

	人均社会融资规模增长率	人均人民币贷款社会融资规模增长率	人均国内生产总值（99 价）增长率	城乡收入差距	基尼系数
人均社会融资规模增长率	1				
人均人民币贷款社会融资规模增长率	0.9052	1			
人均国内生产总值（99 价）增长率	0.1629	−0.0753	1		
城乡收入差距	0.4609	0.2929	0.8131	1	
基尼系数	0.5347	0.4598	0.7060	0.8977	1

财政政策的稳定和公共财政投入的不断增长可以增加基础设施建设，有利于被排斥在外的群体特别是边远地区的人群享受到包括教育、医疗、交通、社会保障等在内的社会服务。我们分析 2000 年后全国财政支出的增长率，发现它和收入差距存在正相关关系。似乎简单地增加财政开支并不能解决收入差距问题。

在更微观的研究中，我们分析了 2031 个县域 2000 年底人均银行贷款余额、人均财政支出、教育水平等指标与 2009 年城乡收入差别的关系，发现除了教育水平的提高可以缩小未来的城乡收入差别外，金融服务和财政支出水平的高低，并不能影响到未来的城乡收入差距。如何通过金融服务促进经济的包容性增长，依然是一个亟待研究的课题。

（三）高储蓄率和投资率

中国人具有储蓄的偏好，无论贫富都普遍具有储蓄的基因。对于一个家庭来说，一方面，储蓄是为了应对未来子女教育、预防疾病、灾害、养老等方面的开支；另一方面，储蓄是资本的形成和积累。研究一再证明，通过储蓄积累资本是永久性脱离贫困陷阱的最好办法。从宏观层面来看，家庭的储蓄也为社会投资积累资本。增加储蓄的一个重要社会条件是稳定的经济环境。在稳定的宏观经济环境中，就业稳定，收入稳定，储蓄率通常比较高。

图 1-4 显示了储蓄的增长与城乡收入差距的关系。很显然，2002—2014 年，人均城乡储蓄增长快的地区，城乡收入差距缩小得比较快，两者呈负相关关系，系数达 0.3854。由此可见，能促进居民储蓄的经济增长模式具有比较高的包容性。

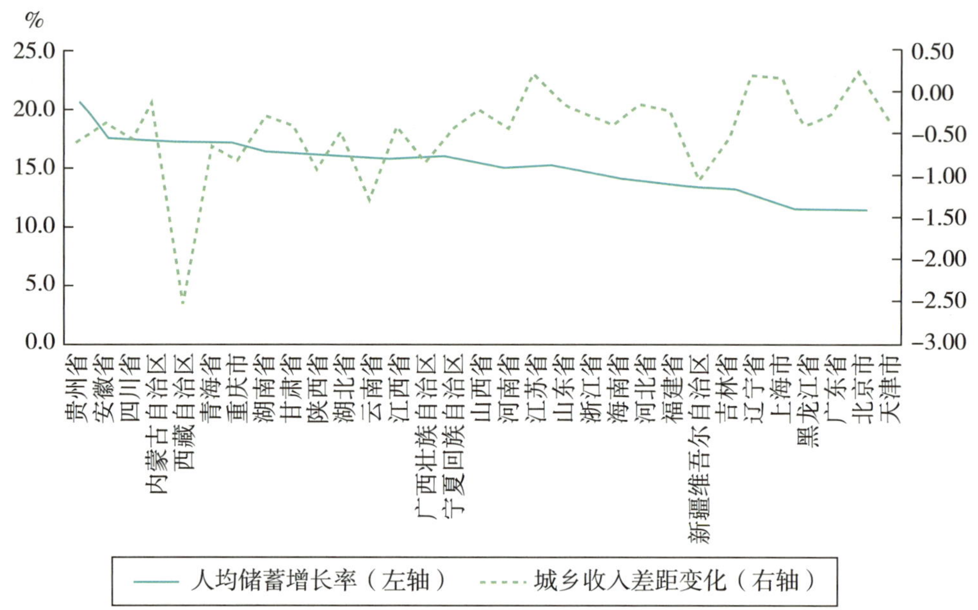

资料来源：《中国统计年鉴》。

图 1-4　城乡储蓄增长与城镇收入差距变化的关系

（四）市场主导

改革开放以来，国家推行的各项改革大多以市场为主导来配置资源，包括国有企业的市场化改制和促进私营部门的成长。国家虽然实施某些引导政策，但基本上遵循“让相对优势发挥作用”的经济原则，没有妨碍生产要素向优势产业部门配置，尤其是资金和劳动力集中投入出口、制造、劳动密集型产业等领域，吸纳了大量过去被排斥的劳动力。

衡量一个经济体的市场化程度是非常困难的事情，我们用国有部门与私营部门的比值作为市场化程度的代理变量来分析市场化程度与城乡收入差距的关系。图 1-5 使用“国有控股工业企业主营业务收入”与“私营工业企业主营业务收入”的比值，考察 2000—2017 年这个比值的变化与城镇收入差距的变化以及 GDP 增长的关系。不难看出，这个时期，凡是比值下降较大的地区，或者说是国有企业占据份额下降越快的地区，其城乡收入差距缩小的幅度越大，与此同时，这些地区的GDP增长速度也更快。很显然，私营部门所占市场份额的增长，不仅有利于经济增长，也有利于缩小城乡收入差距。可见，促进私营部门的市场化是一种包容性的增长模式。

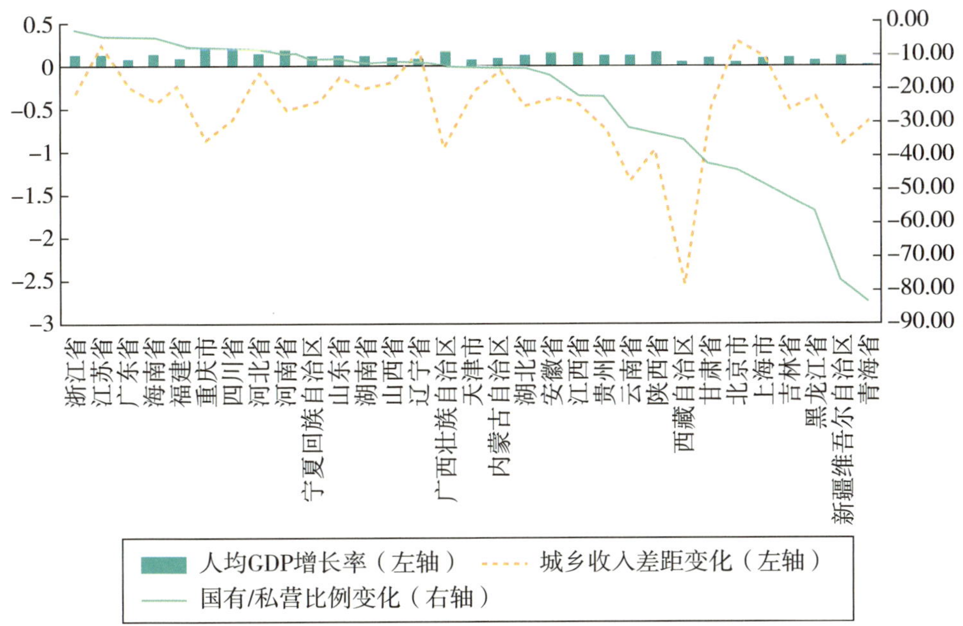

图1-5 国有工业企业与私营工业企业营业收入比例变化与城乡收入差距变化的关系

（五）政府效率高

从40多年改革开放的经验来看，政府在推行改革开放、维持经济稳定和市场秩序等方面保持高效率，是包容性经济增长的重要保障。首先，改革的方向需要政府进行把控，国际上许多从计划经济向市场经济转型失败的案例已经验证了一个高效的政府对经济增长的重要性；其次，上述提到的财政支出，特别是公共服务、社会保障、教育、医疗卫生、环境保护等方面的基础设施建设，都需要一个高效的政府来运作；最后，只有高效的政府才能保证货币、金融和财政政策的有效实行，以保证宏观经济的稳定。

三、普惠金融对包容性增长的作用

普惠金融作为一种发展理念与包容性增长具有天然的关系。两者都是要通过增加对中小微企业和弱势群体的包容性，改善其处境，缩小贫富差距。由于金融排斥性也是社会排斥性的重要组成部分，发展普惠金融、解决金融的排斥问题也是实现经济包容性增长的重要途径。

在微观层面，普惠金融能改善家庭生活福利，增加经济收入。正如安信永的研究显示，普惠金融给企业和家庭带来以下七个方面的好处。一是金融促进经济交换。以支付服务为例，支付体系完善的经济体中，个人或企业可以就近交易甚至通过网络进行移动支付，花费的时间短、交易成本低且风险小。二是有利于日常财务资源的管理。低收入家庭收入少而且不稳定，信贷和储蓄服务可以帮助他们抓住机遇、增加收入、平滑消费。三是改善生活质量。低收入家庭可以使用金融产品来保证教育、健康和日常必需的服务，提高生活水平。四是缓解脆弱性。低收入家庭有很多方面的脆弱性，包括疾病、灾害和失业等。信贷、储蓄、汇款、保险服务都有利于他们免受这些脆弱性带来的冲击。五是有利于增加生产性投入。企业和家庭可以通过信贷和储蓄增加对生产性资产的投入。六是有利于撬动资本。以数字支付为代表的金融科技的发展推动包括个人信用体系在内的金融基础设施的完善，有利于低收入家庭为生产活动进行融资。七是树立经济公民身份。金融服务让人们更加独立、更有能力参与社区和国家的各种活动。

从宏观层面，普惠金融能够在以下五个方面促进经济增长。

第一，加速商品流通，提高经济效率。普惠金融尤其是数字普惠金融，增加了交易的便捷性，缩短了交易时间，减少了交易成本。Beck 等（2009）研究认为，包容性金融可以降低信息和交易成本，改善投资决策，提高储蓄率，促进科技创新，提高长期增长率。更重要的是，普惠金融将很多原来被排斥在外的低收入群体纳入经济活动中，在增加他们收入的同时，扩大了经济总体规模，提高了经济的总体效率。

第二，有利于经济的稳定。普惠金融提供服务时产生了大规模的数据。在数字经济时代，数据具有多方面的用途，其中一个重要用途就是风险控制。数字化的风险控制措施精准且反应迅速，可以减少风控成本，提高风控的有效性，有利于经济的稳定发展。同时，稳定的经济条件也有利于发挥资产的融资杠杆作用，增加全社会投资总量，进一步促进经济增长。

第三，促进社会诚信环境建设。数据的另一个用途就是打造数字信用体系，基于支付表现建立起来的信誉担保，是信用信息体系最基本的用途。建立在普惠金融数据基础上的信用体系，涉及广泛而且准确，信用记录保留时间长，影响深远，对失信行为具有强有力的震慑作用，有利于培育诚信社会。在高度诚信的社会中融资难问题更容易得到解决。

第四，提高政府效率。普惠金融的发展使政府的社会保障和扶贫工作更加精准有效，特别是建立在数字普惠金融基础上的监管，成本更低，效率更高。高效的社会保障和监管为包容性增长提供良好的社会安全保障。

第五，增加就业。普惠金融通过支持中小微企业，为被排斥的劳动力提供就业机会，解决经济发展不充分不平衡问题。

许多研究证明了普惠金融发展可以促进经济增长。Beck、Demirgüç-Kunt 和 Honohan（2009）研究认为，金融可得性的改善不但能促进增长，且有利于减少贫困，缩小收入差距。Beck、Demirgüç-Kunt 和 Levine（2007）及 Littlefield、Morduch 和 Hashemi（2003）研究发现，普惠金融发展已经在实现联合国千年发展目标中发挥了作用，在扶贫、健康、教育和性别平等方面的效果尤为明显。

四、促进包容性增长的普惠金融措施

包容性增长已经成为目前和未来主流的增长模式，我国改革开放以来的经济增长有一定程度的包容性，特别是民营企业的发展为广大农村劳动力提供了大量的就业机会，对缩小收入差距起到明显的作用。但是分析也表明，我国的城乡差距随经济增长的加速而加大，随着经济增长的放缓而缩小，总体而言，随着国民整体收入水平的提高而扩大。发展普惠金融，在微观层面上可以提高低收入人群的收入和福利水平；在宏观层面上可以促进包容性增长，缓解社会不平等。因此，有必要采取措施推动普惠金融的发展，以实现促进包容性增长的目标。

第一，加强数字信息基础设施建设，整合分散在不同机构和部门的数据资源。随着数字经济的到来，数字信息基础设施将成为未来非常重要的公共产品，所以必须打破当前数字孤岛或数字壁垒的格局，建立可以共享的统一数据存储系统。数字信息基础设施的建立，既有利于普惠金融的发展，也能够促进经济的全面增长。

第二，加强数字信用体系建设，促进社会诚信发展。数字信用体系是数字技术最基本的应用，对社会诚信将产生积极而深远的影响。

第三，建立数字化的监管体系，保障经济的稳定和安全。稳定的经济环境对普惠金融和包容性增长都具有积极的意义。历史经验证明，金融危机是经济波动的主要起因，只有处理好普惠金融与金融稳定之间的关系，才能培育包容性的增长模式。

第四，加强金融能力建设，提高弱势群体的生产效率。较低的金融能力使弱势群体无法使用金融产品和服务来提高其生产效率，提高其金融素养和技能可以促进他们收入的提升。而提高中小微企业的金融能力除了可以提高其经营效率，还可以为弱势群体创造更多的就业机会，有利于缩小收入差距。

除此以外，必须强调政府在发展普惠金融、促进包容性增长方面的引导作用。政府在解决市场失灵中发挥不可或缺的作用。Beck 和 de la Torre（2006）研究发现，市场失灵与信息鸿沟有关，对集体行动的协调和集中力量的需要，都意味着政府必须在普惠金融建设中发挥重要作用。

第二章　数字技术的作用机制与局限

【摘要】在人们还来不及弄清其作用机理的情况下，数字技术以爆发式的速度将金融服务送达亿万名普通消费者。这种状况容易让人们对数字技术期望过高。事实上，数字技术也是通过成本、风险控制和市场竞争等金融交易的若干要素来提升金融的包容性，了解数字技术如何通过这些要素发挥作用有助于理解数字金融的局限性。

大量的事实已经让人们意识到数字技术可以大幅提升金融服务的包容性，进而对数字技术寄予厚望，期待数字技术将给金融服务带来颠覆性的变化。变化来得太快，人们还来不及考虑金融服务速度发展的背后是什么机理在发挥作用。对作用机理的探究有助于我们发现数字金融服务可能存在的局限。

一、数字技术促进金融包容性

数字技术对普惠金融的贡献体现在它能够解决金融服务交易双方遇到的诸多问题。成本常常是普惠金融面临的最重要问题。金融服务属于风险业务，能否用较小的成本将风险控制在一定的范围内，考验了风险控制的有效性。在有效的金融体系内，适当竞争是降低成本、提高风险控制的有效性、扩大金融服务的包容性的重要途径。数字技术是否有利于提高金融服务的包容性，要看它能否有助于降低成本、提高风控的有效性和强化竞争。

（一）交易成本降低

在金融服务中，交易双方都要付出一定的成本，交易才能完成。过去，大多数分析只限于分析供应方的成本，而忽略了需求方的成本。当然，供应方拥有更大的能力和技术力量来影响成本，进而决定某种服务的可得性。从需求方的角度看，交易成本包含交易价格和获得服务的附加成本。交易价格取决于供应方成本和利润。需求方的附加成本因人而异，地理位置、交通条件、获得服务所需的时间都会影响需求方的附加成本。数字技术的应用不但降低了供应方的成本，也降低了需求方的附加成本。

1. 需求方附加成本降低

需求方获得金融服务的附加成本包含交通费、时间机会成本和其他成本。在传统的金融服务中，金融机构根据服务能力和服务半径，设置物理服务网点，周围的消费者需要付出交通费和时间到服务网点获得服务。CAFI 在广西的一项调查中发现，在 987 个农户中，有 24%的农户获得金融服务的最近距离为 1～5 公里，有 22.8%的农户最近距离为 5～10 公里，有 30.2%的农户最近距离为 10～20 公里（见图 2-1）。可以设想，在交通工具为步行、自行车和电动自行车为主的农村，农户要想获得金融服务就需要付出较多的交通费和时间成本。当然，为了节约成本，农户会在一次行程中办理多种事务，但是这种状况也会减少服务的频率。总之，农户获得服务的成本和时间明显高于城市居民。

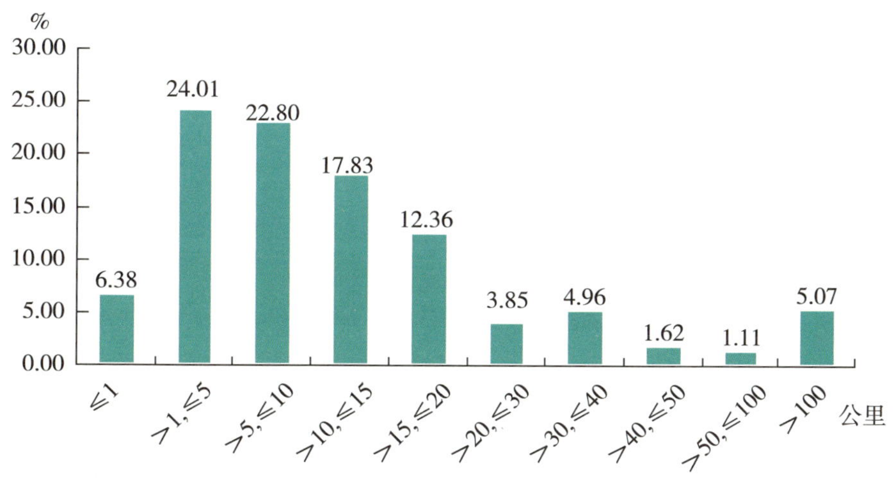

图 2-1　农户获得金融服务的最近距离

图 2-2 显示了农户获得贷款所付出的附加成本。在广西调查样本中有 104 户在 2015 年有银行贷款，平均利率为 7.7%，平均附加成本为 1.1%，总成本为 8.8%。其中，只有 13.5%的农户没有付出任何附加成本，71.2%的农户要付出贷款额 1%的附加成本，约有 15%的农户支付的附加成本超过 1%，附加成本最高的达到 4%。

通过移动终端提供数字金融服务，可以明显增加金融服务的可得性，其主要机理就是降低农户的附加成本。如果农户安装了金融机构的 APP，直接通过它申请并获得贷款，就可以节约上述 1.1%的附加成本。其普惠金融的效果，可以从问卷调查生成的普惠金融（贷款）需求曲线测算。如图 2-3 所示，如果利率水平从 8.8%下降到

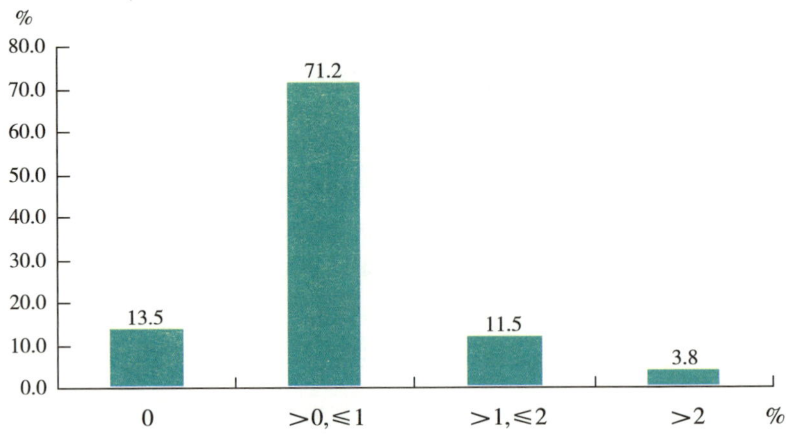

图 2-2　农户获得贷款所支付的附加成本

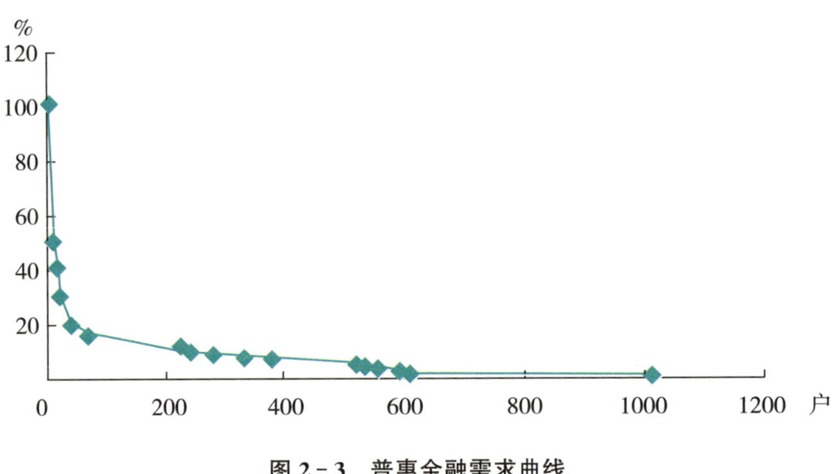

图 2-3　普惠金融需求曲线

7.7%，将有 6.5%的新增农户愿意向金融机构贷款。这样的增长率，对于贷款覆盖率只有 12.3%的贫困地区来说，是一个非常大的发展。

2. 运营成本降低

数字化可以大幅降低成本。其中包括：一是大幅减少一线服务人员的数量，减少人员费用的开支。数字普惠金融通过互联网和手机连接客户，金融机构从自己的渠道和其他服务渠道获得大量的客户信息，通过大数据建模对客户进行数字画像，对客户的需求进行细分，提供个性化的金融服务。二是数字化服务特别是手机银行不需要建设许多物理网点，因此减少了大量的租赁费用和装修费用。同时，也减少了与物理网点相关的物业水电、装修折旧、安保支出、运钞等日常运营成本。根据 McQuinn (2016)，专用 IT 基础设施的建设成本和维护成本分别是传统银行的 60%～80%和 30%～59%，员工数只是传统银行的 10%～15%。

提高效率是数字普惠金融降低成本的主要途径。中国普惠金融研究院对中和农信数字化项目的调查发现（贝多广、李焰、莫秀根，2017），有85.13%的员工认为数字化以后可以让他们腾出更多的时间进行营销，有65.1%的员工认为他们的贷款业务量由此提升。与此同时，如图2－4所示，80%以上的受访信贷员认为数字化服务节约了交通工具的油耗，减少了上门放收款的时间，超过90%的受访信贷员认为数字化服务减少了去银行存取款的时间。此外，信贷员更为关注现金放收款带来的安全问题，90%以上的信贷员认为集中代付避免了保管大额现金、降低了收到假币带来的风险。

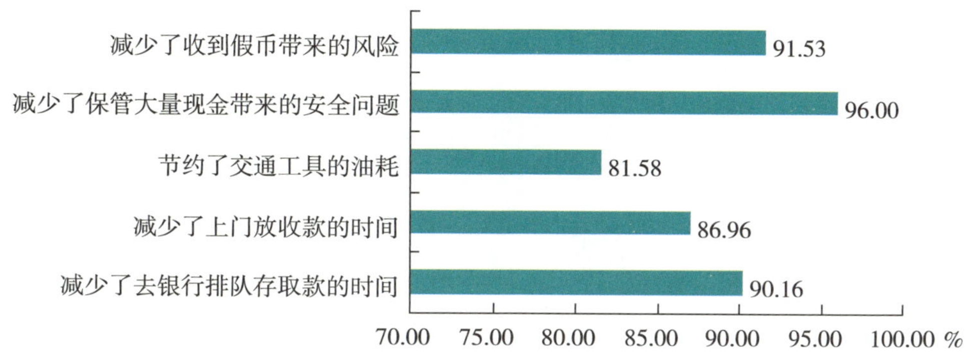

图2－4　信贷员对数字化服务提高效率情况的感受

3. 风险管理成本降低

风险管理是金融服务的中心内容，在获客、放贷和贷后管理等环节中都要围绕风险管理来开展。在信用体系不健全的情况下，金融机构根据客户的个人信用来评估客户是否具有违约风险，并采取合适措施防范金融风险。金融机构之间的信息壁垒导致信息孤岛的形成，使恶意欺诈等问题经常发生。为了避免风险，金融机构只能投入更多的人力层层把关，严格审批程序。成本增加和风险降低是一种负相关关系。综合起来，风险管理成本占据了金融服务成本的主要部分。

大数据应用的核心是金融风控。大数据技术使金融机构对客户的信用情况更加了解。大数据不但能够了解客户的信贷情况，而且能了解客户与信贷相关的经济活动、社交活动和生活消费行为等，依托丰富的数据，金融机构可以建立比较完善的征信体系。例如，由中国人民银行主导建立的征信体系已经在全国范围内防范金融风险方面发挥了重要作用。

截至2014年，国家征信系统收录8.6亿多自然人，有3.5亿人拥有信贷记录，收录企业及其他组织近2068万户（见图2－5）。征信系统采集的企业信息包括贷款、保理、票据贴现、贸易融资、信用证、保函、银行承兑汇票、公开授信等信贷业务，以及与之相关的担保、垫款、欠息、资产接入及资产处置、养老保险参保缴费、住房公积金缴费等信息，涉及的数据项超过200项。采集的个人信息覆盖贷款、信用卡、担保等信贷信息，以及个人住房公积金缴存信息、社会保险缴存和发放信息、车辆交易和抵押信息、法院判决和执行信息、税务信息、电信信息、个人低保救助信息、执业资格和奖惩信息等公共信息，涉及的数据项超过80项。

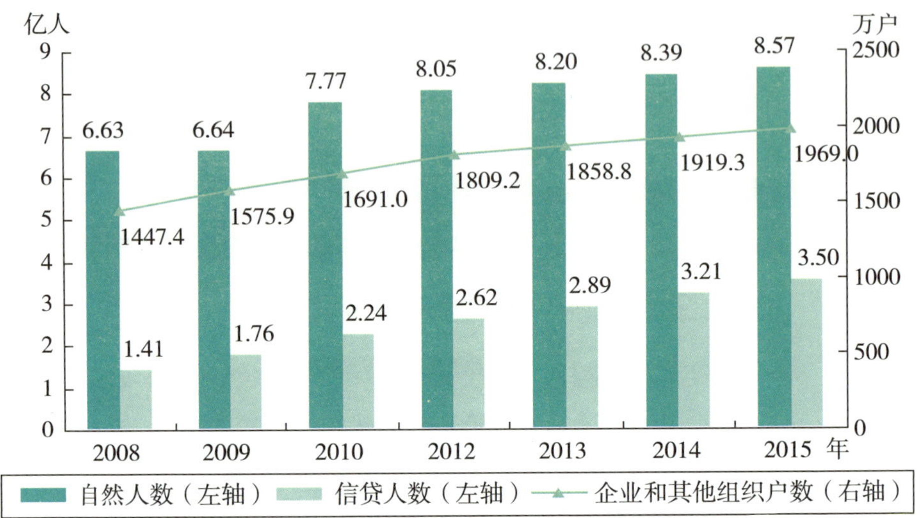

资料来源：中国人民银行征信中心。

图2-5 征信系统收录的企业和个人征信情况

征信系统的信息查询端口遍布全国各地的金融机构网点，信用信息服务网络覆盖全国，形成了以企业和个人信用报告为核心的征信产品体系，征信中心出具的信用报告已经成为国内企业和个人的“经济身份证”，也成为金融机构防范风险必须依赖的主要信用信息来源。

除了国家征信系统，不少企业也利用掌握的数据建立自己的信用体系。根据李焰（2017）对中国官网的统计，目前中国明确表示运用数字技术的征信机构共有79家。从事数字征信的机构分为两类，一类是从事互联网金融、社交网络、搜索引擎平台等互联网公司，出于业务需要开展大数据征信，征信结果自用或者与其他企业交换、共享；另一类是专门从事大数据信用信息服务的机构。

根据不同的信用数据，金融机构可以建立大数据风险控制体系，多维度、全方位地进行风险管理、风险决策，提高审核效率，提升信贷业务质量，降低潜在的信用风险和金融损失风险。

大数据风险管理体系对成本的影响有两个方面：一方面是减少风险管理中的人工成本。大数据技术能够收集和存储金融业务中的各种数据，经过建模技术进行智能化的风险管理决策，因此减少人工成本。另一方面是提高了效率，由于大数据风险管理可以在几秒钟内作出决策，极大地提高了决策的效率。综上所述，大数据风险管理体系大幅降低了风险管理的成本。

由于成本是企业非常重要的机密信息，数字技术带来的风险成本降低的实操数据很难获取。IIF 和麦肯锡（2017）采用模拟的办法推算成本下降的幅度：采用机器人和自动化的风险控制，可以将信用风险管理和风险预警功能的效率提高 10%～20%；由于模型能够更好地对不良信用进行预判，可以将信用风险损失减少 5%～10%；由于自动化减少了人为错误，改善了对员工不适当行为的监督，运营和罚款损失下降 8%～10%；由于资本配置效率提高，储备率降低，资本成本降低 4%～8%，信贷和风险加权资产的比例降低 5%～9%；随着数据管理的优化，用于风险管理的 IT 技术效率可以提高 10%～20%。

（二）风险控制更加有效

对 399 家小额贷款公司的风险情况进行调查发现（具体结果见第十三章），互联网和金融技术的使用并没有像一部分人担心的那样，会显著增加贷款风险。也就是说，在风控成本降低的同时，互联网和金融技术的使用并未增加金融服务的风险。数字金融促进风控效率的提高，主要体现在以下三个方面。

1. 风险识别效率高

数字技术在风险识别方面显现出比较高的效率。金融机构使用数字技术进行风险识别可能包含三个步骤。第一，身份证识别和认证。通过身份证识别系统、人脸识别系统、银行卡绑定和个人网络征信验证等，实现用户信息的交叉验证，有效地识别用户的真实身份，确保用户账户的真实性和有效性。第二，反欺诈侦测识别。通过黑名单拦截系统、灰名单侦测、GPS 定位、IP/MAC 地址侦测、社交关系模型等反欺诈技术手段，对客户在线提交的各项材料，通过信息交叉检验甄别真伪。第三，用户信用评级。通过蜂鸟数据采集技术实现用户授权信息自动采集，能迅速、有效地甄别用户信用级别，从而自动完成风险控制和风险评定。

RegTech 可以提高监管部门对金融风险的识别能力。RegTech 是金融科技的分支，它采用新技术以更高效的方式为满足合规和监管要求提供解决方案，包括大数据分析和数据可视化技术、区块链技术不可更改的分布式账本技术、人工智能及包括任何自然语言和语义分析理解的深度学习。RegTech 通过改进数据处理、客户身份识别、压力测试、市场行为监控和法律法规跟踪等环节，能够提升监管机构的监管能力和降低金融机构的合规成本。

2. 风险分散

缓解风险最有效的方法之一是分散投资。数字技术的应用，不仅能够降低风险管理的成本，提高金融风险识别的能力，更重要的是能够提供多样的小额分散金融产品，投资人可以选择更合适的金融产品组合来降低风险，也使投资人具有承担适度风险的能力。

另外，数字技术也有利于金融信息的透明，为客户提供识别风险的相关信息。通过数字技术的使用，金融服务机构可以提供以下服务：对特定产品风险的相关信息进行查询，了解资产类别和行业等级；基于模拟场景预测风险；根据历史趋势分析比较，帮助客户进行投资组合分析；生成投资组合，并对风险和回报进行预测分析；根据个人或公司对风险和长期投资回报率的容忍度提出建议等。

由于金融技术的进步，信贷服务和保险服务可以有机结合，产生叠加效果，降低金融机构和客户双方的风险。

3. 风险处置效率高

风险处置的基本方法包括回避、减少、转移和接受风险。数字技术的应用使这几种风险处置方法更加有效。高效的风险识别、有效的风险预警机制、风险信息的透明等，让金融机构和客户能在进行金融服务的交易全过程回避风险。分散风险机制总体减少金融机构的风险，小额金融服务也使每一位客户将风险控制在可以接受的范围内。

（三）促进供给竞争

1. 促进供给多元化

数字金融服务实际上已经突破了地理边界，通过网络特别是移动网络，每一位客户可以了解并选择全国其他地方的金融服务，客户有更多的产品选择权，完全可以按照自己的偏好对服务组合进行选择。

金融机构通过采用大数据分析，能够更加了解客户的需求，对客户的需求进行有效细分，设计并提供更加有针对性的产品，提供个性化的金融服务，使金融交易更加符合个性化需求，又增加了金融机构获得的回报，同时提高了普惠金融服务的可持续性。

2. 服务模式融合

经过几百年的经验积累，传统金融开发形成了一种比较完善的金融服务体系，尤其是金融风险控制体系。实践证明，这些风险控制的方法是有效的。但是，传统金融由于成本高、效率低、服务半径小、交易进程慢等原因，自动将中小微企业和弱势人群排除在外。数字技术的应用刚好弥补了传统金融的不足，可以为中小微企业和弱势人群提供可以负担得起成本的金融服务，而且服务质量大大提高。这就使数字金融具有很高的包容性，它的发展将大幅促进普惠金融的发展，增加金融服务乃至经济发展的公平性。

二、数字金融的局限

数字金融也有自身的局限，并不可能解决所有阶层的金融服务问题。数字金融不完全等于普惠金融，两者高度重合，但各有边界。数字化可以明显降低成本，但是仍需供需双方有一定的投入。如图 2－3 所示，有一部分农户只有在成本极低的情况下才愿意使用金融服务。因此，数字化不可能解决普惠金融的所有问题。

（一）数字金融和普惠金融具有不同的边界

对于数字金融服务比较宽松的定义就是所有数字化了的金融服务。按照当前的发展趋势，金融服务几乎可以全部实现数字化。也有比较严格的定义认为，数字化金融服务就是通过互联网和移动网络提供的金融服务。

有时候很难对传统金融服务和数字金融服务作出非常清楚的划分。例如，目前分布在广大农村地区的金融服务点的代理人员可以利用 POS 机，通过互联网或者移动信号与银行连接，为当地的农村居民提供各种金融服务，包括查询、提取现金、转账和购物等。这是一种混合型的金融服务，它在解决当前农村金融服务“最后一公里”问题中起到重要的作用。

数字金融和普惠金融的边界不是完全重合的。数字技术拓展了普惠金融服务边界。一方面，体现在它通过数字技术的发展及互联网基础设施的普及，打破了时间和空间的限制，实现金融在地理上的全覆盖；另一方面，数字技术带来的金融模式创新能够增加普惠金融的资金供给，拓展贫困人群的投融资渠道。随着数字技术金融创新的不断涌现，一些新兴的金融业态如 P2P 网络贷款、众筹等新型金融工具和业务的产生，将普惠金融纳入更广阔的金融市场中，为增加普惠金融的供给提供了更多的融资渠道和选择。同时，数字技术的发展带来了“鲶鱼效应”，加剧了金融业的竞争，特别是它有助于打破我国农村金融体系中农村信用社“一家独大”的状况，有利于提高金融资源配置的效率，更好地满足广大农民的金融需求。

（二）数字鸿沟引起新的排斥

尽管数字技术具有金融普惠效应，帮助缓解传统的金融排斥，但其效应的发挥还是会受到数字鸿沟、知识鸿沟等多方面因素的制约，形成由于新的金融排斥，将一部分人群排斥在数字普惠金融服务之外。总体来看，农村地区数字技术在金融领域的应用可能存在以下发展障碍：

一是地域排斥。数字技术在金融领域的发展与地区经济发展水平息息相关，经济发达地区的数字技术应用和互联网金融发展水平普遍较高，经济落后地区的发展水平则较低。

二是信息排斥。数字技术的应用在金融领域面临评估排斥。由于我国征信体系还处于初创阶段，广大农村地区农民的信用体系建设基本处于空白状态，导致金融机构很多时候无法判断客户的信用状况，形成评估排斥。虽然大数据、云计算技术确实能够降低互联网金融机构的信息搜寻成本，但很多农户并无网购记录或银行账户记录，使大数据很难覆盖这个群体，特别是贫困地区的农户。

三是成本排斥。在推动普惠金融发展的进程中，金融机构面临的最突出的难题就是缺乏优质的资金来源，运营成本较高，而依托数字金融维持运营必然会提高其产品定价，形成价格排斥。例如，P2P 行业在 2015 年以前的“野蛮生长”阶段，为吸引更多的投资者和资金加入，平台综合收益率最高达 17.86%（2014 年），虽然 2015 年其下降至 11.6%，但融资者的筹资成本仍然很高。考虑线下营销、调查、管理的成本，一些平台年化贷款利率达 18%～23%，这远高于同期银行贷款利率，会使一大批贫困人群因价格因素被排斥在数字技术金融服务之外。

四是终端排斥。这是指数字普惠金融服务过程中，由于受众缺少电脑、手机等终端工具未能将其覆盖所导致的排斥。从现实发展来看，许多贫困地区的群众因缺少电子设备而被排斥在金融服务之外，这种排斥也被看作是工具排斥。截至 2016 年底，我国农村地区还有 66.9%的农户未实现互联网覆盖。近年来，各大金融机构纷纷推出网上银行、手机银行业务，这些业务在农村发展相对缓慢，其中一个原因可能是工具排斥。农村地区人群的电话、电脑等电子产品拥有量少且使用能力差，相关费用承担能力不足，制约数字技术在贫困农村地区金融普惠效应的发挥。

五是能力排斥。数字技术应用中还面临服务群体自我排斥的问题。数字普惠金融对于其使用群体的文化素质、金融素养及相关互联网金融技能都有一定要求，而在农村地区，农户获取金融信息的能力及金融素养普遍不高，可能导致他们对互联网金融不了解、不信任或不愿使用。

简而言之，数字技术虽然能够迅速提升金融的包容性，但是它并没有改变金融服务的本质，而是通过改良金融交易的各种要素，特别是降低交易双方的成本、增加风险控制的有效性、改善市场竞争等途径来提高弱势群体在金融服务市场的参与度。数字技术对金融市场各种要素的改善是有限的。因此，数字金融也有它的局限性。

第三章　包容的政策和监管环境

【摘要】互联网金融是把“双刃剑”，实现风险缓释和创新激励协调共进是我国监管部门面临的迫切问题。面对互联网市场快速发展和自身监管问题，我国需要借鉴国外先进的监管经验，从被动监管到主动引导。本章就此提出包容性监管理念，主张从金融排斥到金融包容，涵盖社会的公平正义，接近金融法制的人文精神，也是社会收入分配均等的理性回归，力图探索出一套既具弹性又有规范的监管模式，打造创新和安全平衡的包容性监管环境。

一、概念的提出：包容性监管演化与作用

早在 2002 年，国际货币基金组织的 S. Das 和 Marc Quintyn 开始将监管思想引入金融领域，金融监管治理的理念逐渐流行起来。同年，国际货币基金组织发布了有关金融监管治理机制标准的研究报告——《监管的独立性和金融稳定》和《危机防范和危机管理：监管治理的角色》，提出了良好的金融监管治理的四个标准：监管机构的独立性、责任性、透明化、宽容度。①不难发现，四个标准中的宽容度最能体现包容性监管理念，秉持和践行软法之治，最接近金融法制的人文精神，实现了金融善治的方法与路径，更多地涵盖了社会的公平和正义，折射出善治理念的理性光辉。

（一）包容性监管概念及演化进程

长期以来，在我国政府主导型金融资源配置模式下，金融资金资源采取了偏好城市而忽视农村的不恰当做法，金融资源配置的扭曲拉大了我国城乡之间的收入分配鸿沟，利率、汇率和 IPO 等金融工具更是严重倾斜城镇地区，加剧了农村金融的“空洞化”，使农村地区深陷“贫困恶性循环”怪圈而难以自拔，积重难返的金融排斥问题长

① 赵峰，等．金融监管治理的指标体系：因应国际经验［J］．改革，2010（9）．

期存在，可谓是“冰冻三尺，非一日之寒”。

但是，一种与金融排斥相对的包容性金融浮出水面，其目的在于将“无银行服务”的社会大众纳入金融系统，让贫困人群、个体工商户及小微企业可以享受到信贷、支付和保险等金融服务。简单地说，包容性监管就是打造适应科技金融变化的宽松监管环境，探索出一套既有弹性又具规范的监管模式，其至少包括三层含义：柔性监管、适度监管、差异化监管。

1. 柔性监管

所谓柔性监管，就是对互联网金融市场纷繁复杂的经营行为，根据社会危害性、侵权程度采取民事、行政处罚的方式，不能简单粗暴地将所有不符合现行规定的市场行为统统认定为金融犯罪，采取刑事处罚措施加以惩罚。

金融监管法体现出国家刑事法律的对抗性和市场规范秩序的强制性，[①] 这本身并没有问题。但是，对于互联网金融纷繁复杂的环境和模式来说，不能简单地采取行政处罚措施加以监管，更不能将改革过程中所有不符合现行规定的金融市场行为统统认定为金融犯罪，统统予以刑事处罚，而是应该根据不同的市场行为所产生的社会危害性和侵权程度采取民事、行政和刑事等多种处罚方式进行处置。

在金融监管过程中，法律法规固然可以发挥重要作用，但道德伦理、宗法习惯、乡规民约等非强制性规范的约束功能同样不容小觑，以祖缘、地缘、血缘、情缘为基础形成的关系契约更是成为调整人们金融交易行为的基本准则。[②] 由此，我们有必要在普惠金融治理中引入柔性监管理念，根据中国社会特有的传统与文化背景，打破法条主义、教条主义的治理观，认真对待社会底层中那些鼓励性、协商性、指导性的软法规范，将社会自治规则纳入普惠金融监管体制框架中，采取一种更为宽容的态度对待出现的市场问题，用更为宽容的监管理念化解矛盾冲突，平衡好风险防范和金融创新之间的关系。

2. 适度监管

所谓适度监管，就是在守住不发生系统性风险底线的同时，对互联网金融的监督管理要留有余地。在保障消费者资金安全、信息安全和人身安全的前提下进行监管，而不是一味地从严管控。

我们知道，互联网金融往往具有混业经营的特征，本身涉及交织或嵌套多项金融业务，形态多样易变，不容易准确辨识业务实质。在这种情况下，监管者避免简单采取“一竿子到底”的穿透式监管方式，而是要针对金融科技发展的内在规律，对不同种类的互联网金融采取不同的监管方式，给予互金企业一定的创新空间，实现创新激

---

① 罗豪才，宋功德．软法亦法：公共治理呼唤软法之治［M］．北京：法律出版社，2009.

② 费孝通．乡土中国·生育制度［M］．北京：北京大学出版社，1998.

励和风险防范的协同发展。监管层不宜采取过严的监管政策，应该采用较为温和的监管策略，对互联网金融领域的创新产品进行适度监管，否则可能使大量互联网金融新业务“胎死腹中”。

事实证明，无论是监管过度还是监管不足，都会引发灾难性后果。如果监管过度，必然会扼杀普惠金融的创新动力，使其陷入金融抑制的深渊，无法惠及普罗大众的金融需要。而如果监管不足，则可能导致普惠金融秩序紊乱，甚至会引发系统性金融风险。因此，适度监管应该成为普惠金融的理想监管状态，宽容度也应该成为市场行为和金融创新的主旋律。

3. 差异化监管

所谓差异化监管，就是监管者强调金融环境的多变性、参与主体的多元性、经营方式的多样性，充分考虑互联网金融市场信息和人力资源的各种差异，在监管目标、监管手段等方面具体业务具体对待。

从本质上看，差异化监管是一种融合现代管理理念的多元思维、多元目标的监管方式，它强调金融环境、市场主体的差异，倡导激励监管相容，追求公正与效率的统一。[①] 也就是说，监管者必须强调金融环境的差异性、参与主体的多元性和经营方式的多样性，充分考虑互联网金融市场信息和资源的各种差异，在业务目标、准入条件、资源配置及风险处置手段上采取差异化管理，对不同种类的互联网金融创新采取不同的监管方式，根据不同的违法行为采取不同的监管措施，实现公平与效率的有机统一。

总之，包容性监管的目的不是“保证不出事”，而是促进普惠金融市场更快、更健康地发展。我们将包容性监管引入普惠金融的公共治理中，核心就是搭建起金融机构和公民生活的互联互通，并通过市场准入、市场运营、风险规避的再造，将适度性、差异化与包容度融入普惠金融，这关乎互联网金融市场能否健康、稳定发展的重大现实问题，不仅是对金融市场改革的积极回应，也是对金融监管的大胆创新，更是回应了普惠金融善治的制度诉求，趋向实现公平效率的最终统一。当然，如何找到适度监管、柔性监管和差异化监管在普惠金融中的一个交集点，也是监管者今后一个时期需要深入探讨的重大课题。[②]

（二）包容性监管对普惠金融发展的作用

长期以来，在“严刑峻法”思想的影响下，我国金融监管过于强调金融稳定，对金融行业管制有余而开发不足，处罚有余而激励不够，监管机构防范金融风险的急功近利之用明显。因此，市场治理逐渐蜕变成为“工具主义”的管制之法，不断损害社

① 李庚南．差异化监管：小企业信贷商业化可持续的内在要求［J］．中国农村金融，2011（8）.

② 顾雷．海龟派 PK 土鳖派：互金监管向左 or 向右？［DB/OL］．OBT 商业科技观察，2019—01—10.

会低端人口和家庭获得金融服务的权力，导致了大量非自愿金融排斥增加，缺乏应有的创新气质和人文情怀。迪图斯和克莱因（Dittus 和 Klein，2011）曾经指出，政府监管者应根据不同的金融服务和创新的风险属性来设计不同的监管规则，过度强调金融稳定会阻碍金融创新，不利于金融包容发展。

第一，包容性监管有效提高资源配置效率，在减少社会排斥、实现社会公正方面发挥积极作用，特别是对需要金融服务的贫困人群、偏远地区人群及社会底层人士来说，包容性就显得更加重要，提高基础性金融服务的普及率和使用率，可以让更多的小微企业、个体工商户有能力应对金融危机。

第二，包容性监管有效降低基础性金融服务的门槛，创新金融服务模式和渠道，降低单一借款人在银行贷款资产组合中的规模，不仅降低了顺周期性风险，还能够实现银行利润结构的多元化，减少银行对核心融资的依赖，降低金融体系内部的风险传播性。

第三，包容性监管使普惠金融领域的货币政策传导渠道更为畅通，对微观主体的影响范围更加广泛，不仅有利于货币政策目标的实施，加强统筹规划和顶层设计，更有助于创造包容的政策监管与金融创新并重的市场环境。

二、从概念走向理性：法律如何为普惠金融正名

（一）对穿透式监管的理性反思

反观 2018 年，穿透式监管已成为年度监管的关键词。中国银保监会、中国证监会更是频繁地在一些规范性文件中反复提及“穿透”一词，穿透式监管已经扩展到很多金融领域，尤其是互联网金融行业。

最早的穿透式监管起源于资本市场，主要使用于证券行业和资管行业，通过穿透式信息披露、穿透式经营指标和穿透式处罚手段，统一监管证券及衍生品种的交易、结算活动。以穿透式信息披露为例，可以避免资管市场中的信息不对称，有效保护投资人的合法权益，解决我国资产管理成本过高的顽症。从某种意义上看，穿透式监管确实促进了证券市场的有序发展，这一经验得到了 IMF（国际货币基金组织）和国际证监会组织的认可与好评。于是，中国监管部门强调学习西方国家先进的监管理念，穿透式监管方式自然成为一种首选。

但是，我们必须对穿透式监管可能给市场带来的不确定因素进行理性剖析，不能丧失科学研究的本真。简单地说，所谓穿透式监管，就是对各式各样的金融业务，监管的政策取向、业务规则和管理标准就应该相互一致，也就是采用“一套标准”，不存

在区别对待的情况。[①]

我们认为，我国金融市场的人文环境与发达国家有很大的不同，互联网金融市场也不同于证券市场，不能完全照搬照抄国外资本市场的监管经验，套用他国的监管模式很难走出相同的康庄大道。况且，穿透式监管方式也存在缺陷。按照我国金融监管分类，股权众筹归于中国证监会监管，网络借款归于中国银监会监管，互联网保险归于中国保监会监管（尽管中国保监会和中国银监会已经合并，但其实质的监管分类并没有多大变化）。如果对不同类型互联网金融业务采取一成不变的监管方式，无异于以不变应万变。如果对不同监管机构使用相同的监管规则、监管方式和监管逻辑，也无异于削足适履。显然，这种监管方式能否适应不断变化的互联网金融行业是存在疑问的，至少不能完全适合千差万别的互联网金融经营模式，其单一粗糙的监管方式与精细化市场发展的理念更是格格不入。

可以说，"一刀切"既是穿透式监管的最大标签，也是最大问题。穿透式监管的最大特点是可以打破金融行业分业监管障碍，对互联网金融领域混业经营进行一站式管理。这种一竿子到底的监管方式可以短时期起到整肃互联网金融市场乱象的作用，有效避免监管套利，在一定时期内稳定互联网金融市场，但由此带来的监管过度也会抑制金融创新，造成对互联网金融市场过度伤害也是显而易见的。例如，联合房贷、小额贷款、智能投顾、区块链等细分领域难以找到特定的监管主体，如果一味采取穿透式监管极易"误伤"互联网金融创新业务，尤其对于非银行金融机构能否负担得起长久、高昂的监管成本更是一个严峻问题。

一是考虑互联网金融行业创新多变的实际状况，未来对普惠金融监管原则上应该是一种更为宽松和包容的监管政策，相对提高风险容忍度，有利于为互联网金融机构的发展提供良好的制度环境。2018 年，中国人民银行对互联网金融采取了鼓励的态度，鼓励民间经济开拓市场，对互联网金融创新活动采取了更为宽容的态度。因此，我国互联网金融市场初创发展阶段也一定要避免"误伤"好金融，应该根据中国国情与特点设计监管制度和市场规则，单纯地移植国外监管模式绝对是不可取的。

二是重视民间金融的软法之治，社会共治。在一个"熟人社会"里进行金融监管治理，单靠强硬监管经常会显得捉襟见肘。这是因为，我国农村地区虽然历经多次规制变革，但以"熟人社会"为特征的稳定组织架构并未发生实质性改变，尤其在我国传统农村文化背景下，道德伦理、宗法习惯、乡规民约等非强制性规范的约束功能同样不容小觑，以祖缘、地缘、血缘、情缘为基础形成的关系契约成为调整人们金融交

① 顾雷．海龟派 PK 土鳖派：互金监管向左 or 向右？［DB/OL］．OBT 商业科技观察，2019－01－10.

易行为的基本准则。[①]因此，我们必须打破对纯粹国家主义治理观的盲目崇拜，正确看待乡土社会中鼓励性、协商性、指导性的软法规范，将农村社会共同体的制度化、规范化、程序化的自治规则纳入监管框架中，发掘民间非正式规范的理性作用，使之与法律规范保持良性互动，共同促进农村普惠金融监管效能，确保普惠金融治理机制的弹性与活力。

（二）包容性监管的三大价值观念导向

第一，打破核准主义一统天下的监管格局，适当降低互联网金融平台开展普惠金融的门槛，逐步实行差异化管理。

我国政府在投资主体资格、注册资本、治理结构、内部控制等方面多向传统金融机构倾斜，宽松有余，限制较少，而对规模小、实力弱的普惠金融机构，现实情况是限制有余，灵活不足。在监管理念上，更强调市场安全而忽视经济效率。在监管模式上，更强调权力集中而忽视社会公平。在监管制度上，更强调监管威权而忽视综合治理。例如，当前对普惠金融机构设立实行无差别核准制，无论是村镇银行、贷款公司，还是农村资金互助社，莫不如此。如果说对村镇银行的设立采取核准主义尚能理解，那么，监管部门对小额贷款公司与农村信用社强行采取核准主义，这是否存在过于严苛的监管倾向呢？

值得欣慰的是，2010 年 5 月《国务院关于鼓励和引导民间投资健康发展的若干意见》（国发〔2010〕13 号，以下简称《若干意见》）发布，开始调低注册资本、放宽业务准入条件、调整高管人员准入资格、调整新设法人机构审批权限等方面限制性规定，鼓励和引导民间资本进入基础产业、基础设施领域及金融服务领域，为村镇银行、贷款公司、农村资金互助社等新型金融机构进入农村金融市场开启了大门。

但是，《若干意见》尚处于试点阶段，因其法律效力层级较低而难以有效地指导所有互联网金融监管实践。因此，有必要将行之有效的制度加以总结提炼，明确监管职责和风险防范责任，并推广到互联网金融实践中，逐步建立普惠金融包容性监管框架。

第二，打破传统国有银行“一统天下”的格局，鼓励非正规金融机构和民间资本进入普惠金融市场。

我们知道，传统国有大型银行虽然也响应政府号召，主动采取“下沉战略”，为农村贫困人群和小微企业提供普惠金融服务，但是这些大型银行依然面临一个很大的制约，就是国家对它们的利率有比较明确的限制，大型银行“下沉”成本高，商业价值并不具有可持续性。同时，中小型银行，包括城市商业银行、农村商业银行、农村信

① 费孝通．乡土中国·生育制度［M］．北京：北京大学出版社，1998.

用社，虽然也开展普惠金融业务，但是同样面临严峻挑战。因为这些中小型银行往往缺乏卓越的品牌、过硬的技术和优秀的人才，要在短时间内成为中国普惠金融主力军还有待检验。因此，我们必须按照业务经营行为和业务本质属性，逐渐对我国土生土长的非正规金融机构、金融科技公司及民间资本进行规范性改造，使之与成熟的规范保持良性互动，鼓励非正规金融机构和民间资本进入普惠金融市场。

第三，打破对传统金融机构监管措施简单复制的做法，对普惠金融监管措施重新调整。

长期以来，监管部门对普惠金融服务市场特异性问题缺乏清晰的认知，习惯于将传统金融机构的监管措施简单复制到普惠金融平台机构身上，诸如在适用资本充足率、存款准备金、坏账与呆账准备金等方面，传统与普惠金融机构几乎没有区别，导致我国现行普惠金融服务市场运营监管制度刚性有余而柔性不足，过于强调统一化监管而忽视差异化监管。因此，打破对传统金融机构运营监管措施简单复制的做法，用包容性监管理念对普惠金融监管措施重新调整，是一种更具有深厚社会人文基础的金融实践，在市场准入、治理环节更具备回应普惠金融监管制度诉求的能力。

（三）“监管沙箱”对包容性监管的促进作用

从1995年全球第一家纯网络银行在美国诞生开始，到1998年支付宝“师父”贝宝（Paypal）在美国加利福尼亚州成立；再从2005年全球第一家网络借贷平台Zopa在英国伦敦成立，到2007年全球最早上市的网贷平台Lending Club在美国硅谷诞生并上市，互联网金融科技拥有很强的创新意识与科技能力，已经成为全球金融行业发展最有力的助推器。

值得欣慰的是，在最近十年间，我国金融行业经历了“弯道超车”的喜人局面。以支付宝为例，虽然较贝宝晚五年成立，但目前其规模已经是贝宝的数倍。目前，我国已经进入金融科技发展阶段，呈现出主体多元化、迭代加速化、用户大众化、市场全球化、服务实时化、组织扁平化和要素科技化多方面成就。首先，其产品相对传统金融而言更加简单化、透明化、标准化，其应用场景渗透到用户生活的方方面面，打破传统金融在时间和空间上的限制。其次，客户群体覆盖了之前没有被传统金融服务到的贫困人群、弱势群体，满足了诸如小微企业、“三农”机构或个体工商户的长尾需求。

巨大成就的背后是科技力量在驱动。诸如人工智能、大数据、云计算等新技术，助力互联网金融实现产品创新、存储数据、体验升级、场景扩展和效能提升，及时发现风险并采取有效应对措施，降低银行合规成本，提供自动化合规报告，不间断为监管机构提供实时动态监管。[①]其中一个比较突出的例子就是监管沙箱这种包含监管者审

---

① 李敏．金融科技的监管模式选择与优化路径研究——兼对监管沙箱模式的反思［J］．金融监管研究，2017（11）．

核、监督、评估及对消费者保护的综合性监管方式。

如前所述，普惠金融需要包容性监管，首先必须找到普惠金融领域平衡创新与风险的有效监管手段，向FinTech创新产品提供包容的监督管理机制和政策环境，关键就是在创新测试过程中嵌入监管沙箱，测试创新的金融产品服务而不需要担心带来的监管后果，既可以使创新在较大限度内通过测试，又能够有效降低潜在风险扩散，进一步促进互联网金融市场的创新和繁荣。

截至2017年8月1日，全球范围内已有14个国家（或地区）开始实施监管沙箱，还有两个国家已经宣布即将实施。尽管各国对监管沙箱的定义、特征及实际操作手法存在差异，但实施监管沙箱的总体目标基本上可以概括为支持创新，促进市场发展和竞争，推动经济增长。①

案例

监管创新案例

香港金融管理局（HKMA）最初是将金融科技监管沙箱（FinTech Supervisory Sandbox，FSS）作为现有银行的项目推出的。在运营过程中，HKMA收到越来越多的科技公司要求直接访问FSS的要求，以及收集有关新兴金融科技项目反馈意见的申请。在这种背景下，HKMA在2017年顺应金融市场发展需求，率先将沙箱升级成FSS 2.0版本，包括现有银行和非银行技术公司的扩展接入，为市场参与者提供带有访问、反馈和支持功能的简化版FSS聊天室。截至2018年8月底，HKMA已经收到约170个要求接入聊天室的请求，其中近七成的请求来自中国香港及海外的非银行技术公司，推动了香港地区科技企业的发展。

在美国，消费者金融保护局（Consumer Financial Protection Bureau，CFPB）推出“催化剂项目”（Project Catalyst），主要目的就是通过包括RegTech在内的FinTech等金融创新公司颁布“不行动函”（No-action Letter），为金融创新公司提供良好的政策环境以支持其金融创新。CFPB于2017年9月14日向一家借贷平台Upstart Network颁布第一次行动函，前提是该公司定期将借贷和合规数据信息报送CFPB，这些数据信息将用于创建征信和制定价格，有助于更多的信用信息隐藏和缺乏足够历史信用的人获得贷款。

① 李敏．金融科技的监管模式选择与优化路径研究——兼对监管沙箱模式的反思［J］．金融监管研究，2017（11）。

虽然监管沙箱不是推动普惠金融创新的充分条件，但监管者使用监管沙箱可以从最小可行的产品 MVP 着手，快速启动并提供反馈，增加迭代机会，达到用最小代价创造出最大金融效益，甚至利用区块链和人工智能技术，进行投资者、资管机构身份验证、份额登记、交易流水记录等，使监管部门获得资产管理活动的全貌，监控账户交易、交易种类、价格权限等，重点盯防可疑交易。实际上，来自多个国家和地区的证据都表明，沙盒监管可以有效地防止非法侵害消费者的行为产生，提升普惠金融规范性。[①]

在我国，中国人民银行在 2017 年 5 月成立金融科技委员会，提出强化监管科技（RegTech）的应用实践，积极利用大数据、人工智能、云计算等技术丰富金融监管手段，提升跨行业、跨市场金融风险的甄别、防范和化解能力。中国人民银行、中国银保监会、中国证监会有关部门负责人也多次表达了对 RegTech 的关注和倡导。因此，未来我国建立监管沙箱模式并不是没有可能。所以，互联网金融的核心就是技术进步带来金融业态的变化，传统金融监管思路必须接受新的挑战，打破原有金融业态监管模式故步自封的局面，快速调整为一种更加积极的应对方式。

三、从理性走向制度：建立有效的金融消费者保护制度

2008 年国际金融危机后，世界各国深刻认识到，忽视对金融消费者保护将直接破坏金融机构赖以发展的公众基础，危及整个金融市场稳定。为此，二十国集团、世界银行、经济合作与发展组织、金融稳定委员会、金融包容联盟（AFI）都把金融消费者保护作为一项核心工作。[②]

（一）当今世界金融消费者权益保护概览

2011 年 7 月 21 日，时任美国总统奥巴马正式签署《多德·弗兰克华尔街改革和消费者保护法案》，责令美联储下设消费者金融保护局（Consumer Financial Protection Bureau，CFPB），当金融消费者面临不公平待遇和受到金融欺诈时给予必要的保护，还把以前分散在美联储、证券交易委员会、联邦贸易委员会等机构的消费者权益保护职权，统一集中到新成立的消费者金融保护局，确保美国金融消费者权益今后在受到

---

① MVP 是硅谷的一个老生常谈的概念，它是一个非常简单、能让创业者获得最初市场反馈的产品样本，然后再根据早期用户的反馈来逐步优化的过程，并在这个最小化的可行产品上持续快速迭代。MVP 对于互联网金融创新团队而言十分重要，可以快速验证团队的目标，快速试错。

② 贝多广，顾雷．重塑我国金融消费者权益保护机构［N］．金融时报，2018－07－16.

任何侵害时，有一个强有力的金融消费者保护机构伸出援手。①

英国紧随其后。英国经历了2008年国际金融危机后，“双峰理论”逐渐成为金融监管的主流模式。②2009年，由英格兰银行负责全英金融系统稳定工作，将金融服务局（FSA）的金融监管职能划归英格兰银行，设立审慎监管局全面掌管监管事宜。2012年英国还成立了金融消费者保护机构——金融市场行为监管局（FCA），强调在审慎监管的同时，必须关注金融市场消费者权益保护问题，确保金融消费者享受到及时、有效和高质量的金融服务，推进金融教育的国家战略，并为金融市场消费者提供了一个解决争议的有效方案。

日本也在金融消费者权益保护方面做了很大改进，尤其在1996年日本“金融大爆炸”以后，日本在2006年制定了《金融商品交易法》，作为金融市场消费者权益保护的基础性法律。③日本政府认识到，金融分业管理模式过分强调对行业及企业的纵向垂直监管，这使金融市场金融活动、法律关系被人为地割裂开来，各自为政的行业监管模式已不能适应消费者权益保护的需要。于是，日本在“金融大爆炸”以后取消了金融分业监管模式，一改过去几十年由各自行业协会承担金融消费者保护的格局，逐渐过渡到由日本金融厅为主导、其他监管机构（中央银行、消费者厅和财务省）为辅助的统一监督体制，取得了不错的效果。④

发展中国家也日益关注金融消费权益保护，不少国家纷纷成立了独立的金融消费者保护机构，诸如马来西亚金融调解局（FMB）、墨西哥国家保护金融服务者委员会（CONDUSEF）、秘鲁金融督察专员局（FOS）等。⑤

中国香港和中国台湾同样重视金融消费者保护。2012年6月19日，中国香港成立金融纠纷调解中心，采取“先调解后仲裁”的方式有效解决了金融纠纷，得到了广大金融消费者的普遍赞同。2011年6月3日，中国台湾通过《金融消费者保护法》，专门建立“金融消费争议评议中心”，专门处理金融消费者投诉案件和维权事宜，其裁

---

① 美国消费者金融保护局（CFPB）规定了一般权力、特定权限、州法律保留、强制执行权力、职能移交、监管改进及相应法律修改等内容，目标是：（1）提高消费金融产品服务市场的透明、简单、公平和负责；（2）保证消费者拥有、懂得并能够利用他们需要的信息来对消费金品服务作出负责任的决策；（3）保证消费者免于滥用、不公平、欺骗和歧视；（4）保证消费金融产品服务市场公平而又有效地运行，并能有足够的空间进行可持续增长和创新；（5）确保传统的低阶层消费者和社区能够享受金融服务，最大限度地保护本国金融消费者的合法权益。

② 金融“双峰理论”起源于英国，由1995年经济学家迈克尔·泰勒（Michael Taylor）最早提出。该理论认为，监管的目标是双重的，一是审慎监管目标，起到金融市场稳定作用；二是保护金融消费者的权益目标，起到市场规范作用。金融市场最终目的是保护金融市场参与主体的合法权益不受任何非法侵害。目前，西方主要金融大国都在采用双峰监管模式，强调金融市场消费者权益的保护。

③ 杨东．我国金融消费者保护的统合立法体系的构建——以日本的立法经验借鉴为视角［J］．社会科学，2013（81）．

④ 何颖．日本金融消费者保护制度改革［J］．日本学刊，2011（1）．

⑤ 贝多广，顾雷．重塑我国金融消费者权益保护机构［N］．金融时报，2018－07－16．

决相当于民事判决，具有法律约束力。[①]

2011 年 10 月，二十国集团巴黎峰会公布了经济合作与发展组织牵头制定的《金融消费保护高级原则》，金融稳定委员会发布了《重点涉及信贷的消费者金融保护》及《消费者金融报告》。2012 年 6 月，世界银行出台了《金融消费者保护的良好经验》。这些文件的出台旨在形成一套金融消费者权益保护的核心原则，更好地促进国家间金融消费者保护经验交流及国际规则形成。

综合美国、英国、日本、中国香港及中国台湾对消费者权益保护方面的经验，最明显的一个趋势就是金融消费者保护机构归于统合，形成高度统一的金融消费者权益保护机构，为金融市场参与者提供统一、高效和专业的制度保障和司法救济。这是当今国际金融市场消费者保护的趋势，应该成为我国金融消费者保护关注的重点。

目前，我国在消费者权益保护方面，由中国人民银行、中国银保监会、中国证监会共同开展互联网金融消费者权益保护工作，完善个人信息保护的原则、标准和操作流程，构建在线争议解决、现场接待受理、受理投诉等纠纷解决机制。与此同时，我国各地工商行政管理部门、消费者协会、金融行业协会承担着地方金融消费权益保护职责，开展互联网金融产品合同内容、免责条款等信息披露和金融知识教育培训工作。

与一般金融服务相比，互联网金融是一个海量信息汇集的场域，各种信息鱼目混珠。以数字普惠金融为例，数字普惠金融服务用户基数多，覆盖面广，一旦产品和服务的相关信息披露不全、系统安全性不足，就可能无法维护个人数据保密性，加之数字普惠金融是跨时空服务，服务对象总体素质偏低，其权益保护渠道、发声渠道明显较弱，消费者权益受到侵害以后，更加难以有效保护。因此，确保信息真实，妥善处理数字普惠金融技术、服务、销售渠道以及个人数据处理显得尤为重要。

总之，金融消费者是金融产品和金融服务的最终使用者和感知者。金融消费者受到不公平对待而表达合理诉求，对经营者的批评、建议、检举、控告，不仅是对不合格金融机构的一种提醒和警示，更是对金融机构的一种鞭策，让经营者做到闻过即改、过而能改甚至举一反三、自我加压，体现出对金融消费者的尊重，有效提升金融机构的信用等级。

当然，为了更好地发挥金融消费者的监督作用，为金融消费者提供畅通、便利的监督渠道，激发监督成效，行政资源、司法资源必须适度向“中小微弱”倾斜，尽量消除金融消费者与金融机构之间信息不对称、权利不对等的情况，形成一种包容、平等的消费者监督氛围，让挑剔、蔑视和阻碍消费者监督的行为受到应有惩罚，让消费者敢监督、愿监督、能监督，这应该是 2019 消费者维权主题年的应有之义，也是互联

① 王华庆．完善金融消费权益保护机制［J］．中国金融，2012（22）．

网金融市场知法守法的必然选择。

（二）确立金融消费者保护是普惠金融监管的核心价值观

我国金融业发展起步较晚，目前仍处于转轨期，诞生于特殊历史时期的政治结构和社会结构之中，难免被打上“国家主义”烙印，中央政府赋予了金融系统太多的政治功能，金融机构掌握着绝对支配权，承担了减轻国家财政压力、为国有企业筹资、充实资本金并为国有企业解困等任务，成为国有企业输血机器和社会稳定的减压器。因此，国家立法注重对金融机构利益的保护，对金融消费者的保护往往会被忽视。

互联网金融时代，金融消费者权益屡屡被不法侵犯。如果普惠金融消费者利益得不到应有的保护，就会动摇公众对普惠金融的信心，导致市场趋于萧条和萎缩，危及我国整个金融存在的基础。由此，我们必须强调客户保护原则。在此方面，我国可以借鉴国际上关于金融消费者保护的“七原则”，逐渐消除金融产品和服务的提供者与消费者之间存在的信息不对称，限制信息优势一方欺凌盘剥消费者的渠道和机会，并在设计普惠金融产品时充分考虑定价的合理性、客户隐私保护、有效的仲裁机制等。具体来说，我们需要从以下三大方面体现包容性监管理念。

1. 及时引入金融消费争议 ADR 机制

监管部门进一步完善金融仲裁机制，引入金融消费争议 ADR（Alternative Dispute Resolution）机制，设立专门独立统一的金融消费纠纷处理机构，建立金融机构内部投诉处理机制，成立专司金融消费纠纷非诉讼解决职能机构，从公益角度出发为弱势群体受理小规模索赔金额案件，进一步确保普惠金融服务消费者能够对个人数据进行有意识的选择和保护。互联网金融市场实践表明，方便、高效的 ADR 有助于解决金融消费者遭受欺诈服务、信息不透明的金融服务的维权，通过呼叫中心、网站、网页或社交媒体等科技手段，加大第三方机构（如司法部门、律师团队）解决纠纷的效率，鼓励消费者使用团体诉讼机制，提升消费者权益保护执行力度，这对普惠金融而言意义重大，影响深远。

2. 深化金融消费者适当性原则

有必要确立金融消费者适当性原则，使金融机构从审慎经营角度，以消费者容易理解的方式对所销售的金融产品和提供的金融服务加以说明。简单地说，金融消费者适当性原则可以分为两个阶段：第一个阶段是金融从业人员首先要了解金融消费者，并判断应对其推销何种金融产品，目的在于确认金融消费者对金融服务的认可程度。第二个阶段是在向金融消费者推销相应的金融产品与服务时，金融从业人员以适合其理解的方式对所推销的金融产品加以说明，目的在于使金融消费者理解金融产品与风险进而能够承担相应的法律责任。

3. 探索通过保险机制完善普惠金融消费者损失补偿机制

与传统金融服务对象相比，普惠金融覆盖对象大多是金融知识匮乏的群体，尤其是农村偏远地区人群的金融意识更加淡薄，风险承受能力比较低下，而今天的互联网金融市场跨界服务和交易已成为一种十分普遍的互联网现象，这种横跨行业、产品交叉、信息重叠的创新活动带来了系统安全性隐患、代理商欺诈及个人隐私泄露的风险。因此，监管机构和农村普惠金融服务商通过完善金融消费者损失补偿机制，公平对待缺乏金融服务的弱势群体，充分考虑消费者群体的差异性，不采取歧视性手段，以保障消费者的损失最小化，帮助金融消费者能够及时获得相应的经济补偿。例如，通过引入第三方保险公司为第三方支付的“账户安全险”，为用户账户安全进行承保，确保用户在账户被盗后得到快速理赔。这一做法有利于提振用户对支付安全的信心，快速化解金融科技创新风险带来的客户损失，实现用最合适的方式为金融消费者提供最合适的金融服务的宗旨。

为此，曾经担任美国商品期货交易委员会（CFTC）主席的盖瑞·詹姆斯勒（Gary Gensler）曾经表示，国际金融危机后各国金融监管改革的一个主要趋势，就是设立强势的金融消费者保护机构，对市场投资者利益进行了一个相当完善的保护性制度设计，以应对日益复杂的金融创新带来的各种侵害金融市场消费者权益的不利局面。①

四、从制度走向实践：全力为普惠金融保驾护航

近年来，普惠金融依托于互联网金融支付、云计算、社交网络及搜索引擎等互联网工具，实现了金融、支付和信息中介的完美组合，各种经营模式及金融产品层出不穷，为市场注入了新的活力。但是，对于普惠金融领域的法律法规滞后、监管机制不健全、监管主体模糊不清等问题依然不容乐观。

（一）现实困境：普惠金融从业者和互联网金融平台的尴尬处境

1. 暧昧的管制政策可能会使普惠金融陷入刑事陷阱

企业家刑事法律风险很大程度上来源于我国刑法条文的词义模糊，极具解释空间，例如，“非法吸收公众存款罪”“非法经营罪”在司法实践中往往异化为“口袋罪”，在司法实践中随时可能被扩大解释，成为金融企业家经营创新活动中的“刑事陷阱”，成为“创新”头顶上的“达摩克利斯之剑”，普惠金融企业家极易坠入“刑

---

① 王力为．金融监管改革应设立消费者保护机构［DB/OL］．财新网，2016—04—22.

事陷阱”。

2. 失调的法律体系可能会让普惠金融平台处于泛刑罚化边缘

公平地说，普惠金融作为新兴事物，不应放任自流。普惠金融平台需要监管，不能让其打着金融创新的旗号违反法律，普惠金融从业者也需要树立风险意识，自我保护。但是，也要避免普惠金融平台一直处于刑事法律风险的旋涡。我们需要防止两种倾向：一是防止有些人抓住普惠金融平台一些行为上的瑕疵或轻微的违法行为，就置普惠金融创新业务于死地；二是防止一些人抓住一些鸡毛蒜皮的事情，剥夺普惠金融从业者金融创新试错的机会，利用一些瑕疵来恶意诉讼，就对普惠金融从业者敲诈勒索。这两种倾向都存在普惠金融治理“泛刑罚化”问题，无疑加大了普惠金融从业者和互联网金融平台的刑事法律风险，使刑事法律向业内行规转移，这本身就是对普惠金融最大的伤害。

3. 淡薄的风险意识可能会使普惠金融从业者面临刑事风险

普惠金融从业者是“经济人”，其思维以追求经济利润最大化为特征，往往缺少识别法律风险的敏锐性，极易忽视存在的刑事法律风险，对互联网金融高利益带来的高风险认识不足，对普惠利益与法律风险共存共生的特征体会不深，即便是正当经营的金融企业家也可能不知不觉地坠入刑事陷阱中。

（二）高发雷区：普惠金融从业者和互联网金融平台的刑事法律风险

1. 投资理财模式涉及的法律风险

2014 年，全国注册的 P2P 网贷平台多达 1500 家，截至 2016 年 12 月底，全国 P2P 网贷平台累计达 4329 家，其中仅有 2824 家是正常运营，其余 1505 家 P2P 网贷平台不是涉及虚假广告诈骗，就是存在非法集资等犯罪嫌疑，占比高达 34.76%。

2018 年，全国公安机关共立非法集资案件 1 万余起，同比上升 22%，涉案金额约为 3000 亿元，同比上升 115%，波及全国各个省市，平均案值达 2800 余万元，同比上升 76%。一些案件涉案金额上十亿元甚至上百亿元，造成群众巨大损失，特别是 P2P 网络借贷更成为“重灾区”，不法分子打着“金融创新”的幌子，冒充“网络借贷”新业态聚拢资金，对社会危害更大。为此，2019 年 1 月 29 日最高人民法院、最高人民检察院、公安部联合颁布了《关于办理非法集资刑事案件若干问题的意见》，全面回应当前非法集资违法犯罪中的难点问题，就实体法律适用、诉讼程序、刑事政策和量刑幅度作出具体规定，对于依法打击非法集资违法犯罪、维护人民群众合法权益具有重要意义。

2. 支付模式涉及的法律风险

支付模式涉及的法律风险有盗窃犯罪，即支付账号作为犯罪对象，主要是盗取他人的第三方支付账号进而盗窃其账户内钱财的犯罪。另外，某些虚拟电子货币具有“去中心化”支付功能，其本身就饱受争议，因为它完全是互联网上虚拟出来的，不像现实货币有黄金等硬通货提供支持。随着使用人群日趋庞大，虚拟货币也可以代替真实货币进行交易，甚至可以兑换主要流通的货币，这就很可能为洗钱和转移非法资金违法犯罪提供渠道。

3. 融资模式涉及的法律风险

融资模式下很容易产生诸如非法集资、非法吸收公众存款、金融诈骗等破坏金融管理秩序犯罪。一方面，在网络借贷、网络众筹中，发起人在互联网平台面向全社会不特定的人群发布项目，极易产生吸收公众存款违法行为；另一方面，受到利益驱使，筹资者为了吸引广大投资者，本无融资需求却用虚假项目的高额回报进行广告推送，敛聚钱财，进行金融诈骗活动。

为此，2014 年 3 月 25 日，最高人民法院、最高人民检察院、公安部针对普惠金融从业者和互联网金融平台在互联网信贷、投资理财或者第三方支付过程中，可能会实施危害金融管理秩序、互联网管理秩序和侵犯公共财产或个人财产的行为，颁布了《关于办理非法集资刑事案件适用法律若干问题的意见》，增大了对金融诈骗、破坏金融管理秩序等非法行为的刑事责任风险。

（三）防控提示：普惠金融从业者和互联网金融平台法律风险防范要点

1. 构建普惠金融违法防控综合法律体系

首先，以传统金融业务的规制方式为参照，针对普惠金融违法犯罪新特点，在统筹协调、深入研究、综合考量的基础上，有关部门加快起草制定关于普惠金融监管主体、监管内容、监管方式和处罚手段的部门规章。

其次，对与普惠金融业务相关的《民法》《合同法》《证券法》《票据法》《保险法》《商业银行法》《银行业监督管理法》作进一步完善，对在互联网状态下的禁止性行为重新评价，对传统法律与互联网金融法规进行衔接和协调，避免发生法律冲突。

最后，按照罪刑法定原则和罪责刑相适应原则，在现有法律框架的基础上增加新的罪名，以适应互联网时代新型金融违法犯罪，特别是细化普惠金融领域新出现的、具有严重社会危害行为的认定标准。正如有的学者提出的“合理权衡各个利益方的权利和义务，分配责任、建立惩戒机制，约束各个主体的行为”，以此构筑严密的刑事法网，建立普惠金融犯罪防控的综合法律体系，引导和规范普惠金融事业健康发展。[①]

---

① 门植渊．如何运用大数据防控互联网金融犯罪［N］．检察日报，2016－10－25．

2. 提高分析研判能力，建立健全风险预警防范机制

中央和地方金融监管机构应该通过对互联网金融数据分析，开发监测风险预警系统，形成风险关口前移，观察不同类型的普惠金融违规犯罪在一段时期的发展趋势，分析一定区域内普惠金融违规犯罪特点和规律，对于高发案件的类型、区域、行业等开展专项分析研判，从源头上减少风险隐患，将普惠金融违法犯罪消灭在萌芽阶段。

目前，上海正在建立新型金融业态监测分析平台，可以对互联网金融领域（包括普惠金融领域）一些高风险机构的活动提前预警，及早发现疑似非法活动线索。据悉，该监测分析平台已经归集了行业监测、园区监测、企业全息信息查询及实时监测四个子平台，多维度掌握风险动态，取得了很好的金融风险预警效果。

3. 加大部门间协作力度，建立信息甄别和共享机制

近年来，公安部已经联合中国人民银行、中国银保监会、中国证监会、工业和信息化部、商务部、国家税务总局、海关总署、国家互联网信息办建立互联网金融大数据信息共享平台。①

此外，全国地方金融监管部门定期开展联席会议，汇总分析普惠金融违规情况，不定期对辖区内普惠金融平台进行摸底检查和风险评估，摸清其经营者真实身份及经营规模，形成“一起抓、共同管”的监管格局。加大对利用网络平台进行信贷诈骗、非法集资、非法股权融资等违法行为的打击力度，对那些以“创新”为名从事违法行为的要严加惩罚并将其踢出市场，守住不发生区域性、大规模群体性事件的底线。

4. 法律援助，引入风险防控机制

在普惠金融领域，中央政府、地方政府、互联网金融平台及金融消费者各方利益交错，法律风险源不断叠加，控制难度大。在此种背景下，普惠金融监管者应该树立起“预防才是最好的危机处理方式”意识，保持对刑事法律风险的高度警戒心，转“事后被动补救”为“事前积极防控”，防范刑事风险的最佳方法是建立法律援助和律师服务。从防范刑事风险的角度讲，事前对互联网金融参与者设置严格的审核程序才能有效避免风险。例如，对于融资方提供的身份甄别，关系到金融从业者和互金平台是否被认定为刑事犯罪的问题，马虎不得。

总之，在现实的政商生态、法律环境和社会制度安排下，互联网金融从业者和平台都有可能“不知不觉”地游走在法律灰色地带，由此带来的综合性金融风险仅靠企业家自身谨慎经营是无法完全化解的，需要有法律专业力量的参与，不断提升互联网金融企业家刑事风险防控意识和能力。目前，这一领域才刚刚被挖掘，尚未精细开发，市场潜在需求巨大，同时又是全新的领域，没有前人经验可供借鉴，需要监管者从

① 门植渊．如何运用大数据防控互联网金融犯罪［N］．检察日报，2016－10－25．

"零"开始探索。对法律工作者来说，可谓是机遇与挑战并存。法律援助团队应当抓住机遇，积极探索，通过专业化服务为普惠金融从业者和互金平台合法经营保驾护航，开启法律援助团队普惠金融市场服务的新篇章。

第四章 传统银行[1]普惠金融服务转型

【摘要】普惠金融体系对于经济的包容性增长起着关键作用。作为金融体系中"百业之母"的银行，应当从意愿和能力两方面着力，提供商业可持续的普惠金融服务。银行在提供普惠金融服务的过程中，存在一系列困境，但转型有较大的商业空间，成功的转型需要根据市场需求，寻求合适的突破口，也需要政府进行适当的政策引导。

一、转型的困境

从目前银行[2]实践来看，银行在开展普惠金融服务时，在服务意愿和能力上都存在一定的欠缺。具体而言，存在如下四方面困境。

（一）传统战略调整困境

近年来，随着金融脱媒与金融科技公司加入市场竞争，银行面临边际盈利水平逐年下降的困境。银行的总资产回报率及加权净资产收益率在逐年递减，净息差[3]也在逐年收窄（见图 4－1）。

从图 4－1 中可以看到，2016—2018 年[4]，总体而言，所有样本银行的总资产回报

---

① 本章中的传统银行指的是与互联网银行相对的概念，互联网银行没有线下物理营业网点，只是在线上开展存贷款及其他金融业务，而传统银行一般有大量的线下网点，在线上与线下开展业务。此外，传统银行与互联网银行在账户的功能性上也有不同，在此不做赘述。

② 本章我们选取了 37 家银行作为研究对象，其中 32 家为 A 股上市银行，2 家为香港上市公司，另有 3 家为未上市股份制商业银行；在银行类型上，分为 6 家大型银行、12 家股份制银行、12 家城市商业银行、7 家农村商业银行。

③ 净息差＝净利息收入/平均生息资产规模。

④ 除大型商业银行外，在数据系列中，由于某些银行尚未披露 2018 年年报，因此存在 2～3 个 2017 年的数据，但并不影响总体的趋势判断。

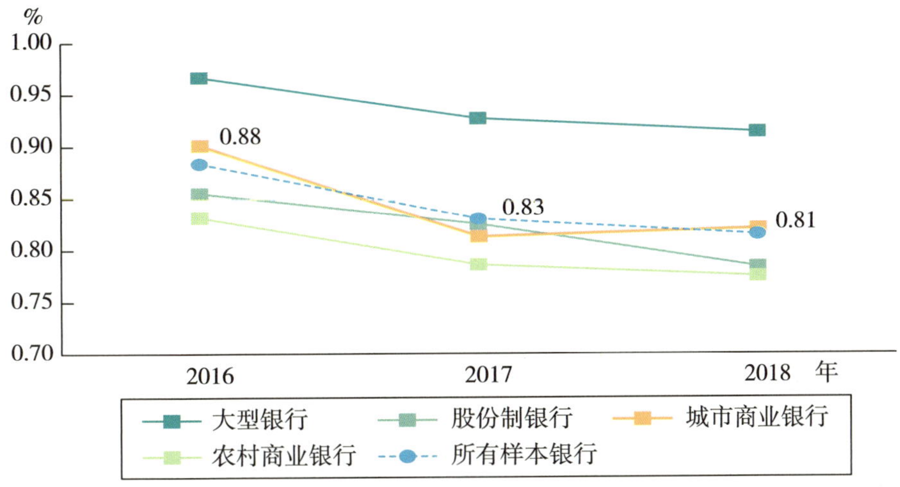

资料来源：Wind、各银行年报。

图 4-1　银行的总资产回报率

率（ROA）均小于1%，处于较低水平，总资产回报率[①]呈逐年下行趋势，从0.88%降到0.81%；除城市商业银行的回报率在2018年有小幅回升（从0.81%增长到0.82%，是否趋于稳定尚有待时间检验）外，其他类型的银行回报率均呈现下降；从结构上看，大型银行的ROA最高，农村商业银行的ROA最低。

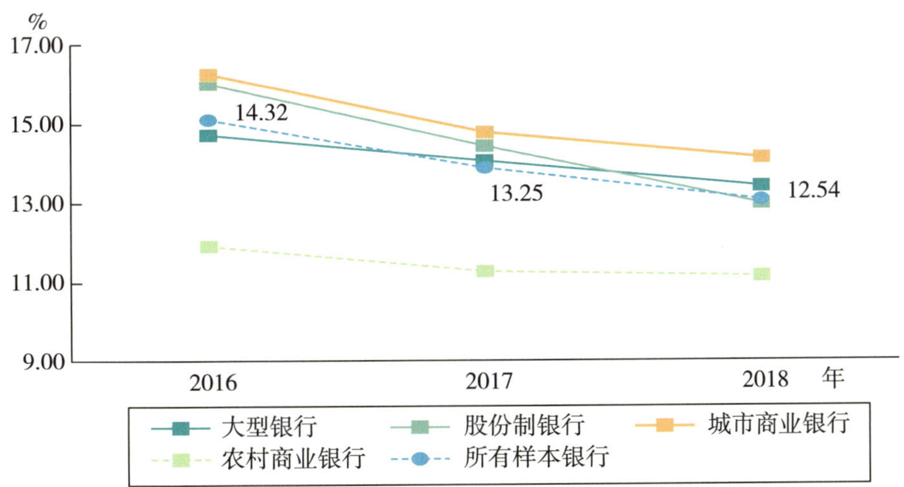

资料来源：Wind、各银行年报。

图 4-2　银行的净资产回报率

① 算术平均回报率。

从图 4－2 中可以看到，2016—2018 年[①]，总体来讲，所有样本银行的净资产回报率（ROE）[②] 虽然数值的绝对值水平不低，但同样呈现逐年下行趋势，从 14.32%下降到 12.54%；所有类型银行的 ROE 增速呈现一致性的下跌趋势；从结构上看，城市商业银行的 ROE 最高，农村商业银行的 ROE 最低。

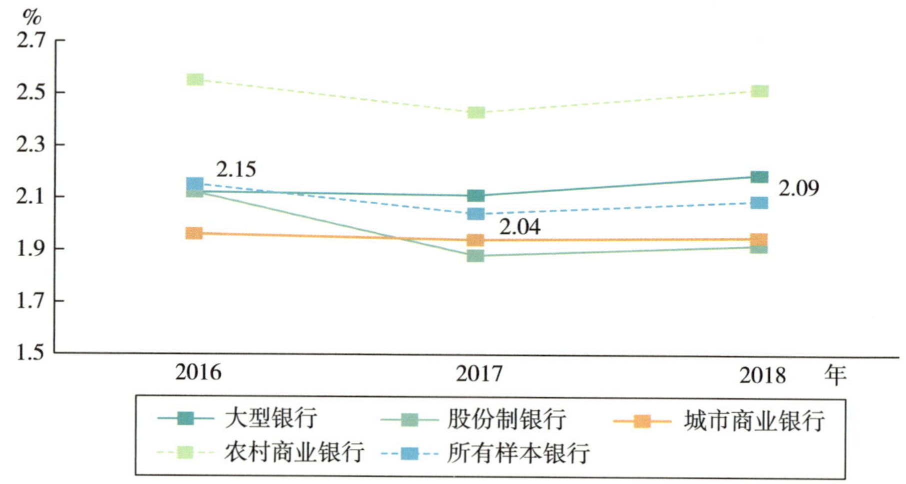

资料来源：Wind、各银行年报。

图 4－3　银行的净息差

从图 4－3 中可以看到，2016—2018 年[③]，总体来讲，所有类型银行的净息差（NIM）[④] 同样呈下行趋势，从 2.15%下降到 2.09%；所有类型银行的净息差 2018 年相比 2017 年有所企稳；从结构上看，农村商业银行的 NIM 最高，股份制银行的 NIM 最低。但无论如何，银行的净息差最近 3 年都徘徊在 2%左右。

以上三个盈利性指标证实了银行的盈利水平近年来确实呈现一致性的下降趋势。这种现象与整体经济结构调整、经济增速放缓有关。以上因素及包容性发展的需要与新的市场主体的加入促使银行不断调整其战略，开拓新的业务群体与产品。普惠金融服务便是传统银行的重要战略之一。

（二）普惠金融能力不足

1. 服务大型企业、高净值客户是传统银行的业务重点

传统银行尤其是大型银行在发力普惠金融服务前，主要服务的客户群体是大型

① 除大型商业银行外，在数据系列中，由于某些银行尚未披露 2018 年年报，因此存在 2～3 个 2017 年的数据，但并不影响总体的趋势判断。

② 算术平均回报率。

③ 除大型商业银行外，在数据系列中，由于某些银行尚未披露 2018 年年报，因此存在 2～3 个 2017 年的数据，但并不影响总体的趋势判断。

④ 算术平均回报率。

企业、高净资产值零售客户。这些客户群体的支付、理财、融资、保险及其他金融服务的需求特征一般是额度大、频次低、期限较长，而且客户数量较少，因此可通过分配专业的客户经理或团队对客户需求进行充分满足，服务与风控流程也以线下为主。

2. 服务普惠金融客户的能力不足

普惠金融的服务对象绝大多数都是长尾小微客户。长尾小微客户数量众多，占到全部企业数量的 90%以上。其金融服务需求一般具有期限短、金额小、频次高、需求急的特点。相对大型企业及高净值客户来说，这会造成同一时间段内的服务需求频次大幅上升。如果按照传统的金融服务做法，众多的长尾客户需要分配更多的人力资源，风控成本也随之大幅上升。因此，传统银行服务长尾小微客户的能力仍然有所欠缺。即使有政策引导，传统银行也很难在短期内达到商业可持续的目标。

（三）风险与回报不匹配

衡量风险与收益回报的综合指标有很多，这里选取较为常见的夏普指数来解释银行在对小微企业和其他类型企业贷款时评估风险与回报的过程。

夏普指数的表达式如下：

$$SharpcRatio = \frac{E(R_p) - R_f}{\sigma_p}$$

其中，$E(R_p)$ 为投资组合的预期报酬率； R_f 为无风险利率； σ_p 为投资组合收益率的标准差。

银行对企业的贷款广义上也是一种投资，其产生的收益率就是其贷款利率，因此在这里以贷款利率作为 $E(R_p)$ 的替代①，为 5.96%；而小微企业与其他企业投资（大中型企业）组合的收益率的标准差 σ_p 在这里分别用三板（全国股转交易系统）与上证 A 股 2010—2018 年的年化净资产收益率（ROE）② 替代，为 1.98%。

无风险利率 R_f 采用 2018 年底一年期银行存款基准利率③来替代，目前为 1.5%；银行 2019 年 4 月对所有小微企业的贷款利率 [$E(Rp_1)$] 为 6.9%④，占比为 24%左右；2019 年第一季度全社会非金融企业及部门贷款平均利率为 5.69%⑤，由此可以推算出银行业金融机构除小微企业外的企业占比为 76%，进一步得出贷款利率 [$E(Rp_2)$]

① 这种替代并不严谨，但此处限于数据的可得性，而且目的只是为说明银行的收益率与其放贷对象的收益率波动的大致关系，因此有一定的合理性。

② 资料来源：Wind。

③ 2018 年银行一年期定期存款利率。

④ 资料来源：2019 年陆家嘴论坛上银保监会普惠金融部主任李均锋的讲话。

⑤ 资料来源：中国人民银行发布的《2019 年第一季度中国货币政策执行报告》。

为 5.31%[①]。

将上述参数代入公式计算出银行贷款给小微企业和其他类型企业的夏普比率，分别为 0.91 与 1.92，可以看到贷款给小微企业的投资效率要远低于给大中型企业的投资效率。由此可见，对小微企业开展金融服务的风险与回报不匹配，投资效率低，因此银行进行普惠金融服务转型的意愿不强。

（四）较难平衡双重目标

普惠金融具有双重目标：一是商业可持续，二是社会绩效目标。社会绩效目标某种程度上可以理解为银行进行社会影响力投资的一部分，这在本报告的其他章节中有详细讨论，这里不再赘述。银行在开展普惠金融服务过程中，由于风险与回报的不匹配，可能会牺牲一部分商业利润，但绝非要以业务亏损为代价。值得注意的是，社会目标是建立在商业可持续的目标基础之上的，而且社会绩效目标的实现可以在长期内对商业目标有正向促进作用，如果将这种正向促进作用计算在银行的社会影响力投资价值中，如带来商誉价值的提高、政策与监管的引导性优惠政策等，其普惠金融服务的价值将因此大为提高，因此银行需要在提供意愿上消除这一疑虑。

二、转型的商业空间

银行在提供普惠金融服务时存在诸多困境，转型可以为银行带来较大的潜在客户群体，且市场风险基本可控，从而使银行利润空间得到较大提升。

为了对银行的普惠金融服务转型有较为深入的探讨，本章中我们以普惠金融主要服务对象“中小微弱”中的“小微”为主对这一问题加以说明。值得指出的是，消费金融存在巨大的市场容量与商业空间，本报告的第二部分“金融健康”中有具体研究与阐述，本章不做赘述。

小微企业概念界定及融资测量指标确定

在开展具体分析之前，我们需要界定几个概念。

第一，关于全口径小微企业贷款。本章中，小微企业贷款的界定与中国银保监会的标准一致，即小微企业贷款余额包含用于小型企业、微型企业、个体工商户、

① 可以通过解方程得到：$0.76X+0.24\times0.069=0.0569$。

小微企业主的贷款余额之和，这是全口径的小微企业贷款。截至 2018 年底，全国全口径小微企业贷款余额为 33.49 万亿元。

第二，关于普惠口径的小微企业贷款。普惠口径的小微企业贷款指的是单户授信总额 1000 万元及以下的企业贷款，2018 年底贷款余额为 9.36 万亿元，有贷款余额的户数为 1723 万户。

第三，选择全口径还是普惠口径的小微企业贷款作为测量目标。在这里我们选择全口径的小微企业的贷款余额作为测量目标。其原因主要是，首先，虽然政策制定部门将普惠口径制定在授信额度 1000 万元以下，但现实中很多小微企业，尤其是初创科技型企业的融资额度很可能大于这个数值，而且数值会随着时间的推移、政策及监管部门标准的改变而不断改变，因此我们最好不要将其锁定为某一个具体数值；其次，全口径的数值也更加能够反映市场的需求总量，便于全面决策需要。

（一）市场需求大于供给

为了科学地衡量小微企业信贷需求，我们利用中国普惠金融研究院（CAFI）在浙江省的小微企业调研数据，在若干假设的基础上，对全国的小微企业信贷额度进行估算。

1. 浙江省小微企业的户均融资需求测算

CAFI 于 2017 年在浙江省的 14 个县区对 2730 户小微企业的生产、经营、普惠金融服务使用情况进行了调研，调研对象包括小微企业、个体工商户、小微企业主等群体，这与官方统计口径一致。

浙江省是我国小微企业和民营企业最为集中的地区之一，在小微金融服务方面取得了一定的成效。因此，用该地区小微企业的融资需求数据测算全国整体的数据具有一定的代表性。

从最终的统计数据来看，2017 年浙江省小微企业的户均融资需求均值为 93.92 万元。从数量结构上看，多数小微企业的融资需求较低，100 万元以下的企业群体占到了 76.4%（见图 4－4）。

2. 全国小微企业 2017 年户均融资额度需求测算

以浙江省的小微企业调研数据为基础，我们需要找到一个折算因子，用于测算全国小微企业户均融资额度。

从融资需求与经济发展程度强相关的经济逻辑出发，我们假设小微企业融资需求

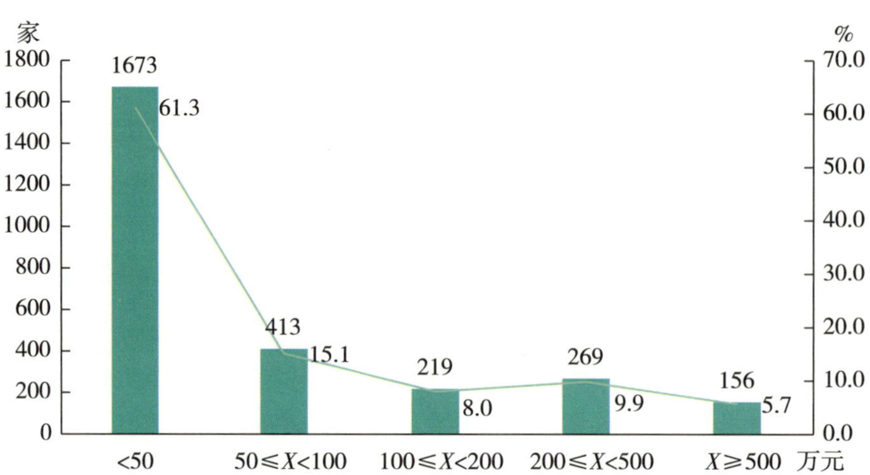

资料来源：中国普惠金融研究院数据中心。

图 4－4　浙江省小微企业融资额度情况

额度与当地的人均 GDP 呈线性相关。根据该假设，测算折算因子为 0.57[①]，那么全国小微企业 2017 年的户均融资额度就是 53.53 万元。

对比中国银保监会的统计数据，截至 2018 年底，普惠口径的小微企业信贷余额为 9.36 万亿元，客户数为 1723 万户，均值为 54.32 万元，与调研数据均值相近。

3. 全国小微企业数量测算

2016—2018 年全国市场主体数量[②]如表 4－1 所示。

表 4－1　2016—2018 年全国市场主体数量　　单位：万户

年份	市场主体总数量	企业户数	个体工商户	农民专业合作社
2016	8705.4	2596.1	5930	179.4
2017	9814.8	3033.7	6579.4	201.7
2018	11020	3474.2	7328.6	217.3

全国小微企业数量占到市场主体的 90%[③]以上。按照 90%的保守数量计算，根据表 4－1 中的市场主体数量进行测算，得出 2018 年小微企业数量约为 0.9918 亿户。

① 2017 年全国人均 GDP 为 5.29 万元，浙江省人均 GDP 为 9.21 万元，折算因子＝全国人均 GDP/浙江省人均 GDP。

② 资料来源：国家市场监督管理总局。

③ 中国人民银行行长易纲在 2018 年陆家嘴论坛上的讲话。

4. 小微企业的银行融资缺口测算

根据全国小微企业主体数量与户均融资需求额度，可以得到小微企业的总融资需求额度为每年 53.09 万亿元。

全国小微企业融资缺口＝全国小微企业融资总需求－现有小微企业信贷余额－（债券融资＋股票融资）－P2P 融资余额－小额贷款融资余额－创业投资增量＝53.09－33.49[①]－0.1783[②]－0.9550[③]－0.7890[④]－0.8873[⑤]＝16.79 万亿元。

（二）市场风险基本可控

很多文献指出，小微企业融资难、融资贵的原因主要归结于小微企业贷款的风险大、不良贷款率较高。然而，随着近年来互联网银行业务的迅猛发展，头部互联网银行的不良贷款率均较低，甚至低于上市银行 2018 年的平均不良贷款率 1.55%[⑥]；净息差较高，维持在 3.9%以上，大于传统银行 2018 年底的 2.1%，而且以小微企业为主要服务对象的网商银行净息差更是比上市银行高 3.3%（见表 4－2）。

表 4－2　2018 年[⑦]互联网银行财务指标

名称	不良贷款率（%）	净息差（%）	资产规模（亿元）	主要客户群体
网商银行	1.3	5.4	959	小微企业、个体工商户
微众银行	0.51	3.9	2200	个人消费为主

反观传统银行的总体不良贷款率，近年来保持相对稳定，但所有类型银行的不良贷款率均比互联网银行的不良贷款率高，如表 4－3 所示。

表 4－3　传统银行近年来不良贷款率　　单位：%

名称	2016 年	2017 年	2018 年
大型银行	2.02	1.43	1.39
股份制银行	1.99	1.65	1.64
城市商业银行	2.16	1.37	1.39
农村商业银行	2.75	1.82	1.65
所有样本银行	2.19	1.55	1.52

① 资料来源：中国银保监会，2018 年底全口径小微企业贷款余额。

② 资料来源：《上海证券报》。其中，股票融资数据为区域性股权市场融资额，小微企业债券融资额非常少，计算中没有计入。

③ 资料来源：Wind。

④ 资料来源：Wind。

⑤ 资料来源：Wind。

⑥ 资料来源：根据上市银行年报数据计算，算术平均数。

⑦ 资料来源：互联网银行年报。

综上所述，小微企业对银行信贷的缺口较大，不良贷款率可以控制在商业可持续的水平，且能够为银行带来潜在利润。因此，银行有理由积极拥抱普惠金融服务。

（三）数字技术扩大利润空间

供需缺口的存在，一个非常重要的原因就是银行与小微企业由于价格原因无法达成市场交易。数字技术可有效降低成本，缩小或消除供需之间的差距，从而扩大银行利润空间，达成交易。

1. 小额贷款公司融资价格

根据中国小额贷款公司协会与中国普惠金融研究院 2018 年对全国 400 家[①]小额贷款公司的问卷调研结果，小额贷款公司的资金加权平均出借利率水平为 15.1%[②]。如图 4－5 所示，在 12 个月以下的贷款中，价格随着借款期限的增加而逐步下降，这主要是由小额贷款公司鼓励客户进行较长时间借贷而形成的。但在 12 个月以上的贷款中，价格又温和上涨，则是由于期限加长带来的风险增加而造成的。

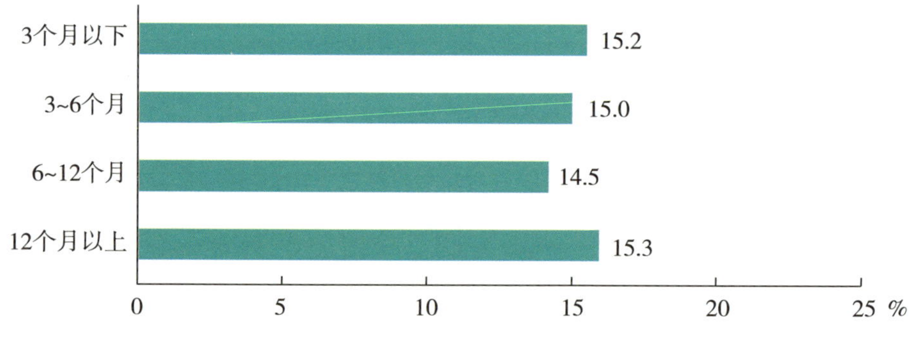

图 4－5　小额贷款公司的利率期限结构

2. 银行融资价格

一般而言，金融机构或企业为小微经济体提供的资金供给价格包含机构的资金成本、运营成本、小微企业的风险溢价、适当的利润率四个部分。为了计算银行可以为小微企业提供的市场价格，我们假设在运营成本、小微企业的风险溢价、适当的利润率上，银行与小额贷款公司无差异，最重要的差异在于两者的资金成本。

根据对 400 家小额贷款公司的调研数据，我们可以测算出小额贷款公司的加权平均融资成本为 6.3%，各种途径的融资成本如图 4－6 所示。对于银行的资金成本测量，

① 这 400 家公司包含传统线下小额贷款公司与互联网小额贷款公司，具有非常强的代表性。根据调研数据，中国普惠金融研究院形成了“小额贷款公司的现状和政策建议”报告。

② 一般有较大借贷余额的互联网小额贷款平台其综合利率较低，而且随着其所占的市场份额逐步扩大，会拉低加权后的市场利率。因此，我们认为市场价格水平在 15.1%是有其合理性的。

我们选取了全部计息资产的平均付息率指标①。根据对37家银行的年报数据进行统计，得出算术平均的指标值为2.35%②。从结构来看，各类型银行的资金成本如图4-7所示。

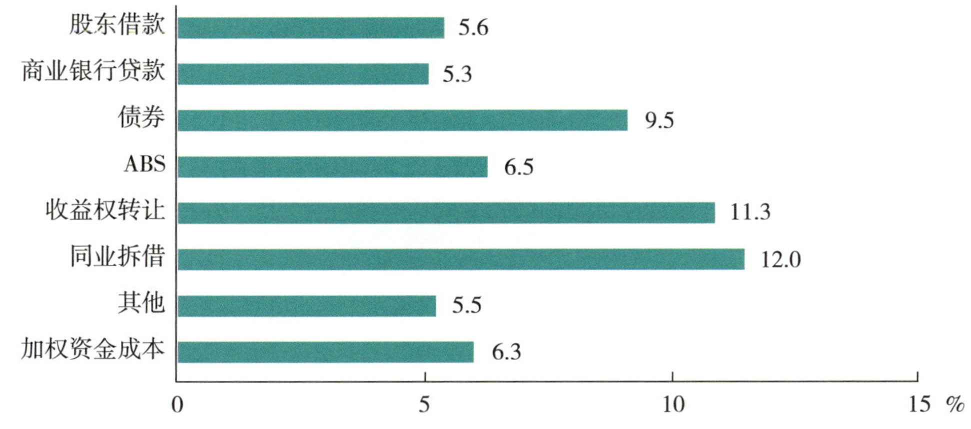

图4-6　小额贷款公司各种途径的融资成本

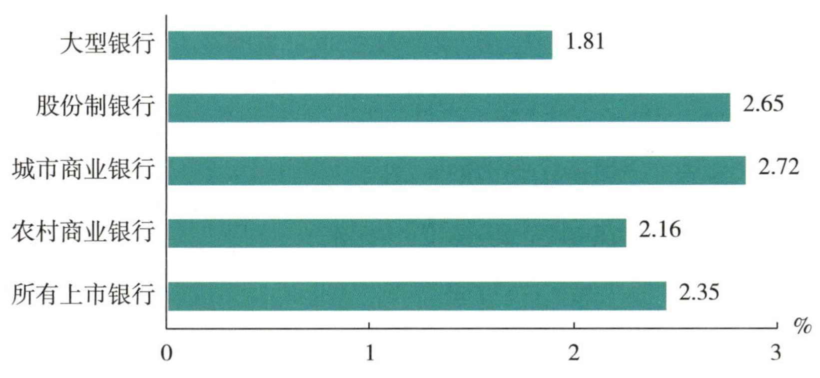

图4-7　各类型银行的资金成本

由上述数据及假设可以测算出，银行的市场化小微贷款利率=15.1%-（6.3%-2.35%）=11.15%。

3. 浙江省小微企业的加权融资需求价格

根据浙江省2730家小微企业需求价格水平，年化的加权需求价格为8.4%。值得注意的是，37%的市场小微主体愿意接受高于8.4%的价格。具体分区间统计数据如图4-8所示。

① 该指标为资金加权平均成本。

② 如果加权平均，该指标值会低于2.35%，因为大型银行的资金成本普遍低于2%。

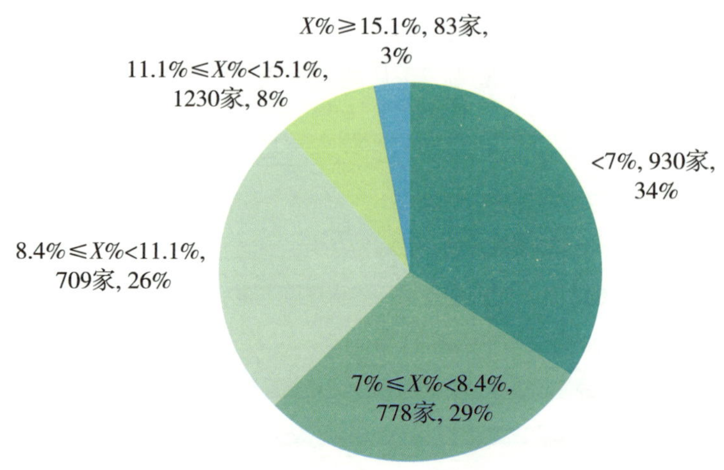

图 4-8　浙江省小微企业资金需求价格构成

4. 银行与小微企业的资金价格缺口

根据以上的测算结果我们可以得到，银行愿意提供的市场价格为 11.1%，而需求方的意愿资金平均价格为 8.4%，二者之间的缺口为 2.7%。虽然有 37%的小微企业客户愿意接受 8.4%以上的价格水平，但这种缺口无疑会在很大程度上造成供给的不足。

根据中国银保监会的统计结果，截至 2018 年底，普惠口径的小微企业贷款平均资金价格为 7.02%。如果我们将供需双方的价格水平放在一起，就可以测算出多个供需主体之间的缺口（见图 4-9）。

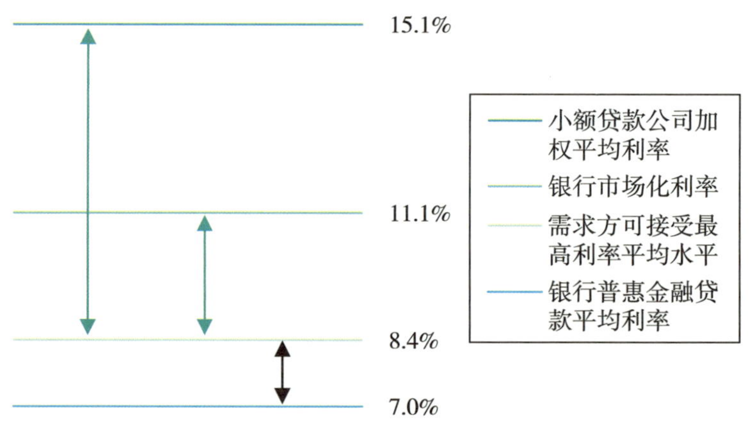

图 4-9　小微企业信贷市场价格

5. 提升金融科技能力可消除价格差距

根据表 4-2 与图 4-3 中所示的 2018 年净息差数据，两家互联网银行的净息差分别大于各类传统银行平均值 1.8 个和 3.3 个百分点①。

① 网商银行 2018 年的净息差为 5.4%，微众银行为 3.9%，而 2018 年所有银行样本的净息差为 2.1%。

这种盈利水平的差异是由什么造成的？其中的影响因素很多，但最为明显也是最相关的因素是由于传统银行与互联网银行的金融科技水平的差异。

我们完全可以推论，在其他因素相同的情况下，如果银行拥有了互联网银行的金融科技水平，那么银行与小微企业之间的价格缺口 2.7%完全可以缩小甚至完全消除。如果按照更加可比的专业服务于小微企业的网商银行的净息差作为基准，如果银行可以达到其金融科技水平，那么银行就可以按照 8.2%[①]左右的价格水平提供服务。那么，图 4－9 就可以修改为图 4－10 所示的情况。

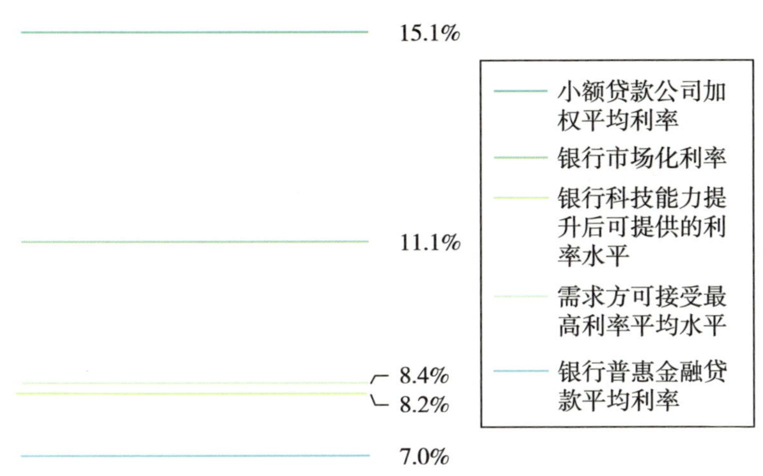

图 4－10　银行可通过科技能力提升服务于小微企业需求

（四）政府政策空间

银行进行普惠金融服务转型是中国经济包容性发展的必然要求。一方面，银行作为最大的资金供给机构有责任提供普惠金融服务；另一方面，政府也可以通过各种政策为银行提供利润空间。

1. 银行转型的责任

银行是中国金融资金供给的最大金融机构。中国的非金融企业资金供给主要来自银行业、证券业、保险业中的金融机构及小额贷款公司、P2P、创业投资等企业。社会融资主要集中在各种间接融资方式如贷款上，占到社会融资规模的 82%，而直接融资[②]比例较小（见图 4－11）。由于普惠金融主要服务对象具有“短、小、急、

① 市场利率构成中包含资金成本、运营成本、小微企业风险溢价、适当利润率等，网商银行 2017 年的资金成本约为 6%，略低于小额贷款行业 6.3%的水平，假设其运营成本、风险溢价与银行一致，利润率差异以净息差代替，那么银行在达到互联网银行的科技水平后，可以提供的小微企业利率为：15.1%－（6%－2.35%）－（5.4%－2.1%）＝8.2%。

② 直接融资包括企业债券、地方政府债券、非金融企业、股票融资。

频”的特征，信贷融资占据了其外部融资的绝大部分，而银行又是信贷资金的主要来源，因此银行在包容性发展过程中必然要承担更多的责任，对于金融体系的健康发展至关重要。

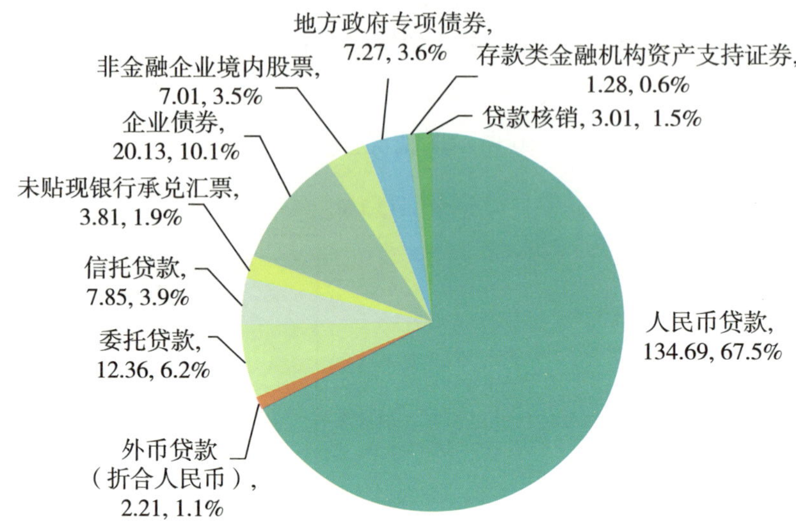

资料来源：Wind。

图 4-11 2018 年底社会融资规模存量结构（单位：万亿元）

2. 优惠政策为银行提供利润空间

近 10 年来，随着政府对包容性发展理解的不断加深，相关政策的出台频率也越来越高。如中国人民银行提供的再贷款政策，包含扶贫、支农支小再贷款，差别存款准备金率政策，差别银行的永续债政策与针对中小企业的再融资政策；财政部对普惠金融服务达标的金融机构实行财政补贴；税务部门对金融机构推行普惠金融业务采取一定的税收优惠；中国银保监会针对普惠金融业务开展差别性的监管政策；中央与地方政府成立融资担保公司与银行共同分担贷款风险等。

这些政策的推出，旨在鼓励传统银行积极开展普惠金融业务，在一定程度上可以减少贷款风险或进行风险补偿。虽然在短期内银行可能会存在一定的利润空间收窄的现象，但无疑从中长期甚至从当前来看，获客量的增大必然会带来银行综合业务量的提升，扩展其商业空间。

三、转型的突破口

从上述分析可知，金融机构的信贷供给与小微企业的需求在量与价上都存在一定的缺口，那么银行如何通过转型突破这两个“缺口”，从而扩大商业空间呢？

（一）细分市场，精准定位

从客户需求特征分析，银行只有通过市场细分和精准定位来识别小微企业并满足其需求，才可获得小微客户，从而产生新的利润增长点。

小微企业的融资需求期限较短，12 个月以内的短期融资需求占 54%，1 年期以上贷款比例占 46%（见图 4－12）。这说明在提供小微企业融资时，要适当地提高融资的期限。

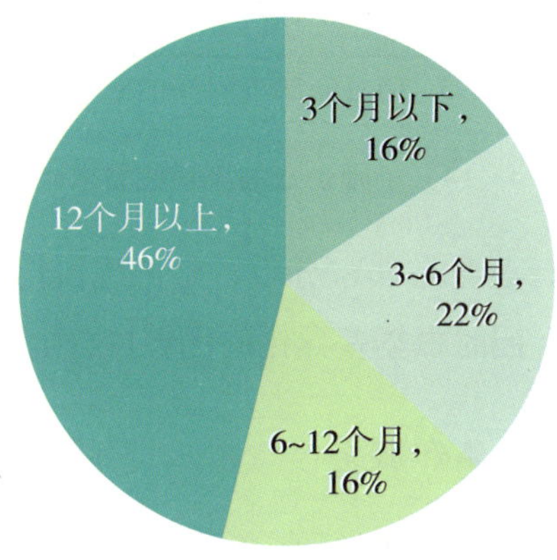

图 4－12　小微企业的融资期限分布

小微企业的借款频率相对较高。2016—2017 年，小微企业的借款笔数分别为 4.3 笔和 3.5 笔[①]（见图 4－13）。这就需要资金供给机构可以随时提供贷款，或提供随借随还的循环贷款产品。

图 4－13　2016—2017 年客户平均借款笔数

与大中型企业的信贷和融资规模相比，小微企业的年融资需求额度较小，约为 53 万元。

小微企业的融资需求相对比较急。该特点可以通过小微企业对融资目的反馈中的“补充流动资金”的出现频率来体现。如图 4－14 所示，小微企业进行融资的目的一般是用来补充流动资金，因此其需求一般都比较急，需要在短时间内获得批准并拿到贷款。

---

① 中国普惠金融研究院 2018 年对 400 家小额贷款公司的调研数据。

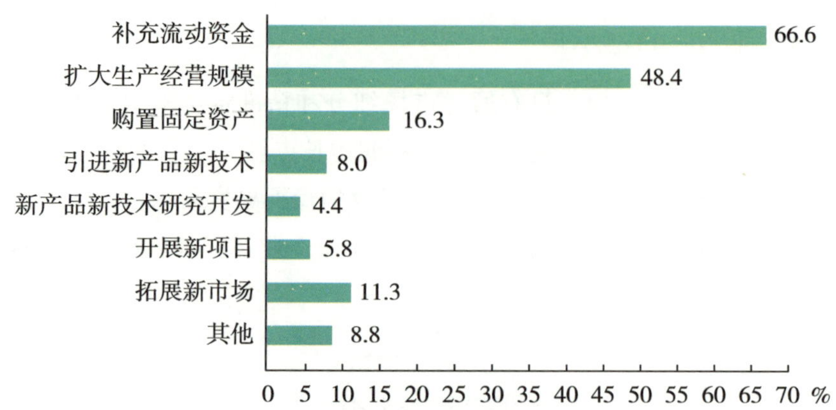

图 4-14　小微企业的流动性需求比例

小微企业的地区分布、行业分布非常分散，是传统银行较难覆盖的长尾群体。这就需要银行不断增加服务场景，同时根据差异化的优势打造生态圈，以增加客户黏性。

（二）以客户为中心的产品和服务

上述的小微客户需求特征，要求银行在产品设计时必须以客户为中心。以客户为中心的产品设计，就是要从客户需求出发，为其提供便捷、成本可负担、全流程体验好的产品。关于该问题，本报告在“负责任金融”部分的相应章节有详尽的介绍，在此不做赘述。

（三）巧用金融科技

金融科技能力的提升在满足小微企业金融需求中发挥着关键作用。小微企业期限中“短、小、频、急、散”的需求特征要求资金供给机构可以快速反应，提供小额、中短期、可以随借随还的产品，同时放款时间短。这就要求银行建立敏捷化组织以应对“急”，以客户为中心的产品设计满足“中、小、频”，以生态圈建设应对“散”，不断获取不同场景的新客户，增加客户黏性。金融科技作为客户数据的存储、分析、信贷决策、贷后管理的手段，在每个环节都必不可少，是银行转型的重要基础设施。

（四）推进能力建设

推进能力建设指的是传统银行的组织改造、管理与从业人员能力的提升。具体可通过以下三点达成。

1. 进行敏捷化组织改造

银行需要通过敏捷化组织来适应客户需求特征，才能获得更多的小微客户。例如，银行普惠金融事业部的建立，就是因为“中小微弱”客户的需求特征、风险控制均与传统的服务大中型企业客户不同，需要的机构服务能力也是迥异的。专门的普惠金融事业部可以较快地进行部门的敏捷化建设而不需要进行整个机构的敏捷化改造。

2. 建设生态圈增加客户黏性

金融服务趋势是将银行变为“主办行”，除去信贷外，保险、理财、支付、购物、生活交费、出行等都通过该行经办，也就是构建场景的“生态圈”，这样可以使客户具有高忠诚度。但是，目前银行的场景与生态圈建设的同质化非常高。只有具有差异化优势的生态圈，才有生命力，才能更好地获客。

3. 管理与从业人员能力的提升

银行服务的提升，需要管理与从业人员能力的提升。一方面，只有人的能力提升才能有效利用金融科技工具；另一方面，人的能力提升可以强化其对普惠金融业务重要性的认识，更加积极地从事该业务。

四、创建有利的政策环境

（一）推行市场化利率

当供给价格低于需求价格时，可能会带来市场主体的套利与本地资金外流等一系列扭曲市场的行为，从而大大降低服务质量，甚至造成中长期的市场萎缩。因此，银行如何有效降低市场的平均价格对于市场与银行自身的健康发展至关重要。

首先，66%的小微企业可以接受目前普惠金融口径下银行提供的7%以上的年化利率（见图4-8），因此适当提高资金供给价格，既可以消除市场主体的套利，也可以防止本地资金的外流，尤其对服务乡村振兴具有积极意义，最终促成市场的资金供给。其次，通过上述分析我们看到，市场自身可以通过“看不见的手”达到供需平衡，有效降低融资价格，因此限制小微企业的融资价格从中长期来看并没有太大的必要。

（二）鼓励多种业务模式

若要充分利用数字技术，需要各种类型银行与互联网小额贷款公司、互联网银行等具有技术优势的企业进行合作。因此，在合法合规的基础上鼓励多种市场主体的存在至关重要。一方面，可以构建多层次的市场体系，更好地促进小微企业良好融资环境的形成；另一方面，应鼓励银行通过多种模式提升其能力，尤其是金融科技能力。

金融科技能力的建设模式主要有三种。一是内生性的。金融机构自建金融科技公司或依赖原先的相关部门，依靠自身资源，提升金融科技服务能力。二是以自我提升为主，与外部合作为辅相结合。三是外生性的，即金融机构与金融科技公司合作为主，自建为辅。

此外，银行在短周期与长周期的金融科技能力的建设也不一致。短中期内与各类同业机构、金融科技企业合作可能是快速扩大有效客户群体的重要手段，因为场景建设有很高的资金和技术门槛。例如，支付宝、微信等为此早已投入了很多补贴，银行尤其是小型银行很难与其竞争。如图 4－15 所示，相对于支付宝[①]、微信等 10 亿户用户的移动应用，大型银行的客户数与之相差甚多，股份制银行差距进一步扩大，城市商业银行和农村商业银行的用户数仅分别相当于单个大平台的 0.0213％和 0.0065％，因此自建金融科技对于中小型银行来说是非常困难的。在资金投入方面，大型银行与股份制银行在资金投入上或许可以和金融科技公司相抗衡，但城市商业银行和农村商业银行由于资金实力的巨大悬殊，只能选择与其他银行和金融科技公司合作（见表 4－4）。

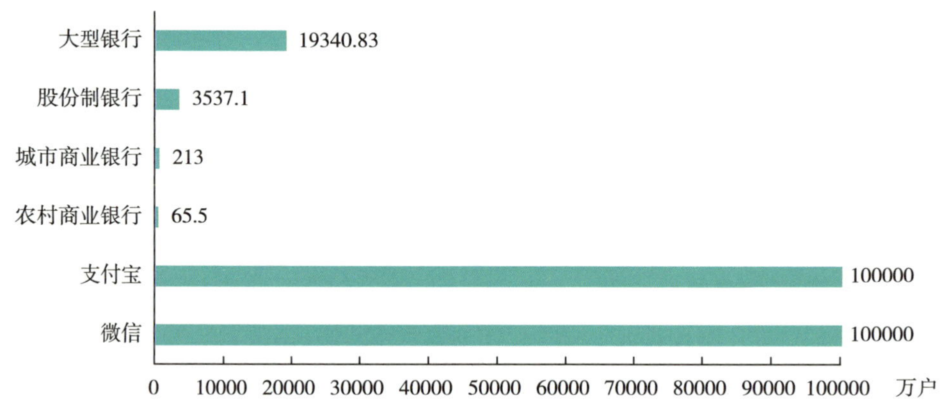

图 4－15　各类型银行与支付宝、微信的移动用户数

表 4－4　银行与金融科技公司的金融科技投资额　　单位：亿元

机构名称	2018 年募资额/金融科技投入额
蚂蚁金服	910
百度金服	279.5
大型银行	87.3
股份制银行	33.7
城市商业银行	3.0
农村商业银行	1.6

① 包含境外用户数。

一般情况下，不同类型的银行会选择以下三种方式提升自己的金融科技能力。

第一，大型银行、股份制银行倾向于内生性提升模式。截至 2019 年 5 月底，共有 8 家银行自建金融科技公司（2 家大型银行、5 家股份制银行、1 家城市商业银行）成立了自己的金融科技子公司。

大型银行由于资本、人才、科技实力较强，一般会自建金融科技公司或依托原有部门提升自身的金融科技能力。这种方式最大的问题在于其“船大难掉头”。大型银行面临股份制银行的威胁，如果未能及时有效地建立敏捷的组织与数字生态圈，将会面临客户流失与新增量不足的问题。在小微企业及零售银行端可能会被股份制银行超越。当然，大型银行除自建金融科技公司外，也可以尝试与金融科技公司开展批发性普惠金融合作，并在合作过程中提升自己的风控能力。

股份制银行属于在资本、公司治理、灵活度等综合能力上相对较强的银行业机构，有可能在金融科技能力竞争中进一步扩大市场份额。

第二，部分股份制银行会采取“自建为主＋合作为辅”的模式。部分规模较小的股份制银行依托原有的信息技术部门构建金融科技能力，同时与外部的金融科技公司开展合作。

第三，“自建为辅＋合作为主”的模式一般以中小型的城市商业银行、农村商业银行居多。它们在自身研发的基础上，采购第三方解决方案，不仅可以提升自身产品科技水平，也可以共同运营，实现流量分成、风险分担。另外，这些银行也会与第三方互联网公司和金融科技公司合作，以联合开发或者外包开发的方式获得相应的服务。

城市商业银行一般地处城区，同时面临股份制银行与大型银行的威胁，必须发力数字技术获客，但限于人才与资本，面临的挑战最大，从而该类型机构大多选择与金融科技企业合作。

农村商业银行与农村信用社有传统的线下网点和县域的地域优势，守住农村阵地，扩大业务范围，发力数字技术，以省联社为金融科技服务的核心是其主要的发展方向，与金融科技公司进行合作也是其快速切入新客群的重要途径之一。

第二部分

金融健康

金融健康要求金融服务必须对消费者有益，帮助他们改进储蓄消费习惯，提升信用意识与金融能力，提高缓冲经济波动的能力，提升生活质量，摆脱贫困，达到可持续的、健康的金融状态。

第五章 定义金融健康

【摘要】金融健康是指金融消费者的金融或财务状况是否处于一个良好的状态，这是普惠金融的更高层次的要求。衡量金融健康既包括客观的指标，如消费者个人的收入与支出、资产与负债的相对情况，也包括对消费者主观态度的衡量，如个人消费者对目前个人财务状况的满意度及对未来个人财务状况的信心。本章详细介绍金融健康这一概念各方面指标具体涉及的问题及其量化方式，并对金融健康与普惠金融领域相关概念及其关系进行梳理，以帮助消费者更有效地改善金融健康的状况。最后，本章根据中国普惠金融研究院对数字金融平台客户的调研结果，对我国消费者金融健康状况的主要影响因子进行回归分析，并提出改善我国消费者金融健康状况的建议。

一、什么是消费者金融健康

近年来，随着我国正规渠道及非正规渠道的个人信贷服务迅速增长，社会对消费者个人因过度借贷陷入循环债务等问题越发关注。提出消费者个人金融健康这一话题，并引导消费者关注自己和家人的金融健康状态成为日益紧迫的问题。金融健康，顾名思义，是指金融消费者的金融或财务状况是否处于一个良好的状态。具有传统思想的中国人大多羞于谈钱。即便是改革开放 40 年的当今，仍有 40%和 44%的中国人认同或非常认同“金钱是所有邪恶的根源”及“金钱是恶魔”的观点①。对金钱概念的不重视，间接导致了我国对个人金融健康教育的忽视，以及资源投入的不足。提高我国居民金融健康水平需要政府机关、社会团体、金融机构、教育机构及居民个人关注等多层次、多方面的努力。

① 数据来源于北京师范大学财经素养教育研究中心的调研结果。

金融健康，是普惠金融领域的更高层次的要求。普惠金融第一层次的要求是金融产品和服务的普及，以求将长尾客户和被传统金融系统排斥的客户包容进来。第二层次的要求是提高消费者的金融知识和素养，让他们了解基本的、与生活相关的金融知识，以便能更好地使用产品和服务。第三层次的要求是改善消费者的金融能力和行为。金融能力的强弱是通过行为来体现的，是其金融知识与素养的外在表现，也是对个人金融状态产生作用的直接方式。个人的金融行为除了受到认知类的金融知识素养的影响，还受到非认知类的个人心理情绪状态的影响。第四层次的要求是金融健康，这是个人金融行为所导致的个人财务状态和结果（见图 5-1）。

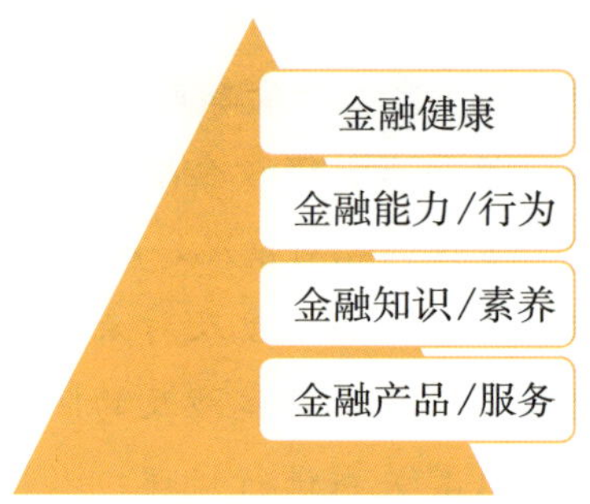

图 5-1　普惠金融相关概念模型

因此，金融健康是指消费者个人可以通过其金融知识、利用金融工具、采取合理的金融行为，以达到的个人财务状态。对消费者财务状态的衡量可以采用客观的方式，如直接衡量消费者个人的收入与支出、资产与负债的相对情况，以判断消费者实际上的财务充足度、灵活度和安全度，以及消费者在多大程度上可以通过其金融管理能力实现个人生活目标。同时，金融健康还包括对消费者主观态度的衡量。单纯的客观衡量指标难以全面地体现个人财务状态对其生活幸福感的作用。个人消费者对目前个人财务状况的满意度及对未来个人财务状况的信心也是综合金融幸福感的重要方面。

具体来说，金融健康的客观衡量因素包括消费者个人的收支、资产、借贷、保险四个方面。收支方面衡量消费者个人是否有稳定、合理的收入和支出结构；资产方面衡量消费者个人是否有足够的应急资金和固定资产；借贷方面衡量消费者个人是否有合理的债务结构和可供获得的贷款渠道；保险方面衡量消费者个人是否有充足、合适的保险。金融健康的主观衡量因素是消费者个人对目前财务状况的满意度及对未来财务状况的信心（见图 5-2）。

国际上，最先提出金融健康（Financial Health）概念的国际机构是美国的金融服务创新中心（Center for Financial Services Innovation，CFSI）。CFSI（2015）[①] 发现，

① CFSI，Understanding and Improving Consumer Financial Health in America，2015.

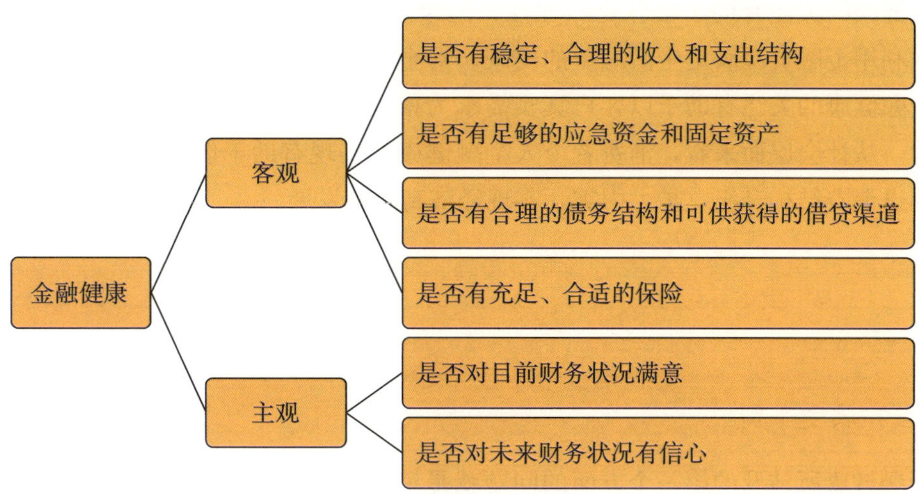

图 5-2　金融健康概念模型

美国人群中，有超过 57%的人缺乏金融健康。CFSI（2016）① 的金融健康概念包括四个方面：消费、储蓄、借贷、计划，而并未涉及消费者个人主观态度。CFSI（2017）创建了另外一套全球框架，设计了一套全球适用的金融健康指标体系。该体系包含六个主要方面，即平衡收入与支出、建立和维持储蓄、管理现有债务并可获得新的债务、计划和确认优先顺序、从财务冲击中恢复、使用有效的金融工具。CFSI 的衡量模型均采用客观衡量的因素，未包含消费者个人主观态度。

一个与金融健康相关的概念是金融福祉（Financial Wellbeing）。美国消费者金融保护局（Consumer Finance Protection Bureau，CFPB）② 认为，金融福祉包含四个主观方面：第一，个人是否可以掌控自己的日常财务活动；第二，未来是否可以抵御财务冲击；第三，现在是否具备享受生活的财务自由；第四，是否可以达成未来的财务目标。在学术领域，Netemeyer 等（2017）③ 用两个主观维度的指标衡量金融福祉：一是目前管理财务的压力，二是对未来财务安全感的信心。笔者发现，消费者个人的财务福祉在很大程度上影响其综合生活福祉。

我们首次在我国提出消费者金融健康的概念，将普惠金融的概念推进到结果、状态的层面。同时，该概念将主观交易与客观变量相结合，形成了更加全面、准确的衡量标准。

衡量消费者个人的金融健康具有重要意义。从消费者个人层面来说，对自己和家

---

① CFSI，Eight Ways to Measure Financial Health，2017.

② CFPB，www.consumerfinance.gov/financial-well-being.

③ Netemeyer et al. How Am I Doing? Perceived Financial Well-Being，Its Potential Antecedents，and Its Relation to Overall Well-Being [J]. Journal of Consumer Finance，2017.

人金融健康的关注有助于培养更加理性、健康的金融行为，能更好地抵御财务冲击，更好地利用金融资源满足生活愿望的实现。对金融机构和金融服务供应商来说，对消费者金融健康的关注有助于以客户真实需求为根本出发点进行产品设计，采取负责任的行为。从社会层面来看，消费者个人金融健康的实现有助于促进社会金融体系的稳定，促进消费结构升级，扩大内需，实现经济高质量发展。

二、金融健康的量化指标

（一）收支平衡

金融健康所涉及的第一个方面的问题就是消费者个人的收入和支出。对成年人来讲，个人收入是财务来源的主要渠道；对于没有收入的学生而言，家庭给予的教育费用也可以算作个人收入。由于我国人口收入水平和不同物价水平相差较大，因此不适宜使用绝对的收入金额作为主要的衡量依据。然而，收入的稳定性，即在多大程度上个人收入是可预期的，能够帮助消费者量入为出，安排个人消费支出。

（二）足够的储蓄/资产

金融健康的第二个方面涉及个人资产情况。资产情况涵盖流动资产，也就是在一周内能筹集多少资金。我们并不采用可筹集到的资金的绝对金额的概念，因为绝对金额在我国不同地区和收入人群中概念不同。相反，我们采用相对金额的概念，即所筹集的资金可以支付多久的生活支出。

（三）合理负债

债务融资渠道是为消费者提供资金来源的重要渠道。使用得当，债务可以提高消费者的生活和生产水平；若使用不当可能会使消费者陷入债务深渊。这里的债务管理包括两个方面的内容：对现有债务资源的管理能力及获取新的债务资源的能力。

（四）适当保险

我国医疗保障体系并不完善，居民的医疗费用占个人及家庭的开支较大，个人或单位购买商业重疾险、医疗保险（补充医疗）是对疾病未来风险的有益对冲。因此，是否购买了充足的商业重疾险、医疗保险是衡量个人未来财务保障的标准之一。

（五）主观态度

对目前财务状况的主观满意度和对未来财务状况的信心程度是 CFPB 和学术领域

对金融福祉的主要衡量方式。就像人的健康包括生理健康和心理健康一样，消费者个人的金融健康也应该在客观指标之外，包含一些主观指标。我们用两个指标来衡量消费者的主观态度：对目前财务状况的满意度和对未来财务状况的信心。

三、金融健康与普惠金融相关概念

金融产品/服务	金融知识/素养	金融行为/能力	金融健康
•基础账户 •电子钱包 •储蓄及理财 •融资与借贷 •保险 •支付 •其他	•单利、复利 •风险与回报率的关系 •分散风险 •货币的时间价值 •通货膨胀 •对贷款、投资等产品利率期限等方面的了解 •其他	•金融素养的行为体现 •合理使用金融产品和服务 •规律储蓄的习惯 •合理风险的投资 •理智借贷 •购买保险 •防范欺诈 •获取建议 •其他	•收支平衡 •充足储蓄 •合理负债 •适当保险 •主观满意

图 5－3　普惠金融领域相关概念

在普惠金融领域，最先提出的概念是金融产品和服务的普及。金融产品和服务包括金融账户、电子钱包、储蓄及理财、融资与借贷、保险、支付等。将这些产品和服务覆盖到尽可能广泛的人群，尤其是传统金融体系所无法触及的人群，是普惠金融早期的核心工作目标。

然而，拥有了获取金融产品和服务的渠道并不能保证消费者可以很好地使用这些产品和服务。对一些基本的金融概念的了解有助于消费者更好地选择适合自己的产品和服务并加以使用，以改善个人财务状况。学术领域对金融素养的常用衡量方式是用一套常规金融常识的问题对受访者进行测试，受访者对问题回答的正确率代表其金融知识水平或金融素养。学术文献发现，金融素养影响消费者的金融行为。例如，当消费者个人需要使用借贷服务时，需要判断金融服务供应商提供的借贷产品的利息、费用、期限等条件是否满足自己的需求，以便在一系列产品中选择性价比最高的产品。这就需要消费者个人对年化利率（Annual Percentage Rate，APR）有所了解。Disney 和 Gathergood（2013）研究发现，消费金融借贷者的金融知识水平普遍低于非借贷者的水平；同时，金融知识较缺乏的消费者更容易拥有高利息借贷产品，如“薪日贷”（Payday Loan）。另外，当金融知识较缺乏的消费者被问到信贷条款的相关问题时会更加不自信。Van Vooj 等（2012）研究发现，具有较多金融知识的个人容易有更加分散化的投资。因此，金融知识或金融素养对金融行为有着显著影响。提高消费者的金融知识与金融素养可以改善消费者的金融行为习惯。

世界银行（2013）将金融能力定义为在一定的社会经济条件下，消费者作出符合自身最佳利益的金融决策的内在能力，包括用于管理自有资源和理解、选择、使用满足需求的金融服务的知识、技能、态度和行为。贝多广等（2017）分别定义了消费者和经营者的金融能力：消费者普惠金融能力是指在面临一系列内部影响因素与外部约束条件下，消费者作出合理判断所需要的金融知识、技能、生态和金融实践的行为；经营者除具备作为消费者所需的金融能力之外，还需要具备特殊的金融能力，包括项目价值评估、现金流管理、融资能力及运用多样化金融工具的能力。

金融能力和金融素养两个概念看似相同，实则存在较大区别。通常而言，金融素养侧重强调知识层面，是对经济、财务、金融等事物的相关知识的理解和掌握。而金融能力的层次更高，除了金融知识，还有对金融知识的应用、对待金融问题的态度及最终所采取的金融行为。金融能力最终是靠金融行为来体现的。

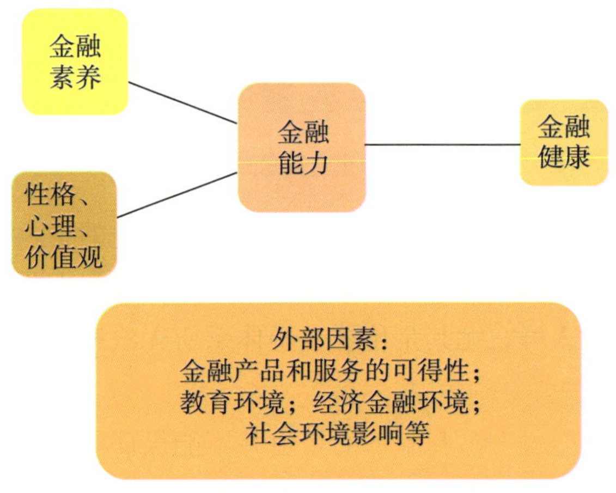

图 5-4　普惠金融领域相关概念之间的关系

金融素养可以提升金融能力。其他影响个人金融能力的因素还包括消费者个人的性格因素心理因素及外部环境因素。金融素养属于认知类因素，即可以通过学习获得；而性格因素、心理因素则属于非认知类因素；价值观也是在成长过程中长期养成的，并非短时间内可以通过学习发生变化的。一个常见的体现金融素养和金融福祉的概念是消费者自我控制力，这属于性格层面的因素。认知和非认知因素在外部因素的作用下共同影响消费者个人的金融能力，并通过金融行为体现出来。

长期的金融行为直接影响消费者个人的金融健康。因此，金融健康是金融行为的良性结果。从横向来看，每一项金融健康的结果都可以由金融能力（行为）、金融素养（知识）及金融产品倒推而来。例如，若金融消费者个人有充足的流动性储蓄和固定资产，则可以推断出该消费者具有良好的储蓄能力和投资或资产配置能力及行为。而且，由此可以推断该消费者对储蓄的必要性、途径、不同投资产品之间的配比、风险的分散等金融知识有较好的掌握，具备较高的投资方面的金融素养。同时，也说明该消费者拥有储蓄账户和投资渠道，并且可能其客户经理还给出了专业的投资建议。

提高金融产品和服务的覆盖率、提高消费者的金融素养和金融能力，其目的是提高消费者的金融健康程度。而金融健康很大程度上决定了消费者个人的整体福祉，且金融福祉对个人整体福祉的作用程度甚至相当于个人其他因素（如工作满意度、身体健康程度及从亲友处得到的支持）（Netemeyer、Warmath、Fernandes 和 Lynch，2017）。金融问题是人生的重要问题，金融健康程度显著影响生活幸福指数。消费者应加强对金融相关知识的学习，形成良好的金融行为和习惯，保持良好的金融健康状态，利用金融这一重要手段来实现美好的人生。

四、我国消费者金融健康状况

在对我国消费者的调研结果中，依照本章对消费者金融健康的定义，3040 名受访者的金融健康平均得分为 67.79 分，中值为 68.83 分，且样本得分的分布近似于正态分布（见图 5－5）。

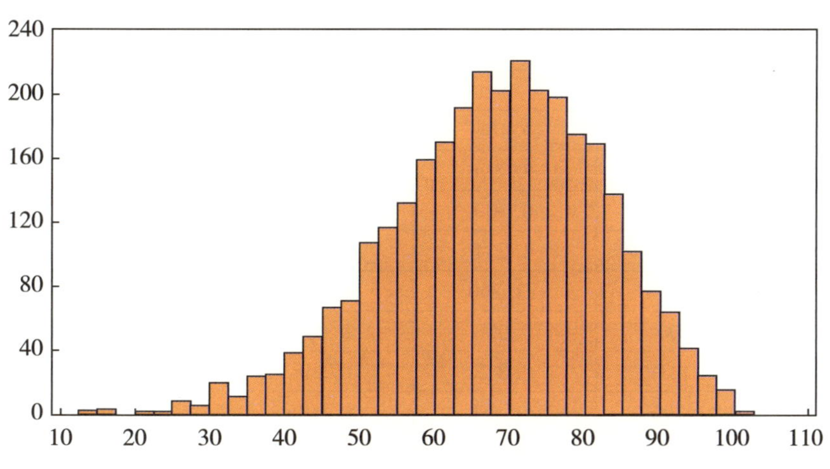

图 5－5　样本消费者金融健康总得分分布

从金融健康的五个子指标来看，平均得分最高的两项分别为收支指标和主观指标，这说明我国消费者样本较重视收入与支出的平衡性与可持续性，且对自身金融状况大体较为满意。其他各项指标的平均分也在 65.2～68.5 分，较为均衡。子指标数值的分布说明，我国消费者样本的收支情况较其他情况略高。通过数字统计计算，我们发现收支指标与其他方面指标的均值和中位数均有显著差别。各子指标中得分最低的为保险指标，这说明我国消费者目前的保险意识有待提升（见表5-1）。

表5-1　样本金融健康子指标得分情况

	收支指标	资产指标	债务指标	保险指标	主观指标
平均值（分）	71.6	68.5	65.2	64.6	69.0
中值（分）	75	68	65	80	70
最高值（分）	100	100	100	100	100
最小值（分）	0	8	10	0	10
样本量（名）	3040	3040	3040	3040	3040

我们对各子指标之间的关系进行了相关性分析。如表5-2显示，各子指标之间相关性均为显著正相关。最高相关性体现于资产指标与债务指标之间，为0.484，其t值也最高。而保险指标与其他各项指标之间相关系数均较低，结合上文保险较低的均值，说明保险配置在我国消费者样本中仍属于较为特殊的类别。

表5-2　金融健康子指标之间的相关性

指标名称	收支指标	资产指标	债务指标	保险指标	主观指标
收支指标	1.000				
t值	—				
p-value	—				
资产指标	0.320	1.000			
t值	18.584	—			
p-value	0.000	—			
债务指标	0.359	0.484	1.000		
t值	21.189	30.496	—		
p-value	0.000	0.000	—		
保险指标	0.174	0.234	0.155	1.000	
t值	9.721	13.290	8.627	—	
p-value	0.000	0.000	0.000	—	
主观指标	0.431	0.348	0.348	0.212	1.000
t值	26.295	20.486	20.435	11.949	—
p-value	0.000	0.000	0.000	0.000	—

为了更进一步地研究影响我国居民金融健康的因素，我们使用回归方程，并用White-Hinkley调整异方差性，得到如下结果。消费者的个人收入和个人支出数额越高，其金融健康程度越高；类似地，其房地产资产与金融资产的绝对值越高，其金融健康程度越高。消费者个人情况方面，年龄越高，消费者金融健康程度越高，女性消费者的金融健康状况显著低于男性，消费者的身体健康状况能够显著提高其金融健康

水平。已婚者的金融健康水平普遍高于未婚者，农村户籍的消费者金融健康显著低于城镇户籍的消费者。

在金融知识和金融行为如何影响金融健康的问题上，我们发现了较为反常的结果。我们期待金融知识和金融行为得分都会提升消费者金融健康水平。然而，回归结果显示，虽然金融行为显著正向影响金融健康，金融知识得分的系数显著为负。为了更好地理解这两个因素对金融健康的作用，我们分别将金融知识和金融行为单独与金融健康情况的得分进行回归分析，发现二者的系数均为正且显著，而金融知识的系数则为负，以及转化为金融行为的金融知识对金融健康的作用反而是负面的。这表明，金融行为对提升消费者个人金融健康的作用更为显著。金融知识如果不导致良好的金融行为，也不足以产生健康的金融结果（见表 5 - 3）。

表 5 - 3　影响我国消费者金融健康的因素

Variable	Coefficient	Prob.
C	18.380	0.000
个人收入	3.376	0.000
个人收入在家庭收入占比	−0.008	0.551
个人支出	−1.037	0.027
个人支出在家庭支出占比	−0.011	0.351
房地产资产	1.135	0.000
金融资产	1.180	0.000
年龄	0.085	0.042
女性	−5.059	0.000
子女数量/家庭人口	−0.358	0.331
健康状况	4.395	0.000
已婚	1.988	0.001
农村户籍	−1.617	0.001
受教育水平	0.235	0.316
金融知识	−0.413	0.005
金融行为	4.994	0.000
R-squared	0.302	
Adjusted R-squared	0.299	
F-statistic	87.274	
Prob（F-statistic）	0.000	
Prob（Wald F-statistic）	0.000	

因此，我们不仅要提倡金融知识的普及，还要倡导消费者将金融知识转换为合理、理性的金融行为，从而有效改善其金融健康状况。

第六章　P2P 与金融健康

【摘要】 P2P 行业从 2007 年开始在中国生根发芽，最高峰时在中国有超过 6600 家 P2P 平台。但是在 P2P 行业快速发展的同时，风险也在不断加剧。从 2018 年 6 月开始的集中暴雷更是引起了全社会的关注，同时也引起了市场对于 P2P 的高度恐慌，更让市场开始反思：P2P 的价值是什么？P2P 对于个人金融健康的发展到底起到了什么作用？本章从借款人和出借人两个角度分别分析 P2P 对于个人金融健康的影响。最后，就如何提升 P2P 客户金融健康的问题，对 P2P 平台和出借人分别提出建议。

一、借款人的金融健康

（一）借款人整体情况分析

金融健康衡量的主要标准包括消费者个人收入与支出、资产与负债的相对情况、应急资金与固定资产、保险情况、对于财务状况的满意程度和对于未来的信心六个客观和主观因素。对于借款人来说，通过 P2P 平台融资直接增加了个人负债，但这个负债额度是否在借款人所承受的范围之内、期限是否适合借款人的生产经营或消费需求、还款方式的灵活性等因素对借款人的金融健康状况也有直接影响。而这些因素也正是 P2P 平台风险控制的重点。我们通过整理相关的行业数据，对于 P2P 借款人的整体情况进行以下几方面的分析。

首先是在借款期限方面。通过图 6－1 可以看出，P2P 行业的平均借款期限有逐年递增的趋势，尤其是在 2018 年 P2P 风险事件后，P2P 的借款期限更加趋于长期。2016 年至 2018 年平均借款期限分别为 7.8 个月、9.2 个月和 13 个月，到 2019 年 3 月更是达到历年最高值 15.48 个月。借款期限与借款人的借款用途息息相关，期限的增长可以更好地适应借款人企业生产、建设、销售的周期和行业特征，为实体经济服务，减少使用过桥贷款的次数和成本。

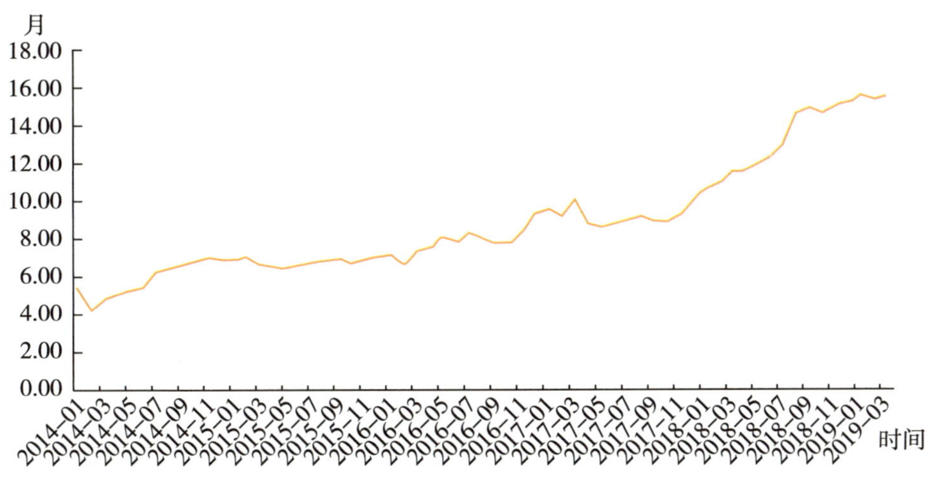

资料来源：Wind。

图 6－1　P2P 平均借款期限

其次是在借款人总数方面。通过图 6－2 可以看出，自 2016 年 6 月 P2P 借款人数突破 100 万人后，于 2017 年 11 月达到峰值 520 万人，之后随着行业风险暴露事件的出现，借款人数开始出现下滑。2016—2018 年平均每月服务的借款人数分别为 120 万人、360 万人和 357 万人，2019 年 3 月服务的借款人数约为 263 万人。虽然 P2P 行业的暴雷对于借款人的影响没有出借人方面大，但是行业的暴雷事件使社会对于 P2P 行业的认知和态度都蒙上了阴影，这也使 P2P 平台在获得新客户方面有了新的挑战。但是，由于 P2P 模式在中国是从线下开始发展的，其行业本身具有一定的客户基础和获

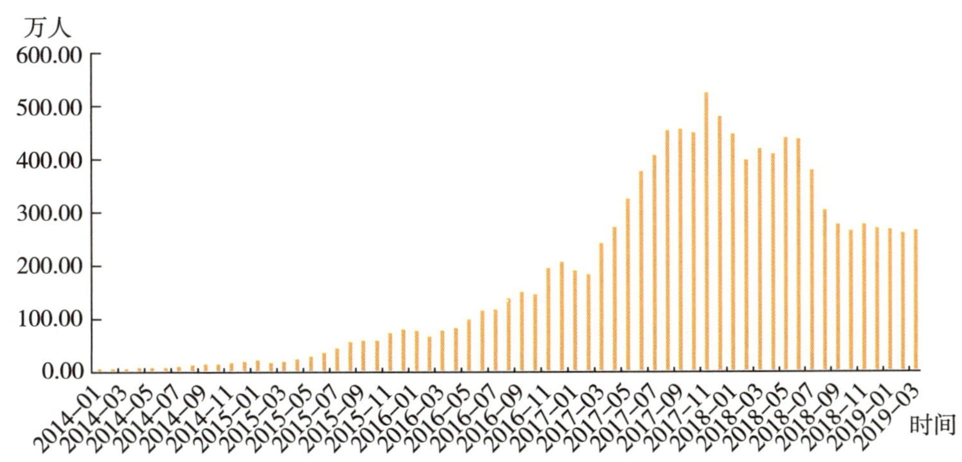

资料来源：Wind。

图 6－2　P2P 当月借款人数

客优势，这也是 P2P 平台在严格监管驱使下开始做助贷业务的基础。

最后是在待还余额方面。通过图 6－3 可以看出，P2P 行业的待还余额曾于 2018 年 5 月达到最高点 10692 亿元。随后，由于风险事件的频出，市场信心遭受较大的打击，导致待还余额呈快速下降的趋势：2018 年底已经跌到 7889.7 亿元。按照中国人民银行表内消费金融贷款余额 10.4 万亿元测算，整个 P2P 行业待还余额占中国消费金融的 7%。

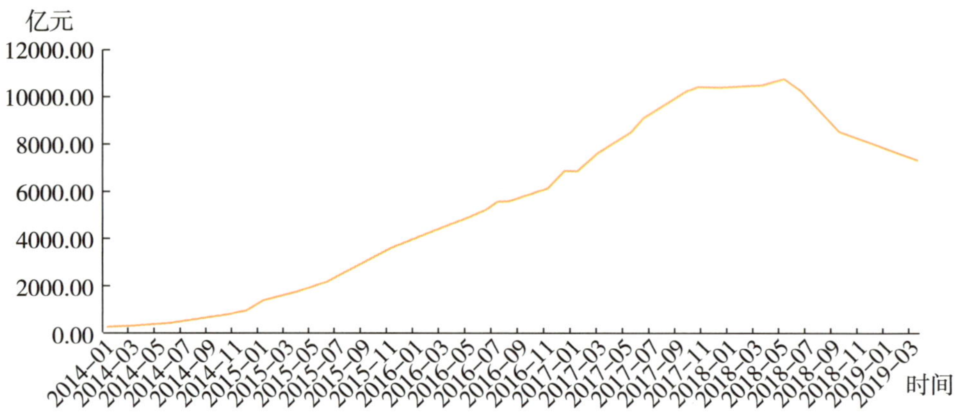

资料来源：Wind。

图 6－3　P2P 待还余额

（二）借款人群体特征分析

根据中国普惠金融研究院的调查结果（以下简称调研），可以分析出 P2P 平台借款人具有以下主要特征：

一是在借款人性别方面，男性的借款需求远大于女性，当然并不排除大量的借款是由家庭一起使用的情况。在年龄方面，借款人主要以 22～38 岁为主，38 岁以上的借款人数量出现了明显的下降。由于 30 岁左右年龄段人群大多已有工作，消费需求相对较为前卫，接受新鲜事物速度较快，是可以接收到多种融资渠道信息的群体，这也体现了 P2P 平台在较年轻人群体中的接受程度较高，他们愿意使用 P2P 平台满足自身的融资需求。

二是在借款用途方面，超过 50%的借款人主要用于生活消费，其余的借款人主要以生产经营为目的。在选择 P2P 平台的原因方面，超过 50%的借款人表示借贷门槛低、通过审批的概率大是他们选择的因素之一。此外，可选择的借贷产品由于期限较多、审批效率高、审批时间短、在线操作方便、不依赖机构网点、流程简单等特点得到部分借款人的青睐。

三是在选择P2P平台借款家数方面，大多数借款人在3家P2P平台以内借款，但是只有31%的借款人只在1家P2P平台借款。在多家P2P平台借款容易造成借新还旧，进而形成多头负债的问题。在借款期限方面，以1年期以内的借款产品为主。在借款成本方面，超过50%的借款人在P2P平台上借款的最高年化利率区间为8%～18%（见图6-4）。

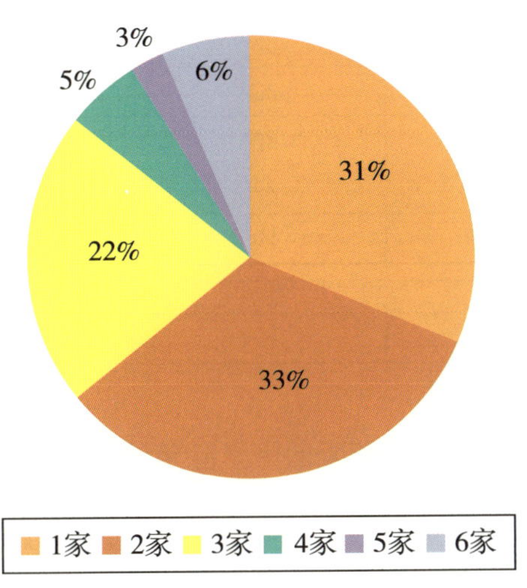

资料来源：中国普惠金融研究院整理。

图6-4 借款人选择P2P平台借款家数

（三）借款人的金融健康分析

根据网贷之家对于8家头部P2P平台借款人的资料分析[①]（以下简称网贷之家调研）可以发现，P2P平台的借款人主要以东部沿海省份为主，再结合前文的借款人特点可以大致得出P2P行业的借款人特征：以东部沿海城市30岁左右的年轻人为主，他们大多数为一般员工，但是已经接受了提前消费的理念，通过使用P2P平台可以更好地平缓他们的收入波动，以达到满足家庭生活或生产需求的目的。

国家统计局和地方统计局公布的《2018年各省居民人均收入》显示，网贷之家调研提到的4个借款人数量排名靠前的省份为山东、江苏、浙江和广东，其各省居民人均收入分别为29205元、38096元、45840元和35810元。通过整理P2P行业内借贷余额排名靠前的10家P2P平台可以发现（见表6-1），它们的人均借款余额约为2.96万元[②]。对比各省的年人均收入情况来看，相当于给借款人增加了0.65～1.01倍杠杆。

① 陈晓俊．揭秘头部P2P平台借款人画像［DB/OL］．https：//www.wdzj.com/news/yanjiu/4394774.html.

② 由于各平台信息披露的数据不同，此处暂且使用借贷余额/当前借款人数量作为人均借款余额。

表 6-1 借贷余额排名前 10 位的平台数据（截至 2019 年 6 月底）

排名	P2P 平台	借贷余额（亿元）	当前借款人数量（万人）	人均借款余额（万元）
1	陆金服	984	147	4.00
2	玖富普惠	480	371	1.29
3	宜人贷	427	89	4.80
4	宜信惠民	377	94	4.01
5	人人贷	328	71	4.62
6	爱钱进	326	160	2.04
7	恒易融	293	63	4.65
8	拍拍贷	195	442	0.44
9	微贷网	154	49	3.14
10	你我贷	154	287	0.54

资料来源：中国普惠金融研究院整理。

对于借款人来说，影响其金融健康的因素除负债金额外，还受到还款方式的影响。通过对前文调研中借款人还款方式的统计可以发现，目前借款人的还款方式以等额本息还款为主，其占比超过 85%。等额本息还款对于 P2P 平台的借款人来说较为合适，由于 P2P 平台的借款人主要是靠工资收入偿还贷款，收入相对较为稳定，所以对偿还一个每月固定金额的等额本息来说，现金流更加匹配。虽然等额本息相比等额本金会支付更多的利息，但是等额本息前期现金流压力较小，在 P2P 平台借款期限逐渐拉长的驱使下，等额本息作为最主要的还款方式成为必然的结果。这也使借款人可以更好地根据自己的工资情况和偿还金额来安排自己的现金流使用。

国家审计署报告显示，民间和网络借贷利率多高于 30%①，按照 30%的利率计算，借款 2.6 万元，借期为 16 个月的产品，平均每个月要还 1990 元左右，占到前文提到的 4 个省份平均月收入的 64%左右。对于一般员工来说，这是一笔较大的开支。因此，P2P 平台的贷款对借款人金融健康程度有重要影响。虽然通过 P2P 平台的贷款可以平缓借款人收入的波动，用于提前消费或商业经营，但后续也为其带来了较大的还贷压力，需要借款人根据自身的工作情况和现金流情况合理使用 P2P 的贷款。

二、出借人的金融健康

通过分析出借人投资 P2P 的风险与出借人个人的风险承受能力的匹配程度，可以

① 国家审计署于 2019 年 6 月 26 日在第十三届全国人民代表大会常务委员会第十一次会议上发布的《国务院关于 2018 年度中央预算执行和其他财政收支的审计工作报告》，http：//www.audit.gov.cn/n5/n26/c133000/content.html。

判断出借人的金融健康程度。如果将本应用于满足基本生活需求的资金或者未来有明确规划的资金用于投资 P2P 平台，显然会造成资产风险与个人风险承受能力不匹配的问题，进而加大金融健康的波动性。本节通过出借人的整体数据情况和调研数据，分析出借人的整体画像、出借人投资 P2P 平台的目的、投资 P2P 平台的考虑因素及对 P2P 平台的风险认识和金融素养问题。本节最后推荐了一种基于目标的资产管理策略，以帮助出借人在保证金融健康稳定的前提下，更好地对 P2P 产品进行投资。

（一）出借人投资 P2P 平台的整体情况

P2P 平台具有操作简便、投资门槛低、收益率高、期限较灵活等特点，受到了大众出借人的青睐。2016—2018 年，每年每月的平均出借人分别高达 333 万人、435 万人和 330 万人。投资 P2P 的人数在 2017 年 11 月达到最高峰：有近 454 万名出借人投资 P2P 行业。大量出借人的涌入极大地激发了民众对于投资 P2P 的热情，也把 P2P 行业推上了风口浪尖（见图 6-5）。

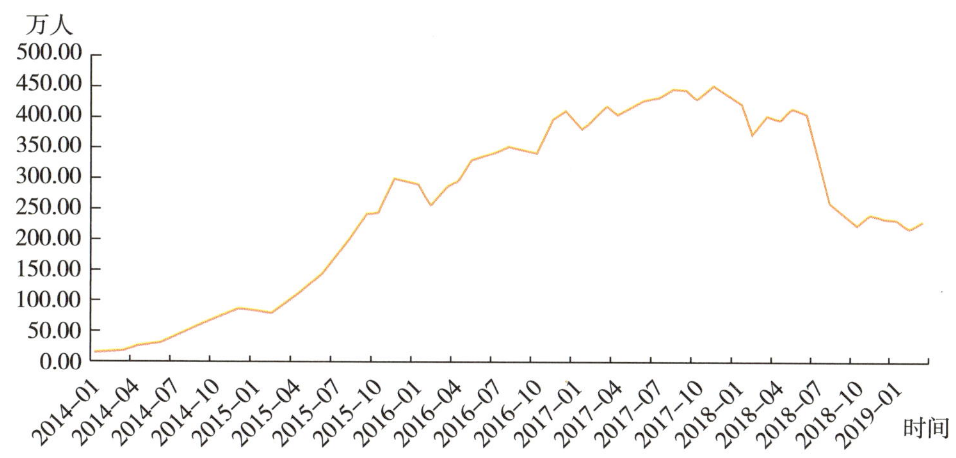

资料来源：Wind。

图 6-5　P2P 每月投资人数的变化趋势

2018 年，P2P 平台暴雷事件集中爆发后，监管日益趋严。目前，P2P 出借人数已出现大幅下滑：2019 年 3 月的出借人数为 229 万人左右，比巅峰时期减少了 50%。在平均投资额度方面，同样以待还余额为依据，可以按月测算出 P2P 行业的平均投资额度。2016—2018 年每年的平均投资额度分别为 16 万元、21.1 万元和 29.9 万元。在 2018 年 10 月后开始出现下降趋势（见图 6-6）。

将 P2P 机构按照银行系、国资系、上市公司系、风投系和民营系区分后可以看出，出借人原本比较青睐的风投系和民营系已经出现了出借人数大幅下滑的现象，银行系 P2P 几乎已从市场退出。在目前严监管趋势日渐清晰的情况下，出借人更多地选择了上市公司系（见图 6-7）。

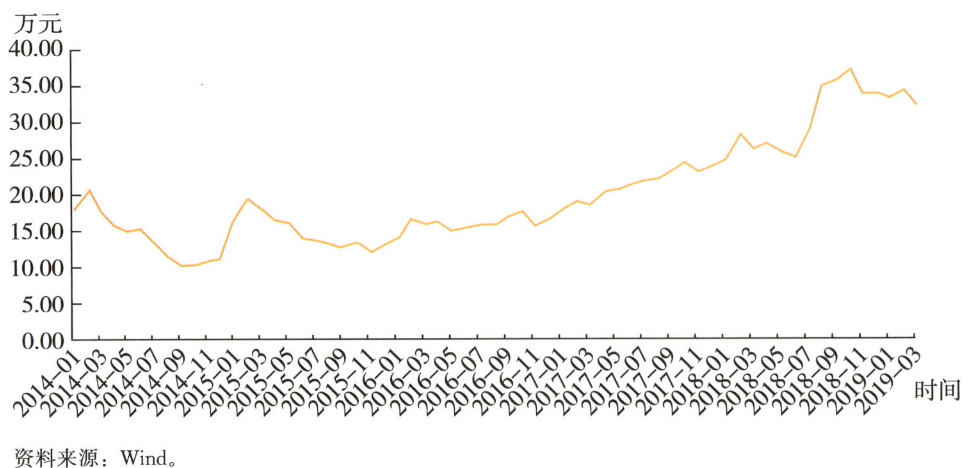

资料来源：Wind。

图 6-6　P2P 行业平均投资额度变化

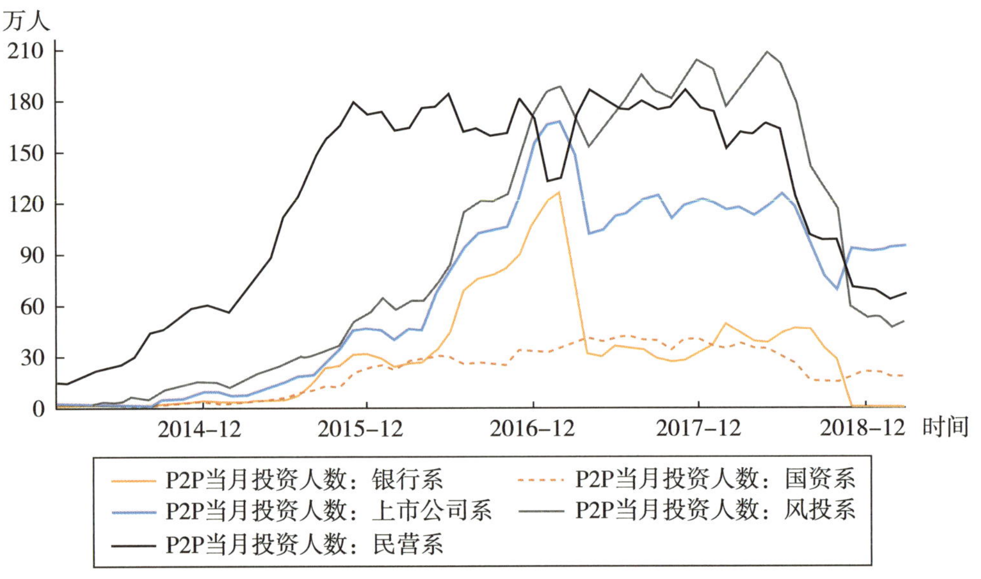

资料来源：Wind。

图 6-7　各系 P2P 平台投资人数变化

（二）出借人的金融健康现状

根据中国普惠金融研究院开展的数字金融平台客户调研，大致可以总结出投资 P2P 机构的出借人整体客户群具有以下特征。

一是性别构成：出借人中超过 55%为男性。

二是年龄构成：以“80 后”“90 后”为主，平均年龄为 37 岁。

三是学历构成：专科及以上学历的客户占比超过 82%。

四是收入构成：在收入方面，接近70%的出借人年收入在10万元以内（包含10万元）；接近23%的出借人年收入在11万～20万元（包含20万元）。

五是收益率构成：接近75%的出借人表示选择P2P平台的收益率为8%～12%。

六是投资期限构成：出借人更加青睐三个月至一年以内的短期产品。

出借人投资P2P平台的集中度分析：

在出借人可以投资的众多金融资产中，投资P2P行业的资金占比如图6-8所示。投资产品的集中度是衡量金融健康的重要指标之一，投资高风险资产的比例应与出借人的风险承受能力有关。对于投资占比在20%以内的出借人，总体来说投资风险相对可控，一旦P2P行业出现流动性等相关风险，对于自身金融资产的损失程度相对较小。对于投资占比在21%～50%的投资人，进一步分析其收入与资产可以发现，其平均年收入为10.7万元，平均金融资产为65.4万元，也就是把1.28～3.06倍的年收入用于投资P2P平台，一旦P2P行业出现风险，其损失相对比较严重。对于投资占比在51%以上的投资人，用同样的方法可以得出投资人把超过3.3倍的年收入用于投资P2P，投资占比在80%以上的投资人甚至将超过40倍年收入的资金用于投资，这种高投资集中度使其金融健康状况堪忧，一旦发生风险，会直接造成不可弥补的损失。

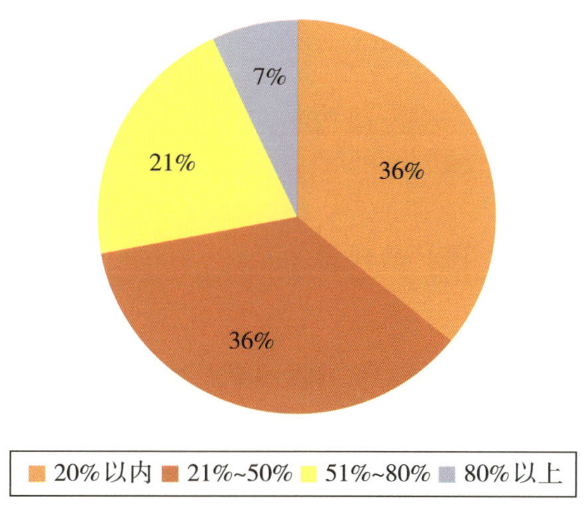

资料来源：中国普惠金融研究院整理。

图6-8 出借人投资P2P平台资金比例

除了投资P2P行业的集中度，另一个指标是投资P2P平台的家数。如图6-9所示，出借人普遍选择投资3家以内的P2P平台，其中以1家和2家最多。原则上，分散投资对于出借人具有一定的风险分散作用，但这不能代表绝对风险的分散程度。具体还应根据投资人所投P2P平台的背景、标的产品的类型、产品的期限、平台在行业的位置等因素，对所投 P2P 平台进行差异化分析，以判定其风险的分散程度。随着 P2P 行业不断出现风险事件及行业的监管趋严，投资者也越来越认清 P2P 行业的风险，投资也会更加趋于理性，选择不同特点的 P2P 平台进行分散投资无疑是有效降低风险的措施之一。

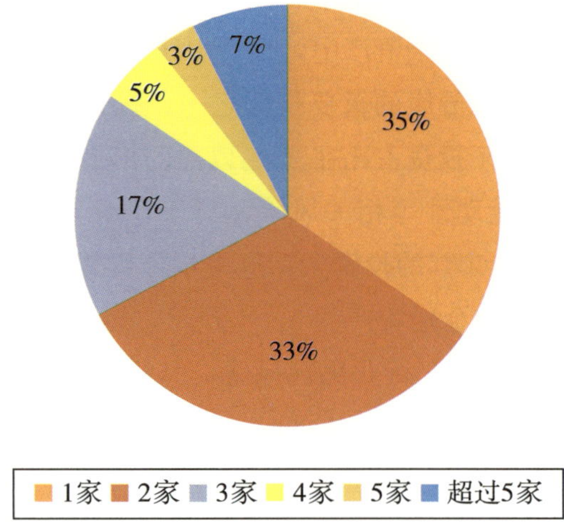

资料来源：中国普惠金融研究院整理。

图 6－9　出借人投资 P2P 平台的家数

三、出借人对 P2P 平台的态度

（一）出借人选择投资 P2P 的理由

1. P2P 行业相对收益较高

出借人投资理财产品，一直较看重其收益率而忽略风险。通过按月统计 P2P 的综合利率可以发现：P2P 的综合利率已从 2014 年的近 22％下降到了 2019 年 3 月的 9.79％；2016—2018 年的平均综合利率分别为 10.62％、9.45％和 9.86％。但是对比其他理财产品的收益率可以发现，P2P 仍是高收益的代表，尤其是在 2015 年中开始，货币市场基金收益率跌破 4％之后，当时 P2P 市场平均收益率在 14％左右，远远超出普通的理财产品。由于个人出借人受外汇管制的限制，无法大量投资美元；银行的理财产品收益率不到 P2P 收益率的一半，偏稳健型的债券类基金和货币市场基金收益率则更低；2018 年股票指数类产品同样跌幅惨重（见表 6－2）。因此，综观各种理财产品的收益率，P2P 成为出借人获得高额收益的不二之选。通过调研也发现，高收益是 83.4％的出借人选择 P2P 行业的理由之一。

表 6-2　2018 年各投资产品收益率　　单位：%

排名	产品	收益率
1	P2P 网贷	9.87
2	美元	5.04
3	银行理财	4.70
4	债券基金	4.16
5	货基宝宝类	3.69
6	黄金	3.60
7	货币基金	3.52
8	QDII 基金	−8.09
9	混合基金	−14.23
10	上证 50 指数	−19.83
11	上证指数	−24.59
12	沪深 300 指数	−25.31
13	股票基金	−25.50
14	创业板指数	−28.65
15	中证 500 指数	−33.32

资料来源：网络整理，http：//www.sohu.com/a/289921181_100034352。

2. 投资 P2P 平台的其他理由

在调查中，超过 65%的出借人表示投资 P2P 平台操作方便，约 60%的出借人表示流程简单，而这种简单上手的用户体验再加上低投资门槛、相对比较灵活的投资期限使 P2P 获得了大量出借人的青睐。

刚性兑付问题也是出借人选择投资 P2P 平台的理由之一。其实从投资端看，我国金融市场长期存在刚性兑付问题，对于 P2P 平台的出借人来说更是如此，不能保本保收益的金融产品市场接受度较低。而 P2P 平台为了快速吸引资金，扩大规模，通过资金池、虚假宣传等违规操作，承诺刚性兑付，进一步加大了出借人对于投资 P2P 平台的热情，使出借人在面对诱人的高收益率 P2P 平台时，往往会失去判断风险的能力和意愿，在投机心理的作用下过度投资高风险产品，却忽略了自身金融健康的客观条件。

（二）出借人对于 P2P 平台的认知

在 P2P 行业多次暴雷事件和严监管驱使下，出借人选择 P2P 平台考虑的因素更加趋于理性。通过调查活动可以发现，超过 87%的出借人表示他们了解所选择 P2P 平台的背景；在P2P平台采用的风控模式方面，只有13%的出借人表示不清楚；在银行资金存管方面，超过90%的出借人表示自己所投的P2P平台是通过资金存管银行汇出；在信息披露方面，71%的出借人表示研究过P2P平台信息披露的相关内容；77%的出借人表示会认真阅读P2P平台出示的网络借贷风险提示书；76%的出借人表示了解P2P平台提供的只是信息中介服务，不承诺保证本金安全。由此可见，对于P2P平台的风险和平台的业务，不到80%的出借人有较为清晰和准确的认知，而这种认知对于出借人投资P2P行业有重要影响，通过考量P2P平台的各种因素，选择适合自己风险承受能力的平台对于其金融健康有重要影响。

虽然P2P行业出现了很多风险事件，但行业中还是有P2P平台坚持服务于“三农”，将自身定位为公益项目。比如，某产品通过与当地公益性小额信贷组织成为合作伙伴，通过合作伙伴帮助平台进行甄选农户、识别风险、收集农户信息、执行放款收款等业务。在此平台上出借人只收取较低的收益作为爱心回报，平台收取极低的费用作为运营成本。这种模式服务的客户群体更加聚焦，依托于公益性组织使其具有很强的社会效益。此外，还衍生出给乡村贫困孩子提供意外伤害保险的公益产品，帮助农户销售农产品的平台等其他公益类项目。

（三）出借人对于P2P平台风险与损失的态度

根据对P2P出借人的调研结果可知，目前仍有大量的P2P出借人将P2P作为主要的理财投资产品进行投资。那么对于P2P存在的高风险，出借人对于损失的态度如何呢？

超过97%的出借人知道P2P平台给其测定的客户风险承受能力是哪种类型。平台出借人以稳健型、保守型和平衡型出借人为主，这也表明大部分出借人可以承受的风险水平不算高，应以低至中等风险类的资产为主（见图6-10）。

在调研数据中，34%的出借人表示损失一点本金都不能承受。接近19%的客户表示发生过逾期且逾期以超过91天为主。这部分用户可以承受的损失如图6-11所示。由此可见，大多数P2P平台出借人所能承受的损失在20%以内，出借人对于P2P风险的承受能力并不强。大多数出借人将自身多年收入用于投资P2P行业，这对其自身金融健康状况有重大影响。一旦发生风险事件，本金的损失可能会超出他们的预期，对他们的生活造成巨大的负面影响。P2P平台普遍存在风控能力偏弱或有违规操作等历史问题，如虚假标的、自融自保、资金池操作、过度包装等，因此，出借人对于P2P平台应抱有谨慎态度。无论平台的宣传和背景如何，都应将其视为高风险的资产，不应存在必然保本的心理预期。

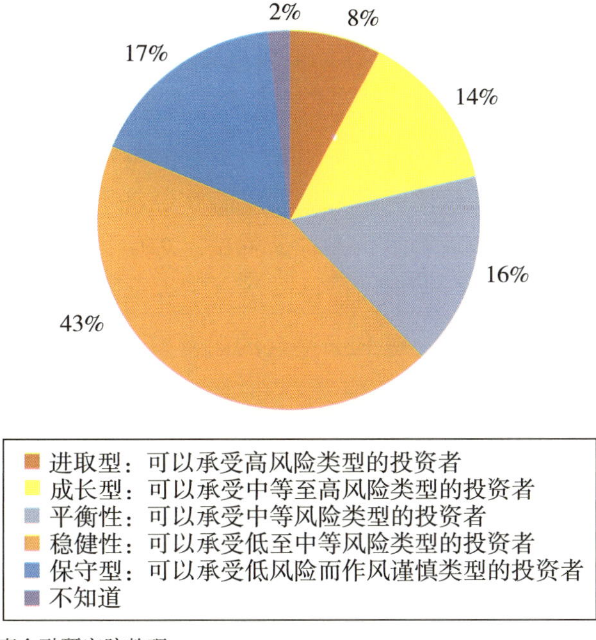

资料来源：中国普惠金融研究院整理。

图 6－10　P2P 平台出借人类型分布

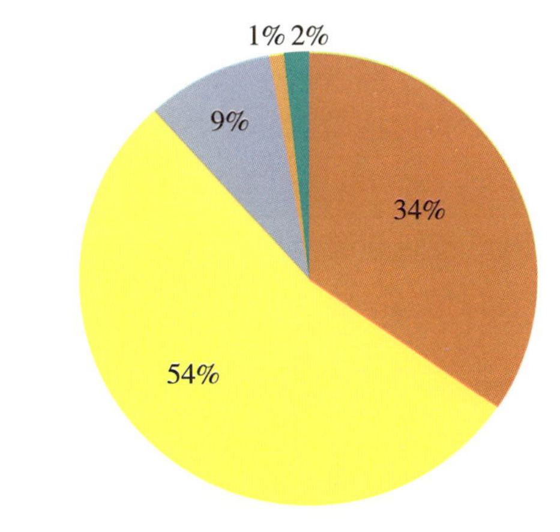

资料来源：中国普惠金融研究院整理。

图 6－11　P2P 平台出借人所能承受的损失分布

四、提升 P2P 客户金融健康

（一）P2P 平台的责任

2016 年在中国银监会等四部委发布的《网络借贷信息中介机构业务活动管理暂行

办法》中规定，P2P 平台是专门从事网络借贷信息中介业务活动的金融信息中介公司。该规定要求 P2P 平台不得提供增信服务，不得直接或间接归集资金，不得非法集资。因此，P2P 平台作为信息中介应承担的是信息披露、风险控制和撮合交易的责任。

然而，P2P 平台在中国发展的过程中衍生了多种业务形态，使其已经远远超过信息中介的业务范围，累积了大量的风险，这些风险在经济下行的情况下就会迎来集中爆发。P2P 平台自身的风控能力有限，在标的筛选过程中，并没有充分考量借款人的信用风险，大量的违规操作使风控形同虚设，信息中介的本质已经成为信用中介。而出借人过度追求高收益，在没有了解 P2P 平台的运营模式和投资标的的情况下盲目投资，付出了惨痛的代价。

P2P 行业目前正在经历监管机构的合规检查，整个行业正处于清理和整顿过程中。2018 年 8 月，P2P 网贷风险专项整治工作领导小组下发的《关于开展 P2P 网络借贷机构合规检查工作的通知》要求全量覆盖、真实准确、查改结合，同时列出 108 条合规检查清单，为 P2P 行业未来能够更加合规地为借款人和出借人提供服务，以及为回归信息中介业务的本源提供了政策保障。

（二）出借人需理性投资

1. 谨慎投资 P2P

从金融健康的角度来说，客户应该将哪些资产用于投资 P2P？依据以目标为基础（Goals-Based）的资产配置方式，客户可以将资产依据不同目标，按照期限、流动性、要求回报率等因素进行分层[①]。不同分层使用不同的投资组合来达到目标，不同的目标也对应了不同的风险偏好。以图 6－12 为例，以基本生活保障为目标的投资，主要

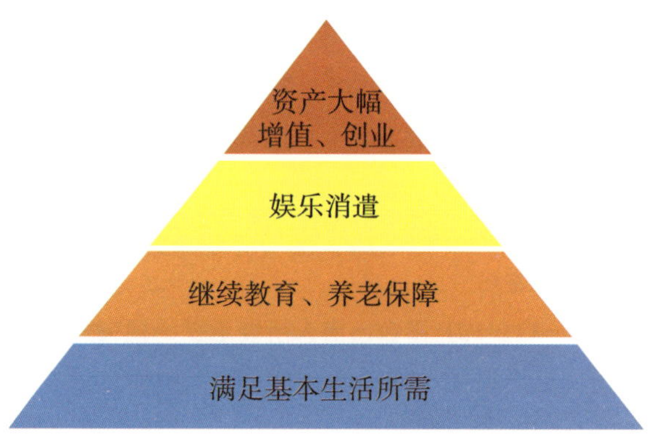

图 6－12　按目标分层的投资

① Brandon Parrish，CFA，CAIA. An Insight into a Goals－Based Asset Allocation Framework，NEPC Private Wealth Whitepaper.

用于满足日常生活、经营开支或突发紧急开支，所以此投资组合应该考虑流动性高、投资期限灵活的产品，如货币市场基金、活期存款等。以继续教育、养老保障为目的的投资应倾向于稳健长期型产品，如养老保险、年金产品、重疾险、分红险等。以娱乐消遣、购买奢侈品、旅游等为目的的资金，主要用来提高生活品质、改善生活质量，因此可以用来投资收益较高的资产，如债券型基金、各类理财产品、资产管理计划等产品。以资产大幅增值或者创业为目的的资金，主要是为了赚取超额收益，因此可以投资风险较高的资产，如私募股权基金、期货、外汇等金融产品。

P2P投资由于具有门槛低，操作流程简单，期限相对灵活，比基金、期货等金融产品更便于理解等特点，受到了大众出借人的青睐。在整个金融资产领域，P2P风险应小于私募股权基金、期货和外汇。因此，从金融健康的角度，个人可以将自己用于娱乐消费的资金投资于P2P，而用于养老、教育和满足基本生活所需的资金则应远离P2P投资。根据调研结果，超过93%的出借人投资P2P行业的目的是让财富保值增值，其次是个人或家庭的财富目标，如置业、购车等。

然而，《中国出借人教育现状调查报告（2018）》[①] 显示，我国超过半数的出借人并未对自己的养老生活作出合理的目标设定和经济规划，仅有46.62%的出借人对自己的养老资产规模有过预期。这表明，多数出借人养老规划意识较为薄弱，缺乏必要的养老资产准备意识，对于未来没有适当的财务规划能力和意愿。

以目标为基础的资产配置方式是一个过程化的分析。随着出借人年龄、资产和能力的增长，其各层的目标和资金也在变化，金融健康的状况也会随之改变。换而言之，这种方法本身是一个动态变化的过程（见图6-13）。因此，运用分层目的管理自身资产，出借人要定期重新评估自身的投资均衡情况，查看投资的金融资产是否符合自身

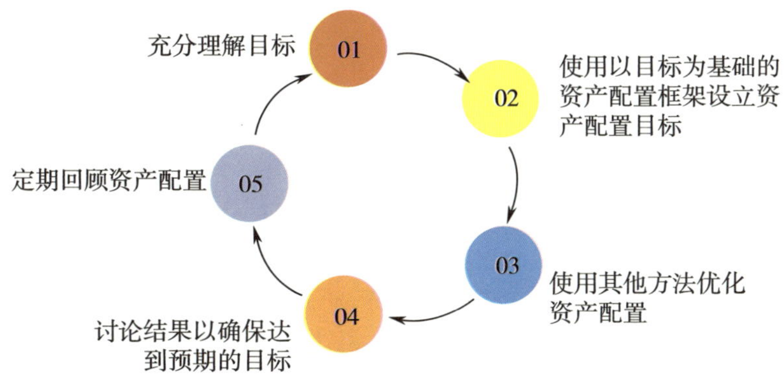

图6-13 以目标为基础的投资流程

① 李建勇，宋明莎．中国投资者教育现状调查报告（2018）[N]．证券时报，2019—03—07.

的定位与规划，在恰当的时候进行资产的重新分配以适应自身的投资需求。

2. P2P出借人的金融素养

经历了P2P行业多次暴雷，出借人得到了血的教训，更让公众意识到培养出借人金融素养的重要性。根据《中国出借人教育现状调查报告（2018）》，我国出借人群体对利率、复利及通货膨胀等基础金融知识掌握较好，但大部分出借人专业金融素养仍未达到及格标准；对于风险分散、无风险利率等专业金融知识，出借人的掌握严重不足。这种情况在P2P投资领域更加突出：出借人只关注高额的收益率和平台背景，对于P2P平台为什么能够给出如此高的收益率、影响收益率的因素、投资标的能否带来高收益的合理性、P2P平台的运作模式等并不了解。再加上行为金融学中的过度自信、可得性偏差等影响，越是金融素养低的出借人越倾向于高估自身的金融能力，从而使他们出于投机心理不顾自身金融健康条件盲目投资，将自身的财务状况暴露于高风险中。

因此，在P2P进入严监管、强制备案的背景下，除强调P2P平台本身和业务的合规性外，也需要进一步加强对大众P2P出借人能力建设的培养。可以结合金融机构、交易所、行业协会和高等院校等多方教育资源，利用新媒体、线上线下融合的方式传播基础金融知识。对于P2P出借人，可以通过专家学者对其进行特定产品的解析和答疑，帮助出借人梳理清楚P2P产品的业务逻辑和风险，使他们更好地分配自己的资产，有助于改善出借人的金融健康状况。

第七章　现金贷与过度负债

【摘要】现金贷产品弥补长尾客户的贷款需求，丰富消费者融资渠道；同时，有助于丰富我国信贷体系层次，从侧面打压地下高利贷，补全社会征信数据。我国应完善法律法规建设和信用体系建设，加强消费者保护与金融消费者教育，使现金贷成为提升消费者金融健康的有力工具。

现金贷是中国普惠金融发展历程中的一种特殊产品。监管部门对现金贷的定义为“无场景依托、无指定用途、无客户群体限定、无抵押”的借贷品种。现金贷以线上产品为主，常见的现金贷产品主要通过商业银行、消费金融公司、网络小额贷款公司或P2P公司发放。现金贷于2014年出现，先后经历了2015—2016年的疯狂增长，到2017年底遭遇严监管行业受到整顿，部分现金贷平台在2018年转入地下演变成超利贷，乃至一部分变异成为2019年“3·15”晚会曝光的“714高炮”。原本为借款人提供短期资金周转的现金贷，缘何将借款人推入超利贷和套路贷的深渊？潮水退去，现金贷这一新生事物是否会因这段黑暗历史而被刻意遗忘？

现金贷并非生来即洪水猛兽，它生而具备完善金融供给体系、丰富金融市场层次的普惠性。本章认为，现金贷对消费者金融健康产生了重要的积极作用，是大量低收入人群重要的融资渠道。现金贷原有客群不应被忽略，他们的借贷需求宜疏不宜堵。若将现金贷比喻为双刃剑，如何扬其利而避其弊也许是超利贷风波之后社会应该冷静思考的问题。

一、现金贷弥补长尾客户的贷款需求

现金贷，顾名思义，是以现金为形式向借款人提供的贷款，它类似于欧美的发薪日贷款（Payday Loan），具有小额、短期、高利率、高风险等特点。2017年12月1日，中国人民银行联合中国银监会发布《关于规范整顿“现金贷”业务的通知》，定义现金贷是具备“无场景依托、无指定用途、无客户群体设定、无抵押”等特征的贷款业务。

现金贷自2014年至2017年中的飞速发展，除了依托互联网的技术发展及社会年轻群体强烈的消费愿望和创业潮流，更深层的原因是这类信贷产品弥补了传统金融体系信贷服务的不足。嘉银新金融研究院①整理数据显示，2017年11月底，中国人民银行个人征信系统收录的人数约为9.5亿人，有贷款记录的约为4.8亿人。这意味着中国大部分人仍无法从传统金融机构获得信贷服务。而这些传统金融服务覆盖不足的个人客户，往往是收入水平较低的弱势群体。

在我国，人们无法从传统金融机构获得信贷资金时，往往通过向自己的亲友，甚至通过地下钱庄借钱来解决短期资金问题。世界银行FINDEX2017的调研数据显示，中国的调研样本过去一年向金融机构借款的比例为9%，而向亲友借钱的比例为28%，是前者的3倍以上。而在美国，这两个数据则分别为29%和15%，这说明美国样本向亲友借贷的人数是向正规金融机构借贷人数的一半。这组数据的对比进一步体现了我国传统金融体系在金融借贷领域覆盖不足。

现金贷的出现正好满足了长尾客户的借贷需求。“无场景依托、无指定用途、无客户群体设定、无抵押”的短期信用贷款方便、快捷，成为长尾客户信贷的重要来源。据一本智库②统计，我国共有1亿名现金贷用户，其中活跃人群为4000万人；规模最大时，头部现金贷公司月放贷款量在100亿元左右，至少有近100家公司的月均放贷款量在10亿元左右。虽然由于严监管态势许多现金贷平台转入“地下”，但是行业公认的市场规模最高达到万亿级，最多时有5000～10000家平台参与。这样巨大的市场规模从侧面证明了长尾市场借贷需求的旺盛。若现金贷产品监管得当，有序发展，会为消费者提供极大的便利，促进其金融健康，提高其生产及生活效率。

这些现金贷正好覆盖的长尾客群，即难以从传统金融体系获得信贷的低收入人群，具备以下特征③：20～39岁年龄段的借款人占总人数的比例为66%。从职业分布来看，公司职员占比最高，为33.84%；其次是工人，占比为16.73%；再次是个体户（14.87%）和企业主管/负责人（11.28%）。现金贷借款人普遍受教育水平较低，大专及以下学历占93%。从工资水平来看，借款人的月收入多在2000～6000元，其中服务员、保安和营业员的月收入分布多在2000～4000元。

中国普惠金融研究院关于网络借贷的研究显示，在借贷渠道中选择“网络小贷或P2P借贷”④ 的受访对象具有以下特征：平均年龄较小、女性占比较低、已婚人数占

① 嘉银新金融研究院．中国个人征信行业现状与趋势展望［DB/OL］．https：//www.weiyangx.com/277673.html.

② 一本智库：《现金贷行业研究报告》。

③ 数据来自互金专委会及一本智库《现金贷行业研究报告》。

④ 在此次CAFI调研中并未询问受访者是否借现金贷，而是用网络借贷的概念进行调研。虽然最新监管不允许网络小额贷款公司与P2P平台出借现金贷，但是我们将此次调研中网络借贷情况作为合规现金贷情况的参考。

比较低、教育水平较低、个人收入占家庭收入占比较低、家庭资产规模较低（见表 7－1）。这一发现与上面的结论相似，即参与网络借贷（互联网小额贷款公司或 P2P 借贷）的人群多为年轻、收入水平较低、教育水平较低的长尾人群。而现金贷刚好满足这部分人群的融资需要。

表 7－1　CAFI 网络借贷情况调研

	互联网借贷者	非借贷者
受访者数量（人）	2093	494
年龄（岁）	27.9	33.7
女性占比（%）	23	26
已婚人数占比（%）	38	47
本科以上占比（%）	27	36
个人年收入（万元）	10.1	11.4
个人收入占比（%）	38	42
家庭资产均值（万元）	142.7	173.1
家庭资产中位数（万元）	100	120

合规的现金贷产品具有线上操作、无须抵押、流程快捷简单等特点。如图 7－1 所示，根据 CAFI 互联网借贷的调研结果，受访客户选择互联网借贷最重要的四个原因：在线操作方便、流程简单、利率低和审批效率高。可见，合规现金贷的特点极大地满足了网络借贷者对借贷产品的需求。

二、现金贷的作用与效果

（一）现金贷对借贷者的作用

在这样一个巨大规模的市场面前，由于缺乏公开统计数据，很难判断在众多借款人中有多少享受到了现金贷带来的便捷，有多少由于借新还旧而深陷超利贷的深渊。我们试图从现有的相关调研结果中探寻现金贷的作用与效果，下面将分别从现金贷（或类似产品）的使用满意程度、逾期情况、对借款人收入的影响等方面进行分析。

首先，我们用 CAFI 于 2018 年在兰州和丽水调研取得的数据分析金融消费者对现金贷的满意程度。研究显示，两地使用过电商提供的消费信贷[①]（如支付宝的“借呗”

① 电商的消费金融产品中有纯消费信贷产品（如“花呗”），也有现金贷类产品（如“借呗”），然而，这两类产品的利率和借款周期非常类似，因而我们认为该样本对电商消费金融的态度可以类比为对电商现金贷类产品的态度。

“花呗”，京东商城的“京东白条”，微信钱包的“微粒贷”等）的受访者占比分别为9.52%和8.82%。在兰州2489个样本中，选择使用过消费信贷的受访对象中有5.49%表示对产品“非常满意”，60.45%表示“基本满意”。在丽水3027个样本中，对电商消费金融服务的使用情况基本相同：有8.82%的受访者使用过电商的消费信贷；在使用过的受访者中，有10.11%的受访者表示对产品“非常满意”，有52.43%的受访者表示“基本满意”。

其次，在现金贷还款情况方面，兰州样本中76.37%使用过消费信贷的受访者表示“可以足额还款”，有12.66%的受访者表示“花得越来越多，快还不起了”。丽水样本中有77.75%的受访者选择可以足额还款，有10.49%的受访者选择“越花越多，快还不起了”。类似地，CAFI互联网借贷调研问卷中，90.4%选择有互联网借贷（互联网小额贷款公司和P2P借贷）经历的受访者表示没有发生过逾期。且发生逾期的受访者中，选择通过申请展期或想办法提高个人收入来解决逾期支付问题的各占50%以上，而选择通过从其他平台借款来偿还逾期债务的占比为30%。这说明大部分参与现金贷或类似贷款的受访者可以负担现金贷的利息成本，不至于由于借贷压力陷入循环债务危机。

最后，现金贷对借贷者个人收入的影响方面，我们可以参考CAFI 2019年的互联网借贷调研数据。在选择互联网借贷目的是“生产经营所需”和“投资”的893位受访者中，有77.6%的受访者选择“通过互联网小额贷款公司和P2P平台的线上贷款，增加了个人收入”。没有通过互联网借贷增加个人收入的受访者仅占22.4%。若现金贷利率及途径合规，互联网借贷对借贷者收入的正向作用同样可见于现金贷。

社会上有人担忧现金贷是造成消费者过度负债的因素。然而，我们认为这种问题并不普遍存在。中国消费者的储蓄习惯和借贷习惯依旧比较保守。对兰州问卷中“如果向金融机构借款能够改善您的生活，而且支付的利息在您的偿付能力之内，您会不会选择向金融机构借款?”这一问题，仅有27.72%的受访者表示会，而72.28%的受访者表示不会。因此，可以推论出，绝大多数长尾客户不会轻易进行借贷行为。王靖一（2018）在研究中发现，贷款申请者对利率变动，即贷款成本有着相当的敏感性，且这种敏感性在多种测试下保持稳健；同时，并未发现明显的风险问题，即借贷者非理性过度借贷导致自身陷入危机的可能性也比较低。因而，所谓的现金贷引发过度借贷的担忧并未得到证实。

（二）现金贷对金融体系的作用

除了对消费者提供额外的信贷渠道、满足长尾客户的借贷需求等作用，现金贷还对金融体系的完善具有正面作用。首先，现金贷完善社会信贷体系，丰富社会信贷服务层级。现金贷的出现由市场需求引发，说明原有供给侧金融市场对这一层级客户需求的关注和满足不够。现金贷弥补了市场空白，丰富了供给层次，提高了金融体系的包容性。

其次，纳入监管而良性发展的现金贷行业有助于从侧面打压地下高利贷，维护社会稳定。在社会需求一定的情况下，若对现金贷类产品全面打压，有可能产生的影响是导致现金贷“地下化”，变为高利贷或超利贷。而地下高利贷或超利贷游走于监管范围之外，利率畸高，伴有暴力催收等行为，严重影响社会安定。因此，得到良性引导并纳入监管的现金贷行业，可以吸收部分借贷市场需求，有助于从侧面打击地下高利贷或超利贷现象。

最后，现金贷业务的合规发展可将原金融体系无法覆盖的长尾客群纳入普惠金融体系中，随着互联网大数据征信的发展，数字化的现金贷产品还有助于补充社会个人征信数据。

综上所述，现金贷可以满足长尾客户的借贷需求，大多数借贷者对现金贷的使用情况表示满意且可以按期足额偿还贷款，且大多数用来满足生产经营和投资所需的借贷者实际上增加了个人收入。同时，现金贷具有完善借贷体系、打压地下高利贷、补足征信等结构性作用。

三、现金贷变异为超利贷的原因

自 2017 年底开始的强监管促使现金贷行业发生一系列变化：部分线上小额短期贷款的产品变成“714”（7 天或 14 天的超短期高利率借贷）、产业链“作坊化”、形态“地下化”。究其原因，可能有以下五个方面。

（一）监管突然收紧

《关于规范整顿“现金贷”业务的通知》（整治办函〔2017〕141 号，以下简称 141 号文）等一系列监管政策的收紧导致许多原有现金贷平台受限于利率红线或牌照条件，转战地下。例如，141 号文要求“各类机构以利率和各种费用形式对借款人收取的综合资金成本应符合最高人民法院关于民间借贷利率的规定，禁止发放或撮合违反法律有关利率规定的贷款。”对一笔期限为 14 天、金额为 5000 元的短期借款来讲，36%的年化利率相当于 75 元的利息（含各种费用）。对于许多现金贷平台或者小额贷款公司来说，这笔收入无法弥补其资金成本、运营成本、数据获取成本及信贷风险成本。因此，即使满足其他监管条件，金融服务供应商也难以继续维持现金贷业务条线的运转。这切断了一部分原现金贷客群的融资来源。若正规金融服务供应商还无法满足其借贷需求，那么他们将被迫选择地下高利贷产品。与之前平均年化158%、最高利率598%的现金贷相比，地下超利贷产品普遍年化利率在1000%以上，借款人的还贷压力更加沉重。对比美国的发薪日贷（Payday Loan），日均利率也在5‰～1%的水平。从年化角度计算，这一利率年化高达180%～400%，属于高利贷范畴。而如果能按时还款，由于期限短，其利息成本低于开“空头支票”和银行信用卡罚息，对借款者而言更加划算。因此，这样高的年化利率也有其存在的市场空间。合理的市场化定价是金融服务供应商向长尾客群下沉，以商业可持续性作为开展普惠金融业务的前提。我国正规金融服务供应商的借贷产品的利率进一步实现市场化定价，也许是现金贷行业的出口之一。

（二）配套法律法规不完善

现金贷自2014年在我国出现至今，仍算新生事物，因而配套的法律法规建设仍不完善。发薪日贷在英国、美国存在时间较长，在历史上也存在没有专门法规监管的时期。然而，随着其市场的发展，英国金融行为监管局（Financial Conduct Authority，FCA）于2014年4月率先颁布了《消费贷款管理细则》。2016年6月，美国消费者金融保护局发布了《发薪日、汽车消费以及特定高成本消费分期贷款法案》，在联邦层面对发薪日贷进行详细规定。同时，建立发薪日贷的贷款平台准入机制，如英国要求发薪日贷的平台具备相关资质，美国则采取备案登记制度进行自律监管。另外，各国对贷款利率、各种费用、贷款额度、展期次数等都有明确要求。

表7-2　全球主要国家现金贷监管政策

	美国	英国	澳大利亚	韩国	日本
监管机构	消费者金融保护局	金融行为监管局	证券及投资委员会	韩国金融服务委员会	金融监督厅、贷金业协会
持牌要求	备案登记	资质认证	持有牌照的非吸储机构	持有牌照的放贷机构	持有牌照的放贷机构
借款限额	开展足额偿还测试或不超过500美元	须进行支付能力核实	不高于2000澳大利亚元	根据借款人的综合资信和收入水平确定额度	贷款人的贷款余额不得超过年收入的1/3
利率限制	长期贷款年利率不得超过36%（含利息、申请费等相关费用），短期年利率根据各州规定	日利率不超过0.8%	期初费用不得超过合同房贷金额的20%（若借款是为了归还另外的现金贷，不得收取），月费率不得超过4%	年利率最高不超过27.9%	禁止超过《利息限制法》规定上限的20%

续表

	美国	英国	澳大利亚	韩国	日本
展期限制	在贷款无法归还时，只能申请展期两次	用户只能申请两次展期，两次展期后其借款总额（含利息）不得超过其原始借款金额的2倍	没有展期限制，但如因展期导致增加了原本约定的借款期限，则必须进行适应性评价	提前10天申请，一次展期	无
罚金限制	无	对用户逾期收取的罚金不得超过以下费用的总和：每天15英镑加上按0.8%的日利率收取的利息，且要求归还贷款（含罚金）的总额不得超过借款金额的2倍	在逾期的情况下，所有收回的金额不得超过调整后的放贷金额的2倍	对贷款者的罚金不能超过当期确定的比率，并综合考虑贷出该笔贷款项，管理逾期贷款的费用及逾期贷款额度、期限、业务种类等确定罚息	无
消费者保护	信息披露风险提示，对用户减轻融资负担或使用其他融资方案替代高成本短期融资的咨询建议	信息披露风险提示，对用户减轻融资负担或使用其他融资方案替代高成本短期融资的咨询建议；必须在至少一家价格比较网站上公示其信息，且必须将公司网站与该价格比较网站建立“显著联系”	借款人签约时要按固定格式提示借款风险	信息披露；严禁欺诈或夸大宣传；指派专人监督金融借贷者保护；侵权损害赔偿责任	信息保护，无正当理由，在不适当的时段，不得拨打电话或至债务人居住处

资料来源：巴曙松，黄文礼，许南燕．现金贷的风险来源分析及其监督［J］．武汉金融，2018（4）．

需要注意的是，英美要求对借款人进行偿还能力审查。英国要求发薪日贷款对借款人进行强制性的可支付能力审查，以确认借款人可以在维持基本生活开支的情况下能够承担还款压力。美国要求借款人接受偿还能力测试，同时禁止向学生等无收入的客群及有犯罪记录的借款人发放发薪日贷。

我国现金贷发展过程中由于缺乏针对这一特殊金融产品的监管法规，市场参与者良莠不齐，对借款人存在严重的诱导消费、诱导贷款的行为。现金贷本是信贷业务，首要考虑信贷风险。然而，在市场乱象中却发展成为流量业务，一方面用高息费覆盖高风险，另一方面诱导借款人借新还旧。防范能力不足的借款人很容易从起初为了弥补一时现金流不足的借贷而多次展期或借新还旧，最终陷入债务深渊无法自拔。

一本智库的调研数据显示，2017 年现金贷客群中仅有 18%的客户借款目的是偿还其他贷款。一本智库在 2019 年完成的另一份针对超利贷客群的调研显示，在 265 万份超利贷样本中，92.7%的贷款原因是因为逾期记录过多用于还款和网贷。仅有 4%的用户借超利贷的原因是为了消费，不到 2%的用户借超利贷用于临时周转。同时，该份调研结果显示，超利贷客群的重复申请率高，7 天内，借款人申请贷款 5～15 次，37.81%的借款人申请 5～9 个平台，23.22%的借款人申请 10～14 个平台。1 个月内，借款人申请贷款 10～35 次，52.43%的申请人申请 15～35 个平台。12 个月内，60.07%的借款人申请 50 次以上。可见，陷入超利贷的客群只能一次次借贷、一步步深陷，对借款人的金融健康造成毁灭性影响。

（三）社会征信体系搭建不足

官方的中国人民银行个人征信系统收录人数为 9.5 亿人，而其中约有 5 亿人是没有信贷历史的“白板用户”。为了弥补个人征信市场空白，符合互联网金融时代发展的需要，在中国人民银行的监督指导下，中国互联网金融协会与芝麻信用、腾讯征信等 8 家市场机构共同发起了市场化个人征信机构“百行征信”。这一征信平台将合并 8 家市场机构的市场征信能力，与中国人民银行个人征信系统优势互补、错位发展。个人征信体系的进一步发展，有助于个人征信信息被使用于现金贷的风险评估环节，同时，借款人的偿还历史也能反馈到个人征信评分。这将有助于提高借款人的违约成本，约束借款人履行还款义务，也有助于提升借款人的征信意识，对借款行为更加谨慎，避免债务陷阱。

（四）消费者保护不到位

在法律层面，应加强金融消费者保护的法律法规的建设，加强产品信息披露，将借款额度、各种费用、年化利率、风险提示等相关信息放在显著位置，避免倾向性、诱导性的产品宣传。在机构层面，金融服务供应商不负责任地推销，引诱借款人过度借贷、借新还旧等行为，也是导致许多借款人陷入债务深渊的原因之一。金融机构要对客户负责任，了解客户的真实需求，推荐适合客户的产品与服务。同时，要注意消费者隐私保护，规范催收行为。

（五）消费并非根本原因

有些社会舆论及媒体批判年轻人过度消费、超前消费的行为，它们认为这些行为是导致许多年轻人深陷超利贷债务陷阱的根本原因。然而，调研数据①显示，现金贷的借款用途中，超过50%的借款被用于资金周转，18%的借款用途为生活急用，18%是为了偿还其他类型贷款，仅有17%的借款用途为购物。同时，超利贷借款样本中，仅有4%是为了消费。可见，以消费为目的的借款在2017年现金贷客群和2018年超利贷客群中都是少数。也有现金贷平台经营人员认为借款原因中，50%是网络赌博，20%是做生意，20%是消费，10%是恶意老赖、撸口子。从侧面可见，导致超利贷的罪魁祸首并非消费，而是网络游戏、赌博等不良生活方式及盲目创业。从这个角度来讲，社会应当全面引导青少年进行健康的生活方式，控制网络游戏、远离赌博、合理消费、谨慎创业，尤其是对没有经济收入来源的学生，更要关注其生活方式和金融健康。

因此，要从根本上避免现金贷变异为超利贷或其他扰乱金融市场秩序的产品，有赖于我国在法律法规建设、征信体系建设、消费者保护方面进一步完善。

四、从现金贷到金融健康

普惠金融首先是金融服务的普及，包括金融账户的开设及储蓄、支付、汇款、贷款等金融服务的满足。在此基础上，是第二层次即金融知识与教育，只有结合金融知识与教育的提供，才能帮助金融消费者更好地选择和使用金融服务。持续的金融知识与教育导致的金融消费者行为变化和能力的提升是第三层次的概念，即金融能力。而金融能力所引发的改善的、长期的结果则是金融健康（见图7－1）。

图7－1　普惠金融中四个递进的概念

① 一本智库：《现金贷行业研究报告》及《超利贷人群画像与老哥上岸》。

因此，如果现金贷属于金融服务的范畴，现金贷与金融健康之间还隔着金融知识与教育，就需要将金融知识与教育转化为金融能力。

CAFI在兰州的调研显示，受访者的平均金融知识水平尚低。受访者为自己的金融知识平均打分为4.7分（1分表示最低，10分表示最高），为配偶平均打分为5.03分。然而，在过去一年里，仅有10.08%的受访者曾经向亲友主动请教学习过金融知识（包括如何申请贷款、如何使用网银和手机银行等）；仅有4.94%的受访者参加过金融知识的培训或宣传（包括银行、信用社等金融机构或政府举办）；仅有6.79%的受访者曾经学习过经济或金融的课程。这种结果说明，我国普罗大众的平均金融能力尚弱，需要面向全社会开展金融知识普及和个人的金融能力建设。

这些缺乏金融知识及金融能力的长尾客群正是现金贷的潜在客群。长尾客群金融知识不足，金融能力欠缺，有其社会原因。但若是同时消费者保护不足，金融服务供应商不负责任地恶意骗贷，就容易将这些客户带入债务深渊。

总之，现金贷产品具有丰富金融消费者融资渠道的作用，有助于社会金融体系的完善，因此需要监管为其留有市场空间。同时，我国应完善法律法规建设、完善信用体系建设、加强消费者保护与金融消费者教育，使现金贷成为提升消费者金融健康的有力工具。

案例

防控用户过度负债是金融科技公司的责任

2018年11月8日，度小满金融CEO朱光在第五届世界互联网大会期间出席“金融科技与社会信用建设”分论坛时表示，防控用户过度负债是金融科技公司的责任。

“信用社会的建设过程中，金融科技公司既要积极参与国家信用数据库的建设，做好信用信息的共享，也要通过技术能力防控用户过度消费、过度负债，降低金融风险。这是金融科技企业共同的责任。”

信用是市场经济的基石，加快建设社会信用体系，是完善社会主义市场经济体制的重要手段。近年来，金融科技的发展，在社会信用体系建设中发挥着独特的作用和价值。“中国社会信用体系的建设，大大提升了金融服务效率，本质上降低了金融服务成本，让老百姓得到了更便宜的金融服务，让更多人有了信用记录，让普惠金融成为可能。”朱光表示。

通过人工智能、大数据等金融科技的应用，可以加强金融信用信息基础设施建设，进一步扩大信用记录的覆盖面，强化金融业对守信者的激励作用和对失信者的约束作用。朱光表示，度小满金融一直在积极参与国家信用数据库建设，定期向中国人民银行征信中心、中国互联网金融协会报送用户的信贷数据。同时，将从自身生态中挖掘到的风险名单、黑产名单等开放给合作伙伴，让更多金融机构可以共享信息，进行风险联动预警，帮助金融机构更好地评估一个用户的负债能力，降低潜在的金融风险。

据了解，度小满已经自主研发了多个模型系统用于防控风险，比如，其建立的信用模型，可在中国人民银行征信数据基础上，将风险区分度提升15%；多头共债监控系统，可提前1个月准确预警用户的共债风险；行业监控和区域监控模型，可动态监测不同行业和不同地域的信用水平变化，有效防止用户过度负债。

金融科技的发展，大大提升了金融服务的效率，让用户随时随地获得金融服务，但用户过度消费、过度负债有可能陷入债务危机，增加生活负担，同时会积累社会金融风险，给金融机构造成损失。作为金融科技公司参与信用社会的建设，除做好信用信息的共享之外，还应该积极运用技术防控用户过度负债，倡导良好的金融用信行为，帮助用户养成珍视自身信用的习惯等，这也是所有金融科技企业共同的责任。

第三部分

负责任金融

除高质有益以外，负责任金融从更高的道德水准要求金融机构必须具有较高水平的使命感和责任感，要为消费者的金融健康负责，提供更加透明、包容和公平的金融产品和服务。

第八章 互联网平台的金融责任

【摘要】根据负责任金融的定义，本章梳理了一个供金融服务供应商、监管部门、金融消费者自查的负责任金融诊断工具。通过总结中国互联网平台发展经验发现，主导价值分配力量的增强、资源使用方式的改变、刺激非正规经济的发展是互联网平台的主要特点。基于这些特点，互联网平台作为数字金融服务供应商，不仅要承担传统金融服务供应商的基本金融责任，还要做好数据保护、跨越数字鸿沟、优化竞价体系等方面的金融责任新要求。在数字经济时代，互联网平台、监管部门、金融消费都需要正视金融责任，共同建设透明、公平、包容的行业环境。

金融健康与消费者的能力具有密切的关系，但是，消费者是金融市场中的弱势一方，不能完全决定金融服务的全部结果。作为市场中的强势一方，金融机构有能力影响金融服务是否给消费者带来有益的结果。要使金融服务产生健康的结果，金融机构在提供服务过程中必须承担一些责任，包括提供必要的信息、公平对待消费者、让金融服务具有较高程度的包容性。

一、负责任金融

也许有些人认为，金融服务也是一种商业行为，商业服务提供商的最大责任就是确保按市场规则提供服务。市场规则就是将服务配置给那些对服务赋予最高价值的消费者。如果消费者赋予某一服务最高价值，往往其出价也是最高的，因此，按出价高低进行优先供给符合高价值优先的市场规则。但是，越来越多的人认识到，金融机构的责任不仅限于此。

金融机构应在产品设计生产、交易和服务的一系列活动过程中承担更多的责任，尤其要对消费者的利益负责，以实现商业和社会的双重绩效。世界银行扶贫协商小组（CGAP）指出，在以负责任为特征的金融世界里，客户利益与金融服务供应商的可持续发展之间的平衡被精心维护，客户保护体现在产品设计与业务的每一个细节中①。

（一）负责任金融的概念

对于金融机构应负哪些责任，已经存在许多讨论。Luara Brix 和 Kathatine Mckee（2010）将负责任金融定义为以透明、公平的方式提供零售金融服务，并认为促进负责任金融发展的策略包括三大支柱（见图 8－1），即行业行为准则和标准、消费者保护法律法规与监管、提高消费者金融能力。Peer Stein、Bikki Randhawa 和 Nina Bilandzic 等（2011）认为，负责任金融是为了促进金融服务的透明、包容和公平，通过金融消费者保护监管、行业自律和金融能力三个领域来实现。后一种定义与普惠金融的内涵比较吻合，而前者提出的实现负责任金融的路径具有较高的实践意义。

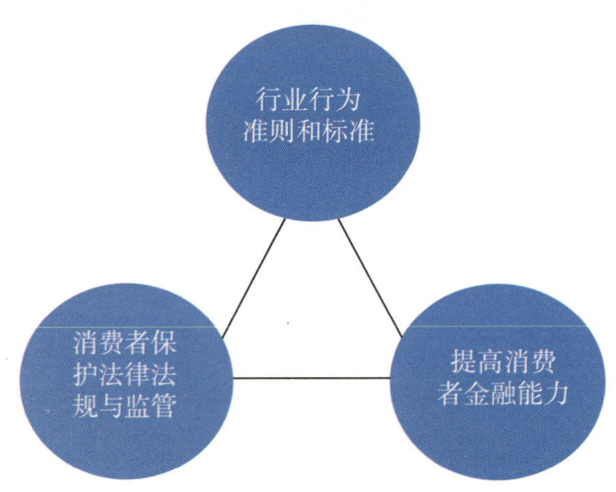

图 8－1　负责任金融的三大支柱

行业行为准则和标准基本是金融机构落实金融责任的重要落脚点。例如，CGAP 倡导的“Smart Campaign”对金融机构在客户保护方面提出了比较具体的要求，要求金融服务供应商应遵循：（1）适当的产品设计与交付方式；（2）防止客户过度负债；（3）透明度；（4）负责任的定价；（5）对待客户公平且尊重；（6）注重保护客户隐私；（7）建立投诉解决机制。金融服务供应商的自律行为对市场良性发展至关重要，这也是从源头上践行负责任金融。

消费者保护法律法规与监管是指监管当局通过法律、法规、制度安排来保护金融消费者的权益。审慎监管和非审慎监管都有助于金融消费者保护。金融消费者保护的非审慎监管用来管理金融服务供应商的市场行为；审慎监管的重点是保持金融业的健康，确保金融机构及整个金融系统的偿付能力（Luara Brix 和 Kathatine Mckee，2010）。金融消

① CGAP. Responsible Finance：Putting Principles to Work. 201109，No. 73.

费者保护的法律法规应当涵盖尽可能多的金融服务供应商，最大限度地减少漏洞。

提高消费者金融能力是指提升金融消费者的知识、态度、技能、行为，以便消费者更好地管理自己的资源，自主地理解、选择、利用金融服务来满足自身需求。仅仅依靠行业自律和法律法规未必可以完全阻止市场上的不当行为，消费者本身的金融能力可以有效防范欺诈、管理财务健康、行使正当权益等。

（二）负责任金融的诊断工具

根据负责任金融三大支柱的要求，表 8－1 可以作为金融服务供应商、监管部门、金融消费者的自我诊断工具。

表 8－1 负责任金融的问题诊断与自查要求

三大支柱	自查要求	针对问题
金融服务供应商		
行业自律	客户风险分析：通过商务尽职调查、实地考察、征信数据调查、互联网数据等进行客户画像	防范客户风险，避免客户过度负债的情况
	以客户为中心的产品设计：符合 KYC 原则，通过定期调查、焦点小组、神秘客户调查、客户流出监控等方式全方位了解客户满意度、回头率、需求等信息	避免产品与客户需求不匹配情况
	负责任的定价：通过市场调查、合适的定价工具等对产品进行合理定价	避免高利贷、高收费，或超出客户承受能力的定价情况
	正当营销与宣传：对产品价格、风险、条件、条款等如实宣传	避免不实宣传，诱导消费者的情况
	公平交易：对待所有客户都公平、公正，交易程序公开透明	避免客户歧视或排斥的情况
	信息披露：对机构财务绩效、社会绩效、产品信息等进行标准化的披露	避免投机、操纵、欺诈等情况
	内审与外审机制：通过标准化的内审与外审流程，发现问题，及时纠错，防范风险	避免机构问题累积，提高机构竞争力
	客户申诉系统与投诉解决机制：建立客户纠错平台，有效追索，调查与解决客户问题	避免客户损失，及时解决客户问题
	客户隐私保护：通过健全的流程，对客户隐私、信息进行严格保密	避免客户隐私与信息泄露情况

续表

三大支柱	自查要求	针对问题
金融服务供应商		
行业自律	逾期处理与催收流程：改变“零容忍”规则	避免暴力催收情况
	员工培训与绩效管理：通过外部与内部的培训体系，对员工开展业务与素质培训，以可行的绩效评估体系进行员工管理	避免低质量服务的情况
	企业内部规章制度：标准化的制度，有利于领导层、员工依照标准行事	避免无标准可参照的情况
	行业行为守则：由行业实践者共同确定可行、可信的行业规则，有利于行业良性发展	避免无章可循的情况
监管部门		
法律法规与监管	透明度法规和信息披露法规：如强制披露并设置高利贷上线，简单明了的合同用语，主要风险提示等，采用张贴公开告示，售前、售后的书面形式或口头形式披露，广告或营销材料等形式	避免消费者不了解获得哪些服务、费用、风险等
	隐私与信息保护法规：如保密法规等	避免损害消费者隐私与数据信息安全
	公平对待的标准：公平对待低收入和缺乏经验的消费者，制定一定标准，如掠夺性销售法规、适用性要求、冷静期、广告真实性法规或指引等	避免欺骗性广告、员工道德、欠款管理和收账、过度销售、垄断定价等情况
	征信部门的法规：建立金融消费者的信用记录、债务记录等	预防过度负债情况
	追索机制的流程与标准：如书面程序、调节机制、投诉监测、问责制度等	避免消费者无法行使追索权
	纠纷与投诉解决机制的流程与标准：如申诉专员制度、投诉热线、争议解决框架等	避免投诉与纠纷无法解决
	违规者处理办法：如点名批评违规者	确保有效监管
金融消费者		
消费者金融能力建设	金融教育：基于决策所需的知识与能力、权利与责任的教育等	避免消费者错误决策

仔细观察表8-1对负责任金融三大支柱的要求，其内容的本质是“以客户为中心”和“客户保护”。虽然国内对负责任金融的专门讨论还很有限，但是“以客户为中

心”和“客户保护”方面的研究文献却汗牛充栋，国内监管部门和金融服务供应商也重点关注这两个方面。

（三）我国负责任金融的现状

行业自律方面，我国金融行业协会数量增加、规模扩大①，包括中国银行业协会、中国保险行业协会、中国证券业协会、消费者金融保护协会金融分会、中国支付清算协会、中国互联网金融协会等。它们积极制定相关行业自律规范、行业标准、行业规范、从业人员管理规范、协会会员管理规范等。不过，行业协会及其制定的行业自律规则会因为有无市场影响力、是否具有政府背景、是否具有强制力而影响协会本身的地位及其规则的执行效率。除了行业协会，本报告更多地从行业实践者的角度讨论负责任金融，包括以客户为中心的产品设计、合适的金融服务价格，后续章节将详细论述。

法律法规与监管方面，《消费者权益保护法》《商业银行法》是我国金融消费者保护的法律基础，《中国人民银行金融消费权益保护工作管理办法（试行）》《中国人民银行金融消费者权益保护实施办法》《国务院办公厅关于加强金融消费者权益保护工作的指导意见》是相关的政策条文。2012 年，中国人民银行内设金融消费权益保护局，成为承担和履行金融消费者保护职责的监管主体。本报告后续章节将从金融消费者隐私信息保护及纠纷解决的角度，详细讨论负责任金融在法律法规与监管实践的具体体现和做法。

消费者金融能力建设方面，2013 年中国人民银行、中国证监会、中国银监会、中国保监会研究制定了《中国金融教育国家战略》，自 2013 年开始中国人民银行每年都组织全国性的“金融知识普及月”，向金融消费者发放《金融知识普及读本》等宣传材料②。

二、互联网平台金融责任的新要求

中国互联网平台的快速成长，为世界各国提供了较为完整而庞大的观测与实验空间。在中国经验的基础上讨论互联网平台的金融责任，将会有更直观有效的结论。

（一）中国互联网平台的发展现状与特点

中国 2017 年全球互联网经济发展综合指数排名位居第二，仅次于美国。德国、

① 崔芙蓉．金融消费者保护行业自律研究［D］．太原：山西大学，2018.

② 资料来源：http：//finance.sina.com.cn/china/20130829/104116603436.shtml。

英国、瑞士、日本、韩国、荷兰、瑞典、芬兰等国分别居第三位到第十位[①]。“独角兽”公司在一定程度上被视作衡量新经济活跃程度的指标。2018 年中国“独角兽”公司有 88 家（包括中国香港），仅次于美国的 151 家，而且蚂蚁金服以 1500 亿美元估值占据超级“独角兽”公司榜单的第一位[②]。从网上零售额来看中国的数字经济（见图 8－2），经济规模呈逐年增长的趋势，截至 2018 年底，网上零售额已超过 9 万亿元。

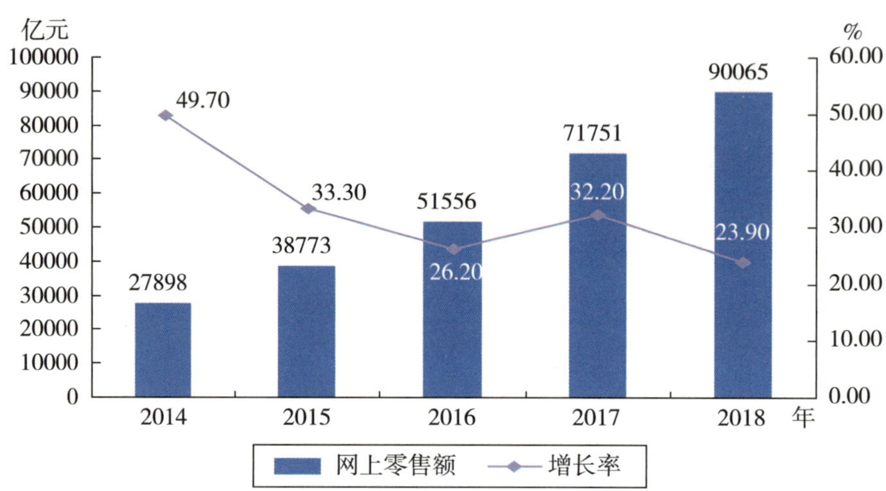

资料来源：国家统计局、中国普惠金融研究院。

图 8－2　中国全年网上零售额情况

互联网平台的特点主要体现在：主导价值分配力量的增强、资源使用方式的改变及刺激非正规经济的发展。

1. 资源急剧聚集，互联网平台主导价值分配的力量增强

观察中国经验可知，互联网平台迅速发展，为数字经济奠定了基础，而数字技术使互联网平台的发展周期缩短，短时间便可以服务于众多买家和卖家，将线下交易搬到了线上。数字技术是传统企业和互联网平台企业的分水岭，从企业生命周期来看，互联网平台企业从初创期、发展期到成熟期的时间确实比传统企业耗费的时间要短许多，互联网平台企业聚集资源的时间也较短。

经济学生产要素理论认为，土地、劳动、资本、组织、知识等是生产价值与扩大人类财富的重要决定因素，而随着互联网科技的发展，技术、信息、数据等也对企业发展与收入分配有着重要影响。互联网平台恰恰可以在较短时间内汇聚海量生产要素

---

① 资料来源：亿邦动力研究院．中国互联网经济蓝皮书：跨境电商成为新热点［DB/OL］．http：//www.ebrun.com/20190114/316723.shtml.

② 资料来源：任泽平．中国独角兽报告：2019［R］．恒大研究院，2019.

和相关资源，包括买家、卖家、数字化劳动力，以及他们提供的商品或服务。通过供需关系形成的平台竞价体系在一定程度上决定了买家、卖家、数字化劳动力及平台自身的盈利，平台主导价值分配的力量得以体现（见表 8－2）。

表 8－2　中国互联网平台与数字化劳动力发展情况

<table>
<tr><th rowspan="2">企业名称</th><th rowspan="2">企业估值范围（亿元）</th><th rowspan="2">行业</th><th colspan="2">数字化劳动力</th><th rowspan="2">个人用户数</th></tr>
<tr><th>类别</th><th>数量</th></tr>
<tr><td rowspan="2">阿里巴巴</td><td rowspan="2">31600</td><td rowspan="2">互联网综合</td><td>商户</td><td>1000 万家</td><td rowspan="2">20 亿人</td></tr>
<tr><td>就业岗位</td><td>1 亿个</td></tr>
<tr><td>腾讯控股</td><td>31417</td><td>互联网综合</td><td>活跃公众号</td><td>350 万个</td><td>10 亿人</td></tr>
<tr><td>今日头条</td><td>5000</td><td>互联网文娱</td><td>自媒体号</td><td>90 万个</td><td></td></tr>
<tr><td>京东</td><td>3338</td><td>电子商务</td><td>商家</td><td>20 万家</td><td>3 亿人</td></tr>
<tr><td>滴滴出行</td><td>3200</td><td>移动出行</td><td>司机</td><td>2100 万人</td><td>5.5 亿人</td></tr>
<tr><td rowspan="2">美团点评</td><td rowspan="2">2500</td><td rowspan="2">O2O 服务</td><td>骑手</td><td>200 万人</td><td rowspan="2">3.1 亿人</td></tr>
<tr><td>商家</td><td>440 万家</td></tr>
<tr><td>拼多多</td><td>1768</td><td>电子商务</td><td>商户</td><td>360 万家</td><td>4 亿人</td></tr>
<tr><td>苏宁易购</td><td>1212</td><td>电子商务</td><td>快递员</td><td></td><td>4.07 亿人</td></tr>
<tr><td rowspan="3">菜鸟网络</td><td rowspan="3">1000</td><td rowspan="3">互联网物流</td><td>快递员</td><td>300 万人</td><td rowspan="3"></td></tr>
<tr><td>校园驿站</td><td>2800 家，
10 万实习岗位</td></tr>
<tr><td>社区驿站</td><td>数万家</td></tr>
<tr><td>京东物流</td><td>800</td><td>互联网物流</td><td>快递员</td><td></td><td></td></tr>
<tr><td>58 同城</td><td>720</td><td>互联网服务</td><td>本地商户</td><td>1000 万家</td><td>4 亿人</td></tr>
<tr><td>阅文集团</td><td>592</td><td>互联网文娱</td><td>创作者</td><td>730 万人</td><td>数亿人</td></tr>
<tr><td>饿了么</td><td>500</td><td>O2O 服务</td><td>餐厅</td><td>130 万家</td><td>2.6 亿人</td></tr>
<tr><td>神州优车</td><td>450</td><td>移动出行</td><td>司机</td><td></td><td></td></tr>
<tr><td>满帮</td><td>400</td><td>互联网物流</td><td>货车司机</td><td></td><td></td></tr>
<tr><td rowspan="2">美菜网</td><td rowspan="2">400</td><td rowspan="2">电子商务</td><td>司机</td><td></td><td rowspan="2"></td></tr>
<tr><td>商户</td><td>100 万家</td></tr>
<tr><td>微医</td><td>400</td><td>互联网医护</td><td>在线医生</td><td>24 万人</td><td>1.6 亿人</td></tr>
<tr><td>平安好医生</td><td>377</td><td>互联网医护</td><td>外部签约名医</td><td>0.47 万人</td><td>2.28 亿人</td></tr>
<tr><td>达达—京东到家</td><td>300</td><td>互联网物流</td><td>快递员</td><td></td><td></td></tr>
<tr><td>VIPKID</td><td>200</td><td>互联网教育</td><td>在线教师</td><td>6 万人</td><td>50 万人</td></tr>
</table>

续表

企业名称	企业估值范围（亿元）	行业	数字化劳动力		个人用户数
			类别	数量	
汇通达	200	电子商务	夫妻店	11 万家	
			农民	50 万人	
喜马拉雅	200	互联网文娱	有声主播	500 万人	4.7 亿人
			有声自媒体大咖	0.8 万人	
银联商务	200	互联网金融	特约商户	826.3 万家	
土巴兔	100	互联网服务	设计师	110 万人	
			装修公司	8 万多家	
微店	100	电子商务	商家	7200 万家	百万人
小猪短租	100	互联网房产	房源	50 万套	
猪八戒网	100	互联网服务	专业人才	1300 万人	
58 到家	70	互联网服务	上门服务人员	160 万人	2000 万户
春雨医生	70	互联网医护	执业医师	50 万人	2 亿人次
丁香园	70	互联网医护	医生用户	200 万人	千万人
好大夫在线	70	互联网医护	医生	20 万人	300 万人
微盟	70	互联网服务	商户	280 万家	

资料来源：《2018 胡润大中华区独角兽指数》、恒大研究院《中国独角兽报告：2019》、各家企业的官网、中国普惠金融研究院。

以阿里巴巴为例，短短十年时间，平台聚集了 20 亿名个人用户，几乎占到全球人口总和的 27%及超过 1000 万家的商户。平台上的“商家—阿里巴巴平台—用户”依托竞价体系完成交易并获得收入。

可见，互联网平台各类参与主体之间的供需关系（见图 8-3）包括但不仅限于“买家—平台—卖家”的三方关系和“买家—平台—数字化劳动力—卖家”的多方关

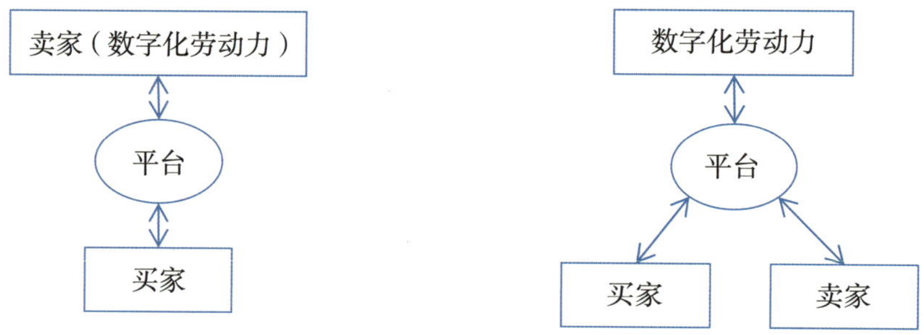

图 8-3　数字化劳动力在平台上的关系

系。各类参与主体通过互联网平台提供产品或服务，进而盈利；通过为买家、卖家、数字化劳动力搭建链接服务，互联网平台向他们收取一定的服务费。

值得注意的是，越来越多的互联网平台通过降低服务费的方式，吸引并留住越来越多的买家、卖家、数字化劳动力，当数量发生从量变到质变的飞跃之后，一方面增强了平台在市场上的竞争力，另一方面进一步增强了平台主导价值分配的力量。

2. 互联网平台催生共享经济，改变资源使用方式

互联网平台的发展催生了共享经济。共享经济被定义为“个人或机构把闲置的资源或服务有偿分享给需求者使用，从中获得报酬，需求者通过使用供给者的资源创造价值”（马强，2016），其内涵是“去中介化和再中介化过程”（郑志来，2016），其核心是“以信息技术为基础和纽带，实现产品的所有权和使用权的分离，在资源拥有者和资源需求者之间实现使用权共享（交易）”（汤天波和吴晓隽，2015）。

如表 8-2 所示，提供移动出行服务的滴滴出行、神州优车，提供互联网物流服务的菜鸟网络、京东物流、满帮等，提供互联网医护服务的微医、平安好医生、春雨医生、丁香园等，提供互联网教育的 VIPKID，提供互联网房产服务的小猪短租，以及提供互联网服务的猪八戒网，都被认为是共享经济的代表性企业（汤天波和吴晓隽，2015；马强，2016）。

共享经济打破了人们对所有制的传统认知，“占有”不再是评价资源价值的最重要指标，实现资源循环利用、最大限度地发挥资源价值，反而可以获得人们的更大认同。

3. 互联网平台承载数字化劳动力，刺激非正规经济的发展

随着互联网平台多元化发展，平台加载的功能越来越多，包括电子商务、金融服务、物流服务、O2O 服务、房产服务、生活服务、文娱服务、医护服务等。其中，人的劳动力也开始了数字化转化进程，依托平台为平台、买家、卖家等多方提供服务，以获取报酬。因此，云工作（Cloud Work）、零工工作（GIG Work）、群体工作（Crowd Work）、数字化劳动力（Digital Labour）等对传统工作模式形成深刻变革的工作模式引起人们越来越多的注意①。

互联网平台的发展大大刺激了非正规经济的发展。国际劳工组织对非正规经济的定义是“缺乏劳动法规保护和社会保障的从业人员”②。全球在非正规经济中就业的工

① Friedman（2014）、摩根大通（2016）、Baltimore 等（2016）、Huws 等（2017）、Drahokoupli 和 Piasna（2017）、中国普惠金融研究院和 BFA（2018）、世界银行（2019）等学者和机构，对新型数字化工作模式有了较为系统的研究。

② 黄宗智，李强，等．中国非正规经济（上）[J]．开放时代，2011（1）．

人有 20 亿人[①]，中国的非正规就业人员超过了 2 亿人[②]，其中有 7500 万人[③]是数字化劳动力。这就意味着，如今中国至少有 7500 万人通过互联网平台提供服务，如果加上互联网平台上的商户（包括中小微企业商户、个人店、夫妻店等），则中国非正规经济的数字化规模远远超过这个数字。

一方面，中国越来越多的劳动力依托互联网平台提供服务，互联网平台直接影响了个人或家庭的收入情况。如表 8－2 所示，聚集百万以上个人数字化劳动力的平台有 9 个，如滴滴出行、美团点评、菜鸟网络、阅文集团、喜马拉雅、土巴兔、猪八戒网、58 到家、丁香园等，其中滴滴出行上聚集了 2100 万名司机，猪八戒网上有 1300 万名专业人才。

另一方面，互联网平台上也聚集了数量众多的小微型商户（包括中小微企业商户、个人店、夫妻店等），吸纳了大量的劳动力。这些在线商户相当于劳动力的“聚合器”，将劳动力“打包”进行数字化，进而参与到数字经济中。如表 8－2 所示，聚集百万以上商户的平台有 10 个，如阿里巴巴、腾讯控股、美团点评、拼多多、58 同城、饿了么、美莱网、银联商务、微店、微盟等，其中阿里巴巴、58 同城、微店上聚集的商户超过了千万家。

（二）互联网平台与金融服务的关系

综上所述，互联网平台承担的角色越发多样化了，如图 8－4 所示，包括非金融服务供应商、数字金融服务供应商、数字化劳动力的雇主或使用者及社会关系网络的连接者。

第一，互联网平台为平台上的买家、卖家、数字化劳动力等提供数字化的非金融服务，包括电子商务、移动出行、物流、文娱、医护、房产、餐饮、酒店旅行等，即互联网平台承担了非金融服务供应商的角色。

第二，互联网平台在合规的基础上为平台上的买家、卖家、数字化劳动力等提供各类数字化的金融服务，包括支付、理财、融资、保险、众筹、信用等，即互联网平台承担了数字金融服务供应商的角色。

第三，互联网平台通过雇用或使用数字化劳动力为平台上的买家和卖家实现各类数字化服务的现实转化，此时互联网平台承担了数字化劳动力的雇主或使用者的角色。

---

① 资料来源：世界银行．世界发展报告 2019［R］．世界银行，2019.

② 资料来源：共享经济浪潮下，如何保障 2 亿非正规就业人员的医疗保险？［DB/OL］．http：//www.sohu.com/a/280120876_100291829.

③ 资料来源：国家信息中心分享经济研究中心．中国共享经济发展年度报告（2019）［R］．国家信息中心，2019.

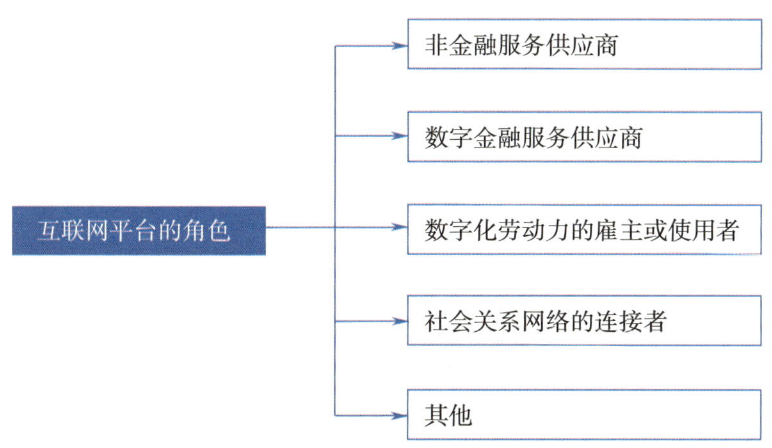

图 8-4 互联网平台角色示意

第四，互联网平台为平台上的买家、卖家、数字化劳动力等建立数字化的通道，为各类数字化服务及其现实转化，提供了解决方案，即互联网平台承担了社会关系网络的连接者的角色。

当互联网平台上形成了交易生态，以数字支付为基础的金融服务成为支持互联网平台交易生态在线高速运转的基石。可见，互联网平台承担着非金融服务供应商、数字金融服务供应商、数字化劳动力的雇主或使用者、社会关系网络的连接者四种角色，并不能轻易地排他存在。从这个意义上说，互联网平台与金融服务密切相关。

（三）互联网平台金融责任的新要求

互联网平台承担数字金融服务供应商时，区别于传统金融服务供应商，其金融责任的新要求主要体现在数据保护、跨越数字鸿沟、优化竞价体系等方面。

1. 严格执行数据保护，保障金融消费者的金融资产安全

在大数据时代，如果拥有足够的数据，数字世界完全可以复制出一个个鲜活的虚拟人物，与真实世界的个人有着相同的喜好、社会关系网、时间表、行动轨迹等。如果数据控制者、使用者、接受者可以随意调取和使用任何人的数据，那么所有人就毫无隐私可言。从这个意义上说，数据保护关乎每一个人的隐私，甚至是生命财产安全。

2018 年 5 月 25 日正式生效的《欧盟数据保护通用条例》（*General Data Protection Regulation*，GDPR）被称为最严格的数据保护立法，对数据类型、数据主体的权利、处理数据的基本原则、数据控制者与数据处理者的义务、一些特别的规定（如被遗忘权）、处罚等作了详细规定。该条例无疑给数字世界的虚拟人物撑起了保护伞，虚拟人物与真实世界的个人一样，拥有了保护隐私的武器。

当然，对《欧盟数据保护通用条例》的主要质疑在于该条例遏制了互联网创新。

该条例直接影响了在欧盟国家有业务往来的互联网企业，严格的数据保护给企业增加了不小的成本。如何取得数据保护和互联网创新之间的平衡，是欧盟及其他各国需要面对的问题。

对于数字金融供应商来说，“在获取和持续使用数字金融服务的过程中，健全的消费者和数据保护框架对构建消费者信任和信心必不可少，尤其是对于那些金融素养不高或承担损失能力有限的消费者”①。

2. 跨越数字鸿沟，实现数字机会均等

关于数字鸿沟最早的论述是雅克·巴尔岑所描述的，人口被分为两组，一组人有能力处理技术产品和精通自然科学，尤其是数学，另一组人则没有这种能力②。经济合作与发展组织（OECD）将数字鸿沟定义为，在不同社会经济发展水平的地域条件下，个人、家庭、企业获取信息、通信技术及使用互联网开展各种活动的机会差异③。

虽说引起数字鸿沟的原因有技术因素也有社会因素，但要跨越数字鸿沟，技术研发、基础设施建设、设备普及、金融消费者技能培训等依然是先决条件，往往需要政府部门承担更多的投入，尤其对贫困地区和中小微弱群体。实际情况是，从人群来看，老年人和低收入人口容易被数字技术边缘化；从地区来看，偏远地区、农村地区、牧区等区域容易发生数字鸿沟的问题。

在数字金融服务占半壁江山的今天，如何服务于传统金融机构难以触达的那部分人群，使越来越多的人通过数字金融服务实现金融机会均等，数字普惠金融被寄予厚望。虽然基础设施建设和设备普及未必是商业化数字金融服务供应商力所能及的工作，但是技术研发和金融消费者技能培训值得重点投入。

3. 形成公平、透明、包容的竞价体系，兼顾平台多个利益相关方权益

互联网平台的竞价体系主要基于买方、卖方、数字化劳动力、平台本身形成的供求关系。在此基础上，当互联网平台的规模达到一定程度时，互联网平台的议价能力就远远超出了作为个体的买方、卖方、数字化劳动力，即前文所述互联网平台主导价值分配的力量不断增强。正因如此，互联网平台遵循公平、透明、包容原则来制定竞价体系，即是对买方、卖方、数字化劳动力的让渡。

相对于买方和卖方来说，数字化劳动力的角色显得更弱势一些。以美团骑手④为例，他们中的75%来自农村、18.4%来自贫困县、84%受教育程度在职高/中专/技校和高中以下、87%有养育子女的重任等，骑手的工作对他们来说非常重要，与家庭金

① CGPI，G20 2016 CHINA. 二十国集团数字普惠金融高级原则．2016.
② 阿斯法克·伊萨克，兆雄，译．论全球数字鸿沟［J］. 国外社会科学文摘，2002（3）.
③ OECD. Understanding the Digital Divide［R］. OECD Digital Economy Papers，No. 49，2001.
④ 美团点评研究院．新时代 新青年：2018年外卖骑手群体研究报告［R］. 美团点评研究院，2018.

融健康状况息息相关。从这个意义上来说，美团作为一个大体量的互联网平台，其竞价体系如何使每一位骑手都能有所得，是维系美团交易生态的重要因素。

（四）从 P2P“兴衰周期”看互联网平台金融责任现状

从 2007 年中国第一家 P2P 平台拍拍贷成立至今，短短十多年，中国网络借贷行业发展大致经历了起步探索、快速发展、风险爆发、规范调整几个阶段，可谓走过了一个完整的“兴衰周期”。网贷之家统计数据显示，截至 2019 年 5 月底，中国正常运营的 P2P 平台数下降至 914 家，累计问题平台数增加到 5703 家，占比超过 87%，其涉及投资人数 267 万人，涉及贷款余额 2104.3 亿元。

从 P2P 平台的“兴衰周期”看，诱发 P2P 平台各种问题的原因①在于：第一，未被满足的投资需求与借贷需求巨大。出借人积极寻找提供更高收益的投资渠道，借款人则寻找更方便、快捷、灵活的借贷渠道。在如此巨大的需求面前，逐利资本，甚至违法资本，便想办法削尖脑袋挤入市场，意图分一杯羹。第二，准入门槛低且长期处于监管真空状态。准入方面，在 2016 年《网络借贷信息中介机构备案管理登记指引》印发之前，P2P 平台的设立主要完成工商登记注册即可；该指引印发之后，P2P 平台除需完成工商登记注册外，还要及时到地方金融监管部门申请备案登记，完成备案登记后再到通信主管部门申请增值电信业务经营许可，以及与银行业金融机构签订资金存管协议。在 2016—2018 年的“一个办法三个指引”和“108 条”之前，2012—2015 年，监管环境宽松，在巨大的市场需求和利益的驱动下，P2P 平台野蛮扩张，风险不断积聚并最终爆发出来。第三，金融科技加速了“跑马圈地”。P2P 平台借助金融科技的力量，大大缩短了触达时间、降低了成本、提高了效率，切切实实助力 P2P 平台业务呈指数级增长。但无论是银行系、国资系、上市系，还是风投系、民营系，在“跑马圈地的”时代，问题 P2P 平台不惜踩踏红线，借道金融科技，能捞一把是一把。最终，金融科技成为问题 P2P 平台走向覆灭的加速器。

从行业自律的角度看，问题 P2P 平台并未践行金融责任，反而沦为逐利资本、违法资本的工具；从法律法规与监管的角度看，由于一段时间的监管真空状态，为问题 P2P 平台提供滋长的机会，而现如今以“清退”为主要方向的监管政策与法律法规，又使合法合规的 P2P 平台也处于艰难境地；在消费者金融能力建设方面，问题 P2P 平台的出借人和借款人对风险的识别仍有待加强。

（五）改进建议

在数字经济时代，互联网平台、监管部门、金融消费都需要正视金融责任，共同

① 赖丹妮，张亦辰．P2P 网贷机构的问题、诱因与可持续发展对策［J］．中国经贸导刊（中），2019（3）．

建设透明、公平、包容的行业环境。

第一，倡导行业自律，作为数字金融服务供应商的互联网平台应当清醒地了解平台责任的重要性。除传统金融服务供应商的基本责任之外，互联网平台还承担更新的金融责任，包括数据保护、跨越数字鸿沟、竞价体系等。这就要求互联网平台在提供金融服务的过程中，始终坚持经济绩效与社会绩效的平衡。也只有从创立之初就具备金融责任意识的互联网平台，才能最终成长为行业标杆，既创造巨量的财富，又为社会带来正向效益。

第二，鉴于互联网金融创新的超前性，监管部门需要更好的“平衡术”，一方面能更有效地识别并监控风险，另一方面能包容合法合规的互联网金融创新。中国数字支付、数字借贷（包括 P2P 撮合业务、助贷业务、互联网小贷、互联网消费信贷等）、数字保险、数字理财等领域取得了不同程度的发展，数字金融相关政策与法律法规也逐渐趋于成熟，尤其在“兴衰周期”的刺激下，监管部门对数字金融违规业务及其风险有了更深刻的认识，政策与法律法规的制定也将更有针对性。在此基础之上，监管部门才能更好地练就其“平衡术”。

第三，金融消费者需要以开放的心态学习互联网与数字金融知识，提升金融资产保护与配置能力。从目前来看，数字化进程不会止步，还有可能加速前进。金融消费者只有适应瞬息万变的数字技术变化，才能真正保护自身金融资产的安全，才能从根本上解决数字机会均等的问题，在平台竞价体系下赢得更多报酬。

第九章　消费者隐私信息保护与纠纷解决

【摘要】数字技术在金融领域的应用促进了金融的包容性，但是数字技术的普及也带来了消费者隐私信息泄露的问题。隐私信息泄露不仅给金融消费者的日常生活带来了困扰，更使部分消费者遭受巨大的财产损失。本章首先介绍目前消费者隐私信息泄露的主要途径及目前消费者遇到金融纠纷时的解决途径，继而对保护消费者隐私信息和解决金融纠纷提出相关建议，以帮助读者更好地理解金融消费者隐私信息泄露的问题及解决办法。

一、消费者隐私信息泄露问题

（一）消费者隐私信息泄露现状

数字技术的发展与繁荣，一方面为用户提供了良好的信息互动平台，信息获取更加容易，给用户工作和生活带来了极大的便利；另一方面，用户信息的传播范围和传播速度也不断加大，隐私信息通过网络快速而广泛地传播，极大地压缩了用户的私人空间。如本报告第一章中所提到的，移动互联网和信息技术等数字技术的飞速发展及其在金融领域的应用促进了金融的包容性，但也带来了消费者隐私信息泄露的问题。被泄露的隐私信息通常被非法使用于非法获利和精准营销等活动，如人们在日常生活中经常遇到的金融诈骗电话和广告骚扰电话等，都是隐私信息泄露的结果。隐私信息泄露不仅给个人的日常生活带来了诸多困扰，甚至还使很多人遭受巨额财产损失。

在2018年对浙江省普惠金融发展的调研中，我们发现，有近一半（48.04%）的受访者接到过金融诈骗电话（见图9－1），如果考虑广告骚扰电话的情况，这个比例还会更高。由此可以看出，目前隐私信息泄露的情况非常普遍；有3.40%的受访者因为金融诈骗而遭受了实际损失（见图9－2）；在调查受访者没有使用手机银行的原因中，我们发现害怕电信诈骗（28.79%）是金融客户放弃使用手机银行的第二大原因

（见图 9－3）。数字技术可促进金融的包容性发展，推动普惠金融发展，但是如果不能做好消费者隐私信息保护且在出现纠纷时缺乏完善的解决机制，金融消费者则会对隐私泄露产生顾虑，从而减少数字金融的使用。因此，金融机构在提供金融产品时，尤其需要考虑如何确保消费隐私信息安全并提供负责任的金融服务。

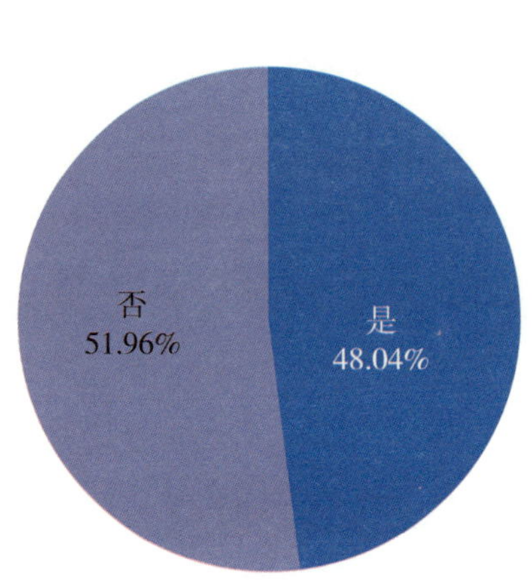

图 9－1　是否接到过金融诈骗电话

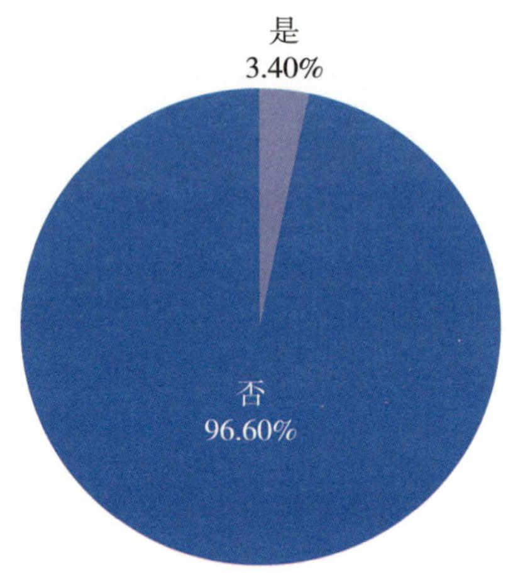

图 9－2　是否因为金融诈骗而遭受损失

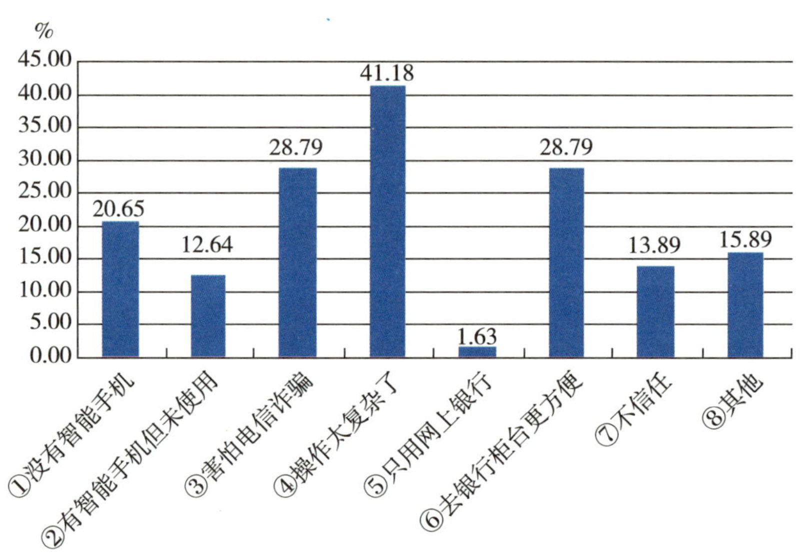

图 9－3　不使用手机银行的原因

（二）消费者隐私信息泄露途径

1. 不当收集造成的消费者隐私信息泄露

在消费者使用互联网的过程中，消费者的隐私信息可以在多种情况下被悄无声息地收集。一是通过首次注册收集隐私信息。一方面，互联网平台会要求消费者在注册时提供身份信息、联系方式、通讯录、工作情况、家庭情况等隐私信息，但是多数情况下这些信息是非必需的；另一方面，在首次登录APP时，APP会要求消费者允许读取识别码、调用摄像头、允许开启定位、打开运动数据等，大多数情况下如果消费者拒绝则会影响软件的使用。二是通过互联网技术收集隐私信息。例如，通过技术手段获得消费者的密码、上网习惯等信息，全面了解消费者的网络活动习惯，从而进行精准营销，为平台获利。美国著名社交网站Facebook（脸书）的创始人兼首席执行官扎克伯格曾在接受美国国会听证会质询时公开承认，出于安全考虑，Facebook会收集非注册用户的信息。三是通过黑客技术非法收集隐私信息。如果平台的安全防卫技术不过关，会造成黑客入侵盗取个人隐私信息的案件发生。黑客入侵平台后台后，能够轻易地获取其消费者信息数据库的隐私信息，而且目前的技术无法彻底杜绝这种违法行为。

2. 不当使用造成的消费者隐私信息泄露

互联网平台收集到消费者的隐私信息后，应根据获取信息的条款合理使用信息数据库，以更好地提供服务。然而，在现实中很多互联网平台没有遵守条款，侵害了消费者的权益。一是非法过度开发消费者隐私信息。一般在消费者提供信息时，对这些信息的使用授权仅限于当次的活动，并没有授权平台对这些信息的再次开发和利用。但实际上，有些平台会将这些隐私信息纳入自己的信息数据库中，用于为其经营决策行为提供依据。平台擅自将消费者信息进行再开发和利用，实际上已经侵害了消费者的权益。二是不当泄露消费者隐私信息。由于互联网平台的数据安全意识淡薄及安全防卫技术不过关等原因，导致消费者隐私信息数据库因保存不当而被窃取。三是不当交易隐私信息。因为互联网平台可以通过消费者的隐私信息了解客户的习惯偏好，帮助其作出更合理的经营决策，增加平台经营利润，因此消费者的隐私信息对平台是有价值的。在现实中，有些平台会通过与合作平台交换数据的方式来扩大自己的数据库，有些平台则会通过出售消费者隐私信息的方式来获利，这些行为使消费者的隐私信息泄露的范围越来越大。例如，2017年曝光的现金贷平台通过向数据公司购买数据产品，再通过爬虫技术获得用户的社交网络行为轨迹作为平台放贷前用户风险评估的依据。这就是消费者隐私数据在企业之间交易的案例。而这种交换和交易消费者隐私数据的行为大部分都没有事先征得消费者的同意，侵犯了消费者的隐私权。

从浙江省普惠金融发展调查的数据中可以发现：从年龄看（见图9-4），20岁以下的受访者中接到金融欺诈电话的比例最高，达到57.89%①。随着年龄的增长，接到

① 接到金融欺诈电话占比$=\frac{(0，20]\text{岁受访者接到金融欺诈电话的人数}}{(0，20]\text{岁的受访者人数}}$，其他年龄段的计算方法相同。

金融欺诈电话的人数占所在年龄组总人数的比例逐渐降低，而年龄超过 80 岁的受访者接到金融欺诈电话的比例最低，为 20.83%。因金融诈骗遭受损失的受访者中，趋势与接到金融欺诈电话的情况相同。年龄在 20 岁以下的受访者中因金融诈骗遭受损失的比例最高，达到 5.26%①。随着年龄的提高，因金融诈骗遭受损失的人数占所在年龄组总人数的比例逐渐降低，而年龄超过 80 岁的受访者因金融诈骗遭受损失的比例最低，为 2.08%。这两组数据显示，年轻人较年长者更易遇到金融欺诈电话和遭受损失。在现实生活中，年轻人因接触互联网的途径和时间更多，隐私信息被泄露的情况更严重，由此也更易遭遇金融诈骗。

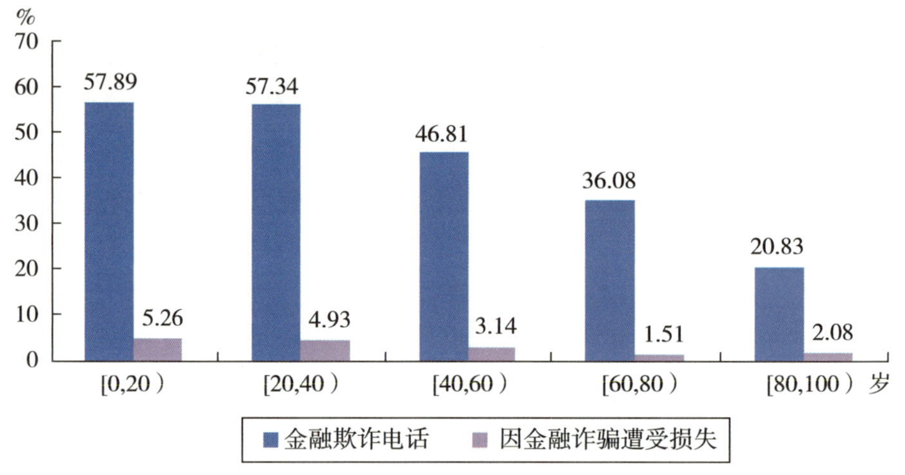

图 9-4　年龄分组

从受访者所在的家庭文化层次来看②，所处家庭中接受高等教育成员人数占比越高的受访者接到金融诈骗电话的比例越多。其中，所处家庭中接受高等教育家庭成员人数占比低于 20%的受访者接到金融欺诈电话的比例为 44.99%，所处家庭中接受高等教育家庭成员人数占比高于 80%的受访者接到金融欺诈电话的比例为 59.92%。因金融诈骗遭受损失的家庭文化层次分布与接到金融欺诈电话的情况相似，所处家庭中高等教育成员人数占比越高的受访者因金融诈骗遭受损失的比例越大，并且所处家庭高等教育家庭成员人数占比最高组（［80，100））的受访者因金融诈骗遭受损失的比例达到了最低组（［0，20））的 2.4 倍。这两组数据显示，家庭文化层次的提高并没有使消费者防范隐私信息泄露的能力增强，反而因为其在生活中接触互联网的机会和途径更多，更易接到金融欺诈电话和遭受财产损失。因此，在保护消费者隐私信息的

① 因金融诈骗遭受损失占比 $=\frac{(0，20]\text{岁受访者因金融诈骗遭受损失的人数}}{(0，20]\text{岁的受访者人数}}$，其他年龄段的计算方法相同。

② 家庭成员中接受高等教育的比例 $=\frac{\text{专科文化程度人数}+\text{本科文化程度人数}+\text{研究生学历人数}}{\text{家庭总人数}}$。

工作中，仅仅依靠消费者通过自身防范是不够的，还需要互联网企业、行业和政府的共同努力。

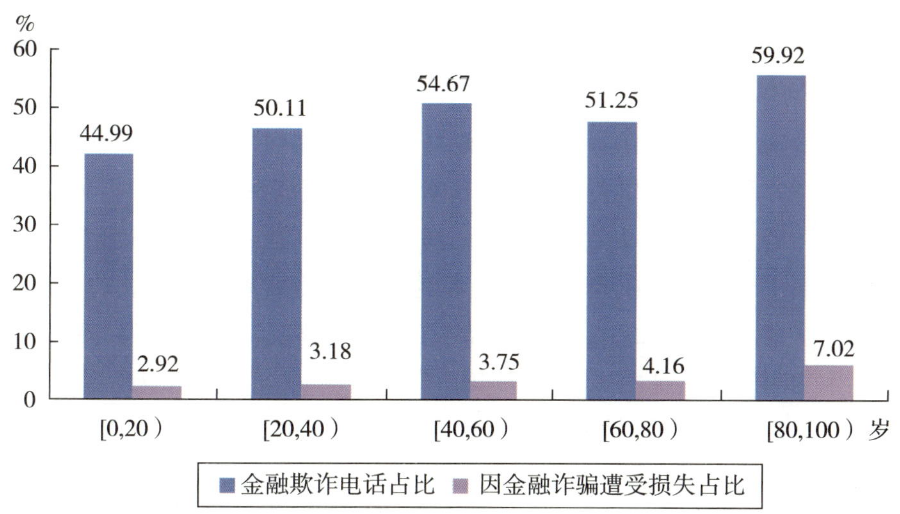

图 9-5　高等教育分组

二、消费者隐私信息保护

通过以上对消费者隐私信息泄露的途径分析可以看出，无论消费者年龄长幼、学历高低，都无法避免在接触互联网后遭受隐私信息泄露的风险，消费者不具备保护自身隐私信息的能力。大多数隐私信息泄露都和互联网平台的经营管理有着密切的关系，消费者隐私数据管理不善不仅会使消费者遭受损失，对平台的信誉及长期发展也有负面影响。因此，保护消费者隐私信息应是企业的义务，也是其经营发展中负责任的体现。企业在保护消费者隐私信息安全中，应具有以下四个方面的义务：

一是提前告知义务。在信息收集环节消费者的隐私信息泄露主要是因为互联网平台在消费者不知情的情况下过度收集、秘密收集信息造成的。根据我国《网络安全法》的知情同意原则，互联网平台应明确告知收集信息的目的、方式和范围，且收集使用消费者个人信息必须经消费者“明示同意”后，即在信息主体通过勾选、点击、发送、拨打等形式作出声明的情况下，才可以进一步收集使用消费者个人信息。

二是安全保障义务。互联网企业对信息保护的忽视和安全技术不过关会造成消费者信息的泄露和丢失。根据《网络安全法》第四十二条的规定：互联网企业应当采取技术措施和其他必要措施，确保其收集的个人信息安全，防止信息泄露、毁损、丢失。在发生或者可能发生个人信息泄露、毁损、丢失的情况时，应当立即采取补救措施，按照规定及时告知用户并向有关主管部门报告。

三是合理使用义务。如果互联网企业对消费者信息的使用出现超过消费者授权范围的情况，如擅自修改、删除、披露、转让、出售，则严重侵害了消费者的权益。根据《消费者权益保护法》《网络安全法》的规定：互联网企业收集、使用消费者个人信息，应当遵循合法、正当、必要的原则。也就是说，互联网企业应通过正当手段，杜绝暗中收集，收集的信息应符合特定的收集目的，并应在承诺的范围内使用。

四是限期持有和妥善销毁义务。数字技术的发展使消费者隐私被收集、储存和传播变得更容易，消费者随时面临数据泄露的风险，互联网企业不应将消费者信息当作自己的资产长期持有，而应在完成与消费者约定的用途后妥善销毁，防止出现隐患。我国《信息安全技术公共及商用服务信息系统个人信息保护指南》《侵权责任法》《网络安全法》中均明确了信息主体有正当理由时，可以要求互联网企业删除其个人信息。这种删除权也适用于互联网企业收集个人信息的特定目的已经完成或双方约定的期限已经届满的情形。

三、我国金融消费者纠纷保护现状

隐私泄露最直接的负面影响是威胁了消费者的人身财产安全，造成金融纠纷和恶劣的社会影响。当消费者的信息落入不法分子手中后，最常见的行为是通过隐私信息获取消费者信任后进行电信诈骗，如电话诈骗、网络诈骗、短信诈骗等。2016 年轰动全国的“徐玉玉案”就是电信诈骗带来的恶果。除了电信诈骗，盗用消费者隐私信息进行违法犯罪活动也非常普遍，如盗刷信用卡、用他人身份办理银行卡进行违法犯罪活动等。当消费者遇到此类纠纷时，应该如何处理纠纷、挽回损失呢？在浙江省的调查中，我们发现当受访者因金融诈骗遭受损失后（见图 9－6），47％的受访者在遭受

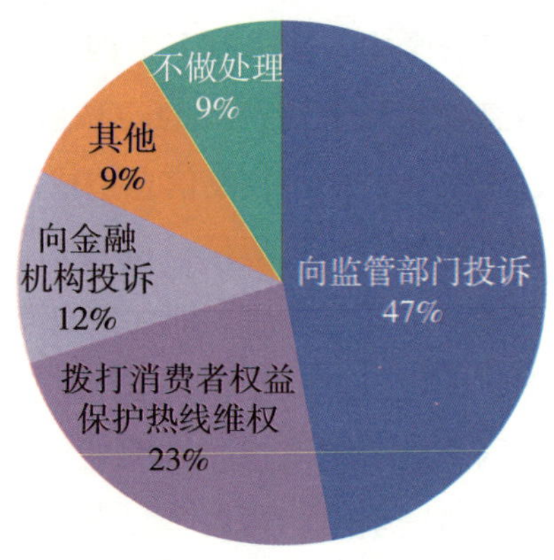

图 9－6　遭受损失后，会寻求的挽回损失途径占比

损失后会向监管部门投诉，23%的受访者会拨打消费者权益保护热线进行维权，12%的受访者会向金融机构投诉，9%的受访者采取其他手段，另外还有9%的受访者不做处理。可见，大部分人在因金融诈骗遭受损失后都会积极采取措施挽回损失。

目前我国消费者遇到金融纠纷时，主要有以下四种途径解决纠纷：

（一）金融机构内部投诉解决

我国的金融机构大都设立有内部的消费者纠纷投诉处理机制，包括但不限于设立专门的客服投诉电话、网络投诉反馈平台以及在网点柜台配置专职的客服人员和大堂经理等投诉处理渠道。一般情况下，这些内部投诉处理机制会成为消费者在纠纷发生后最先寻求帮助的重要渠道。作为最基础的纠纷解决机制，绝大多数的日常纠纷都能通过这个渠道得到解决，但是一旦消费者遭遇到较大的实质性经济损失时，内部投诉处理机制往往很难有效地解决问题。一方面，内部纠纷解决部门的执行权力不足，机构内部部门协调效率低。当涉及金额较大时，内部纠纷解决部门需要向上级主管部门汇报有关情况，而上级部门需要充分了解纠纷的前因后果后才作出决定，这一系列的过程耗时长，不利于损失的追回。另一方面，是饱受诟病的金融机构既当“运动员”又当“裁判员”问题，这在客观上使机构难免出现偏袒自身的情况，使消费者在主观上难以相信其公正性。

（二）行政申诉解决

我国现在的金融监管机构——中国银保监会除了对分管行业内的机构进行监管，还下设消费者权益保护局，其责任包括拟定行业内消费者权益保护的总体规划和实施办法、调查处理损害消费者权益案件、组织办理消费者投诉及开展教育工作。中国人民银行同样设有一个名为金融消费者权益保护局的部门，负责居中协调处理跨市场、跨行业的金融产品和服务涉及的消费者保护问题。除上述的监管机构之外，中国消费者协会也是进行行政申诉的主要对象。上述的行业监管委员会及其下属的消费者权益保护局看似涵盖了金融市场的方方面面，但是在保护金融消费者权益的实际操作中却仍旧困难重重。虽然中国银监会与中国保监会实现了合并，跨出了混业监管的第一步，但是面对已经高度交叉创新、混业经营的金融市场及复杂的金融消费纠纷案件，纠纷解决的成效和效率依然较为低下。

（三）仲裁和诉讼等法律方式解决

当金融消费者内部投诉得不到解决且行政申诉也没有成果时，就会转向仲裁机构或法院来寻求公道。仲裁不同于诉讼，它需要争议双方自愿达成协议才能进行，同时仲裁一经作出即发生法律效力，即便当事人对裁决不满，也不能就同一案件向法院起诉。由此可以看出，仲裁具备公正、高效的特点，且保密性强，收费往往较诉讼更为低廉。但在现实中，金融仲裁并未被消费者广泛采用。其原因在于市面上大多数金融产品的合同上对于争议解决方式都是默认为法院诉讼，消费者基本没有选择的权力。金融机构这么做的原因就是故意规避消费者使用仲裁这一机制，因为相对于消费者而言，金融机构往往配备有相应的法务处理部门，具备有优势的资金、能力和人员处理漫长的纠纷事务，快速解决纠纷对其而言并没有显而易见的好处。相反，在与金融机构漫长的斡旋中，消费者往往会因为各种压力选择放弃，拖延得越久对机构越有利。

（四）公众舆论维权

随着互联网技术发展的深入，大众传媒的发展越发多样化，同时民众也逐渐意识到媒体具有不可估量的社会影响力，可以凝聚社会各界的力量和智慧来“声讨”不公事件，并促进问题的解决。因此，不少消费者会选择向媒体曝光违规金融机构，并利用微信传播、微博转发、网上发帖等方式给金融机构制造舆论压力，迫使其更积极地解决纠纷问题。然而，这样的做法很容易激发金融机构与消费者间的对抗情绪，甚至可能会使金融机构转变思路变本加厉地想办法从源头进一步剥夺消费者维权的能力，站在消费者的角度，长期的舆论对立也可能导致群体性事件的发生，造成恶劣的社会影响。

四、消费者隐私信息保护与纠纷解决建议

（一）消费者隐私信息保护的建议

1. 提升保护技术

网络技术的发展使互联网企业拥有庞大的消费者信息数据库，但是如果对数据库管理不当，不仅会对消费者造成巨大的损失，也会影响自身的信誉与发展。同时，由于法律对消费者信息保护立法的压力，多数互联网企业会通过增加技术研发力度来保护消费者的隐私信息，如加密技术、匿名发布技术、时空融合的角色访问控制、附加第三方审计技术等。互联网企业对于消费者信息保护在任何时候都不能掉以轻心，应随时根据行业发展的新变化做好隐私信息保护技术的升级与创新，确保对消费者信息负责任。

2. 建立统一法律

目前，我国有关个人信息保护的法律分散于各部门中，尚未专门制定个人信息保护的法律，如《刑法》中规定将非法获取和提供个人信息入罪。《消费者权益保护法》

《网络安全法》等也都规定了对个人信息权的保护。这种分散化的立法模式使个人信息保护在实践中缺乏协调性，导致保护的责任义务不清、打击力度不够、执行困难等问题。因此，建议构建统一的消费者信息保护法律体系，明确在消费者信息保护过程中各方的责任，监督行业的规范发展。

3. 规范行业自律

由于统一法律体系在短期内很难建立，而保护消费者信息迫在眉睫，建议设立行业自律组织作为保护主体来保护消费者的个人信息。一方面，行业自律组织作为业内统一的监管和协调机构，能够更准确深入地了解业内的发展与变化，及时发现不合规现象，帮助法律政策的贯彻和落实，同时弥补了法律滞后性的缺陷，避免了实际操作与监管制度之间出现脱节的情况。另一方面，行业自律组织通过建立行业内统一的标准，能够逐渐统一行业的隐私保护水平，避免不同机构之间隐私保护能力差距过大，有利于提高行业的整体消费者隐私保护能力。

（二）解决金融纠纷的建议

1. 金融机构提高重视度

金融机构是金融消费者遇到金融纠纷中最先求助的部门。由于机构内部牵扯的部门众多且缺乏监管机构，金融机构在应对消费者的投诉时效率很难提高。为了更好地帮助消费者解决纠纷，首先，机构应该赋予内部纠纷解决部门更高的权限，确保在解决纠纷的过程中可以调动各个部门的配合。其次，将消费者金融纠纷解决效果作为绩效考核的内容之一，提高机构内配合解决纠纷的积极性。最后，加强外部监管机构对金融机构的监督，确保金融机构会重视消费者权益的保护。

2. 打通诉讼通道

当消费者遭遇金融纠纷时，大部分人都会采取法律诉讼的手段维护自己的权利。为了保护消费者的权益，挽回消费者的损失，不仅需要立法严惩违法犯罪行为，也要打通消费者的诉讼通道。按照我国现行的诉讼制度，消费者权益诉讼严格执行诉讼程序规定，耗时长、成本大。为了帮助消费者更有效地维权，一方面，应简化诉讼程序，通过设立专门的巡回法庭等方法帮助当事人尽快解决纠纷，让消费者及时诉讼，早日挽回损失；另一方面，应建立有利于消费者维权的诉讼费用制度。根据现行诉讼法律规定，所有诉讼需缴纳一定费用，如果原告败诉需自行承担诉讼费。在很多涉及金额较少的纠纷中消费者因顾虑诉讼费用而放弃法律途径维权。因此，应考虑通过降低相关诉讼费用的方式保护弱势群体。

3. 引导消费者增强自我保护意识

很多消费者遇到金融纠纷的原因在于对自己的隐私信息没有保护意识，同时无法识别因此产生的金融诈骗，最终导致纠纷产生。政府职能部门要加强对消费者的宣传力度，让消费者提高警惕性，不断学习保护个人隐私信息的知识，熟悉金融诈骗的特征，掌握遭遇金融纠纷时的解决途径。例如，充分利用网络媒体、宣传册、条幅等形式让大众逐渐提高自我保护意识，减少遭遇金融纠纷的可能。

第十章　以客户为中心

【摘要】以客户为中心的理念是一种商业模式思维。在生产者、消费者、投资者等角色组成的整个经济生态系统中，客户是制定公司策略、重大决定、组织设计和运营的核心。[①] 以客户为中心不仅仅是一种产品设计思路，更是一种企业的文化和管理观念，企业无论处在何种战略方向，都不应只追逐利润，而应将服务客户作为所有工作的重中之重。金融机构通过以客户为中心的理念进行产品开发可以达到增加客户采纳率和使用率、改善市场地位、降低成本以满足特定细分客户群体的需求、满足客户安全和监管要求，以及履行社会责任义务等目标。为帮助读者更好地理解以客户为中心的理念，本章首先讨论了以客户为中心的必要性及难点，进而讨论了以客户为中心的产品设计方法和企业管理理念。最后以中国民生银行为例，详细解释了其小微金融以客户为中心的产品设计思路。

一、以客户为中心的必要性

以客户为中心的理念在《中国普惠金融发展报告（2018）》[②]（以下简称《报告》）中就已提及。《报告》认为，要解决普惠金融“最后一公里”问题，首要方法就是要在思想上转变，把“最后一公里”当成客户服务的“第一公里”，也就是强调做普惠金融服务一定要回归初心，把客户当作服务本体，从以产品为导向转变为以客户为导向。

首先，普惠金融服务的是“中小微弱”等传统金融机构无法服务的客户群体，由

① CGAP. Customer Centric Guide Executive Summary［R］. 2017.

② 贝多广，莫秀根 . 中国普惠金融发展报告（2018）——攻坚“最后一公里”［M］. 北京：中国金融出版社，2018.

于不同人群所需的服务不同，使用产品的方式和自身理解能力也存在较大差距，故将传统金融机构现有服务直接套用在普惠金融客户群体上会出现成本过高、风险较大等问题，这些因素使传统金融机构为这类群体提供服务的动力不足。因此，传统金融机构要想提供普惠金融服务，必须改变现有的面向原有客户群体服务方式，以客户需求为导向和出发点，重新设计产品架构和服务体系。

其次，数字普惠金融的发展极大地降低了普惠金融服务成本，增强了普惠金融的可得性，但同时要求服务提供商能够以客户为中心进行产品设计，尽量减少数字鸿沟，在便捷性、易用性、安全性上均以客户为核心，增强产品竞争力①。例如，互联网小额贷款公司提供的纯信用贷款，通过互联网技术的广覆盖性，依托其自身的大数据技术的风控审核能力，在前端对各种场景进行嵌入匹配，极大地降低了提供普惠金融服务的成本。再加上随借随还的产品灵活性和良好的用户体验，快速获得了大量用户的青睐。

再次，以客户为中心的产品设计更加强调针对不同的客户，根据客户群体的特点，提供不同的金融服务，即注重给客户提供个性化金融服务。而传统的金融服务，尤其是面向大众的零售金融服务，往往是以产品为门槛和依据将客户强行区分，这也就造成对于客户服务的内容并没有任何区别。普惠金融服务往往门槛较低，客户群体多样化，不同的客户所需要的服务种类、数量和产品差异化较大，个性化服务由此产生。例如，格莱珉银行的第一笔贷款是穆罕默德·尤努斯教授将 27 美元借给 42 个贷款者②，这与传统的银行贷款有着巨大的差异。格莱珉银行一开始就将目标客户定位于贫困家庭的妇女群体，已服务约 830 万名借贷者客户，发放贷款总额超过 71 亿美元，其中妇女客户仍约为 98%。格莱珉银行的客户定位非常清晰，就是服务那些非常贫困的社会边缘人群，尤其是妇女和农村地区的穷人，为他们提供小额无须抵押品的贷款，以促进现有的或新建的创收项目。此外，格莱珉式银行后续也开始增加贷款品种，引进房贷、教育贷款等。除了贷款产品，格莱珉银行还帮助贫困人群积累自己的资产，培养储蓄的习惯和能力③。除了格莱珉银行，市场上目前也有大量的信贷产品，灵活的还款期限也是为了更好地满足生产经营的需求，将生产周期与还款周期相匹配，也体现出了普惠金融服务要根据客户提供差异化服务。

最后，普惠金融服务的群体具有可变性④，即普惠金融服务的群体范围是随着金

① 莫秀根．国际普惠金融前沿趋势与经验启示［J］．中国银行业，2018（6）．

② 潘素梅，周立．格莱珉银行的反传统模式及金融普惠［R］．银行家，2016（1）．

③ 穆罕默德·努鲁·阿拉姆，迈克·葛图比，安德里亚·芬德利，等．格莱珉模式小额信贷项目创建和运营指南［M］．格莱珉基金会，2012．

④ 贝多广，李焰．中国普惠金融发展报告（2015）——好金融 好社会［M］．北京：经济管理出版社，2015．

融供求平衡的变化而变化的，这也就要求提供普惠金融服务的产品能随着客户群体范围的变化而作出相应调整，除产品功能性和易用性需要不断完善外，还需时刻明确服务的客户群体范围，了解客户群体行为特征。不应试图改变或挑战客户既有的使用习惯，而应迎合和引导客户，才能让产品保持旺盛持久的生命力。

目前，有些公司市场策略是通过高频度宣传和资本运作，最大化扩张客户群体数量，忽略客户质量，不做客户定位细分，在客户基数足够大后再寻求流量变现的商业模式。对于企业来说，无论是服务资源还是管理资源均是有限的，客户群体的扩大必然会占用企业更多的资源。在技术高速发展的前提下，资源的边际成本可以无限趋近于零，但不代表企业可以为所有潜在客户提供优质服务，因此企业应针对服务的目标客户群体制定不同的产品线和策略。

二、以客户为中心的难点

企业初期往往以产品为中心，尤其是管理层面，注重的是产品竞争力。它们关注如何增加产品功能点、如何快速扩张产品线、增大客户群体基数从而抢占更多的市场份额等，并以这些因素来驱动促进产品迭代升级。但是，随着版本更新、企业规模逐步扩大，管理重心也在发生转变。比如，更加注重成本控制、管理机制规范化、资源整合协作等，即更加注重企业自身发展，而将客户需求和感受抛诸脑后，与客户距离越来越大。取而代之的是各种复杂的内部流程和业绩报告，最终不可避免地落到 KPI（关键绩效指标）导向，以客户为中心的理念越来越淡薄，实现难度也越来越大，最终导致大企业病。

在以产品为中心的发展模式积累了一些成果后，企业开始注重市场需求：收集销售、客户服务等渠道反馈回来的信息；通过市场调研对用户行为进行分析研究。此时产品研发可能会以竞争对手产品为导向，即依据市场热点或者跟随竞争者产品特性来指导产品开发。这种做法虽然能少走一些用户需求调研的弯路，也确实可以满足一部分客户的需求，但未针对自身客户群体需求进行细致分析，仅仅是为了拓宽产品线，以多功能为卖点去盲目开拓市场，最终导致同质化的恶性竞争。产品变得越来越庞大复杂，多数功能对多数用户来说都是用不到的，这对客户来说是一种巨大的浪费。这也是市场上一种很常见的现象：某软件或服务取得一些业绩后，就会放弃专注度而开始不断做加法，只为了扩大客户基数。

以客户为中心的理念强调的是产品的开发和业务机制要从客户需求出发，以用户需求驱动产品设计和迭代，在客户个性化需求与商业价值之间取得平衡。企业在提供高质量、安全服务的同时，能保障客户正当权益和优秀的使用体验。用户数量并非越多越好，给产品功能做减法远比做加法难得多，为 80%的用户群做到 200%的满意度比为 120%的用户群做到 60%的满意度更重要。目前的企业都加速了产品的更新迭代以确保竞争力，客户需求和期望越来越受到企业重视，也就逐渐汇聚成了市场需求，以市场为中心的经营思想与以客户为中心的产品开发理念正在走向统一。

三、以客户为中心的产品设计方法

（一）以客户为中心的产品设计原则

客户的真实需求需要经过高度提炼和理解后，才能转化为产品需求。因此，以客户为中心的产品设计原则就是在能力范围内最大限度地满足客户的需求，并且针对普惠金融客户的特点，在产品设计时要充分考虑用户的理解能力、使用习惯等因素，针对特定客户群体开发出符合用户特点的产品。当然，在实际研发和设计的过程中，往往会受到技术、成本、时间等因素的制约，这就需要开发者在商业价值和用户需求之间取得平衡。

（二）以客户为中心的产品设计流程

以客户为中心的产品设计主要步骤包括但不限于：用户需求分析、系统/业务设计、产品开发与实现、产品生命周期管理等，具体开发流程如图 10－1 所示。

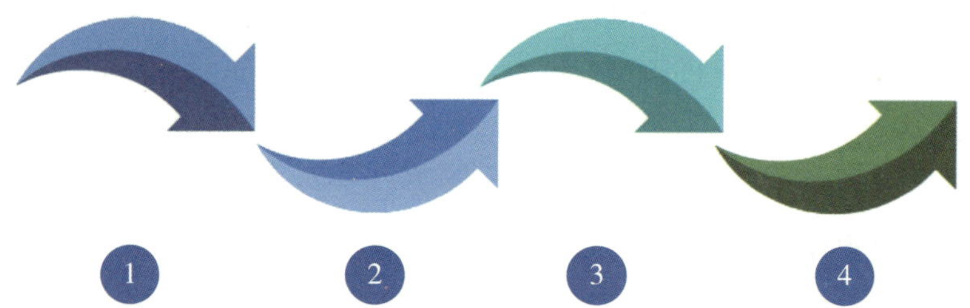

图 10－1　以客户为中心的产品开发流程

1. 用户需求分析

在做设计时要充分了解客户。要获得新的市场机遇或提高客户满意度，需要对目标客户群体的需求、使用产品的动机和期望有充分了解。有研究表明，客户满意度每提升 1%，厂商的投资回报率会提高 2.37%；客户满意度每降低 1%，厂商的投资回报率会降低 5.08%[①]。了解客户是整个产品设计思路的依据与来源，企业可以从定量和

① CGAP. Customer Centric Guide Executive Summary [R]. 2017.

定性两个方面对客户进行分析。

定量是分析客户历史数据以便精准描绘客户群体画像，从而提炼出客户总体特征。在此基础上可以做客户数据的深度挖掘，对客户的发展趋势作出预测性分析。随着产品和服务的版本更替和发展实施，不同客户群体对产品的接受度和使用习惯也在发生变化。竞争对手产品特性异同和使用场景细分使用户越来越难以引导，所以培养、尊重用户使用习惯从而巩固客户忠诚度、加强客户黏度非常重要。企业可依据上述要素作出分析，有针对性地提出产品的未来开发规划。

除了使用历史数据对用户进行定量分析，对用户的定性分析也同样重要。定性分析包括了解客户使用产品和服务时的用例场景、不同客户群体对产品的关注点和使用习惯、客户选择使用/不使用产品和服务的理由等，这些定性信息涉及心理学、行为金融学等内容，可以描绘客户对于产品的看法，而使用产品时的心理变化，对于分析和培养用户的使用习惯及产品的发展方向有重要的参考价值。

在数字普惠金融领域，头部的数字金融平台已经累积了大量的客户数据。这是平台分析客户画像的宝贵资源，应充分利用并作出预测性和战略性的分析。有些企业会直接聘用市场调研机构去做客户调研，通过调查问卷等方式，将答案进行分类汇总，当作客户需求的参考。但这种方式受到调查问题、调查环境和被调查群体心态等因素的影响，往往只能得到片面的或有修饰的需求。以客户为中心强调的是要准确理解客户的需求，而不是只听市场调研的一面之词，应花费更多时间与客户深入交流，无论是当前的优质客户、历史客户还是潜在客户，均可在定性方面了解他们真实的需求和偏好。

除了解客户真实需求，将客户的众多需求进行提炼深化，挖掘其背后的潜在逻辑也是以客户为中心理念的重要步骤。多数客户并不能准确表述出自己的需求且带有强烈的主观性，所以在提炼真实需求时要有良好的产品感和用户思维。这一点在普惠金融领域尤为关键：普惠金融服务的群体以“中小微弱”群体为主，这类群体的需求一般比较直接、单一，注重实用性且关注点相对集中，对产品的其他需求和要素表达能力偏弱，因此更需要不断追问和引导，挖掘出他们的真实需求。之后，在众多普惠金融群体看重的需求点中将真实需求进行重要性排序，再结合产品需求，制定出符合客户需要的产品。在集成产品开发（Integrated Product Development，IPD）模式中，有八个方面可以衡量客户对产品的关注和重要性：价格、可获得性、包装、性能、易用性、保证性、生命周期成本和社会接受程度①。

① PITTIGLIO RABIN TODD，MCGRATH. 产品及生命周期优化法［M］. PRTM公司，1986.

2. 系统/业务设计

有了客户细化分析后，就可以着手设计相应的金融产品解决方案，即以合理的方式将客户需求产品化。首先要做的是把需求分析转为产品的功能点/业务点，初步建立起系统架构，然后落实为技术基础属性。在做产品基本技术基础属性分析时，要梳理出产品的核心技术构成，然后从系统架构角度总结产品的基本技术需求。为增强产品的竞争力，往往会为产品增加一些企业自己的创意属性，甚至不只是纯技术方面的创新，还可能包括服务、营销、购买便利性等其他与用户相关的功能点。接下来就需要将用户的真实需求进行优先级排序，梳理最高优先级的需求，并依据现有的开发框架、团队资源等客观因素进行相关分析并计算出产品各个功能设计的权重值。针对权重值较高的产品功能进行评估，如果与预期用户需求符合，则确定设计方案，反之则需要调整产品功能点/业务点。在系统和业务设计过程中，也需要设计人员反复与产品的特点相结合，通过产品实现的过程不断更新系统和业务设计思路，进而作出真正符合客户需求的产品。

3. 产品开发与实现

在开发与产品实现过程中，一定要在客户和产品需求两个方面作出权衡取舍，即规划出产品的发展方向、成本、商业目标等与客户的真实需求进行最大限度的匹配，以提升产品竞争力。在此过程中，需要不断强化产品核心流程，优先实现客户最核心的需求。在产品实现过程中，由于普惠金融客户对金融知识的掌握不够丰富，故需要着重考虑客户使用习惯、理解能力和对新产品的接受度等因素。将金融业务的术语和流程进行简化、通俗化，以方便客户理解使用。

下面以互联网金融产品为例，分析在服务普惠金融客户时，以客户为中心的产品应考虑哪些因素。

针对普惠金融客户，要强调金融产品的风险性。在互联网金融产品中，风险性、收益性和流动性都是非常重要的产品特点。尤其是风险性，是多数企业重点关注的，要充分提示客户各金融产品风险，不能只强调高收益和便捷性。由于金融产品具有专业性和复杂性，与普惠金融服务群体的距离感较强，因此在用户使用普惠金融产品时，能否产生安全感非常重要，这要求普惠金融产品在设计过程中充分考虑用户的理解能力和关注点，将关乎用户切身利益的重要信息简洁、清晰、准确、完整地展示出来，让用户易于理解且不能出现歧义，对于产品也有可控感和确定感，这也要求设计师对产品和业务有深刻的理解。比如，直接告诉用户采取等额本息的方式还款，会让用户困惑这是什么还款方式。不如将还款日和还款金额等信息直接列出，让用户更加清楚自己未来的还款安排。另外，为满足风险控制和监管要求，在购买产品时往往需要客户填写个人信息并验证真实性，这给客户带来了个人信息的不安全感。金融产品都有相应的政策要求，要取得符合政策规定、满足用户需求和商业利益三者之间的平衡。这就需要产品经理在业务流程框架下做好细致的设计，减少不必要的信息噪声，将政策要求及时准确地呈现给用户；在流程中尽量减少不必要的信息录入；可使用导航或者标签页方式让客户知道目前处于业务流程中的哪个环节；通过操作界面给客户带来流程的安全感和确定感。除此之外，用户在查看、购买产品时也需要系统反馈信息的呈现，以提高客户对产品的掌控感和信任度。由于普惠金融产品的群体对于金融产品要素较为陌生，故需要较多的信息反馈来提示客户如何操作。同时，还可辅以短信、微信、手机 APP、电话等方式进行系统通知①。

4. 产品生命周期管理

在将客户需求产品化后，就进入了优化迭代更新的产品生命周期管理阶段。此阶段仍需通过定量与定性的方式梳理客户新增和变更的需求，不断积累，为下次产品迭代升级做好准备。例如，持续观察用户数据的变化，利用数据分析客户在哪些环节流失较多，在哪些环节出现的问题和投诉较多，有针对性地进行修改或优化。优化的方向大到产品的流程、小到产品样式等均需结合用户反馈和已有用户习惯仔细考量。在此过程中，需要进一步结合反馈对新客户、老客户和已流失客户等客户类型进行分析调研，了解用户在产品使用过程中的真实感受，比如哪些地方设计得比较成功，哪些地方比较烦琐，哪些地方让用户没有安全感等。尤其是针对普惠金融的客户，由于客户在表达需求时往往不够清晰准确，客户与金融产品的距离感也比较强，故在客户真正使用后的感受比最初需求调研阶段更加直观，也就更加具有参考价值。了解客户的产品真实使用体验有利于不断完善用户体验。我们强调要以用户需求驱动产品迭代，但最终目标还要落实到商业目标上，好的产品可以把商业价值和用户需求完美结合，并且能带来持续性效益，从而保证产品的可持续发展。

由于普惠金融客户群普遍需要更好的帮助和引导，且在服务过程中随时可能需要技术支持，即使是在服务后，相应的售后或者催收服务仍是关系到客户体验的关键。所以普惠金融产品除了在设计时要考虑用户体验，相应的配套服务也要做到为客户负责。但目前运营的普遍目标是充分利用客户一切可能的商业价值，而对于客户的真实需求与感受并不在意，甚至会出现虚假宣传、诱导消费、把客户作为广告资源等情况。

用户的生命周期管理主要是为了提升用户的参与度、提升生命周期中每个节点的转化率。这本应是用户自主选择的权利。当通过数据发现某种特征的客户群体正在流失时，应该及时通过用户需求分析，了解他们不选择产品的原因，并及时在产品上作出规划改变，而不是通过红包、折扣或小礼物等方式留住客户，这些方式对于改善用

① 腾讯 Fit Design. 价值在定义——腾讯金融产品体验设计之作［DB/OL］. https：//www.fitdesign.com/，2018.

户体验没有任何意义。用户本身就存在一个从引入期、成长期、成熟期、休眠期最后到流失期的过程，要想长期让客户保持在成长期和成熟期，必须让产品对客户有足够的吸引力，成为用户刚需，形成客户高黏性。即使是已流失的客户，根据不同的阶段也可以分为新手用户流失、成长客户流失和成熟客户流失，针对不同阶段的流失客户，可以制定相应的需求分析方法，了解客户流失的痛点以提高用户体验，形成客户群转化的正向循环。

四、以客户为中心的企业管理理念

企业要想做到以客户为中心的管理，其核心就是要打破传统企业中各个部分单线工作的业务模式，强调为了客户的需求，多个部门之间通过跨部门合作，此时给予客户的服务也不再是某种单一的产品，而是一套全方位的服务体系。例如，从开始接触客户的咨询、选择适合客户的多个产品，到形成产品组合，再到协调多个部门共同为客户提供一整套服务，还包括后续的售后管理服务和增值服务等，进而形成“千人千面”的全流程金融服务。

要想做到以客户为中心的管理理念，就需要管理层将此战略自上而下一起梳理制定，这离不开企业各部门的支持。在人员方面，以客户为中心的发展战略更是强调企业全员参与，使企业中每一位员工都成为客户服务的拥护者，积极与客户交流，获取客户需求信息，即使在不同部门也要协同响应客户的反馈和诉求。在这种战略理念的作用下，可以逐步形成以客户为中心的经营模式和企业文化。

IPD是一套产品开发的模式、理念与方法。核心思想可概括：以客户为开发导向，通过市场驱动来开发产品，把产品开发当成一种投资来管理[①]。IBM公司在应用了IPD的方法后，显著缩短了产品研发周期，降低了产品成本，研发费用占总收入的比率降低，人均产出率大幅提高，提高了产品质量并且浪费在夭折项目上的费用明显减少。客户需求分析和优化投资组合成为市场管理理念。其中，优化投资组合的本质是在客户需求分析后，对产品开发进行有效的投资组合分析，包含投资利润率、成本及资金的对接等。同时，也有跨部门合作、结构化流程、异步开发等对于产品设计而言重要的实际开发理念，将以客户为中心的理念融入公司的治理中。IPD管理框架如图10-2所示。

由于IPD的研发流程体系主要针对大而复杂产品的中大型企业，对于中小型企业并不适用。但是在目前普惠金融的市场中，有头部BATJ[②]这种金融科技公司，也

① 资料来源：https://blog.csdn.net/yy19890521/article/details/82348920。

② BATJ是百度、阿里巴巴、腾讯、京东四大互联网公司的简称。

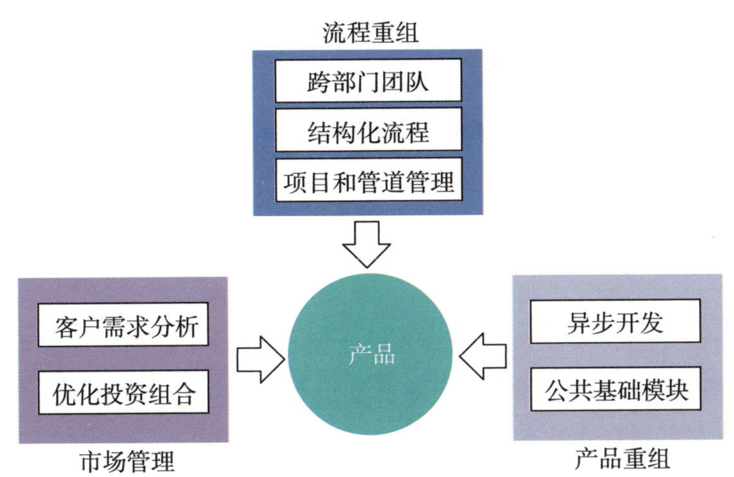

图 10-2 IPD 管理框架

有中小型金融机构和类金融机构服务提供商，更有大型银行开始逐步下沉，纷纷设立子公司或事业部来开展普惠金融业务。这就要求各种大型机构在开展普惠金融业务的同时，公司管理模式不能只是单纯照搬原来的管理体系。由于普惠金融服务群体的特殊性，更需要注重以客户为中心的产品设计理念，这要求大型机构下沉后，必须重新审视自身的管理理念，从企业的价值定位、使命、企业文化等多方面重新规划。不能单纯依靠咨询公司给出的管理解决方案，而是要根据公司已有的业务情况和特点、领导层的战略思路等才能作出真正以客户为中心的普惠金融服务产品①。不能只是形变而神不变，只学习借鉴市场上已有的产品进行研发，而企业的管理方法、对客户的态度和重视程度完全没有变化，这种经营思路对企业长期经营并不利。

总之，金融本身就是伴随信用、风险和杠杆的产业，而普惠金融的客群对于这三点的理解力偏弱，这增大了普惠金融的风险，甚至可能会影响客户金融健康度。例如，2018 年中的 P2P 平台暴雷违约事件，造成了大量客户血本无归。此事件也让人们意识到普惠金融低门槛、高获得性的反面就是风险受众面更广。由于用户风险识别能力较弱，被五花八门的宣传手段和市场技巧所诱惑，造成的损失往往更加巨大。这给普惠金融产品上了重要的一课：一定要在符合政策法规和机构定位的前提下，合理开展业务，对客户负责。企业只有做到以客户为中心进行产品设计，才能使产品得以持续发展，实现商业价值和社会价值的双重目标。

① IPD 在华为成功的 6 个原因［DB/OL］. http://baijiahao.baidu.com/s?id=1598685286567116016.

案例

民生银行小微金融以客户为中心的产品设计思路

民生银行在服务小微客户方面有10余年的发展历程，从开始的单个信贷产品，到后续为小微客户提供多样化、个性化的综合金融服务，逐步探索出了富有民生银行自身特点的小微金融服务模式。在不断更新产品与服务的过程中，民生银行坚持以客户为中心的理念，结合中国小微企业发展的特点和规律，逐步推出了“商贷通”“乐收银”“随身银行”等多种产品服务。

一、民生银行小微金融发展历程

（一）1.0阶段（2008—2011年）：着力推广“商贷通”品牌

在小微金融1.0阶段，民生银行着力打造并推广“商贷通”金融产品，突破传统金融主要服务“高富帅”的窠臼，为小微企业提供融资服务。为降低经营成本，提高服务效率，控制金融风险，此阶段主要针对商圈市场、供应链等小微客户，借助商会、协会、市场管理方，发动全行力量，批量拓展小微商户，快速将贷款规模扩大至2000余亿元。

（二）2.0阶段（2011—2016年）：推进流程再造，并随经济周期进行风险结构调整

在小微金融2.0阶段，民生银行推出“乐收银”等小微结算服务，探索流程再造与集中作业，着力提升作业效率与服务体验，并在2012年推出互助基金贷款后，实现贷款规模快速增长。此外，民生银行不断总结业务经验，加快在风控模式、工具、手段方面的研发与更新的步伐，以增强小微金融可持续经营的能力。

（三）3.0阶段（2017年至今）：数字化推进客群综合经营

从2017年起，民生银行进入小微金融3.0阶段，着力打造小微金融新模式。小微金融3.0新模式内涵是围绕客群细分经营的核心发展逻辑，充分运用大数据、移动互联等新兴技术，打造以智能化、线上化、综合化、专业化为特征的服务体系，构建以主动获客、数据化决策、自动化处理、全流程风控为特征的管理体系，实现小微金融从传统金融向数字金融转变，从融资服务向综合金融服务转变，全面提升客户体验与市场品牌，实现小微金融的健康发展。在此阶段的五大变化如下：

一是多元化的小微企业融资服务。在大数据支持下，民生银行不仅可以为存活时间长、信誉卓越的小微企业提供更富有弹性的融资方案，而且依托数据的集成，为更多初创小微企业提供多样化、个性化的便捷融资支持。

二是基于小微企业习惯的移动金融平台，即小微企业“随身银行”。民生银行

着力增加手机银行APP在小微企业家手里的高频率使用，成为提升企业财务管理的智能终端和财富管理的利器，实现“让数据多跑路，让客户少往返”。

三是首创的“小微红包”。民生银行借鉴互联网企业在用户体验上的成功经验，在主动降低财务负担的同时，创新推出“小微红包”，使金融服务更加人性化，同时陆续打通企业主与其家属、企业的账户互通，从多方面着力解决小微企业“融资贵”。

四是智慧支付系列解决方案。民生银行通过市场调研发现，越来越多的小微企业急需高效、快捷的收付款管理，尤其是在民办教育培训、特色专科医疗、连锁超市收银、房屋中介服务等便民领域均有较大需求，为此民生银行小微金融整合科技优势资源，为广大小微企业提供“智慧支付”系列解决方案，帮助提升生产效率、降低运营成本。

五是创新深度个性化的小微金融服务。民生银行除了在财富管理、投资、子女教育、VIP服务等方面深度拓展，还基于小微企业主能力建设、管理提升、事业拓展等需求，创新相关行业特色服务。

二、以客户为中心的重点产品及服务

（一）搭建完整产品体系，提供差异化、专属化产品服务

经过多年的探索与创新实践，已建立完整的小微金融产品体系，覆盖小微客户的综合服务需求，根据客户实际情况及个性化要求，提供可靠、便捷、差异化、专属化的产品与服务。

一是在支付结算服务方面，为小微客户开发了二维码收银台、智能POS机等小微专属支付结算工具，提供“校付通”“享乐租”等行业结算应用，满足小微客户结算及财务管理需求；为小微企业提供低成本、便捷化开户服务，解决小微企业“开户难”，小微企业“云账户”产品，可以做到3分钟线上申请、3小时审核通过、30分钟网点交付。

二是在综合服务方面，通过专属理财、保险及基金等财富管理产品，其中包括针对小微客户资金灵活使用、进出频繁的特点，推出流动性强、安全性高的小微专属存款及投资理财产品；针对小微客户保障需求特点，推出“借款人+”系列保险，为企业债务和家庭之间建立“防火墙”，隔离风险，传承财富；推出团体重疾险、终身寿险、医疗险等保险品种，为小微企业主、小微企业及家庭提供综合保障。此外，民生银行还提供了经济与行业资讯及账务管理、税务代报等增值服务，帮助小微客户解决内部控制不健全、财务管理工作薄弱的问题。

（二）持续优化业务流程，提升客户体验

民生银行小微金融持续优化业务流程与作业标准，多措并举压缩小微企业信贷

业务所需的办理时间。推广集中运营等标准化作业模式，充分运用新兴技术，通过移动PAD运营方式，实现作业模式提升变革，提高作业效率，同时推动运营成本与操作成本的持续降低；根据客户、产品、金额等不同维度，制定并实施材料收集、业务受理等方面的标准化、差异化流程，提高审批效率和一次通过率；积极对接房管、社保、税务等当地政府服务平台，秉承“让客户少往返”的思想，优化审结到放款的业务流。

（三）非金服务，助力小微企业客户成长

除了金融服务，民生银行小微金融也在发展非金融服务，以更好地为小微企业主服务。2017年，民生银行小微金融开展了“致美小微”大型品牌营销活动，活动以发现、寻找的镜头，鼓励现有的民生银行小微企业主讲述自己为梦想打拼、一路走来的艰辛与奋斗历程，赋予成功独特意义的正能量故事。民生银行小微金融作为见证企业发展的金融服务机构，助力小微企业在市场中的推广，由民生银行小微金融出资，将企业的真实情感故事拍摄成短视频，帮助小微企业主塑造企业品牌形象，并运用多种线上媒体进行传播，沉淀品牌阶段性传承核心素材，为企业提供不一样的非金融增值服务。

第十一章 合适的金融服务价格

【摘要】普惠金融强调引导整个金融体系全面参与，均衡配置社会资源，满足各个层面客户的金融需求，实现长远的可持续发展。合理的金融服务价格主要由客户的需求和金融机构的供给能力决定。客户的需求可以从个人特征、金融行为、金融能力等维度的变量来判断，而金融机构的供给能力则应充分考虑资金成本、运营成本及风险成本。价格管制会造成贷款难、过度贷和民间融资盛行等问题，违反了普惠金融包容性的原则。以客户为中心开发金融产品、有效利用市场机制定价才能真正提供既普又惠的金融服务。

一、金融服务需求

（一）包容性曲线

有需求才有市场，金融服务需求是决定合理金融服务价格的重要因素。有效需求是指有能力并且愿意按某一价格购买商品或服务。通过对影响需求的诸多因素进行分析，我们可以对不同客群的需求进行预测，进而制定合理的市场价格。中国普惠金融研究院于2018年在浙江省丽水市展开了针对普惠金融发展状况的调研。下面我们以调研所得的3027份数据为基础，深入分析金融服务的需求弹性及需求影响因子。

金融市场利率是资本使用权的价格，即借贷资本的价格，它是金融资产价值的表现形式。根据调查问卷中贷款年化利率及可接受贷款人数数据，我们近似画出样本中个人对贷款服务的需求曲线。对于普惠金融分析来说，这个需求曲线具有非常重要的意义，它揭示的不是价格与数字的关系，而是价格与金融服务参与者数量的关系，表示着价格的降低，在多大程度上能够增加信贷服务的包容性。

如图11－1所示，当可以接受的贷款利率大于30％时，价格需求弹性非常小，意

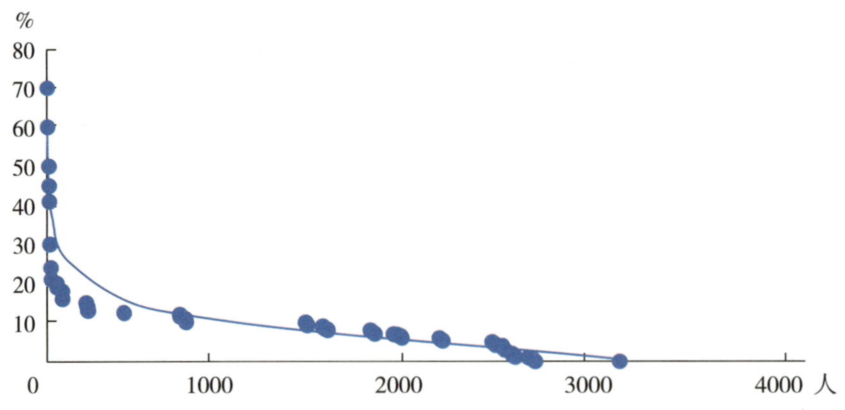

图 11－1　贷款年化利率与可接受的贷款人数的关系

味着金融服务需求者对价格非常不敏感，这部分消费者愿意为了得到相应的金融服务而付出较高的价格。或者说，当利率水平大于 30%时，利率变化不影响金融服务的包容性，当利率低于 10%时，价格需求弹性则较大，意味着处于这一区间的金融服务需求者对价格非常敏感。降低利率可以大幅增加贷款业务的包容性，反之亦然。对于可接受利率为 10%～30%的消费者，其价格需求弹性相对更接近单位弹性，即适度的贷款利率的变化会导致适度的金融服务需求变化。值得注意的是，被调研者中，处于不敏感区间的人数很少，只有 0.5%；超过一半（54.76%）的被调研者对贷款利率的变化处于非常敏感的区间（见图 11－2）。

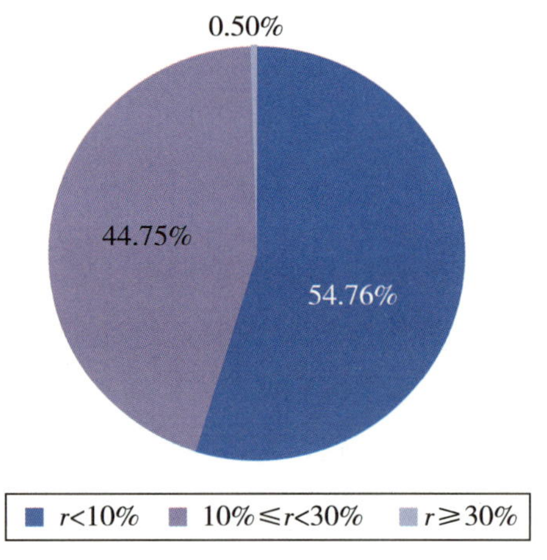

图 11－2　最高可接受利率人数分布

（二）包容性曲线的影响因素

为了进一步了解决定金融服务需求的变量，我们对调查问卷中的个人特征、金融行为及金融能力等相关变量进行回归分析。其中，个人特征变量包括年龄、性别、受教育程度、是否有配偶、是否为户主、子女数、工作性质、年收入、家庭成员数、医疗保险情况；金融行为变量包括互联网使用情况、储蓄或理财习惯、过去贷款经历、储蓄卡及信用卡数量、ATM及银行服务可得性、第三方支付使用情况、网上购物情况；金融能力变量包括过去学习金融服务的情况、过去向他人请教金融知识的情况、风险承受能力及家庭信用等级。我们选用OLS模型对上述变量进行回归，结果如表11-1所示。

1. 个人特征变量

年龄与可接受最高贷款利率呈负相关关系，即年龄越大可接受的最高贷款利率越低。这可能是由于相对于年轻人，年长者收入来源更多，对贷款的需求比较小，对风险的意识比较强。相对于只接受了初等教育的人群（初中及以下），接受过高等教育（大专、本科和研究生教育）的人群可接受的最高贷款利率更低；而接受了中等教育（高中）的人群可接受的最高贷款利率则与初等教育人群无显著差别。工作性质对消费者可接受的最高贷款利率也有显著的影响。与从事务农的人群相比，从事私营工商业的人群可接受的贷款利率更高。个人年收入也与可接受最高贷款利率呈正相关关系：年收入越高的人群，其可接受的最高贷款利率越高。类似地，家庭成员数越多，其可接受的最高贷款利率越高。相对于有社会医疗保险的人群，没有社会医疗保险的人群可接受的最高贷款利率更低。其他的个人特征变量如性别、有无配偶、是否为户主、子女数等对可接受的最高贷款利率无显著影响。

2. 金融行为变量

贷款经历、互联网使用频率、金融服务的可得性及第三方支付的使用情况都是影响个人可接受最高贷款利率的因素。相比上一年无贷款经历的个人，上一年家里有向银行申请贷款经历的个人可以接受更高的贷款利率；而相对于低频或从不使用互联网的个人，每天都使用互联网的人群可接受的最高贷款利率更低。附近银行或农村信用社网点越近，说明金融服务的可得性越高，回归结果也证明金融服务可得性越高，个人群接受的最高贷款利率越高。相对于不使用第三方支付的人群，使用电脑或手机进行第三方支付的人群可以接受更高的贷款利率。总体而言，对金融服务可得性和使用频率更高的人群，能够接受的最高贷款利率更高，这可能是由于这部分人群对金融服务的需求、了解程度与使用满意度比较高。

3. 金融能力的变量

值得注意的是，体现金融能力的变量都对可接受最高贷款利率有显著影响。我们发现，相比过去一年没有向别人请教过网银和手机银行等服务的人群，有请教过的人群可以接受更高的贷款利率；然而，相比没有学习过经济或金融课程的人群，学习过相关课程的人群可接受的最高贷款利率反而更低。这种结果可能是由于个人对金融服

表 11-1　OLS 回归结果

变量	参数值	标准差	变量	参数值	标准差
个人特征（Intercept）	6.416***	1.139	金融行为		
年龄	−0.03693**	0.013	家里开通了有线互联网	0.407	0.260
中等教育（高中）	0.0089	0.273	家里的闲置资金有用于储蓄或理财	0.019	0.219
高等教育（大专、本科、研究生）	−1.038713**	0.397	个人拥有智能手机	0.0419	0.413
女	−0.355	0.251	互联网使用频率（每天）	−0.606767*	0.263
无配偶（离婚、丧偶、未婚）	0.464	0.394	互联网使用频率（从不使用）	0.0958	0.424
是户主	−0.024	0.276	银行存折数量	−0.0614	0.077
子女数（独生子女）	−0.265	0.367	银行储蓄卡数量	0.0259	0.072
子女数（两个及两个以上）	−0.549	0.410	信用卡数量	0.034	0.111
工作性质（私营工商业）	1.185346***	0.283	最近银行或农村信用社距离（公里）	0.0576*	0.024
工作性质（其他）	−0.190	0.222	最近 ATM 距离（公里）	0.005	0.023
个人年收入	0.160791***	0.043	使用手机端的第三方支付	0.861929**	0.278
家庭成员总数	0.185933*	0.074	使用电脑端的第三方支付	1.542544*	0.721
其他类型医疗保险	0.287	0.400	进行网上购物	−0.444724	0.252
无社会医疗保险	−1.029141*	0.474	使用过电商提供的消费信贷	0.438	0.376

续表

变量	参数值	标准差	变量	参数值	标准差
未来 6 个月内有借款需求	0.217	0.269	曾经学习过经济或金融的课程	−0.653695*	0.302
使用移动支付的频率（每天）	−0.416	0.344	过去一年有向亲戚朋友等请教学用网银和手机银行等	0.489983*	0.224
使用移动支付的频率（每周 1～4 次）	−0.275	0.325			
使用移动支付的频率（每月 1～3 次）	−0.376	0.329	为了获得极高收益而承担极高金融风险	−0.298	0.362
储蓄习惯（不储蓄，花的比赚的多）	−0.334	0.426	为了获得高于平均水平的收益而承担高于平均水平的金融风险	−0.230	0.307
储蓄习惯（不储蓄，赚多少花多少）	0.436	0.445			
储蓄习惯（每月规律储蓄）	0.277	0.268	为了获得平均水平的收益而承担平均水平的金融风险	0.762823**	0.258
金融能力					
家庭信用等级（AA 级）	−0.035	0.243	为了获得略低于平均水平的收益而承担略低于平均水平的金融风险	1.048112***	0.303
家庭信用等级（A 级）	0.260	0.258			
家庭信用等级（非信用户）	−0.739	0.351	曾经因为金融诈骗而遭受损失	−0.861	0.471

注：＊＊＊表示为 $P<0.01$；＊＊表示为 $P<0.05$；＊表示为 $P<0.1$。

务和产品的认知不同所造成的。课程相对更系统，可以使个人对金融知识的掌握更全面；而请教他人的结果则相对比较片面，个人可能对风险等因素缺乏全面的了解。至于家庭信用等级变量，调查结果显示，具体处于哪一等级（如 AAA 级、AA 级、A 级）对最高可接受贷款利率并无显著影响，但是相对于有家庭信用等级的人群来说，没有家庭信用等级的人群可接受的最高贷款利率更低。另外，风险承受能力也是个人可接受最高贷款利率的决定因素之一。我们通常认为，可接受的风险越高，可接受的最高贷款利率就越高。然而，我们的调研数据显示，与不愿承受任何金融风险的人群相比，愿意承受相对较高金融风险的人群可接受的最高贷款利率水平并无显著差别；而愿意接受平均或偏低金融风险水平的人群，则能够接受更高的贷款利率水平。

通过对浙江丽水市的案例分析可知，金融服务消费者的个人特征、金融行为及金融能力等都会对他们的金融服务需求产生不同程度的影响。若不考虑特定客群的特定特征，则很容易错误预测金融服务消费者的需求，进而导致不合理的市场定价。同时我们也发现，一些理论上会对消费者可接受最高贷款利率造成影响的因子，如储蓄和理财的习惯，实际上并无显著影响。因此，金融机构应对不同金融产品的目标客群进行精准画像，从而更好地对金融服务消费者的需求作出判断。

二、金融服务供给

在经济学中，产品的供给由生产者的边际成本决定。就金融产品而言，其边际成本一般包含资金成本、运营成本及风险成本。合适的金融服务或产品的价格应该能够充分覆盖资金成本、运营成本及风险成本。下面分别对这三类成本进行讨论。

（一）资金成本

资金成本是指金融机构通过各种途径获得资金的占有和使用时所要支付的费用。换而言之，资金成本是资金所有者凭借其对资金所有权向资金使用者索取的报酬，如股东的股息、红利、债券及银行借款支付的利息等。

相比其他金融机构，商业银行的资金成本相对较低。商业银行的主要资金来源是客户的存款，资金成本主要是利息成本，是银行以货币形式直接支付给存款人或债权人的报酬，如支付给客户存款的利息、同业拆借资金利息及中央银行贷款利息等。在第二章我们提到，根据对 37 家银行的年报数据进行统计，得出不同种类银行的资金成本，其算术平均值为 2.35%（见图 11－3）。对于网贷、小贷，乃至持牌消费金融公司等主要服务于不能从传统农金融机构获得金融服务的小微企业和个人，资金成本较高。根据对 400 家小额贷款公司的调研数据，我们测算出小额贷款公司的加权平均融资成本为6.3%，各种途径的融资成本如图11-4所示。

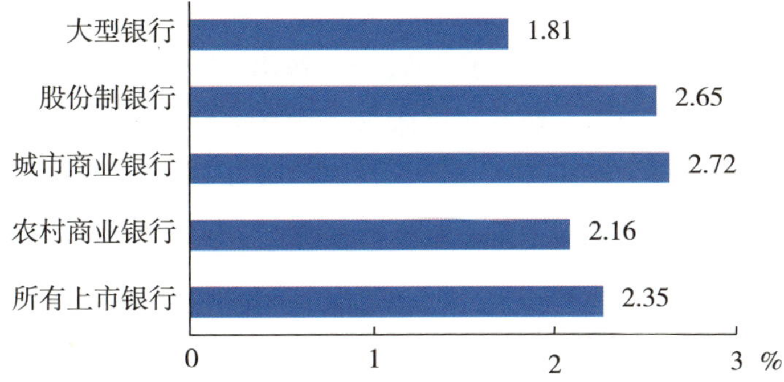

资料来源：37家商业银行2018年年报。

图11-3 银行的资金成本

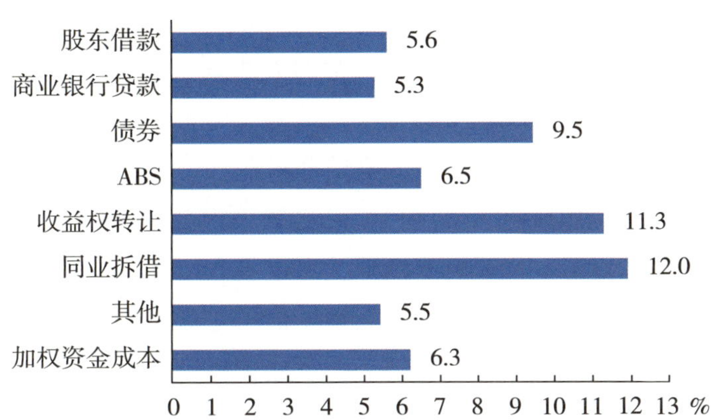

资料来源：CAFI 2019年对于400家小额贷款公司的调研数据。

图11-4 小额贷款公司各种途径的融资成本

（二）运营成本

运营成本是指金融机构花费在负债上的除资金成本之外的一切支出，主要包括管理成本及执行成本。管理成本即金融机构为了维持中小企业贷款业务正常进行而投入的费用及职员的薪酬福利等，如银行对企业进行贷前尽职调查、贷中监督、贷后监管所发生的费用。由于中小微企业在管理水平、财务信息等方面普遍存在较大问题，金融机构对中小微企业贷款调查监管力度相对更大，从而导致管理成本增加。执行成本具体指两个方面：一是金融机构在贷款前的广告宣传等费用；二是贷款后为化解信贷风险、减少风险损失通过各种途径对企业的资产进行查封、扣押、拍卖等过程中所发生的费用。

在金融科技不断革新的背景下，利用数字化手段可以有效降低金融机构的运营成本。首先，在获客能力上，利用金融科技手段可以更精准地找到特定的目标用户，快速地、大规模地获取用户，减少传统广告宣传等费用，降低获客成本。其次，在批贷环节，金融科技公司可以利用大数据风控体系，结合多维度信息（如财务数据、纳税数据、交易数据等）审理，减少人工审核，从而降低运营成本。最后，在贷后监管环节，还可以充分利用第三方支付工具。基于第三方支付，贷款者不能直接控制已贷出资金，而借款者也无法直接接触资金，因此可以凭借当前成熟的第三方交易平台技术确保借款资金定向使用，降低坏账风险。与此同时，也可以减少信贷机构大量人工成本和考核成本，便于机构的信息数据统计，完善贷款者的信用记录。

（三）风险成本

当金融机构贷款给企业或个人时会承担一定的风险，因而风险成本也是决定金融服务供给的重要因素之一。衡量风险时，通常的方法就是将无风险利率与其他高风险的投资利率相比较。高于无风险利率的报酬风险溢价，即投资者要求对其自身承担风险的补偿，称为风险溢价。风险越高，风险溢价越高。

风险成本主要来自信用风险。信用风险是借款人因各种原因未能及时、足额偿还债务而违约的可能性。对于有优质资产抵押、固定收入担保的贷款申请者，金融机构通常可以提供一个较低的价格。中小微企业由于信用记录不全、缺乏优质抵押物、技术开发上投入不足、管理水平不足等原因，企业经营风险和财务风险都较高，到期无法归还银行贷款的概率较大。在这种情况下，金融机构通常选择高价来覆盖风险。

风险溢价的准确性依赖于可收集信息的真实性和广度。健全的征信系统及金融科技的使用有利于金融服务供应商准确分析计算每个客户的风险与价值，实施精准的风险管理，从而显著降低风险成本。例如，蚂蚁金服提供的短期借贷产品“借呗”，在决定借贷申请人的借贷额度、利率与期限计算上综合了借贷申请人的多项财务与非财务数据。财务数据包含申请人在该平台的交易信息、资金余额、消费习惯等信息；非财务数据则包含申请人日常生活的多项风控相关数据。借助金融科技手段，可以实现精准的个人化定价，使消费者享受到与之信用评级相对应的、合理价格的金融服务。

三、市场均衡价格

根据经济学原理，货币市场的供求是影响金融服务价格（利率）高低的最重要的因素。市场上对资金的供给和需求的变化导致利率的波动，并促使利率逐步接近均衡水平。在完全市场经济条件下，资本供大于求，利率下降；反之，利率上升。当市场上的储蓄量与投资量相等时所形成的资金价格，决定了均衡利率水平的高低。在该利率水平下，每个资金需求者都可以如数获得贷款，每个资金供给者都愿意满足所有借款需求（R_0）（见图 11－5）。

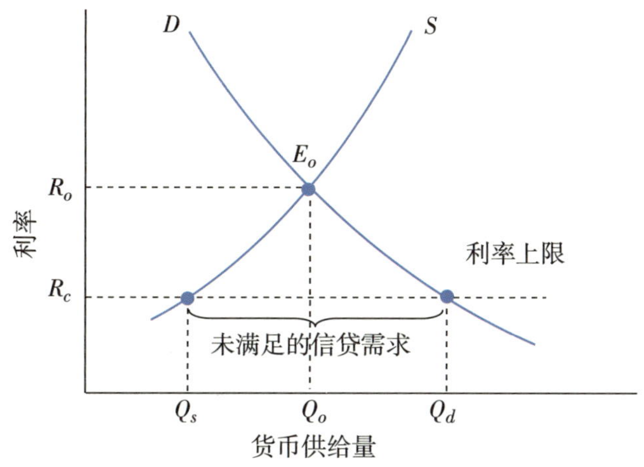

图 11－5　金融服务供给与需求曲线

四、利率管制的影响

鉴于中小微企业在国民经济发展中的重要地位及在获得金融服务方面的弱势地位，长期以来，政府通过设置贷款利率上限对中小微企业融资执行高度保护政策。例如，中国人民银行规定，对于民间小额信贷机构，自营贷款利率和接受的委托贷款利率，必须控制在中国人民银行公布的同期同档次贷款基准利率 4 倍以内。2015 年 8 月 6 日，《最高人民法院关于审理民间借贷案件适用法律若干问题的规定》明确指出，借贷双方约定的利率未超过年利率 24％的，出借人有权请求借款人按照约定的利率支付利息；但如果借贷双方约定的利率超过年利率 36％的，则超过年利率 36％部分的利息应当被认定无效，借款人有权请求出借人返还已支付的超过年利率 36％部分的利息。换而言之，民间借贷利率 24％以下受法律保护，36％以上则不受法律保护。

根据经济学原理，市场利率与边际生产率相等。由市场自由竞争所决定的利率将自动分配资本到那些回报高的投资上，而低于均衡边际生产率的企业会因其支付不起利息负担而退出借贷市场。因此，自由市场竞争能发挥推动产业优化升级的作用，自动淘汰回报低的投资。当政府规定一个低于市场均衡利率的价格上限，一些资本分配到生产率较低的投资项目上，造成低效资源配置及无谓损失。因此，利率管制政策虽然在一定程度上降低了中小微企业的融资成本，但同时也限制了竞争利率的选择机能，妨碍了小额信贷应有绩效的发挥。具体而言，利率管制主要导致了以下三大问题：贷款难、过度贷及民间融资盛行。

（一）贷款难

在图 11－5 中我们可以看出，在利率管制的背景下，政府将管制利率控制在市场均衡利率水平以下（R_c），会导致资本供给量（Q_s）小于资本需求量（Q_d），这意味着利率管制可能会导致更大的融资困难。通常情况下，小微企业主的贷款风险非常高。金融机构在承担高风险的同时，如果因为利率管制而不能从其业务上获得利润，这会导致金融机构不愿意为其贷款。例如，36％是一条政策的红线。如果 36％的利率不能覆盖申请贷款的小微企业的风险，即便贷款申请人愿意接受高于 36％的利率，理论上金融机构也会放弃这笔业务，因为利率水平超过 36％时，出借方的权益是不受法律保护的。这就出现了利率虽然控制在一定水平之下，但是低收入人群反而借不到钱的情况。

对于低收入人群，他们可能更在乎小额信贷的可得性而不是利率水平。从图 11－1 我们可以看出，有一部分小额信贷客户的信贷需求是无弹性的，他们对利率变化并不敏感。无论利率水平是 30％还是 50％，对贷款的需求几乎没有改变。中国人民银行赣州市中心支行课题组（2006）通过实证研究证明，至少在利率市场化初期，利率变化对解决民间融资问题的作用是微不足道的。因此，当小额信贷对多数小微企业而言属于刚性需求时，利率管制反而会减少尾部小微企业借贷的机会，对小微企业的发展造成负面影响。

（二）过度贷

利率管制不仅会导致尾部小微企业出现贷款难问题，还会增加头部小微企业过度贷的风险。当融资成本足够低时，即使一些小微企业没有融资需求，也可能会因贷款成本低而过度借贷。如果贷款人将多余的贷款投资到高风险的股票市场或其他高风险的投资项目上，很容易造成不良贷款率上升，从而使小微企业的融资环境进一步恶化。

我们在浙江省的调研数据也证实了过度贷风险的存在。通过对浙江省 2729 个中小微企业的问卷数据进行回归分析，我们发现企业营业收入与资产的比例越高，越容易出现信用贷款违约。类似地，具备良好教育的法人、经营年限、流动资金贷款等，都与信用等级呈负相关关系。这些指标增加了金融机构对企业的信任，对其进行过度贷，同时也增加了违约风险。

（三）民间融资盛行

当利率管制将尾部小微企业排斥在正规金融服务之外、融资需求不能通过正当途径满足时，个人或小微企业主就会被迫使用其他融资渠道，于是民间借贷市场就会出现。我们的调研数据显示，在金融市场较发达的浙江地区，消费者通过小额贷款公司或其他民间渠道获得的贷款成本比银行的贷款成本高 60%。而在金融服务较不发达的兰州市，消费者通过民间渠道获得的融资要比正规金融机构价格高 140%。在这种情况下，普通消费者或小微企业主不仅没有在利率管制政策下获益，反而成为受害者，这与利率管制政策的初衷相悖。管制利率水平离均衡利率水平越远，资金黑色借贷市场就越盛行。

综上所述，不符合市场规律的利率管制使富裕群体得到了便宜的贷款，而真正需要小额信贷的穷人得不到贷款，被迫成为黑色借贷市场的受害者，这严重违背了普惠金融的包容性原则。为了有效地利用好市场机制，提高资金的边际产生率，应全面放开对贷款利率的管制。在自由市场竞争中，金融机构可以按照收益覆盖风险的原则自主定价，资金会流向实体经济中的高效部门，刺激贷款有效需求，从而提高小微企业贷款的可得性。此外，贷款利率放开后，市场竞争将更加激烈，客户的选择权也更加充分，充分的金融服务供给还可以平抑过高的民间利率，维护金融市场的稳定。诚然，市场化定价也可能导致小额贷款机构利润率受到挤压，部分从事弱势产业的小微企业主也可能无法承担上涨后的高利率（刘成玉和徐丹，2014）。这就要求无论是小额贷款机构还是小微企业都要加快自身的能力建设，增强自身的竞争力。前期政府部门可对此类机构和企业予以一定的补贴，为低收入群体带来金融服务可得性，帮助低收入群体实现金融素养的提升，而此种提升会促使其获得更好地管理自身财务的能力。随着后期贷款服务市场化程度的提高，财政补贴政策会逐步退出贷款服务市场，商业金融机构提供的产品也可以完全满足其金融服务需求。

第四部分

普惠金融与社会发展

小微经济的发展是乡村振兴的关键环节。信用建设可以帮助小微经济融资，以提高生产效率；小额贷款公司可以在风险可控的前提下提供小额便捷的信贷服务。

第十二章　普惠金融在乡村发展中的作用

【摘要】乡村产业的发展是包容性经济发展的重要部分，普惠金融服务有效地支持了乡村产业的发展。我国样本乡村小微企业的账户拥有情况基本满足其需求，新型农村金融机构的兴起有助于进一步提升金融服务的包容性；样本乡村小微企业的借贷需求基本得到满足且利率水平较低。因此，样本乡村小微企业的金融服务包容性较强。然而，企业现金流管理、财务记账等与金融健康密切相关的指标尚需加强，部分企业需要关注避免过度负债的问题，应进一步促进非现金支付方式的使用，促进数字科技在金融服务中的应用，并提高农村小微企业的金融健康水平，以进一步促进农村普惠金融的发展，助力乡村振兴的实现。

为了化解城乡发展不平衡不充分的矛盾，破解城乡二元结构，我国制定了乡村振兴战略促进农村发展。乡村振兴有助于促进"全面建成小康社会"和"全面建设社会主义现代化强国"目标的实现，而普惠金融是实现乡村振兴战略的重要抓手。普惠金融对金融资源进行优化配置，有助于缓解农村地区小微企业及低收入群体的融资约束，刺激农村地区的经济活力，改善人民生活水平，发展普惠金融对乡村振兴战略的实施具有重要意义。

本章以 CAFI 调研数据①为依据，分析我国乡村小微企业金融服务的包容性与小微企业的金融健康状况，讨论农村金融对乡村振兴的作用，并提出促进农村普惠金融发展的措施。

---

① 本章所参考的调研项目包括北京及周边地区调研项目和浙江省丽水市调研项目。北京及周边地区的农村小微经济调研是由中国普惠金融研究院与智惠乡村服务中心合作，在北京、内蒙古、河北等地区的 217 个贫困村开展的。调研对象主要是这些地区贫困村的小微企业（共 617 家），旨在对乡村整体资源、产业发展、基础设施、小微企业金融服务使用情况进行了解。浙江丽水调研项目全称为"浙江丽水农村金融改革试点评估调研"，是中国普惠金融研究院与人民银行丽水支行、当地金融机构（农村信用社、农村商业银行、商业银行）合作，在丽水市的云和县、景宁县、莲都区开展的。调研对象是当地的家庭、个人、中小微企业，旨在对该地区的金融服务需求方的金融服务使用情况进行了解。调研由农村信用社、农村商业银行、村镇银行、商业银行的工作人员具体执行，共收集了 3027 份家庭（个人）问卷，616 份中小微企业问卷。

一、样本乡村小微企业的金融服务包容性

在衡量我国农村地区金融服务包容性的问题上，我们着重讨论小微企业账户覆盖率、支付工具覆盖率及借贷服务的包容性。

（一）账户拥有率基本满足需求

1. 乡村小微企业基本账户情况

如图 12－1 所示，在北京及其周边农村地区调研的 617 家小微企业中，开立了基本账户的数量占比为 78.3%。从开户行的结构来看，农村信用社、农村商业银行依然是农村金融服务的主力军，占比为 42.5%；扎根于农村的大型银行有一定优势，农业银行及邮储银行分别占比为 12.5%和 7.1%；工商银行及建设银行各有一席之地，各占 5%左右；村镇银行作为新型农村金融服务机构，企业开户占比 2.9%。其他大型银行及股份制银行在农村金融服务中占比非常小。

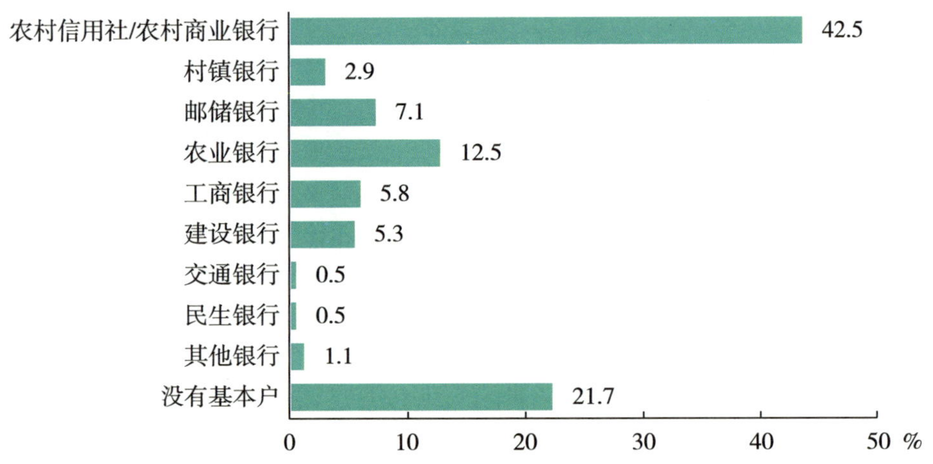

图 12－1　企业开立基本账户的机构类型

未开立基本账户的小微企业大多为个体工商户，占 80.6%（见图 12－2）。小微企业未开立基本账户的原因可能是这类经济体对支付的需求基本都是现收现付，且对公账户结算需求较少，涉及延时支付及对公转账的业务也较少。

2. 乡村小微企业一般账户情况

在北京的调研样本中，有 51.4%的企业未开立一般账户。企业开立一般账户的金融机构分布与基本账户的情况基本一致（见图 12－3），仍然是以农信系统为主，农业银行、邮储银行、村镇银行均占比为 12%以上，其他商业银行占比较低。

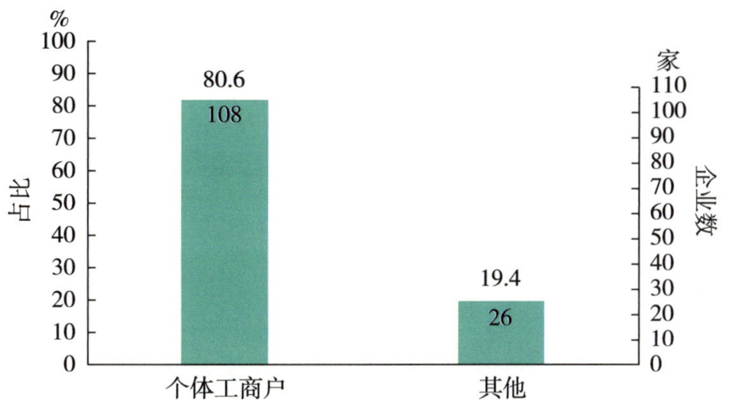

图 12－2　未开立基本账户的企业结构

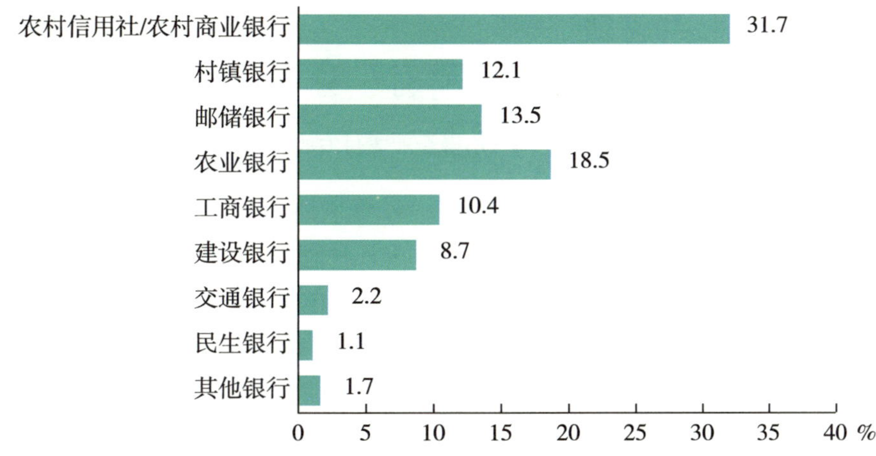

图 12－3　企业开立一般账户的金融机构分布

从以上基本账户及一般账户的开立结构来看，账户覆盖率基本满足小微企业的需求；传统农村金融服务的主力军农信系统、农业银行、邮储银行仍然占据主导地位。村镇银行在基本账户开立的占比较工商银行、建设银行、交通银行等大型银行并没有优势，且与邮储银行、农业银行差距较大，但小微经济体在村镇银行开立一般账户占比较高，超过工商银行、建设银行及交通银行，与邮储银行相近。这说明作为新型机构，村镇银行在获客能力上提高较快。随着农村金融机构的种类增多，在一定程度上会带来包容性的增强。

（二）非现金支付比例仍有待提高

1. 非现金支付比例较大

在支付方式的使用上，北京的调研样本中，小微企业现金支付平均占比为

32.1%[①]，在单一支付方式中占比最高，但如果将银行渠道（POS机、ATM、网银、手机银行、汇票）及第三方支付加总视为非现金支付，则可以发现非现金支付的比例为39.8%，大于现金支付（见图12-4）。

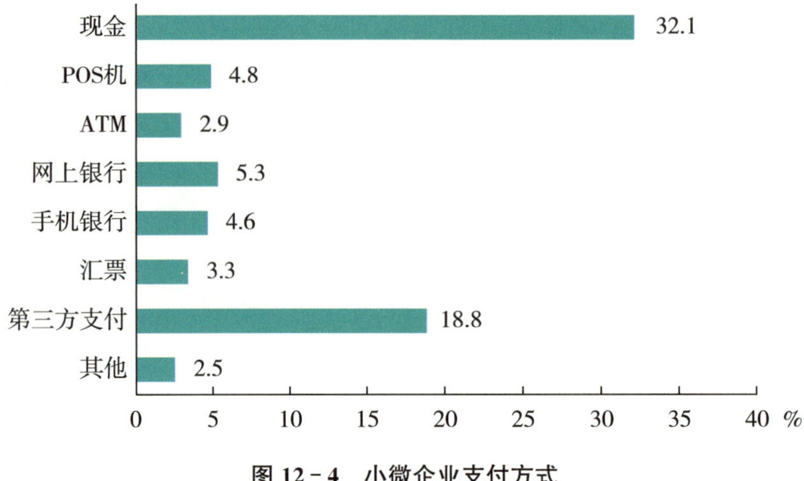

图12-4 小微企业支付方式

非现金支付方式相比现金支付方式而言，具有快捷、安全、不受时间和空间限制等优点，因此，非现金支付方式的比例提高，在某种程度上反映了金融服务包容性的提高。而乡村地区的现金支付比例仍然较高，一个原因可能是个体工商户的占比较高，另一个原因可能是小微经济的主要销售地仍然在农村，从而农户的现金支付比例较高。

2. 选择支付方式时的考虑因素

在支付方式的选择上，对北京的样本小微企业来说便捷、安全、费率是主要的影响因素（见图12-5）。而非现金支付在这三个方面相对于现金支付有明显优势，因此提高非现金支付的使用比例对基础金融服务包容性的提高具有重要意义。

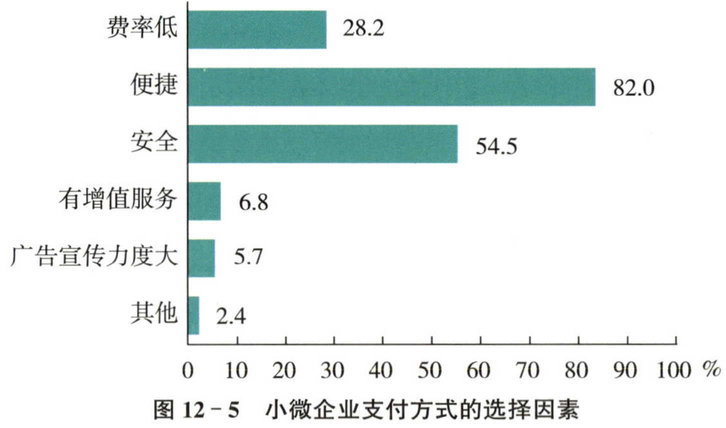

图12-5 小微企业支付方式的选择因素

① 由于一些无效数据的存在，各种支付方式加总比例小于100%，但从中可以看出支付方式的基本结构。

（三）乡村小微企业融资服务包容性

1. 融资目的分析

从北京样本小微企业的融资目的来看，其最主要的目的是补充流动性需求、扩大生产规模及购置固定资产（见图 12－6）。

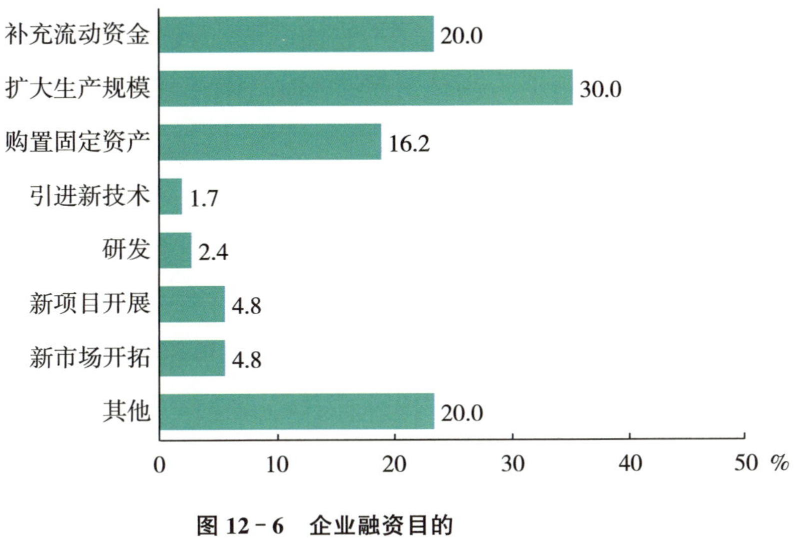

图 12－6 企业融资目的

流动性资金的补充有利于企业增强风险抵御能力；扩大生产规模和购置固定资产有助于企业增强自身竞争力；对新技术的引进和开发有助于企业的长远发展。无论从哪个层面来讲，只要融资成本可负担，合理融资将为企业提升综合实力提供机会。而小微企业综合实力的普遍提升，对于提振乡村经济发展和提高农民生活水平都具有非常重要的意义。

2. 融资情况分析

（1）创业初始资金来源

我们将小微企业创办初始资金募集途径分为传统渠道、互助渠道、新型金融机构渠道。传统渠道包括自有资金、银行贷款、亲朋好友借款等。互助渠道包括资金互助社和标会。新型金融机构渠道包括小额贷款公司、支付宝、微粒贷等借贷渠道。如图 12－7 所示，北京样本小微企业创办时融资渠道占比最高的是自有资金、亲友、银行贷款等传统渠道，占比为 51%，其中自有资金占比最高，为 25.8%；新型金融机构占比为 23.9%，其中小额贷款公司、支付宝、微粒贷三种新型机构各占比为 8%左右；互助渠道占比为 15.5%，其中资金互助社、标会等各占比为 8%左右。

由图 12－7 可以看到，虽然传统的融资渠道仍然占据了半数以上的比例，但随着新型金融机构和数字金融技术的出现及发展，小微企业的融资渠道正在不断拓宽。此外，互助性质的融资渠道也是重要的补充。

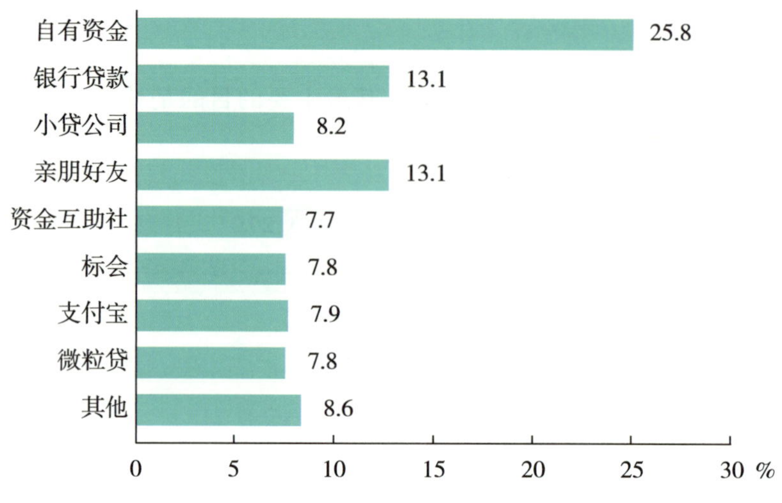

图 12－7　小微企业创办时的融资渠道

（2）融资渠道分析

我们利用北京和浙江省的两份调研问卷的结果来分析小微企业实际的融资情况，问卷中对小微企业在 2017 年最大额度的两笔融资进行的调查来反映其融资情况①。北京的调研样本中，617 家受访企业中只有 14 家在 2017 年同金融机构进行过融资，占比仅为 2.2%；在浙江省丽水市的调研中，616 家受访企业中有 348 家在 2017 年进行过融资，占比为 56.5%。相比北京周边，浙江省作为经济大省，其经济活跃度和金融服务活跃度明显高于北京。

就融资渠道而言，在北京样本中，样本企业最大一笔融资的主要来源仍然是农业系统的金融机构，如农业银行、农村信用社和村镇银行，共占比为 72%；浙江省样本中，这一特征却并不明显，仅有 33%的受访企业向农业银行、农村信用社和村镇银行进行借贷。从其他商业银行的贷款占比情况来看，北京样本中，有 14%的企业从其他商业银行获取了贷款，而在浙江丽水样本中这个比值为 52%。这一数据对比并不能全部归结于地域差别。进一步分析得知，丽水的样本企业规模普遍大于北京的样本企业规模。可推测，虽然同属于普惠金融的范畴，不同金融机构主要覆盖的企业客户层次是不同的。农业银行、农村信用社和村镇银行面对的是更加偏远、规模更小的企业，而其他类别的商业银行主要覆盖规模较大的企业。因此，金融机构类别的丰富和多样有助于提升农村小微企业借贷服务的包容性。

① 由于北京样本中在 2017 年进行过融资的企业仅有 14 家，为丰富样本数量我们同时考虑北京和丽水市的调研数据。本章其他部分不涉及 2017 年的实际融资情况时，讨论仍以北京样本为主。

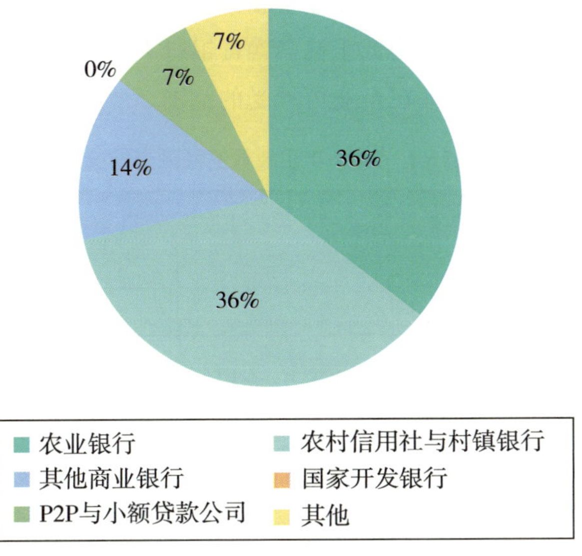

图 12－8　北京样本小微企业 2017 年的实际融资渠道

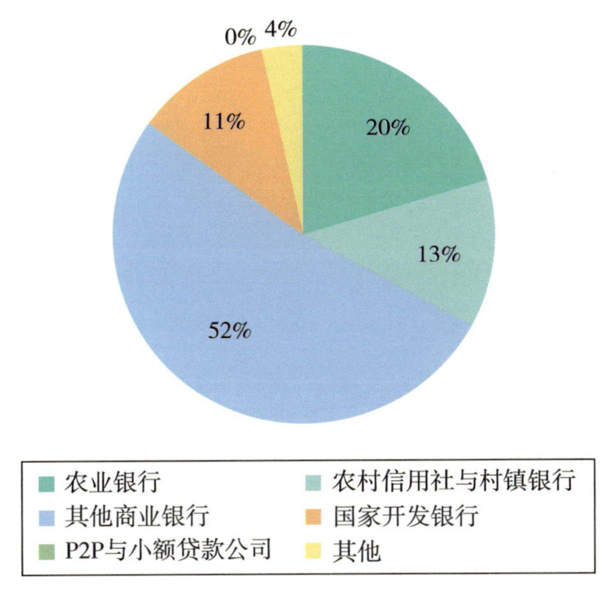

图 12－9　浙江丽水样本小微企业 2017 年的实际融资渠道

（3）融资额度与利率

在融资额度方面，2017 年进行过融资①的北京和丽水样本企业的借贷额度、期限、年化利率的中位数如表 12－1 所示。北京样本的融资金额中位数为 8.5 万元，期限中位数为 12 个月，年化利率中位数为 5.60%；丽水样本企业融资规模大于北京样本企

① 样本企业在 2017 年融资额最高的一笔融资。

业，而融资期限和利率与北京样本企业非常相似。

两个样本的贷款利率中位数均低于社会融资银行平均贷款利率的 6.6%①，这说明金融机构对小微企业的贷款利率在企业可承受的范围。

表 12-1　2017 年企业最高额融资情况②

样本地区	数量（家）	融资金额（万元）	期限（月）	年化利率（%）
北京	14	8.5	12	5.6
丽水	348	30	12	5.44

对于小微企业的融资需求，根据其可以承担的最高利率，可以得到融资需求曲线（见图 12-10、图 12-11）。融资利率高于 20%时，需求量较小；融资利率低于 20%时，需求量激增。而且，虽然北京和丽水的样本规模与借贷额度有所差别，但是二者的需求曲线却非常相似。这再一次证明金融机构对小微企业的贷款定价、小微企业自身可承受的最高利率水平并未受到企业规模的影响，这体现了我国金融机构对小微企业借贷服务的包容性特征。

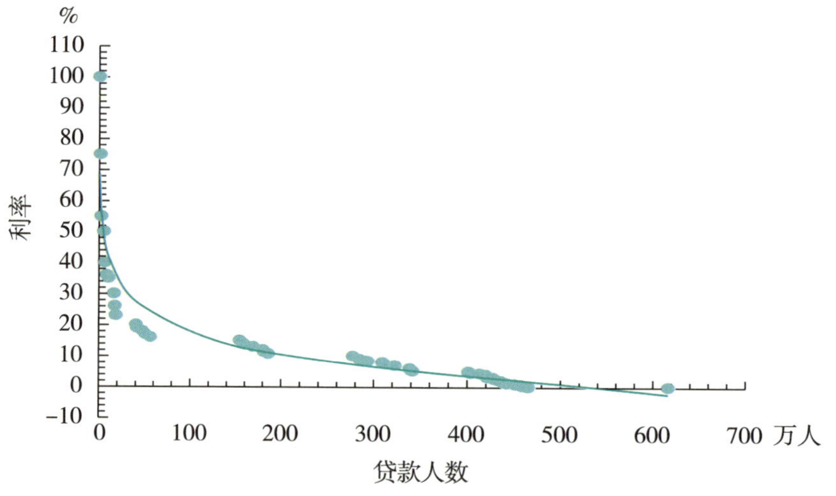

图 12-10　北京样本融资需求曲线

（4）民间借贷作用分析

此外，值得特别指出的是，尤其是在北京样本中，民间借款渠道仍然在小微企业的融资过程中发挥着非常重要的作用。如表 12-2 所示，在北京样本中，调查时仍然有民间借贷的小微企业 56 家，约占调查样本总量 617 家的 9%。而在丽水样本中，持

① 数据来源为中国社会融资成本指数。该指数由清华大学经管学院中国金融研究中心等机构发起，于 2018 年 2 月 1 日在北京发布。

② 此表中数据均为中间值，避免极值对平均值的影响。

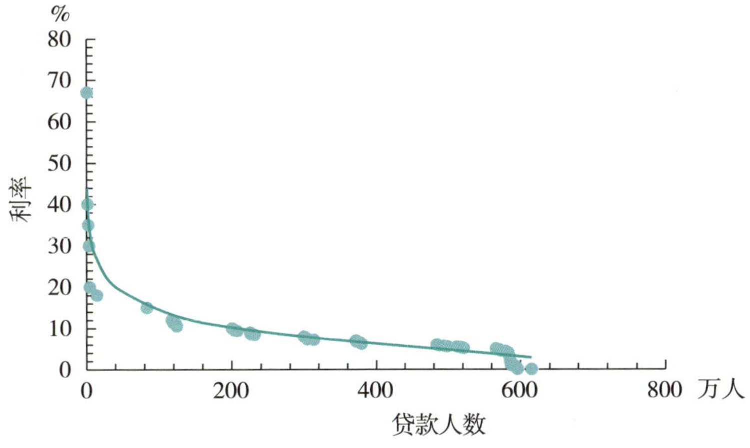

图 12－11　丽水样本融资需求曲线

有民间借贷的企业占比不足 2%，而借贷额度显著大于北京。两个样本中地区民间借贷期限的中位数均为 12 个月，与金融机构借贷的期限相当。然而，由于地区文化不同及样本企业的规模和民间借贷规模不同等原因，北京样本中的小微企业借贷往往以免息或低息方式进行，而丽水样本中的小微企业民间借贷却有着市场化的利率水平。

表 12－2　民间借款的融资特征①

样本地区	数量（家）	额度（万元）	期限（月）	利率（%）
北京	56（9%）	6	12	0
丽水	12（2%）	90	12	12

（5）融资担保方式

北京样本小微企业在 2017 年最高额融资的担保方式中（见图 12－12），70%的小微企业采用的是无抵押的信用借款方式，其次是将商品房、宅基地和土地使用权抵押等方式。之所以信用贷款在该地区的群体中占比较大，可能是由于很多企业主利用当地的普惠金融政策，以个人名义进行贷款，但具体的原因仍然需要深入考证。但不可否认的是，在融资方式上，金融服务的包容性是比较强的。

综上所述，调研样本的小微企业账户及支付方式基本可以满足企业需求。第三方支付和新型金融机构（如村镇银行）的加入丰富了市场主体层次，带来支付方式的数字化和融资渠道的多元化，增强了金融体系的包容性。同时，仅有不足 5%的受访企业的贷款申请遭到拒绝，且小微企业融资利率中位数处于较低水平，说明借贷服务对样本小微企业的包容与友好。而无抵押的信用担保在小微企业中的广泛使用提高了小

① 本表格中的数据为样本的中位数。

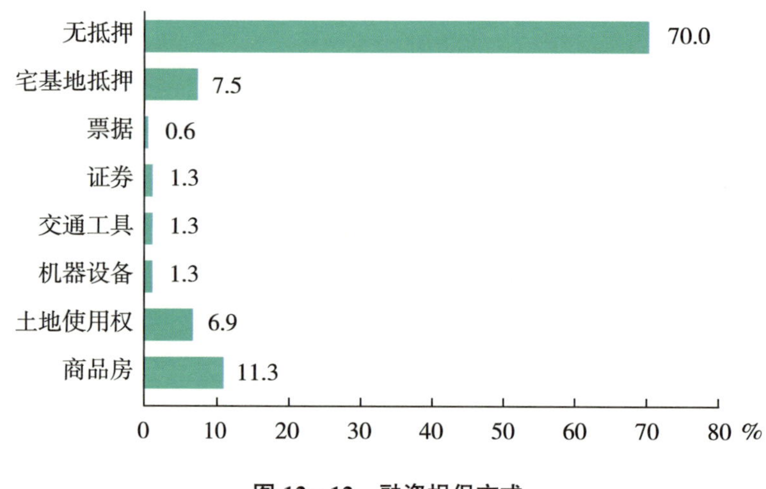

图 12－12　融资担保方式

微企业融资方式的包容性。

3. 融资难原因探讨

在北京 617 家样本企业中，有 28 家企业申请贷款未获批准，占比为 4.5%；在丽水样本中，616 家受访企业中仅有 25 家企业申请贷款未获批准，占比为 4%。这说明两个样本地区的小微企业的借贷服务的包容性较强，融资难的问题只有少部分小微企业会遇到。

在北京样本中，企业未获批准的主要原因是无抵押、无担保和信用等级不足，总共占比为 72.3%，这说明小微企业融资难的主要症结仍然是缺乏抵押、担保、信用等级等评定（见图 12－13）。丽水样本的结论与北京非常相似。

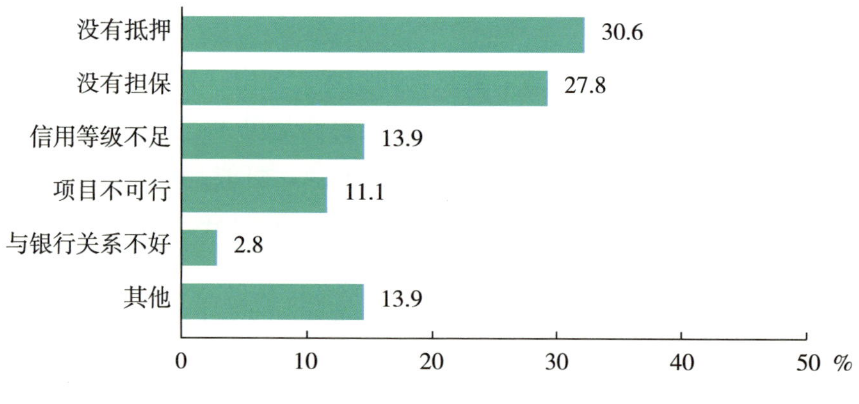

图 12－13　小微企业融资难的原因

在信用等级评定中，企业没有完整、准确的财务信息记录也是其融资难的原因之一。本章第二节将会讨论如何改善小微企业的财务记录情况，采取电子支付方式将有助于提高金融借贷服务对于部分小微企业的包容性。

二、样本乡村小微企业的金融健康

（一）样本企业盈利水平较好

总体而言，乡村小微企业的经营情况较好。北京样本乡村小微企业的年平均营业收入非常小，为 18.58 万元。平均净利润将近 12 万元，净利润率较高（见图 12－14）。

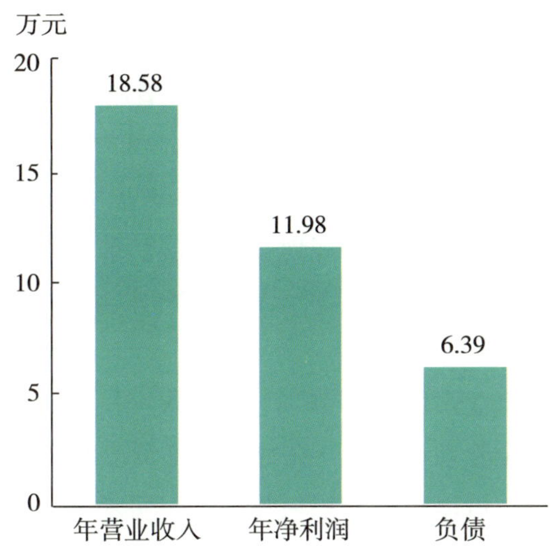

图 12－14　企业平均年营业收入、年净利润、负债金额

按照上文中平均净资产 30.92 万元计算，乡村企业的净资产收益率较高，为 38.7%，这一现象可能与其销售产品的周转率较高有非常大的关系。如小超市单个商品毛利率虽然低，但由于一年内的商品周转率可能有 5 次左右，就会产生较高的净资产收益率。乡村企业的平均负债为 6.39 万元，资产负债率为 20.7%，负债率相对较低（见表 12－3）。

表 12－3　企业净资产收益率及资产负债率　　单位：%

净资产收益率	资产负债率
38.7	20.7

（二）经营现金流管理情况不太乐观

经营现金流对于企业来讲至关重要，我们以应收账款与应付账款为例来说明这个问题。一般而言，企业总是希望应收账款越少越好（对需求方有议价能力），而应付账款越多越好（对供应商有议价能力），这可以反映企业对上下游厂商的管理能力。如图 12－15 所示，乡村小微企业的平均应收账款 8.87 万元大于应付账款 6.99 万元，这说明其经营现金流情况不太乐观，但由于其金额较小，这一问题并不是非常明显。

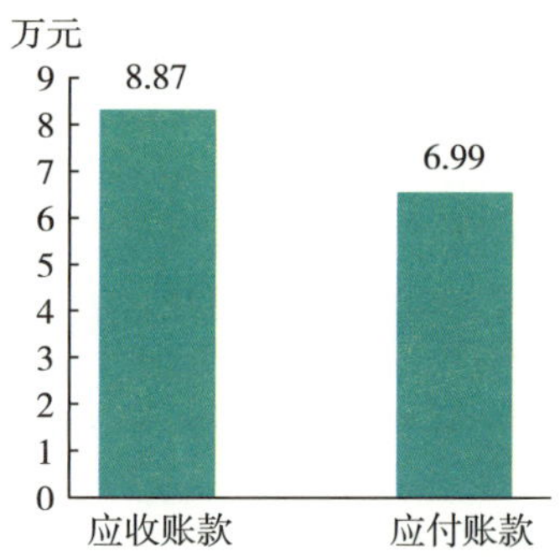

图 12-15　小微企业现金流管理

（三）财务记录非常欠缺

财务记录是有效管理现金流与合理规划企业发展的前提，也是金融机构了解企业经营情况的重要信息渠道。如图 12-16 所示，北京样本乡村小微企业的财务记录普遍比较缺乏。

首先，有财务记录的企业占比仅为 48.3%；其次，只有 16.2%的企业有独立的财务机构负责财务记账及资金管理；最后，在数字就是资产的数据时代，仅有 14.4%的乡村企业有财务管理软件，可以将财务记录数字化。而未来财务软件如果与外部机构进行数据对接，可以在一定程度上提高企业的财务透明性，增加其融资的可能性。

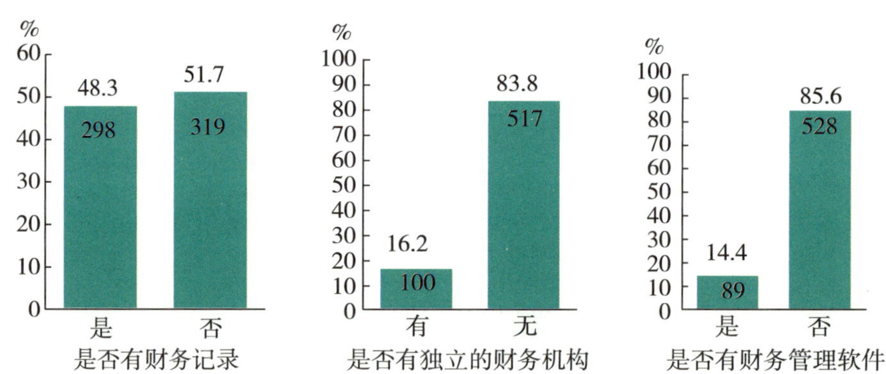

图 12-16　北京样本乡村小微企业财务记录情况

（四）部分企业实际融资额超过需求额度

在北京及丽水调研样本中，实际融资企业的实际融资额度[①]与计划融资额度如表 12-4 所示。总体而言，企业的实际融资额度在其计划之内，但北京与丽水均有 21%

① 我们将样本企业 2017 年实际进行的两笔最大额融资加总作为实际融资总额。

左右的企业实际融资额度大于其计划融资额度。如果计划融资额度代表企业理性范围内需要借贷的额度，那么实际融资额度高于计划融资额度则说明这些企业存在一定的过度负债现象。而由于问卷设计所限，我们暂时无法进一步探究为何企业实际融资额度高于预期。解决这个问题需要进一步调研分析。结合前文北京与丽水样本均有约5%的企业贷款申请没有获批的发现，可以得知在我国乡村企业样本中，借贷不足与过度借贷的情况在一定程度上并存。

表 12-4 企业 2017 年融资需求均值与实际融资额度均值

样本地区	融资需求均值（万元）	实际融资额度均值（万元）	超额融资企业数量（家）
北京	36.8	35.2	3（21%①）
丽水	452.4	285.2	72（21%）

综上所述，乡村小微企业的盈利率水平总体较好，但经营现金流的管理能力较弱，同时财务记账非常不规范，有部分企业实际融资数额超出计划数。乡村小微企业可以通过改善现金流管理，完善财务记账的规范性，避免过度借债等措施来提高自身的金融健康程度。

三、农村普惠金融与乡村振兴

（一）普惠金融促进乡村振兴

1. 支撑乡村振兴战略实施

乡村振兴战略是我国现阶段重要的战略部署。在推行乡村振兴战略的过程中，资金可以发挥源头活水的作用，因此推进普惠金融对实现乡村振兴战略是有重要意义。普惠金融的发展不仅有助于解决农民融资难问题，帮助农民发展生产，而且从长远来看普惠金融的推进有助于建立良好的金融服务体系和良性的金融生态，对实现农业农村的现代化建设、彻底解决“三农”问题、实现乡村振兴具有重要意义。

2. 提高乡村经济活力

在我国金融市场中，金融机构追求金融的效率以实现商业利润最大化，而忽略了金融资源的公平配置，导致“中小微弱”群体遭受融资约束而难以发展生产，拉大了社会整体的贫富差距。普惠金融立足公平、包容的原则对金融资源进行合理配置，让长期被传统金融体系排斥在外的农村小微企业有机会获得金融服务发展生产，从而提

① 超额借贷企业数量占 2017 年借贷企业数量的比值，下同。

高这些地区的经济活力，提高就业水平，助力乡村经济发展壮大。

3. 帮助农村脱贫，改善居民生活

普惠金融有助于乡村振兴战略最终目标的实现，帮助农村贫困人口实现脱贫。普惠金融的发展让各个阶层的人们都有机会获得平等的金融服务，特别是过去遭受金融排斥的贫困人口可以获得金融支持，缓解融资约束。贫困人口在获得金融支持后有更多的机会和能力发展生产、提高收入、改善生活，从而摆脱贫困，因此发展普惠金融有助于消除农村贫困问题。

（二）促进农村普惠金融的发展

为了促进普惠金融的进一步发展，可从以下三个方面着力。

1. 进一步促进非现金支付的应用

如前所述，目前乡村中非现金支付占比已经超过现金支付。非现金支付的应用至少有两个方面的好处：一方面，随着企业交易与支付线上化，企业现金存取手续费用、来往银行柜台的交通费用、人工服务费用及时间都被大大节省，降低了企业的经营成本并提高了效率；另一方面，线上交易可以积累企业的交易行为等数据，让金融机构直接了解企业的销售收入、现金流等财务数据，帮助企业积累一定的信用数据，为授信提供依据，增加小微企业融资的可获得性。

2. 通过数字金融技术缓解融资难问题

数字金融技术的发展，可以改善小微企业的融资难问题。如前述数据所示，融资难在乡村小微企业中依然存在，且无担保、无抵押是融资难的重要原因。与传统的贷款风控基于抵押、担保等不同，新型数字金融技术更多地从行为数据出发，对信用评分比较高的潜在客户进行预授信，在客户产生信贷行为后机构对其进行动态评级，并以此提供纯信用贷款，这就在很大程度上解决了无抵押、无担保的问题，促进融资需求的满足。引入数字金融技术进行融资是产业振兴的必然要求。

3. 提升农村小微企业金融健康水平

如前所述，小微企业的金融健康情况不容乐观，现金流管理、财务记账、负债管理等都存在一定的问题，这对于其发展会有一些隐患，也制约了小微企业获得融资的机会。同时，部分企业在一定程度上存在过度借贷的现象。一方面，需要提高产业管理者、企业员工的金融能力，提升企业的金融健康水平；另一方面，金融服务乡村实体经济的力度将逐渐增强，企业可获得的融资资金数量会逐渐增加。在这种情况下，需遵循市场化定价、使利率可以覆盖风险，这将有助于金融机构控制借贷风险，同时减少企业由于融资成本较低可能产生的过度借贷问题。

案例

发挥农担政策作用　破解“三农”小微主体融资问题的实践

平安普惠作为平安集团旗下专注于为小微企业主和消费者提供个人借款服务的科技平台，深耕个人信贷领域14年，将服务小微的成功经验逐步应用于“三农”人群，助力乡村振兴。截至2018年底，平安普惠低息“三农”贷款产品应运而生。

一、服务模式探索

平安普惠与省级农业信贷担保公司（以下简称农担公司）合作，共同开展《财政部、农业部、银监会关于做好全国农业信贷担保工作的通知》（财农〔2017〕40号）（以下简称40号文）政策性农业融资业务，提供资金、分担风险。相关产品在2018年第四季度上线，试点期提供单户100万元以内的短期产品，在1年内按月付息，到期还本。后续根据试点情况扩大规模、优化产品形态以符合借款人的实际需求。服务对象是符合40号文政策性业务标准的适度规模经营主体，要求经营情况稳定，无不良征信记录，符合农担公司申请条件。信贷资金仅限于经营用途。资金使用的综合年化成本不高于40号文要求的8%，按项目来源、行业、地区进行阶梯定价，可提前还款（无违约金）。产品目前已经在重庆落地，并已与海南、贵州遵义的农担公司签约。

这种业务模式与传统“银担模式”的区别在于，在平安普惠低息“三农”贷款产品业务模式中，省级农担公司和平安普惠融资担保公司采用共保模式合作，分担农户信用风险，作为资金方的小额贷款公司承担担保方违约风险。由于农担公司是非营利政策性机构，享有贴费政策，担保费率比传统“银担模式”大幅下降。

此种模式将非营利性农担公司的政策性作用与平安普惠在小微信贷方面的经验及产业优势充分结合，双方在各个业务环节充分协同，搭建起线上线下相结合的服务模式，由农担公司发挥服务网络下沉的优势进行线下获客，避免获客渠道重复建设，成本大幅降低。根据政策要求由农担公司参与风控并承担主要担保责任，可大幅降低并分散风险，帮助农担公司更充分地落实财政贴息、贴费政策，形成政策乘数效应，为更多的“三农”“小微”人群带来便捷、低成本的融资服务。

二、创新特点

平安普惠低息“三农”贷款产品作为平安普惠开放聚合式借贷服务模式的实践，将过去由单一机构独立完成的诸多信贷环节模块化，搭建以金融科技为基础的开放式平台，通过与农担公司在内的多方协作，将各自在业务属性、服务网络、数据积累、风险管理、科技研发、金融资源等方面的差异化优势融入各业务环节，以协同方式消除业务短板，为“三农”人群提供多元化、价格可承担、体验便捷的服务解决方案。

（一）营销获客环节

在营销获客环节，商业银行主要依赖线下网点和客户经理团队开展人工服务，其优势在于银行多年来积淀的放心、可靠的品牌形象和大量的客户资源，但同时存在流程复杂、时效性差等不足，其服务范围仅能辐射网点周边有限的区域，且由于风险偏好因素，银行提供的借贷服务存在下沉不足问题。而小额贷款公司也无法有效覆盖“三农”人群，并缺乏“三农”信贷业务经验。无论银行或小额贷款公司单独进行“三农”获客，成本将非常高昂。

在平安普惠低息“三农”贷款产品中，获客环节联合各类主体协同进行，在平安普惠多年业务积累的基础上，引入农担公司等机构合作方，充分发挥它们服务下沉的优势，聚焦农村小微客群。

农担公司在日常工作中下到基层，坚持“根植农村、专注农业、服务小微”的宗旨，以贴近农业农村融资需求为导向，以乡镇（村社）为单位，进行业务开发及挖掘。根据建档立卡情况，在县、乡政府和村委会的支持和帮助下，通过摸底调查、村镇公示层层把关，把分散的、碎片化的农业适度规模经营主体的信息梳理整合，掌握其真实情况，为平安普惠低息“三农”贷款产品提供数据支撑。

产品获客方面的合作方除了省级农担公司，还有公益组织、农业基层专业机构等，通过基层组织推荐符合要求的农村小微融资需求。

（二）风险评估和风险承担环节

风险评估环节由平安普惠、增信方和资金方分别独立进行。平安普惠依托 14 年借贷业务运营经验沉淀，依托自身大数据对借款人进行初步风险评估。农担公司借助其基层经验积累和产业数据优势对信贷底层资产进行风险评估和承保决策。小额贷款公司基于其风险管理能力和偏好作出最终借款决定。多方评估使对借款人的风险画像更立体、更精准，从而解决了因“三农”人群资产不充足、结构性数据缺失带来的风险识别难题，提高了各方机构整体的风控质量和服务“三农”人群的能力。

农担公司作为主要增信方，按照备选、培育、不良等标准对适度规模经营主体进行信用级别初步分类，提前做好风险防控工作。农担公司和合作机构根据经营主体的贷款需求、信用状况进行尽职调查，对符合条件者按规定迅速办理手续，及时提供贷款。

农担公司与平安普惠融资担保公司采用“共保模式”合作，根据 40 号文要求，农担公司承担主要担保责任，双方按协议规定分摊责任。双方审核通过后，由小额贷款公司完成放款。其中，农担公司负责借款申请材料的收集及现场尽调、核保，承担协议约定担保责任和贷后催收、回访职责及对坏账进行理赔及追偿。平安普惠担保机构基于农担审批结果进行核保，承担协议约定担保责任。对坏账相应理赔，再与农担公司共同追偿。

（三）资金来源环节

在初期，由小额贷款公司提供稳定、快捷的资金，有效地降低“三农”人群获取借贷服务的成本。在未来，产品将开放资金端，包括引入社会公益资金在内的灵活、多元的资金来源，提供充足的低成本资金。

三、结语

平安普惠低息“三农”贷款产品的业务创新重点是围绕融资难、融资贵、融资慢问题探索可行的解决路径。

针对传统信贷模式融资慢与农业生产季节性、资金需求时效性强的矛盾，平安普惠从三个方面加以改进：一是加快审批。通过计算机系统自动化审批，快速完成审批及放款。二是简化流程。委托农担公司出面进行资料收集和签约，平安普惠与借款人无新增沟通环节。三是优化体验。通过网页即可申请，未来将支持借款人全线上操作。通过这些措施，让农户在最短时间内拿到所需资金，不误农时。

第十三章　小额贷款风险与金融稳定

【摘要】小额贷款公司肩负社会和商业双重使命。基于 399 家小额贷款公司的问卷数据，我们发现小额贷款公司重点服务于低收入人群和微型经济体，激活了民间资本，打通了经济体系的“毛细管道”，发挥着维持生计和稳定就业的作用。此外，小额贷款公司促进了金融科技的创新和普及应用。对小额贷款公司的监管，应该以风险程度为依据执行分类监管，尽量避免按传统商业金融机构的监管框架来监管具有普惠金融性质的小额贷款机构，重视监管科技的应用，以监测为主，放松限制。

最近，党中央和国务院要求金融机构进一步加大对民营和小微企业的金融支持。事实上，小额贷款公司是其中一支不可忽视的力量。小额贷款公司是根据《中国银行业监督管理委员会　中国人民银行关于小额贷款公司试点的指导意见》（银监发〔2008〕23 号）（以下简称 23 号文）而成立的，在不吸收存款的情况下，主要用股东的资本服务“三农”客户，具有自负盈亏和自担风险的特点。十年来，小额贷款公司已经积累了相当丰富的服务“三农”和小微企业的经验。

通过对 399 家小额贷款公司调查发现，小额贷款公司确实已经在普惠金融发展中发挥了先锋作用，最为突出的成绩就是促进了金融科技的发展和金融服务的普及应用。小额贷款公司在经济发展中的作用还包括稳定就业、缓解小微企业风险、为小微企业提供发展所需要的金融支持。

在服务小微企业的同时，小额贷款公司也要维持自身的可持续发展。小额贷款是一种风险业务，要获得商业上的可持续发展，小额贷款公司必须要有较强的风控能力。通过分析样本中的小额贷款公司的数据可以发现，小额贷款公司总体风险可控，且一部分小额贷款公司具有非常专业的风险控制能力。虽然小额贷款公司和监管部门的目标都是对风险进行有效控制，但是小额贷款公司自身的风险控制强调的是业务层面，而监管政策强调的是将整个行业的风险控制在可承受的范围。

小额贷款公司是在不损害商业可持续发展的前提条件下，最大化其社会效益。通过分析认为，对小额贷款公司的监管不同于传统金融机构的监管。最重要的是，应避免采用对传统金融机构的监管原则来监管承担社会和商业双重使命、具有普惠金融性质的小额贷款公司。根据这些原则我们提出八项监管建议。

本章以调查结果为依据，以社会发展和商业可持续为主线，讨论小额贷款公司在普惠金融发展中的贡献，着重分析小额贷款的风险及识别风险的源头，并在此基础上提出政策建议。

一、小额贷款行业的使命与贡献

（一）服务小微，弥补不足

小额贷款的起源就是为了解决中小微企业的融资和弱势群体的生计问题，肩负促进社会发展和维持自身商业可持续发展的双重使命，这也是普惠金融发展的使命。在传统金融体系中，中小微企业和弱势群体往往没有足够的机会获得适当的金融服务，丧失了很多发展和改善生计的机会。这种局面的存在是社会不平衡不充分发展的重要原因之一。

小额贷款行业的发展填补了传统金融的不足。在中华人民共和国成立后的一段时间内，在政府的倡导下，国有金融体系确实强调了金融服务的社会使命和商业使命的结合，但是随着改革开放的不断深入，迅速发展的经济活动对金融服务产生巨大的需求，吸走了传统金融机构绝大多数的金融资源。在大力发展经济政策的引导下，大多数金融机构进行了使命漂移，逐步从农村撤出其分支机构，服务“中小微弱”、服务“三农”不再是传统金融机构优先履行的使命。很多金融机构变成了农村资本的抽水机，成为资本从弱势群体向富裕阶层、从农村向城市、从微型经济向大型经济转移的“管道”。近几年，在政府普惠金融政策的指引下，这种状况有所好转。除传统金融机构开始转向服务“中小微弱”之外，小额贷款公司在其中也发挥了很重要的作用。

第一，小额贷款公司是为服务“三农”而诞生的。“三农”是普惠金融最主要的服务对象之一，贷款难、贷款贵是该领域金融服务的特征。23 号文要求，小额贷款公司在坚持为农民、农业和农村经济发展服务的原则下自主选择贷款对象。小额贷款公司发放贷款，应坚持“小额、分散”的原则，鼓励小额贷款公司面向农户和微型企业提供信贷服务，着力扩大客户数量和服务覆盖面。

我们对 399 家小额贷款公司进行问卷调查发现，其中有 35％的小额贷款公司将农林牧渔业作为首要的服务对象；有 60％的小额贷款公司将零售批发业作为排列前三位的服务对象。这证明了大多数小额贷款公司仍然坚守服务“三农”的使命，支持区域经济发展。

第二，小额贷款公司的大部分贷款被投放到小微企业和个体户的生产经营活动中。2017 年，这 399 家小额贷款公司发放贷款 31246094 笔，服务 11106927 位客户（包括企业和个人），平均每家服务 27837 位客户。根据中国人民银行公布的 2017 年第四季度数据，全国有 8551 家小额贷款公司，由此可粗略推算，小额贷款公司全年大约为 2.38 亿名客户提供贷款服务。根据本次调查的样本数据，用于生产经营活动的贷款占小额贷款公司总贷款的 78%，而且有 52%的小额贷款公司投放的生产经营贷款占各自贷款总额的 90%以上。这些经营活动大多数由小微企业和个体户完成。

第三，小额贷款公司绝大多数的客户属于低收入人群和微型经济体。表 13-1 是对 399 家小额贷款公司客户结构分析的结果，该结果清晰地显示，49.85%的客户贷款额度在 1 万元以内；48.17%的客户贷款数额为 1 万～5 万元。实际上，借贷数额为 1 万元以内的客户，多数属于低收入人群。如果将借贷数额为 1 万～100 万元的视为典型微型经济客户（包括从事农业生产的农户、个体工商户、小微企业），则有 49.9%的客户属于微型经济客户。据此推算，全国 8551 家小额贷款公司服务了约 1.19 亿名微型经济客户。

表 13-1　339 家小额贷款公司客户结构分析

贷款额度（万元）	客户比例（%）	客户数（户）
≤1	49.8480	5536578
>1，≤5	48.1671	5349888
>5，≤10	0.7905	87796
>10，≤50	0.8517	94595
>50，≤100	0.0782	8691
>100，≤200	0.1120	12440
>200，≤500	0.0900	9991
>500，≤1000	0.0194	2157
>1000，≤2000	0.0413	4591
>2000	0.0018	200

如此庞大的微型经济体的融资问题本来就是普惠金融应该解决的问题。如果将 1 亿多低收入人群和 1 亿多小微经济体所牵涉的总人口及他们生计的稳定和生活的改善加以考虑，就可以理解小额贷款在国计民生和在普惠金融发展中的重要性，也就多了一份把小额贷款服务纳入国家金融体系中加以考虑的紧迫感。

（二）拥抱科技，促进创新

金融科技在推动传统金融和普惠金融发展方面的作用是显而易见的。不可否认，在使用金融科技方面，传统金融机构起步最早。例如，POS 机、ATM 的推广使用，都是由传统金融机构首先引进和使用的。互联网时代，在国际上也是传统金融机构首先使用网上银行。但是在中国，小额贷款公司的入场迅速且大幅扩大了金融科技的覆盖面。

小额贷款公司在带动科技金融创新和使用方面，作出了以下重要贡献：一是金融科技丰富了服务产品，提供各种小额、期限灵活的产品以满足客户的各种借款需求；二是金融科技提高了金融服务的客户体验，使小额贷款流程更简便、办理更快捷，使客户更加方便地使用信贷服务，如“310”服务；三是金融科技大幅降低成本，小额贷款公司通过金融科技平台提供金融服务的成本很低，边际成本几乎为零。由于使用了移动终端，客户不需要亲自到线下网点获得金融服务，客户成本也大幅降低；四是金融科技打破地域限制，依托互联网平台，将小额贷款公司的信贷业务送达任何有互联网的地方。

金融科技在普惠金融发展中的作用在我们调查的 399 家小额贷款公司的数据中得到了充分体现。在 399 家小额贷款公司中有 55 家属于互联网小额贷款公司，它们服务了小额贷款行业 98.9%的客户，客户平均贷款额为 2.1 万元；其余的 344 家常规小额贷款公司，仅服务了 1.1%的客户。

（三）改善民生，稳定就业

调查发现，大多数小额贷款公司的最大股东是民营企业，约占 55%，另有 20%的小额贷款公司的最大股东是个人。以国有企业或外资企业作为最大股东的，分别占 14%和 11%。由此可见，小额贷款公司股东主要由民营企业和个人组成，通过小额贷款的方式，他们将自有资金用于帮助微型经济的发展。

当前，在政府的号召下，许多传统金融机构纷纷探索服务微型经济的路径，尝试以自己的资金优势扩大对微型经济服务的份额。然而，由于传统金融机构长期以来没有把微型经济作为服务的战略对象，缺乏针对微型经济的有效服务模式，在面对普惠金融的服务对象时，部分机构感到力不从心。同时，有一部分传统金融机构正在与小额贷款公司结成伙伴关系，将小额贷款公司作为通道，通过助贷或联合贷款的模式，为微型经济提供服务。小额贷款公司就像毛细血管一样，将自有金融资本和外来金融资本不断地输送给微型经济，保证微型经济的持续发展。

调查发现，小额贷款公司提供的贷款中有 78%是用来进行生产经营的。同时，有

99%的客户是低收入人群和小微企业。对于自谋生计的个体人员（包括农业生产、家庭农场、个体工商户）来说，小额贷款公司是他们在自谋生计过程中除自有资金以外的主要资本来源。对于小微企业来说也是如此，他们从传统金融机构获得贷款的机会很少，小额贷款公司提供的贷款使他们能够稳定地开展经营活动，为就业人员提供就业机会。

（四）缓冲风险，纳入监管

小额贷款公司用股东的自有资金，为“中小微弱”客户提供信贷服务，实际上分担了“中小微弱”群体在生产经营中的部分风险。如果没有小额贷款公司的介入，风险爆发造成的全部后果都要由“中小微弱”群体自己承担，甚至可使小微企业经营濒临倒闭。由于小额贷款公司阻隔了部分风险向金融系统的传递，从而减少了引发更严重的金融危机。传统金融则不然，风险爆发的后果可以直接传导到金融机构，然后传导给储户和大众。

金融服务的不足迫使“中小微弱”群体通过民间借贷来解决营业和生计上遇到的困难。这种不规范的借贷关系增加了其经营和生计上的不确定性，提高了经济风险。小额贷款公司的借贷活动取代了部分民间借贷，而且是在政策的规范和监督下经营，实际上是将民间借贷行为纳入政策规范和监督之内。

二、风险要素特征分析

小额贷款本身属于风险业务。在诸多风险中，对小额贷款公司而言最重要的风险包括流动性风险、利率风险、资本风险和信贷风险。下面将根据调查结果，分类描述当前小额贷款公司的风险水平。

（一）流动性风险差别较大

小额贷款公司的流动性风险主要表现为没有足够的资金来满足客户贷款要求，不能及时补偿意外损失。根据有关规定，小额贷款公司只贷不存，资本来源为注册本金和融资。有部分网络贷款公司虽然没有吸收存款，但是其部分资本仍具有公众资金的特征，如从银行获得融资。另外，小额贷款公司贷款具有“小额、快捷”的特点，资金发放的速度往往大于回收速度，很有可能出现资金紧张的状况。如果流动性风险发生，容易触发更严重的信用风险，因此流动性应该成为一个重要的监测指标。

由于小额贷款公司具有特殊性，因此通常用来衡量商业银行流动性的四个指标

（流动性覆盖率、净稳定融资比例、贷存比和流动性比例），显然不适用于小额贷款公司的状况。本报告采用资金满足率，即贷款需求与可用资金的比例来衡量小额贷款公司的流动性，即

资金满足率＝3个月内新增贷款额/（总资本－贷款余额）

图13－1是调查的399家小额贷款公司的资金满足率分布情况，代表现有的资本是否能够满足未来3个月新增贷款的需要。在计算时，假设未来一年新增的贷款需要与上年持平。如图13－1所示，比值为0，代表在过去一年中该公司没有新增贷款，这部分公司比例为17%；比值大于0而小于1，代表公司有充足的资金，数值越小，资金闲置的可能性越大；比值大于1，表示该公司现有资金不足以满足未来3个月新增贷款的需求，公司需要增资或放慢贷款速度，数值越大，流动性风险越大。

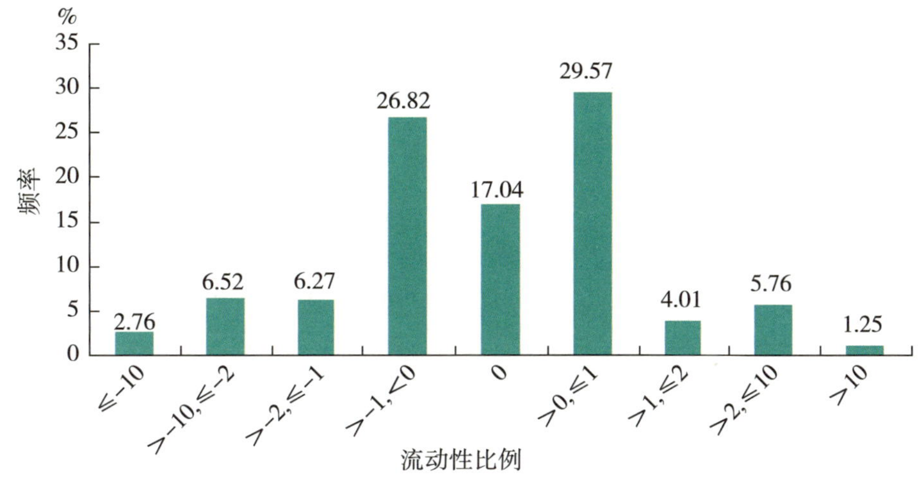

图13－1 小额贷款公司贷款需求与可用资金比例

值得注意的是，有42.36%的公司出现负值，意味着它们的贷款余额大于资本总额。总资本额包含注册资金和全部融资资本，贷款余额超过资本总额只能解释为公司另有表外资金来源。如果是这种情况，那么这部分小额贷款公司的资金充足情况实际上比报表反映得好。

流动性风险还可以用不良贷款与资本总额的比值（见图13－2）来反映。当用不良贷款总额与资产总额（注册资金与各类融资额的总和）进行比较时，发现有13.8%的小额贷款公司不良资产已经超过资产总额。或者说，这部分公司可能已经濒临资金链断裂。

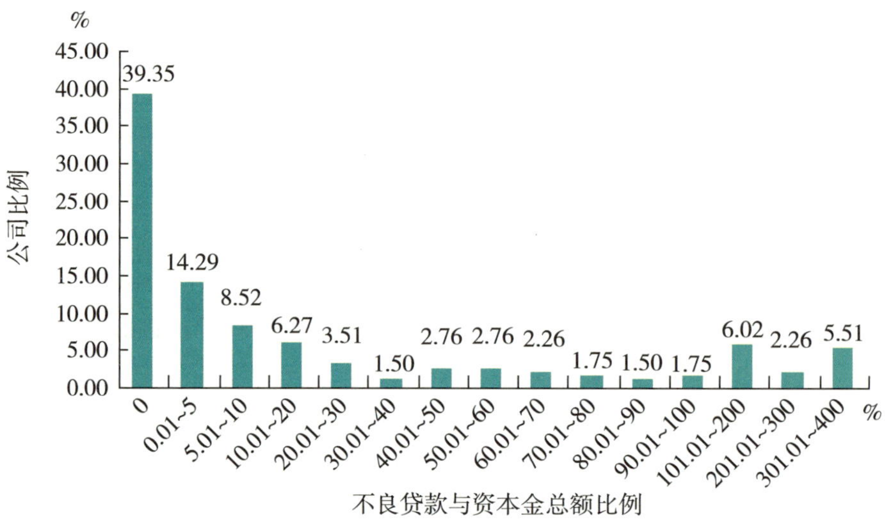

图 13-2 小额贷款公司不良贷款与资本总额的比例

（二）利率风险温和

利率风险是衡量利率变化对小额贷款公司的影响。通常利率风险等于利息敏感性资产和利息敏感性负债的比值。当比值大于 1 时，表示利息敏感性资产大于利息敏感性债务。在这种情况下，市场利率的上升会造成利润的增加；反之，当比值小于 1 时，市场利率的上升会造成利润的减少。

小额贷款公司的资本金主要是股本，政策不允许小额贷款公司从市场融资，监管政策将杠杆率限制在 0.5 以内，个别省份放松对杠杆率的要求，允许小额贷款公司的最高杠杆率为 3。即便如此，由于受到监管政策的限制，小额贷款行业的杠杆率都比较低。因此，利率敏感性负债并不是很大。

小额贷款公司的利率敏感性资产主要是借出去的贷款，因此我们用贷款余额代表利息敏感性资产。在负债方面，除了注册资金，其他资本都是通过各种融资渠道获得，需要支付一定的利息成本，因此，可以用贷款余额和注册资金的差额代表利率敏感性负债。利息风险＝贷款余额/（贷款余额－注册资金）。

图 13-3 是当前小额贷款公司的利率风险情况。其中，52.9％的利率风险资产比值大于 1，在提高市场利率水平的情况下，这部分公司由于借出的资产大于融资的资产，在大多数情况下，负债的利息低于借贷的利率，比例越大，利润越大。因此，这部分企业希望放开利息的限制。47.1％的小额贷款公司，其比值小于 1 甚至为负值，表明这些企业有大量的资本积压没有借出。如果市场利率水平提高，由于其不能将利率敏感性资产借出，就有可能出现利息支出大于利息收入的情况，存在

利息亏损的风险。

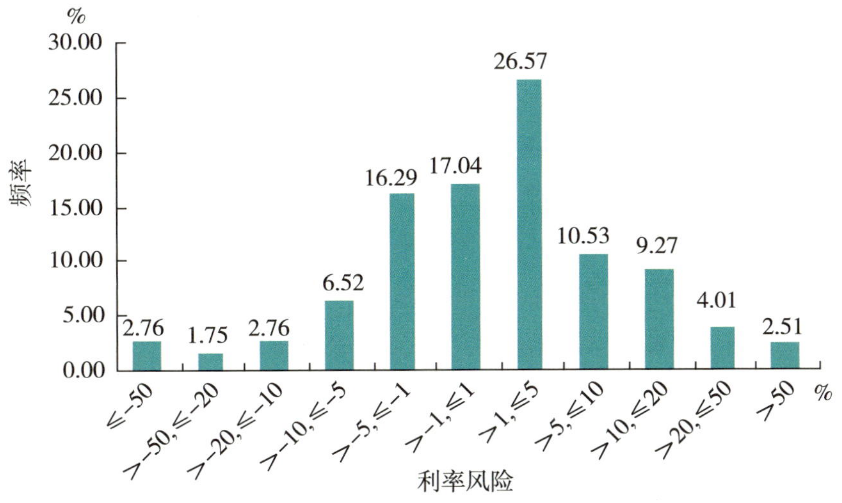

图 13-3　小额贷款公司利率风险

（三）资本风险不高

资本风险是衡量偿还风险资本的能力。由于小额贷款公司的杠杆率被限制，小额贷款公司的资本风险水平不高。如图 13-4 所示，最高的杠杆率为 89%，79.45%的小额贷款公司没有进行融资，完全用注册资本金运作，不存在风险资本的偿还能力不足的问题。

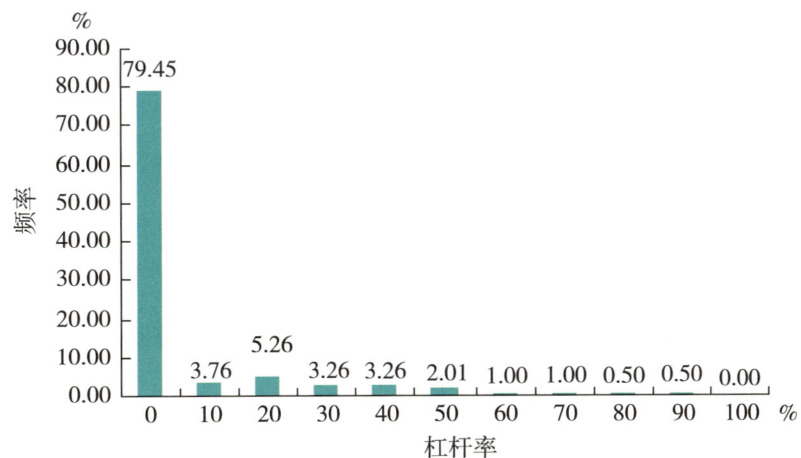

图 13-4　小额贷款公司杠杆率

（四）信贷风险两极分化

我国《贷款风险分类指导原则》中，把贷款风险分为正常、关注、次级、可疑和损失五个等级。虽然不是刚性的规定，但部分金融机构将逾期和风险等级对应看待，并将逾期不超过 90 天的贷款视为关注类贷款，逾期 90～180 天的贷款视为次级贷款，逾期 180～360 天的贷款视为可疑类贷款，逾期超过 360 天的贷款视为损失贷款。通常逾期超过 90 天的贷款即视为不良贷款。

1. 逾期贷款率和不良贷款率的两种极端分布

用逾期贷款率和不良贷款率来衡量小额贷款公司的风险情况可以发现，小额贷款公司的风险水平有明显的两极分化趋势。我们将逾期时间分为 30 天以内、30～90 天、90 天以上三类问题贷款。如图 13－5 所示，调查的 399 家小额贷款公司的信贷风险分布有非常明显的两极化现象。三种逾期类型综合来看，29.6％的公司表现非常优秀，没有出现任何逾期贷款；约 15.3％的公司能够将逾期贷款率控制在 1％～5％；另有 26.8％的公司有 90％以上的贷款处于逾期状态；剩余的 28.2％的公司逾期率分布在 5％～90％。

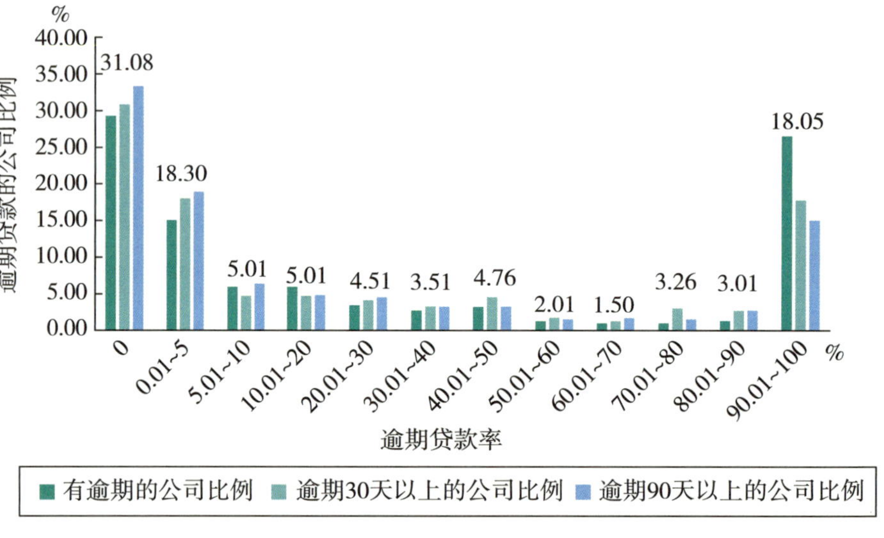

图 13－5 小额贷款公司的逾期贷款率和不良贷款率情况

从不良贷款指标来看，33.6％的公司没有不良贷款，19％的公司出现 1％～5％的不良贷款，约 15.3％的公司不良贷款率高达 90％以上，32.1％的公司不良贷款率在 5％～90％分布。

2. 短期逾期贷款率不一定增加不良贷款率

长期逾期贷款或不良贷款通常是由短期逾期贷款发展而来。因此，不良贷款率高的企业，其逾期贷款率也应该很高。如表 13－2 所示，30 天内逾期贷款率和 30～90 天的逾期贷款率确实存在显著的相关性，其相关系数达 0.353，但是与逾期 90 天以上（不良贷款率）的比例没有显著关联。类似地，逾期 30～90 天的与逾期 90 天以上（不良贷款率）的比例也没有显著相关性。

表 13－2　短期逾期贷款与长期逾期贷款的关系

相关性	逾期 30 天之内	逾期 30～90 天	逾期 90 天以上（不良）
逾期 30 天之内	1		
逾期 30～90 天	0.353	1	
逾期 90 天以上（不良）	−0.053	0.013	1

这种意外的结果暗示短期逾期贷款与不良贷款率是由不同因素引起的。短期逾期贷款比例高的公司，其不良贷款率不一定高。这可能是因为不良贷款率高的公司，在当前监管整顿的环境或者迫于自身不良贷款率高的压力下，采取自我整顿措施，在近期减少或停止发放新的贷款，所以没有短期逾期贷款发生。

三、小额贷款风险要素实证分析

控制风险是小额贷款公司生存发展的头等大事，也是监管的首要目的。最有效的监管方法是能够鉴别出影响风险的要素，然后通过对相关要素进行监管和控制，以达到控制风险、保持金融稳定的目标。如表 13－3 所示，股本收益率（ROE）与风险呈正向的非线性相关关系，说明小额贷款公司的回报是冒适度的风险获取的。因此，影响风险的因素也决定小额贷款公司的生存发展。当然，除此以外，还有其他因素也影响小额贷款公司的生存发展，出于数据和篇幅的原因，这里重点分析风险因素如何影响小额贷款公司的生存发展。

（一）风险要素

我们从理论上识别如下因素可能会对风险产生的影响：区域、注册年限、是否为上市公司、大股东份额、员工教育结构、风险控制员工的比例、是否为互联网小额贷款、是否使用 FinTech 技术、贷款用途、风控措施、还款模式、贷款期限、利率、杠杆率、户均贷款额度、员工人均放贷额、贷款使用的行业、回报率、客户的特征等，表 13－3 列出了代表这些因素的主要指标。我们利用所调查的 399 家小额贷款公司的问卷数据建立数学模型来分析这些因素与不同类型风险之间的关联性。

表 13-3　回归模型分析结果

解释变量	因变量：30 天内逾期贷款率			因变量：30～90 天逾期贷款率			因变量：90 天以上逾期贷款率		
	系数	标准差	显著水平	系数	标准差	显著水平	系数	标准差	显著水平
(Intercept)	3.5580	5.7930		2.2820	4.3910		48.8100	13.9600	***
福建	−4.0400	2.8870		−0.3002	2.1880		10.6500	6.9580	
甘肃	3.7300	4.1690		4.3650	3.1600		−12.4900	10.0500	
广东	−7.7810	4.3040	*	5.4130	3.2620	*	8.7910	10.3700	
广西	−3.2130	4.0750		−3.5100	3.0890		6.9830	9.8210	
河北	−3.1550	4.3660		1.4550	3.3100		−5.6430	10.5200	
江苏	−4.6850	6.0370		0.8007	4.5770		24.8800	14.5500	*
江西	−4.3640	3.9950		−1.0730	3.0280		−1.7700	9.6270	
辽宁	−6.9230	3.4410	**	−2.0060	2.6090		4.9180	8.2940	
内蒙古	−5.8050	3.3060	*	−1.8960	2.5060		23.6700	7.9680	***
重庆	−3.5520	2.6870		1.5290	2.0370		20.5700	6.4750	***
天津	−5.2750	4.3160		−1.6030	3.2710		27.3200	10.4000	***
浙江	−3.8350	4.1350		−0.0945	3.1340		10.4800	9.9640	
公司注册年限（年）	0.4248	0.3562		0.0089	0.2700		−2.3550	0.8585	***
目前已经上市	0.2233	3.5930		4.6000	2.7240	*	8.1770	8.6600	
最大股东股本比例（%）	−0.0181	0.0196		−0.0091	0.0149		−0.0361	0.0473	
杠杆率（%）	0.0472	0.0590		0.1081	0.0447	**	0.0128	0.1422	
大专员工比例（%）	0.0535	0.0500		0.0260	0.0379		−0.1155	0.1205	
大学员工比例（%）	0.0248	0.0451		0.0250	0.0342		−0.1595	0.1087	
研究生以上员工比例（%）	−0.0136	0.0770		0.0284	0.0584		−0.4366	0.1855	**

续表

解释变量	因变量：30 天内逾期贷款率			因变量：30～90 天逾期贷款率			因变量：90 天以上逾期贷款率		
	系数	标准差	显著水平	系数	标准差	显著水平	系数	标准差	显著水平
风控部门人数比例（%）	0.0263	0.0553		0.0064	0.0420		0.1061	0.1334	
互联网贷款公司	5.5110	3.2720	*	−0.5204	2.4810		−1.1760	7.8870	
应用 FinTech	1.5860	2.8200		0.4302	2.1370		2.4230	6.7950	
用于生产经营贷款比例（%）	−2.15E−04	1.40E−03		−1.31E−04	1.06E−03		2.82E−03	3.38E−03	
无指定用途贷款比例（%）	0.1293	0.0651	**	0.1096	0.0494	**	−0.2183	0.1569	
信用放款比例（%）	0.0098	0.0237		0.0078	0.0180		−0.0819	0.0572	
小组联保比例（%）	0.0598	0.0721		0.0722	0.0546		0.0652	0.1736	
到期一次性还本付息比例（%）	−0.0054	0.0197		0.0075	0.0149		−0.0368	0.0474	
分期等额本金比例（%）	−0.0084	0.0497		−0.0026	0.0377		−0.0639	0.1198	
分期等额本息比例（%）	0.0118	0.0300		−0.0441	0.0227	*	−0.1249	0.0723	*
3～6 个月贷款比例（%）	−0.0362	0.0381		0.0131	0.0289		0.1607	0.0917	*
6～12 个月贷款比例（%）	−0.0478	0.0267	*	−0.0109	0.0202		−0.0092	0.0643	
12 个月以上贷款比例（%）	−0.0679	0.0377	*	−0.0216	0.0286		−0.1215	0.0909	
综合贷款利率（%）	0.0989	0.1145		0.0724	0.0868		0.1654	0.2759	
户均贷款额（2017，万元）	5.09E−04	1.20E−03		5.12E−04	9.08E−04		8.27E−04	2.89E−03	
员工平均放贷额（2017，万元）	−6.99E−06	1.49E−05		−7.14E−06	1.13E−05		−1.58E−05	3.60E−05	
农林牧渔业（排序）	0.0773	0.2285		−0.1033	0.1732		0.1036	0.5507	
批发零售业（排序）	−0.4878	0.2292	**	−0.0298	0.1738		−0.0046	0.5524	
住宿餐饮业（排序）	0.1201	0.2662		−0.2090	0.2018		0.5566	0.6414	
股本收益率 ROE（2017）	−0.4064	0.1941	**	−0.2140	0.1472		−1.5500	0.4679	***
股本收益率 ROE^2（2017）	0.0259	0.0078	***	0.0114	0.0059	*	0.0441	0.0187	**

下面将逐一描述哪些因素对信贷风险产生影响。需要说明的是，为了获得更加可靠的结论，在判断哪些因素确实与信贷风险存在关联时，我们采用了更严格的统计学方法。如表 13－3 所示，* 所对应的因素，是通过统计学检验证明对信贷风险具有影响的因素。* 越多，表示可信度越高。表中系数的正负号表示影响的方向，正号（+）表示该因素的指标值增加，风险增加；负号（-）表示该因素的指标值增加，风险减少。

（二）风险要素的表现和影响

1. 地域差异形成不同的生存环境

从逾期小于 30 天、30～90 天和大于 90 天三种不同风险程度来考察区域的差别可以发现，对于 30 天内的逾期贷款率，广东、内蒙古和重庆的系数值为负数，而且统计学检验系数不为零的概率达到显著水平（见表 13－3），说明它们的逾期贷款率显著低于其他省（自治区、直辖市）；对于 30～90 天的逾期贷款率，广东省的逾期贷款率明显高于其他省（自治区、直辖市）；对于大于 90 天的逾期贷款率（不良贷款率），天津、江苏、重庆、内蒙古四个省（自治区、直辖市）的逾期贷款率都显著高于其他省（自治区、直辖市）。

这个结果表明，一是在短时间逾期方面各省差异不明显；二是不良贷款率高的地区，短期逾期率不一定高。需要深入分析的是，为什么高不良贷款率集中出现在天津、江苏、重庆、内蒙古四个省（自治区、直辖市）。

实际上，国家层面没有对小额贷款公司业务进行统一监管，监管职能主要由地方金融监管部门执行。虽然 23 号文是各地对小额贷款公司进行监管的主要政策依据，但各地在实施细则上有所不同，加上社会、经济和文化的差异，各地的小额贷款公司的风险程度会有一定的差异。但是，当差异达到显著水平时，说明其中有一些重要因素在发挥作用。

不良贷款率的提高也与当地金融监管部门准入的宽松程度有关。如图 13－6 所示，上述四个不良贷款率高发区中，只有江苏省是小额贷款公司高度密集的地区。内蒙古、辽宁、安徽、广东等省份也是小额贷款公司比较密集的地区，但是，其不良贷款率没有明显高于其他地区。

各地在实行监管的过程中，对杠杆率的要求也有所不同，有些地区提高了杠杆率的上限。如图 13－7 所示，我们用小额贷款余额与实收资本的比例代表杠杆率，可以看到，重庆的杠杆率最高，小额贷款余额与实收资本比例达 2.00；广西的这个指标达 1.79；广东为 1.31；安徽为 1.22，它们的不良贷款率水平并没有显著高于其他地区。

上述情况产生的原因是否是由于某些地区平均小额贷款余额超出了员工能力？如

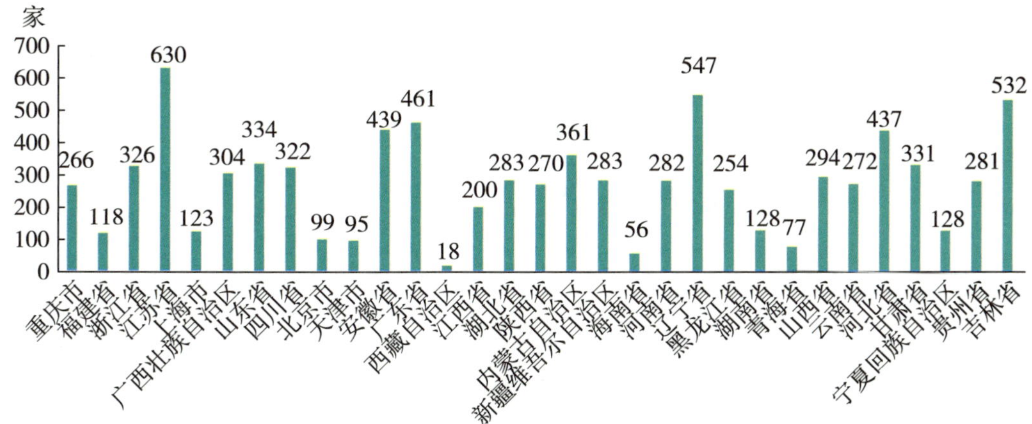

注：由于批准设立与正式营业并具备报数条件之间存在时滞，统计口径小额贷款公司数量与各地公布的小额贷款公司批准设立数量有差别。

资料来源：中国人民银行发布的“小额贷款公司分地区情况统计表”，http：//www. pbc. gov. cn/goutongjiaoliu/113456/113469/3470011/index. html，2017—12—31。

图 13-6　2017 年底全国小额贷款公司数量

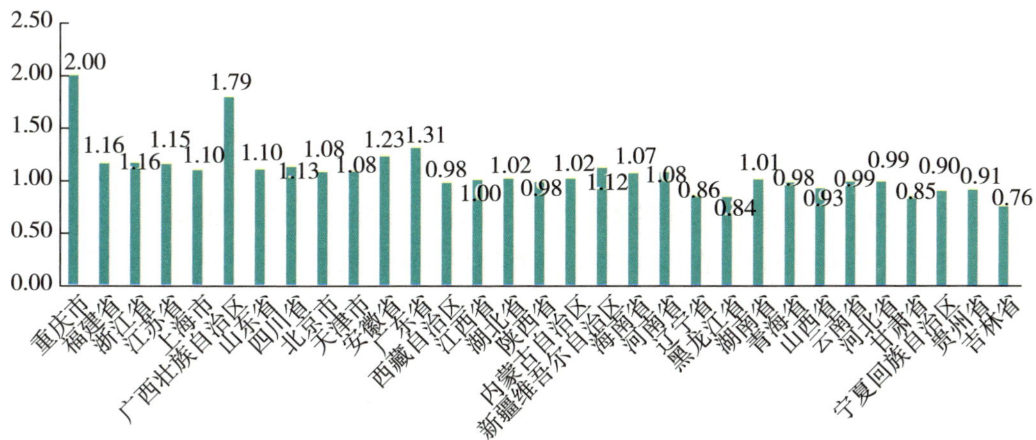

资料来源：中国人民银行发布的“小额贷款公司分地区情况统计表”，http：//www. pbc. gov. cn/goutongjiaoliu/113456/113469/3470011/index. html，2017—12—31。

图 13-7　2017 年底全国小额贷款余额与实收资本比例

图 13-8 所示，各省份小额贷款余额与员工的比值，重庆再一次领先其他省份，员工平均贷款余额为 2322 万元/人；江苏也达到 1610 万元/人的较高水平；内蒙古和天津处于全国平均水平。同时我们也发现，福建达到 2119 万元/人，浙江达到 1955 万元/人，后者的风险水平并不是很高。

通过上面的分析，我们意识到监管的差异与不良贷款率存在某种关联，但在众多复杂的外部环境下很难给出明确的结论，或许是各地经济发展水平、社会诚信风气、

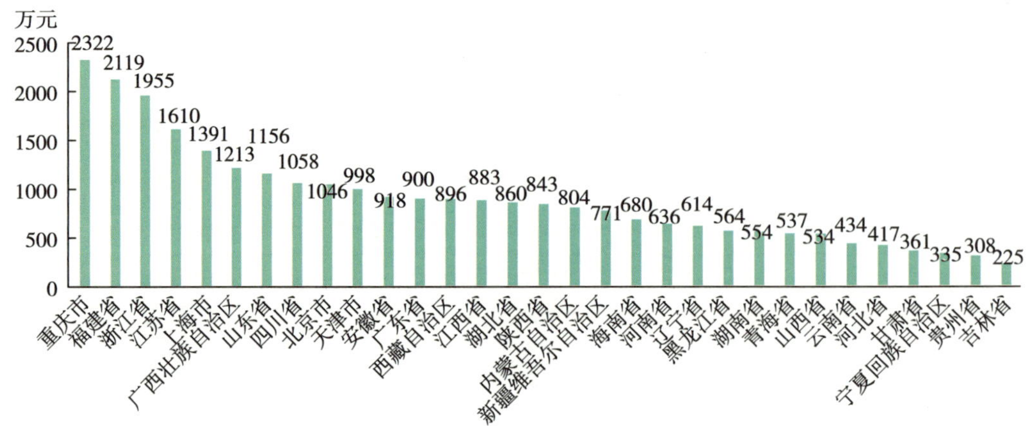

资料来源：中国人民银行发布的“小额贷款公司分地区情况统计表”，http：//www.pbc.gov.cn/goutongjiaoliu/113456/113469/3470011/index.html，2017—12—31。

图13-8　2017年底全国各地小额贷款公司员工平均贷款余额

信用生态环境、金融基础设施等条件的差异导致了风险水平的地区差异，或许是因为各地区的小额贷款公司的某一种共同特征导致风险的区域性差别。

2. 成熟度提高公司的生产能力

风险管控需要经验积累，一个公司从初创到成熟需要经历一定的时间。如表13-3所示，注册年限在逾期90天以上的分析模型中的系数为负值，而且统计学检验达到显著水平。这说明小额贷款公司的不良贷款率随着注册年限的增加而降低。

中国的小额贷款公司是在2008年以后逐渐成立的。如图13-9所示，注册年限最长的已有13年，最短的只有1年。在样本小额贷款公司中，98%已经有4年以上的运作经验，已经达到了成熟阶段。如图13-10所示，从全国小额贷款数量的增长情况来

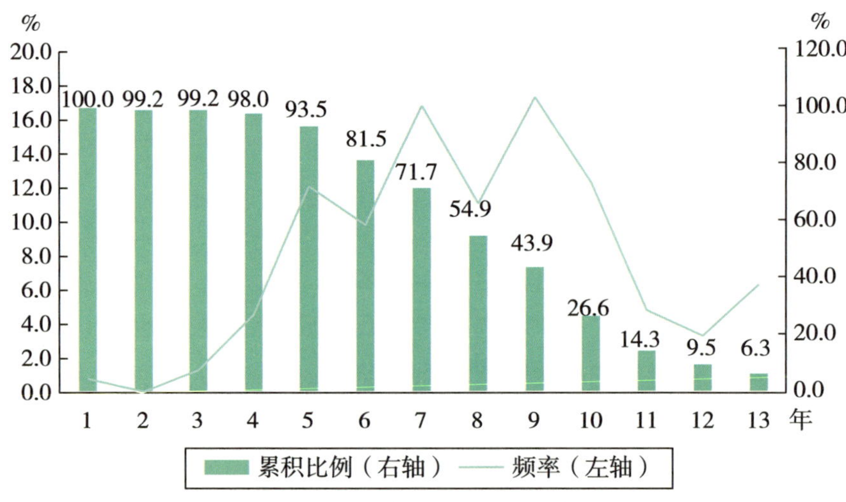

图13-9　小额贷款公司注册年限

看，2015 年以前是直线上升的趋势，这与我们调查的样本情况基本一致。

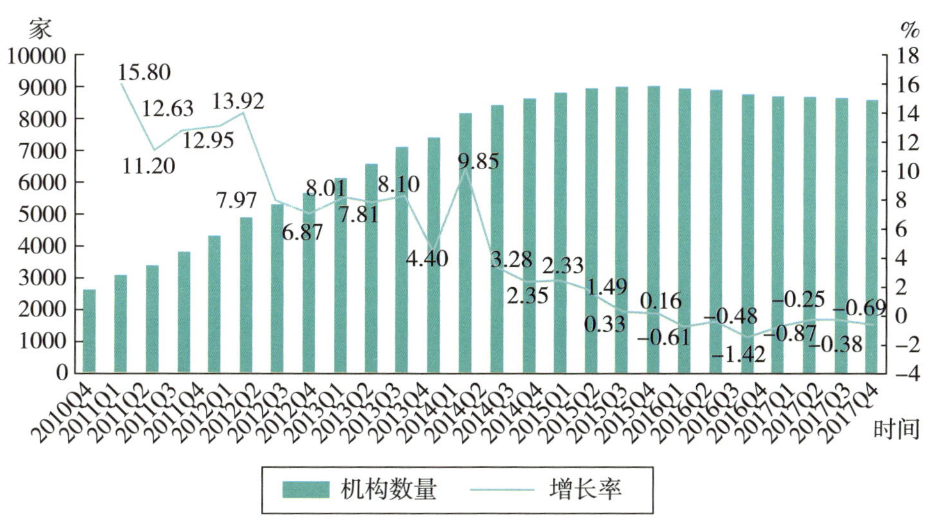

资料来源：中国人民银行。

图 13－10　小额贷款公司数量及增长情况

随着小额贷款公司的成长，业绩也将会增加，我们分析了小额贷款公司注册年限与年底贷款余额的关系，证明两者之间呈正相关关系，系数为 0.1235，统计学检验达到显著水平。

这些结果都说明小额贷款行业正在走向成熟。从监管的角度来看，应该给予小额贷款公司发展成熟的时间。相对于银行业上百年的历史，13 年时间对于小额贷款公司来说不算太长。未来，小额贷款公司应该会更加稳定、更加成熟。

3. 融资是生存发展的关键

资本构成对小额贷款公司成长有非常重要的影响。前面已经讨论，资本结构不当将给企业带来不同的风险，如利率风险和资本风险，这些风险不一定与信用风险有必然的联系，但是它们之间可以相互影响。例如，利率风险爆发可能导致企业的收入产生波动，信贷风控能力下降，信贷风险上升。

在调查的样本中，由于数据获得的原因，只能用是否是上市公司、最大股东所占的资本比例、杠杆率三个指标来衡量小额贷款公司的资本结构。按照 23 号文的规定，小额贷款公司不能从公众融资，最大股东持股比例及杠杆率也受到限制。但是，由于各地情况不同，部分地区在实行过程中放松了部分限制。

图 13－11 为最大股东持股比例分布图，持股比例最大的达 100％，企业数占总数的 18.55％。60.4％的小额贷款公司其最大股东持股比例在 50％以下。民营企业作为最大股东占比较大，约占 55％；其次是个人，占 20％；再次是国有企业，占 17.8％。

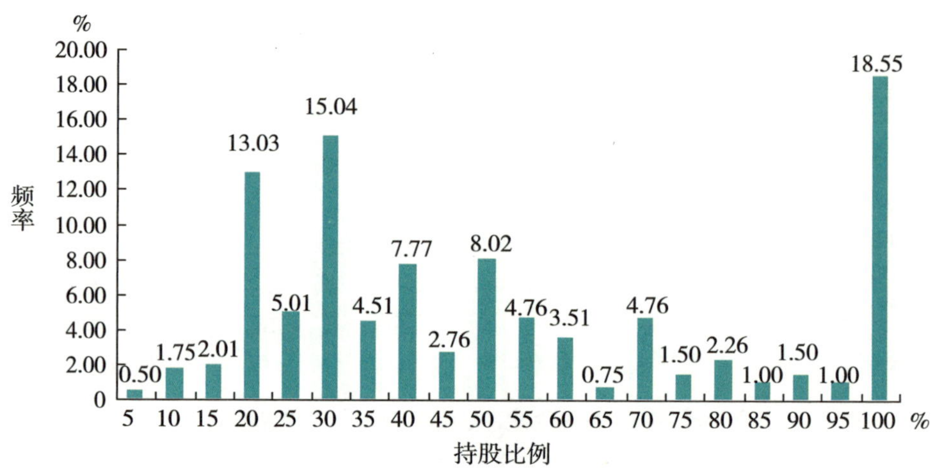

图 13-11 最大股东持股比例分布

金融机构能否持续生存，杠杆率是一个非常关键的因素。小额贷款公司也是一样，需要通过金融杠杆来撬动资本，通过利差获得利润。同时，能否使用好金融杠杆也体现了小额贷款公司的经营能力。如图 13-4 所示，在调查的样本中，79.45%的小额贷款公司杠杆率为零，在杠杆率非零的小额贷款公司中，最大的杠杆率为 89%。这显然是杠杆率限制的结果。尽管如此，图 13-12 显示了杠杆率与总收入之间的正比例关系，它们的关系系数高达 0.5173。可见，杠杆率对小额信贷公司有着生死攸关的影响。

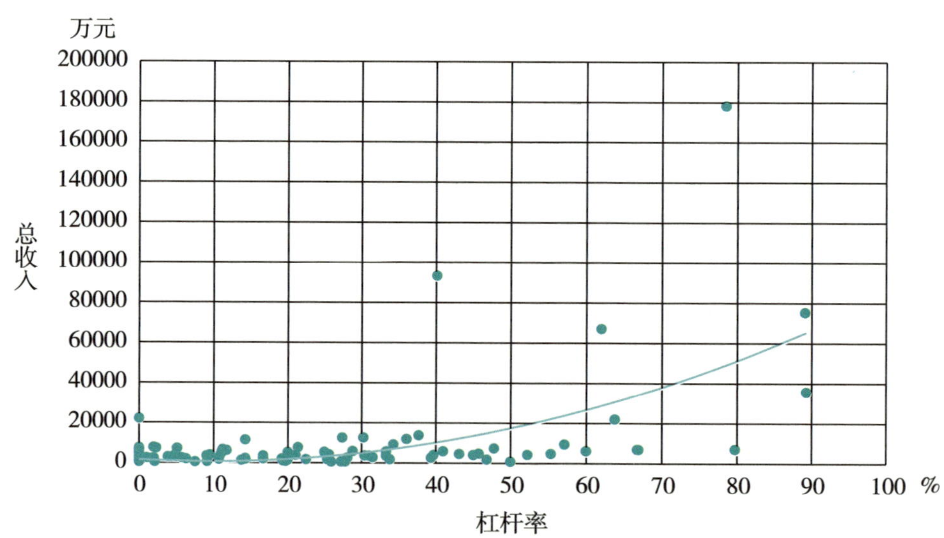

图 13-12 杠杆率与总收入的关系

放松融资限制是否会增加风险是我们重点关注的问题。如表 13－3 所示，20 家已经上市的小额贷款公司，其 30～90 天逾期贷款率明显高于非上市公司；最大股东持股比例与风险没有显著关联；增加杠杆率也显著增加了 30～90 天的逾期贷款率。但是，无论是上市还是增加最大股东持股比例和杠杆率，都没有显著增加不良贷款率。

4. 高素质人才至关重要

一般而言，控制风险需要投入更多的人力。可是，表 13－3 的分析结果告诉我们，小额贷款公司投入风险控制的人力比例与各逾期贷款率和不良贷款率没有显著相关；大学以下学历的员工比例对控制逾期贷款率和不良贷款率也没有显著的效果；不过，增加研究生以上学历的员工比例可以显著降低不良贷款率水平。因此，高素质人才对风险控制至关重要。

5. 信用贷款和担保抵押一样稳妥

担保抵押已经成为传统金融机构认可的具有标杆性的风险控制手段。信用贷款通常被认为是一种风险很高的贷款类型。事实上，担保抵押只能减少金融机构的损失，并不能降低风险。如表 13－3 所示，信用贷款和小组贷款在贷款组合中比例的大小，与抵押和质押相比，并没有显著增加逾期贷款率和不良贷款率。

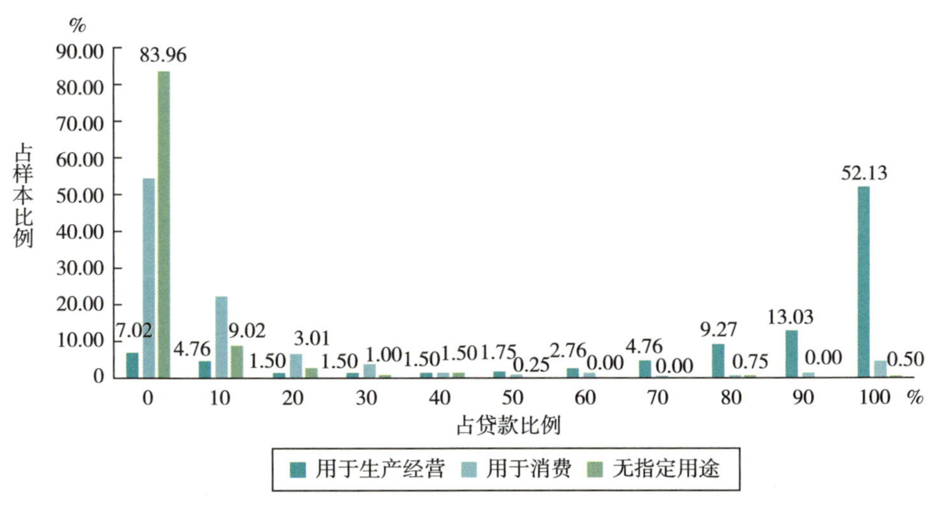

图 13－13　小额贷款公司贷款用途结构

6. 现金贷并不可怕

2017 年底引起监管部门关注的现金贷，是一种无指定用途的小额贷款，被认为是一种高风险的金融产品。监管部门出台专门的文件禁止小额贷款公司从事现金贷业务。如图 13－13 所示，对大多数小额贷款公司来说，无指定用途贷款所占的比例非常小。样本中，84％的小额贷款公司没有开展无指定用途贷款业务；9％的小额贷款公司开展无指定用途贷款业务，但这部分贷款业务占其业务总量的 10％以下；有 3 家公司的无指定用途贷款比例占70%～80%；有2家公司专门做无指定用途贷款业务。

在贷款组合中，大多数贷款用于生产经营。生产经营贷款比例达70%以上的小额贷款公司占样本数量的74.4%。45%的小额贷款公司开展一定程度的消费贷款业务，其中6.27%的小额贷款公司以消费贷款为主要业务，占其贷款业务的80%以上。

分析发现，生产经营贷款比例没有显著影响贷款的逾期率和不良率。表13-3中，生产经营贷款比例与三种不同的逾期贷款率都没有显著的相关性。实际上，无指定用途贷款比例与30天内的逾期贷款率和30～90天的逾期贷款率有显著相关性，关系系数均为正值，表示增加无指定用途贷款比例会提高逾期贷款率。但是，无指定用途贷款比例与不良贷款率的系数为负值，这暗示着增加无指定用途贷款的比例有利于减少不良贷款率。但是这种关系没有达到统计学的显著水平。无指定用途贷款确实增加了逾期贷款率，但不会增加了不良贷款率。

7. 分期等额本息有利于还款

小额贷款公司的还款方式有4种：到期一次性还本付息、分期等额本金、分期等额本息、分期付息到期还本。如图13-14所示，还款方式的分布呈现两个极端的现象，说明小额贷款公司通常比较单调地使用一种还款方式。56.4%的公司采用分期付息到期还本的还款方式，其中使用率为100%的公司占44%；28.8%的公司采用到期一次性还本付息的还款方式，其使用率为100%的公司占20%；19.8%的公司采用了分期等额本息的还款方式；只有5.8%的公司采用了分期等额本金的还款方式。

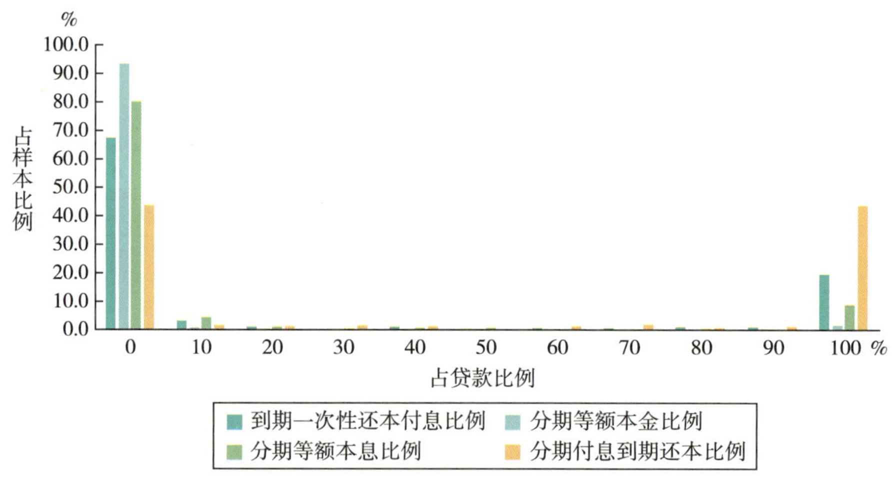

图13-14　小额贷款公司还款方式分布

在表13-14所示的结果中，我们发现分期等额本息还款方式对30～90天逾期贷款率和不良贷款率都有显著的影响，其系数均为负值，达到统计学显著水平。也就是说，随着分期等额本息贷款比例的增加，逾期贷款率和不良贷款率会随之减少。其他还款模式对不良贷款率没有显著影响。

8. 贷款期限影响公司生存

贷款期限短是小额贷款的特征之一，如图 13－15 所示，当前小额贷款公司以 6～12 个月期为主打产品。图 13－16 进一步分析了各种产品的贷款期限在小额贷款公司中占比的分布，产品期限是 6～12 个月期的小额贷款公司占 81.2%；其次是 3～6 个月期的占 74.44%；3 个月期以内的占 68%；12 个月期以上的只有 44.6%。相对来说，6～12 个月期贷款分布比较均匀。23.3%的小额贷款公司其 6～12 个月期贷款占总贷款额的 70%以上。

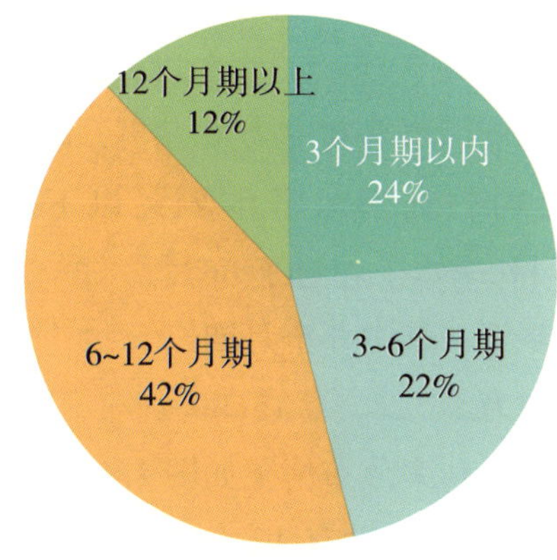

图 13－15　小额贷款公司不同贷款期限产品结构

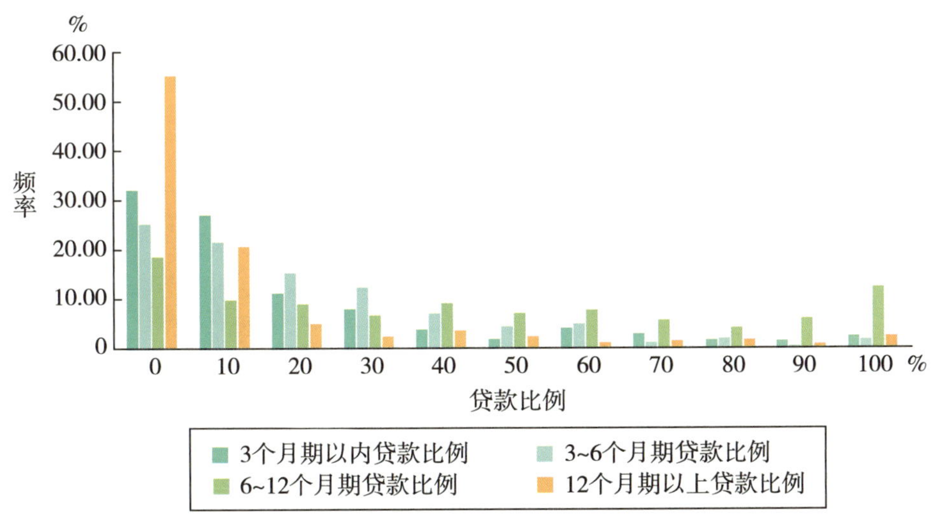

图 13－16　产品的贷款期限占比分布

贷款期限与风险之间是一种非线性关系。如表 13－3 所示，贷款期限长有利于降低短期逾期贷款率，贷款期限短则容易导致不良贷款率升高。具体来说，6～12 个月、

12 个月以上的贷款比例分别与 30 天以内逾期贷款率呈负相关关系，也就是说，随着 6 个月以上贷款期限比例的增加，可以减少 30 天以内的逾期贷款率。当考察表 13－3 中的系数时也发现，贷款期限长，系数相对较大，其降低短期逾期贷款率的效果更好。无论是哪一种贷款期限，都没有影响 30～90 天逾期贷款率，6 个月以上的贷款比例也没有影响不良贷款率。

影响不良贷款率的主要是 3～6 个月期贷款。表 13－3 中，3～6 个月期贷款与 90 天以上逾期贷款率的系数为正值，表示随着 3～6 个月期贷款比例的增加，不良贷款率随之增加。

9. 绝大多数公司综合利率合规

小额贷款的利率问题受到比较广泛的关注和讨论。我们将 399 家小额贷款公司不同产品的利率情况进行综合测算，综合利率为 15.6％。除了 10.7％的公司没有发放贷款，利率为零外，87％的公司的利率水平在 24％以下，1.3％的公司利率水平在 24％～36％，剩余 1％的公司利率水平超过了 36％。

不同产品的利率有一定差别，其中 3 个月期、3～6 个月期、6～12 个月期和 12 个月期以上贷款的综合利率分别为 16.28％、15.50％、15.29％和 15.51％。短期贷款的利率水平稍高一些。不同产品的利率分布情况如图 13－17 所示，图中零利率表示这些公司没有这类产品，如 49.1％的公司没有 12 个月期以上的贷款产品；同时也能看出 6～12 个月期贷款相对普遍。

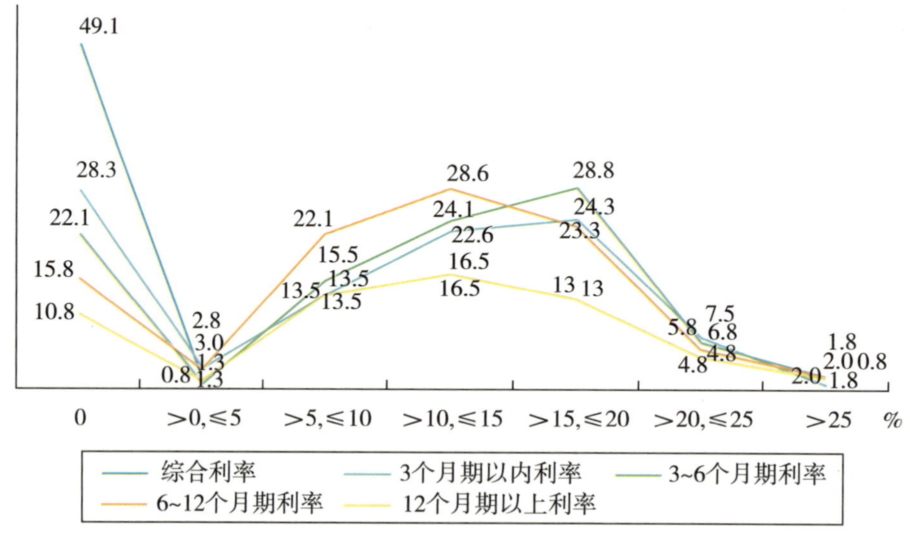

图 13－17　不同期限贷款产品利率

普遍认为，贷款利率应随贷款额度的降低而提高，理由是单位成本随贷款额度的减少而提高。如表 13－4 所示，最下方一栏是各贷款额度利率的算术平均值，该数值确实具有随贷款额度减小而上升的趋势，但是升幅非常有限。

额度和利息之间的取舍关系到公司的商业可持续性。在当前市场条件下，31%的公司把贷款额定在11万～50万元，同时收取10%～15%的利率，这可能是最佳的获利方案。不管是哪一种贷款额度，小额贷款公司收取的利率范围主要是5%～20%。从合规利率水平的角度看，利率超过24%的非常少。

表13-4 贷款额度与利息 单位：%

利率（%）	301万元及以上	101万～300万元	51万～100万元	11万～50万元	6万～10万元	5万元以下
0	41.9	28.1	26.1	20.1	39.3	45.6
＞0，≤5	3.0	2.5	2.3	3.0	2.5	1.5
＞5，≤10	15.0	17.3	17.8	16.8	12.3	9.5
＞10，≤15	17.0	24.8	26.1	31.1	21.6	21.1
＞15，≤20	17.8	21.3	21.3	22.1	16.8	16.8
＞20，≤25	4.8	5.3	6.0	6.5	7.0	5.0
＞25	0.5	0.5	0.5	0.5	0.5	0.5
0	41.9	28.1	26.1	20.1	39.3	45.6
＞0，≤24	57.6	71.2	73.4	79.4	59.9	53.9
＞24，≤36	0.0	0.8	0.3	0.3	0.8	0.5
＞36	0.5	0.0	0.3	0.3	0.0	0.0
算数平均	13.4	13.5	13.7	13.7	14.0	14.2

由此可见，即使利率上限设在36%，在市场机制的作用下，很少有公司把利率水平设在政策的上限，而是根据市场竞争的需要设置利率水平。显然，目前的利率上限基本处于市场均衡利率水平之上，并没有严重影响市场作用的发挥。通过表13-3可以发现，利率大小与风险没有直接的相关关系，放开利率限制并不会增加风险。相反，过低的利率会损害小额贷款的商业可持续性。

10. 小额度客户的信用一样好

小额贷款公司的户均贷款大小与风险高低没有显著的关联（见表13-3）。额度小通常被认为与高风险有关联，其假设是弱势群体信贷需求额度小，也就是小额度贷款以弱势群体为主体客户，弱势群体偿还能力弱、信用差，因此，额度越小，风险越高。但是很多实践已经证明，此种假设并不总是成立。

11. 农林牧渔业也很讲信用

小额贷款公司成立的初衷就是要服务“三农”、服务县域经济，农业是其最重要的服务对象，当然它也服务农村的其他产业，如批发零售业和餐饮业。表 13－5 是涉农行业在小额贷款公司业务上的排序情况。35％的小额贷款公司将农林牧渔业作为首要的服务对象；49％的公司将农林牧副渔业排在前三位；60％的公司将批发零售业排在前三位。

表 13－5　涉农行业在小额贷款公司业务上的排序　　单位：％

排序	农林牧渔业	批发零售业	住宿餐饮业
1	35.1	20.6	1.3
2	7.5	28.6	5.8
3	6.3	10.5	12.5
4	6.0	5.5	10.0
5	5.3	3.3	6.0
6	4.3	2.0	7.5
7	3.5	0.8	4.0
8	2.3	0.5	1.8
9	1.8	0.3	0.8
NA	28.1	28.1	50.4

如表 13－3 所示，在小额贷款公司业务中，农林牧渔业和住宿餐饮业的排序和比例对风险没有影响。换句话说，农林牧渔业和住宿餐饮业的风险程度，与其他行业没有显著区别。批发零售业的地位对 30 天以内的逾期贷款率有影响，排位越靠后，逾期越低，这说明批发零售业的风险比其他行业高。所幸批发零售业的地位与 30～90 天逾期贷款率和不良贷款率之间没有显著的关联。因此，涉及“三农”的小额贷款业务，其风险并没有显著区别于其他行业。

12. 互联网贷款是未来的希望

在调查的 399 家小额贷款公司中有 55 家互联网小额贷款公司，它们服务了近 99％的客户，平均贷款额度在 2.1 万元左右。如表 13－3 所示，互联网小额贷款公司 30 天以内的逾期贷款率的系数为正，而且达到了统计学显著水平，表明其短期逾期贷款率明显高于其他常规小额贷款公司。与此相反，与 30～90 天的逾期贷款率和不良贷款率的系数为负，表明互联网金融不会提高长期逾期贷款率，但是这种关系并没有达到统计学的显著水平，只能认定它们之间没有显著的关系。

四、政策建议

在过去一段时间，小额贷款行业出现的一些事件引发社会的关注，引起了监管的高度重视。不少人认为，严监管是唯一正确的选择，甚至把小额贷款公司误解为高利贷和地下钱庄。根据上述分析结果，我们提出以下对小额贷款的监管建议。

（一）监管原则建议

1. 依据风险进行监管

众所周知，监管的目的是防范金融风险，特别是防范系统性风险爆发。从历史经验来看，风险事件爆发往往激发新监管政策的制定和出台。防范金融风险爆发不能等同于防止金融机构倒闭。对小额贷款公司的监管也是如此，应该以风险爆发的可能性和危害程度作为监管的主要依据。我们希望上述对风险的分析能成为制定监管政策的重要依据，进而根据风险的潜在危害程度进行分类监管。

系统性风险往往起源于经济波动，通过金融体系放大，导致更大的经济波动。特别是在资本来源于公众（如存款、股市）的金融体系中，受风险爆发事件影响，很容易通过金融体系放大，因此需要进行审慎监管，避免造成经济更大的波动。

经济上的任何波动，是否会通过小额贷款这种特殊的金融服务体系传导和放大到整个经济体系？从国际经验来看，即使小额贷款出现严重的风险事件，对政治、经济乃至社会可能产生一定程度的影响，但是大多数情况下这种影响是短暂而局部的。

当然，这不是放松监管的理由。对于那些与公众资本有关的小额贷款公司而言，有必要对其风险进行密切监测，应参照银行采用审慎监管的措施。一般来说，对于那些没有吸纳公众存款的小额贷款公司，没有必要采用审慎监管的原则进行监管。这一类小额贷款公司的风险控制责任在于其股东和理事会，而不是监管机构。

2. 兼顾社会和商业使命

小额贷款从成立之初就肩负服务“中小微弱”群体的社会和商业双重使命，两者之间大多数时候需要取舍，对其监管的措施应有别于传统的金融服务机构。要在风险可控的条件下，让小额贷款公司充分发挥其社会使命，不能因为过度监管而削弱“中小微弱”群体获得金融服务的机会。

3. 善用金融科技手段

无论是对传统金融机构，还是对小额贷款公司，监管应该考虑到金融科技这一重要因素。上述分析证明，金融科技的使用并没有造成逾期贷款率和不良贷款率的增加。当然有些担心是值得关注的。例如，金融科技的广泛使用加速了信息的传播，这可能使原来不容易传播的风险事件，很容易通过互联网传导到整个金融系统和经济系统，造成风险事件影响的扩大。反之，金融科技也为风险防范提供了有效的手段，特别是基于大数据的风控模型的应用还可能改变金融风险的特征，减少风险的危害。

4. 以监测为主，放松限制

金融科技已经渗透到金融服务的方方面面，基于风险防范的金融监管应该以风险监测为主，特别是用监管科技进行有效监测。对于不可避免的风险事件，应该根据监测信息控制其不良后果的传播和放大。监管科技的发展已经为穿透式的监管提供了条件。各种监管限制有望被数字化的监测和及时迅速、有针对性的应对措施所代替。

5. 将风控核心责任交给企业

小额贷款公司是风险控制的第一责任者，也是风险爆发后果的承受者。实际上，监管者不可能比小额贷款公司更了解它们的风险，更不可能在第一时间感知风险的爆发和危害。前面我们也证明了过去的一些监管措施并不能有效地控制风险。因此，应该将风险控制的主要责任交给小额贷款公司自己。

（二）监管政策建议

根据上述对小额贷款公司的贡献、风险的分析及对监管原则的思考，我们提出如下监管政策建议。

1. 将小额贷款公司纳入国家普惠金融体系

无论在国内还是国外，小额贷款公司已经在推动普惠金融发展中发挥重要作用。实践证明，它们在解决民营和小微企业的融资难问题、金融科技的创新和普及应用、稳定就业维持生计等方面起到有效作用。国家应将小额贷款公司的服务纳入普惠金融服务体系中，特别是要确认小额贷款公司“非存款类金融机构”的属性和法律地位，这将有利于它们在税收、司法、财产处置等方面获得公平的待遇。

2. 在中央统一政策加强监督的前提下按属地进行监管

中央出台政策、地方承担监管和风险处置的责任是当前行之有效的监管模式。在一定程度上，局部地区的小额贷款公司问题与当地监管的有效性有关。因此，有必要对地方监管部门实行中央监管政策的情况进行监督。

3. 建立健全全国监测网，促进监管科技的应用

对互联网金融的监管，应充分考虑其巨大的普惠金融价值。通过互联网开展金融服务，并没有改变其金融的本质。上述分析也证明，通过互联网开展放贷并不会增加小额贷款公司的逾期贷款率和不良贷款率。

对互联网金融的担心主要是其跨地域性可能带来的问题。实际上，随着数字技术的发展，不仅仅是金融服务，其他任何服务都已经或将打破地域的边界，对金融服务

进行线上和线下的划分将很困难。将来无论是对传统的小额贷款业务，还是对互联网小额贷款业务，进行地域限制都将是无效的。按小额贷款公司的登记地进行监管，允许跨区经营，采用数字化监管更加符合未来的发展趋势。

风险事件的爆发往往都是从局部开始的，然后其影响逐步扩散到其他地区，限制跨区经营有利于将风险事件的影响控制在本区域范围内，允许跨区经营可能会加速风险事件的传播。然而，在互联网时代，无论是否允许跨区经营，要将风险事件的影响控制在一个区域范围内实际上非常困难，最有效的办法是要求小额贷款公司进行全国性备案，同时建立全国性的监测网，以便掌握全面的小额贷款风险动向。

4. 适当放松对杠杆率的限制，拓宽融资渠道

鉴于小额贷款公司的社会服务和商业可持续性的双重使命，虽然提高杠杆率可能会导致逾期贷款率在一定程度上的增加，但是它没有显著增加不良贷款率。适当放松对杠杆率的限制，有利于小额贷款公司增强其商业可持续性，扩大其在普惠金融发展中的作用。而且，如果杠杆率的限制妨碍了小额贷款公司的生存和发展，反而迫使小额贷款公司采用其他手段进行融资，可能会增加资本风险。经济学理论和实践已经多次证明，采用统一的最高杠杆率限制可能会伤害经济效率，特别是在没有涉及公共资本的情况下，限制杠杆率的做法没有理论依据。杠杆率的决定权及其可能带来的风险控制权，应交给小额贷款公司的董事会。我们建议在放松限制的基础上，可以根据监测结果采用分类灵活的监管措施。

小额贷款公司与银行开展包括联合贷款和助贷等形式的合作是一种行之有效的模式，具有银行、小额贷款公司和客户多方共赢的特点，应给予放开和鼓励。在实践中，由于客户的风险分别经过银行和小额贷款公司双方的风险识别，风控质量较高。这种合作方式将银行尤其是大型银行的资本通过小额贷款公司这种“毛细管道”，及时有效地送达中小微企业和弱势群体，将金融体系的包容性提高到一个全新的水平。

除此之外，在风险可控的原则下，可以适度放开其他融资渠道，以拓宽融资渠道，加速中国普惠金融的发展。

5. 丰富金融产品，适度对现金贷进行监管

普惠金融客户是一个复杂的群体，对金融的需求千差万别，不是几个金融产品就能满足的。以客户为中心的产品开发设计已经被国际上证明是增加金融机构商业可持续性的核心理念。应该鼓励小额贷款公司积极推动产品创新，改善客户体验，对不同客户进行差异化服务。

无指定用途的贷款是金融产品的一个重要类别。根据上文的分析结果，它确实增加了一定程度的信贷逾期风险，但是没有显著增加不良贷款率。由于这种贷款常常是平滑不稳定收入的重要资源，市场需求量大，对提高人们的生活水平特别是促进消费

具有重要作用，而且其风险基本可控，不应该采取过严的监管措施。

6. 由市场决定利率，通过竞争降低贷款价格

利率是贷款的价格，在市场经济条件下对利率进行限制，可能会导致两种结果：一种是最高利率高于市场均衡利率水平，利率限制不起作用，利率仍然由市场决定；另一种是最高利率低于市场均衡利率水平，利率限制产生作用，结果是金融供给不足，部分客户不能获得服务。

从普惠金融发展的角度来看，利率限制具有导致部分客户群体被排除在金融服务体系之外的风险。理论和实践都已经证明，竞争才是降低贷款价格的有效手段。

7. 将信息安全和客户保护作为监管核心

金融科技赋予信息价值，未来小额贷款公司之间的竞争将是信息的竞争。收集、保存和使用用户的数据是小额贷款公司基本的能力。信息给公司和客户都带来一定的利益，但也增加了信息泄露的风险。监管部门对客户的信息安全保护具有不可推卸的责任，在制定相关政策时应将信息安全和客户保护作为监管核心。

8. 加强小额贷款公司的能力建设

能力建设是小额贷款公司长期健康发展的关键。前面分析证明，小额贷款公司的经验积累和高级人才都有利于它的经营发展。因此，应制定一些激励政策，鼓励小额贷款公司培养行业人才，这对小额贷款的发展乃至普惠金融的发展都大有益处。

第十四章　小微企业的增信和违约风险

【摘要】常用的信用评价指标能够反映企业的可贷性，但是不能有效地反映小微企业的贷款需求，信用和实际贷款的转化率低。更值得警惕的是，有些指标在增信的同时也增加了违约风险；普遍认为与信用和信贷需求都有关系的指标，如利率，其实与一些信用和需求指标没有显著的关系。这些问题可能是数据可得性的原因造成的。数字化信用评价为解决这些问题提供了有效的方法。从多维度给企业细致画像，使信用评价同时反映其可贷性和信贷需求。基于这些分析结果，本章还提出小微企业的增信建议。

小微企业在经济发展中的地位和作用是众所周知的。在提供就业机会和提高低收入人群的生活水平、减少贫富差距和减缓贫困等方面，小微企业都发挥了重要作用，它也将成为乡村振兴的中坚力量。通常小微企业是指以商品生产和服务为主的规模比较小的经济实体，它包括小型企业、微型企业、家庭作坊、个体工商户、合作社和家庭农场。划分小微企业的各种具体标准差异较大。本报告将采用国家统计局的统计标准，对分析样本进行规模类型划分。

融资难是当前社会对小微企业比较普遍的印象，也是阻碍小微企业发展的重要因素。普惠金融的主要目的之一就是要解决小微企业融资难的问题。基于其对国计民生的重要性，国家出台了针对小微企业的专项金融政策，各类银行也设置专业部门为小微企业提供服务。

作为解决小微企业融资难的基础设施，小微企业信用建设受到相当高的重视。政府已经将小微企业纳入企业征信体系。各种互联网平台争相建立基于大数据的小微企业信用评价体系。但是，我们要提出的一个关键问题是，信用评价在多大程度上解决了小微企业的融资难问题？信用评价和小微企业的贷款需求是不是一致？信用评价有没有可能对小微企业融资产生误导？

关于小微企业信用的分析通常会受到数据可得性的限制，小微企业一般在统计之外，企业信用评价结果一般只对企业自身开放，小微企业自身也缺乏规范的财务记录。幸运的是，我们拥有浙江省 2729 家中小微企业的问卷数据，使我们的分析得以顺利进行。分析发现，常用的企业信用评价指标与小微企业实际融资情况没有显著关系。换而言之，信用评价结果可能显示某企业“值得贷款”，而企业认为“不必贷款”。这种信用评价与信贷需求脱节的现象，降低了信用评价的信贷转化率。将信用和信贷需求的共同因子纳入信用评价体系可能是解决这个问题的有效办法。分析也发现了值得警惕的问题，在使用信用评价结果时，有可能受到增信指标的误导，反而增加违约风险。一些通常认为对信用和信贷需求敏感的指标，如利率，实际上并没有对融资情况产生显著影响。

建立数字化信用评价体系是解决问题的最佳途径，也是必然的趋势。它可以更加广泛、更多维度、更加深入地对企业信用进行画像，从而使信用评价的使用范围更加广泛。

一、信用评价指标与数字化

企业信用评价是对偿还贷款能力和意愿的综合评估，用来衡量企业债务违约的可能性和损失的大小程度。金融机构根据信用评价的结果来决定是否应该给企业进行贷款。企业也可以根据信用评价结果来决定是否申请贷款及贷款的额度。企业信用评价极大地依赖于数据掌握的广度和精度，然而数据的获得常常是信用评价的难点所在。数字化经济的兴起，使信用评价更加具有预见性。

（一）信用评价指标

对企业信用全面评估是信用评估的基本要求，通常包含企业素质、信用记录、财务状况、经营管理水平、成长性和潜在风险等内容（洪玫，2006）。比较常用的信用评估指标包括财务结构指标（如资产负债率、负债与产权比例、股东权益比率、有形净值债务率、流动资产率等），营业效益（如销售利润率、资产利润率、资本金利润率、成本费用利润率等），偿债能力（如流动比率、速动比例、现金比率、利息保障倍数等），经营能力（如存货收转率、应收账款周转率、总资产周转、固定资产周转等），现金流量（净现金流量偏离标准比率、现金流量充足率、现金流量对流动负债比率、现金流入及流出比率）等。

根据坏账概率模型，在评价潜在借款人尤其是小微企业的信用时，信贷机构应该考虑的几个财务指标包括现金与资产比例、税息折旧及摊销前利润与资产比例、偿债备付率、负债与资产比例、净收入与销货净额比率。

现金与资产比例是衡量流动性和备付率的一个关键指标。小微企业的现金与资产比例越高说明企业坏账的可能性越小。现金与资产比例显示企业应用现金或流动账户进行良好投资的灵活性。如果手上有现金，企业可以对投资机会作出快速反应。

税息折旧及摊销前利润与资产比例，是衡量小微企业信用的另一个关键性指标，它衡量企业的盈利能力，即企业能够应用设备等资产创造多少收入和现金。

偿债备付率等于税息折旧及摊销前利润除以当前长期负债和应付利息。借款人通常要设定一个可以接受的最低比例，作为借款或合约条件。这个比例越高，越容易获得贷款。类似于放贷中最低月收入与最低月按揭还款的关系，要求企业具有最低程度的金融健康以确保当前债务的偿还。

负债与资产比例是用来比较企业负债与总资产，显示企业资本结构中的股本缓冲情况。比例越大，缓冲能力越小，如果出现冲击现象，企业很有可能倒闭。小微企业的负债与资产比例越低，说明缓冲能力越强，信用评级越高，越容易获得贷款。

净收入与销货净额比率也称销售净利率，它是借贷的底线，是销售收入去除所有费用后的剩余。与其他指标一样，不同产业之间变化很大，行业之间很难进行比较。

在实际操作中，通常信息可得性限制了信用评价的全面性，只能基于可以获得的信息来进行评价，尤其是小微企业包含相当比例的个体工商户，要获得他们的内部信息相当困难。贝多广等（2017）认为，36%的个体工商户没有记账的习惯。即使有财务记账，其信息也是残缺不全的。运作不规范性严重限制了信息的可得性和可靠性。

除了内部信息外，国家征信体系建设也在一定程度上解决了小微企业的信用记录问题。但是，其他外部信息的获得还是一个问题，如税务信息、水电费信息等。部门之间存在信息孤岛，从而增加了获得这些信息的难度和成本。

（二）信用评价数字化

金融科技的发展为小微企业的信用评价提供了一种新的手段。数字信用评价建立在大数据的基础之上，互联网和通信网络的广泛应用，为大数据的收集提供数据源。大数据不仅解决了数据源的问题，也大幅扩展了信用评价的深度和广度，对企业的刻画更加精准，增加了企业风险的预见性，是未来信用评价的主要方向。数字信用评价可以解决当前信用评价中的一些主要问题和矛盾，并进一步建设一个更适合小微企业的信用体系。

二、“值得贷”与“需要贷”

（一）小微企业的定义

在分析小微企业的信用之前，有必要对“小微”进行界定。虽然国家统计局公布了大中小微型企业划分标准（2017 年），但是由于企业的规模处于动态过程，再加上信息掌握的问题，在实际操作中，金融机构无法对企业规模类型作出非常明确的界定。然而，在分析小微企业的信用状况时，我们需要作出明确的划分。国家统计标准从三个维度对企业的规模进行划分：资产总额、营业收入和员工人数。对不同产业的划分标准设有不同的阈值，每一个产业只采用其中两个指标进行划分。大型、中型和小型企业须同时满足所列指标的下限，否则下划一档；微型企业只需满足所列指标中的一项即可。用这个标准我们对在浙江调查的 2729 家民营企业进行分类，如表 14 - 1 所示。

表 14 - 1　企业规模统计分类

企业类型	按员工人数分类（家）	按资产总额分类（家）	按营业收入分类（家）	综合规模分类（家）	比例（%）
微型	1880	46	1090	1984	72.7
小型	619	11	901	692	25.4
中型	17	5	422	53	1.9
大型	—	4	28	0	0.0
合计	2516	66	2441	2729	100.0

资料来源：CAFI 浙江问卷调查。

调查结果表明，即使是在工业比较发达的浙江省，民营企业也几乎很难达到大型企业的统计标准，中型企业也只有 1.9%。微型企业占比将近 3/4。如果普惠金融以“中小微”为服务对象，我们调查的 2729 家企业都属于该服务的范畴。

（二）贷款难与过度贷共存

不是所有的小微企业都有贷款需求，浙江调查样本中只有 62.7%的公司有不同程度的贷款需求。其中，约 54%的小微企业有贷款需要，约 85%的小型企业及中型企业有贷款需求，相差 31 个百分点。表 14 - 2 是 2017 年具有贷款需求的企业的贷款满足情况。总体来看，15.4%的中小微企业的贷款需求没有得到任何满足，21.4%的中小微企业的贷款需求得到部分满足，完全满足贷款需求的中小微企业有 52.7%，有 10.5%的中小微企业的实际贷款超过了企业主认为的贷款需求数额。由于问卷没有进一步追问超额贷款的原因，无法判断为什么会出现这种情况，最有可能的原因是贷款为上年度申请下年初放贷，由于经济形势发生变化，企业主在贷款结束后意识到并不需要那么多的贷款。贷款的实际数额超过需求数额，不一定就是过度贷款。是否为过度贷款，需要根据贷款的额度与企业的现金流和资产情况来判断。

表 14-2 中小微企业贷款满足率

贷款满足情况	中小微企业		小微企业		微型企业		小型企业		中型企业	
	企业数（家）	占比（%）	企业数（家）	占比（%）	企业数（家）	占比（%）	企业数（家）	占比（%）	企业数（家）	占比（%）
没有贷款	264	15.4	261	15.7	198	18.4	63	10.7	3	6.7
部分满足（1%～90%）	366	21.4	348	20.9	178	16.5	170	28.9	18	40.0
完全满足（100%）	902	52.7	884	53.1	597	55.4	287	48.7	18	40.0
超过需求（大于100%）	179	10.5	173	10.4	104	9.7	69	11.7	6	13.3
合计	1711	100.0	1666	100.0	1077	100.0	589	100.0	45	100.0

比较企业规模与贷款满足情况的关系可以发现，完全没有满足的企业比例随着企业规模变小而明显增加：中型企业为6.7%，小型企业为10.7%，微型企业则为18.4%。部分满足和贷款超过需求的情况则相反。这表示部分微型企业存在贷款难问题。

然而，对比不同规模贷款满足率，并没有让我们得到微型企业贷款难的结论，而是企业越小越容易满足。分别有40%的中型企业、48.7%的小型企业、55.4%的微型企业的贷款需求得到完全满足。如果将实际贷款额大于贷款需要纳入考虑，超过53%的中型企业、61%的小型企业、65%的微型企业的贷款需求处于饱和状态。

综合考虑，在当前信用评价体系下，小微企业贷款需求资质低，更容易被银行排斥，存在贷款难问题。然而，一旦小微企业被银行接纳，小额度的贷款需求更容易获得满足，甚至过度饱和。

（三）“值得贷”与“需要贷”矛盾

由于资产信息和收入信息比较容易获得，它们常常是企业规模划分的重要指标，也是信用评价的基础指标。通常认为，企业的资产越小，收入越少，其信用额度越低，获得的贷款额度越小。但是，在我们调查的2729家小微企业中，这种关系并不明显。

如表14-3所示，企业资产总额、营业收入、收入资产比、销售利润率四个常用来评价信用的指标，与融资借款需求、实际贷款、满足率之间的关系系数几乎为零。这个结果表明，企业的资产和收入只是在金融机构眼里“值得贷”的考虑因素；在企业主的眼里，并不是“需要贷”的考虑因素。

表 14-3　企业资产和收入与信贷之间的相关系数

		资产总额	营业收入	净利润	融资借款需求	实际贷款	满足率	收入资产比	销售利润率
微型企业	资产总额	1							
	营业收入	0.0056	1						
	净利润	0.0013	0.4409	1					
	融资借款需求	0.0012	0.0106	0.0087	1				
	实际贷款	0.0020	0.0240	0.0050	0.2541	1			
	满足率	0.0079	0.0741	0.0240	−0.0032	0.5159	1		
	收入资产比	−0.0020	0.0929	0.0862	0.1564	0.0037	−0.0029	1	
	销售利润率	−0.0009	−0.0038	0.2308	−0.0036	−0.0043	−0.0032	−0.0030	1
小微企业	资产总额	1							
	营业收入	−0.0002	1						
	净利润	−0.0021	0.1852	1					
	融资借款需求	−0.0008	−0.0010	−0.0016	1				
	实际贷款	−0.0009	−0.0004	−0.0017	0.9893	1			
	满足率	−0.0006	0.0311	0.0213	−0.0014	0.0341	1		
	收入资产比	−0.0015	0.0393	0.0760	0.0050	−0.0009	−0.0021	1	
	销售利润率	−0.0016	−0.0029	0.2224	−0.0016	−0.0017	−0.0025	−0.0023	1
中小微企业	资产总额	1							
	营业收入	−0.0002	1						
	净利润	−0.0020	0.1853	1					
	融资借款需求	−0.0008	−0.0010	−0.0016	1				
	实际贷款	−0.0008	−0.0004	−0.0016	0.9893	1			
	满足率	−0.0005	0.0311	0.0214	−0.0014	0.0341	1		
	收入资产比	−0.0015	0.0393	0.0760	0.0050	−0.0009	−0.0021	1	
	销售利润率	−0.0016	−0.0028	0.2225	−0.0016	−0.0017	−0.0024	−0.0023	1

进一步分析发现，企业的营业收入有助于信贷需求得到满足。如表 14 - 3 所示，中小微企业营业收入与信贷需求满足率的关系系数为 0.0311，微型企业的此系数还要高（0.0741），这表明在有信贷需求的时候，营业收入较高的企业尤其是微型企业，其小额的信贷需求更容易得到满足。当然这样的关系是非常微弱的，其稳健性需要得到进一步证明。

显然，如果按规模将企业划分为中小微等级，对信用评价并没有很大的帮助。金融机构可以根据企业资产和收入的情况来判断是否“值得贷”，可是企业不完全基于其资产规模大小来决定是否“需要贷”。在需要贷款的情况下，营业收入只是对能否成功获取贷款具有些许帮助。

三、信用、信贷需求与违约风险

提高信用转化为贷款的效率，最好的办法就是找到影响信贷需求和信用评价的共同因子，将信用评价建立在这些共同因子之上。同时，还需要防范过度贷的问题。由于数据的缺乏，我们以收入资产比、销售利润率、过去贷款还款情况、融资借款需求、贷款满足率等指标分别作为信用和贷款需求的代理变量进行回归分析，了解信用、信贷需求和违约风险的关系。

回归模型的解释变量包括法人年龄、性别、受教育程度、企业营业年限、当前注册资金、合同工和临时工人数、员工工资、经营场所面积、应收账款、水电费、企业类型、营业收入、净资产、财务记账、银行账号、支付的利率、抵押和信用等贷款条件，以及补充流动资金、扩大营业规模、启动新投资项目等贷款目的。诊断没有发现这些因素具有共线性。由于篇幅的原因，这里直接对回归模型的结果进行讨论，不描述建模过程和提供模型分析结果。

（一）良好信用可能暗藏违约风险

营业收入与资产比例、销售利润率都是最常用的判断信用的指标。回归分析发现，营业收入与资产比例与企业行业类型、新项目、法人受教育程度和企业经营年限具有显著相关性。新项目增加了营业收入。但是，法人受教育程度和企业经营年限与营业收入资产比例具有负相关性。类似地，销售利润率也与作为流动资金用途的借贷呈负相关关系。这种负相关性都出乎我们的预料。

在样本中，有 77 家企业报告了不能及时还款的情况。在两笔最大的贷款中，其中有 55 家一笔不能及时还款，有 22 家两笔都不能及时还款。回归分析发现，营业收入与资产比例、信用贷款两个变量与之有相关性。营业收入与资产的比例越高，越容易出现违约；信用贷款也会增加违约的风险。

我们更容易接受信用贷款可能增加违约的结果，但是对于营业收入和资产比例与违约的关系，一般的理解是它们之间应该呈负相关关系。这里出现正相关，可能是因为过度贷款造成的。在金融市场竞争比较激烈的浙江省，各金融机构都根据企业的营业收入表现作为信贷决策依据，忽略了企业的其他风险，导致一定程度的过度贷款，从而增加了违约风险。

良好的信用度在给企业增信时，也导致过度贷款的风险。类似地，具备良好教育的法人、经营年限、流动资金贷款等，都与信用等级呈负相关关系。这些指标增加了金融机构对企业的信任，放松了对风险的警惕，在增加贷款可得性的同时，也增加了违约风险。

（二）信用评价与信贷需求的共同影响因子

除了企业行业类型外，对企业贷款需求有显著影响的还有新投资项目。如前所述，这两个因素同样影响营业收入与资产的比例。新项目不但增加贷款需求，还提高资产收入比例，暗示着资产效率的提高。

贷款的满足率与营业收入总额有关，营业收入总额高的企业贷款需求更容易得到满足；同时，当企业为了扩大营业规模而融资时，其申请信用贷款也比较容易得到满足。

值得一提的是，贷款利率水平对贷款需求、满足率、利润率都没有显著的相关性，这说明小微企业对利率的变化并不敏感，只与营业收入与资产比例之间有比较高的负相关系数，统计检验接近于10%的显著水平。类似地，抵押并没有明显增加信贷需求和满足率，这可能是由于金融科技的应用在一定程度上满足了小微企业的信贷需求。

综合上述分析结果，信用评价指标和信贷需求存在共同的影响因子，例如，企业行业属性、新项目开发等因子既影响融资需求又影响企业的营业收入与资产比例。扩大营业和营业收入总额的增加有利于提高贷款的满足率。需要警惕的是，通常用来增信的指标，如营业收入与资产比例、企业主的受教育程度、企业经营年限、较多的信用贷款和流动资金贷款等，在改善信用的同时，也可能增加违约风险。值得反思的是，利息高低和抵押多少并不显著影响信贷需求和信用。

四、小微企业数字化信息体系

数字经济时代已经到来，客户为了获得商品，不仅要支付货币，还要支付数据信息。商业机构通过积累大量的数字信息，对客户进行更加精确的画像，判断客户的信贷需求和信用，使信用评价和需求评估的相关性更强。基于强大的人工智能和数据存储能力，信用评价可以从更加全面的维度进行，从而构建更加完善的数字化体系。

小微企业是一个比较特殊的经济体，类型复杂，介于正式与非正式之间，有效的财务信息数据相对难以获得。对于小微企业而言，非财务信息覆盖的范围相对更加广泛，也更加全面。若要有效地对小微企业进行信用评级，更好地化解“值得贷”和“需要贷”的矛盾，应根据小微企业不同类型的信息，分别构建有针对性的信用评价模型。下面我们对完善数字化信用评价体系所需要的多维度信息分别进行讨论。可以用来对小微企业信用进行评价的信息包括财务信息、税务信息、行业信息、企业主信用信息及交易记录信息。

（一）财务信息

小微企业的履约能力和成长性是信贷机构决定其企业信用的核心因素。信贷机构通过分析企业的财务数据可以判断企业运营资金需求、经营能力、偿付能力等指标，进而对企业信用进行评级。例如，根据企业的资产负债率、流动比率、资本收益率、收入增长等财务指标可以对借款人的还款能力进行分析判断。然而，由于我国的社会信用基础比较薄弱，大多数小微企业的财务透明度比较差，财务制度不规范，甚至部分微型企业根本就没有财务报表，这类小微企业即便能够提供一些财务数据，失真度也比较高，显著增加了贷款违约概率（何光辉和杨咸月，2015）。因此，依赖财务数据来评估小微企业信用通常会导致小微企业的信用评级低、信息不对称、还款风险大等问题，从而导致银行放弃贷款，企业失去融资机会。

（二）税务信息

2015 年 7 月，国家税务总局和中国银监会在全国范围内开启“银税互动”，鼓励税务部门和银行业金融机构探索建立专线、搭建系统平台等方式实现数据直连，通过企业税务信息对企业进行授信。税务数据中有大量可以反映企业第一还款来源的直接信息。按照纳税人、课税对象或纳税环节分类，在我国现行的 18 种税中，与企业经营直接相关的税种包括 5 种，其中增值税、企业所得税是对企业经营情况的直接反映。此外，税务数据更新频率高，增值税相关数据可按月更新；企业所得税相关数据可按季度更新（清华大学互联网产业研究院，2019）。税务信息用于小微企业融资时可输出的企业信息维度包括企业主营商品分析、采购商品分析、销售额排名区间、水电支出等信息。

清华大学互联网产业研究院统计（2019），截至 2018 年 12 月底，千亿元资产规模以上的 89 家银行（包括国有银行、股份制银行、城市商业银行、农村商业银行和民营银行）陆续推出 97 款信贷产品；截至 2018 年 3 月，全国银行业金融机构已累计发放“银税互动”贷款 7933 多亿元。与此同时，第三方金融科技平台也与税务局和银行合作推出“银税互动”信贷产品。在该模式下，第三方金融科技平台基于自身的风控技术优势提供税务信息输出风控模型处理后的企业征信报告。典型的第三方平台包括微众税银、东方微银。据统计，截至 2018 年 11 月，微众税银累计服务 180 万名用户，累计授信额度 400 亿元（艾瑞咨询，2018）。对于“银税互动”等信贷产品，小微企业的税务信息无疑会对小微企业的信用评级产生重要影响。

（三）行业信息

小微企业所处行业的属性对企业信用和违约概率有显著影响。相对于第三产业，制造业通常有一定的场所、机器设备等固定资产，因而信用评级更高，更容易获得贷款；农业企业受惠于政府服务“三农”的政策导向，其受到信贷抑制的可能性也弱于其他行业（王静，2012；何光辉和杨咸月，2015）。对于一般服务业和批发零售业，小微企业处于这些行业的低端市场，其竞争激烈，附加值低，规模较小且抵抗市场波动能力较弱，因而信用评级较低，违约概率较高（何光辉和杨咸月，2015）。

（四）企业主信用信息

相比小微企业数据采集难，对企业主的征信信息的采集更容易实现。个人的信息采集和评估系统相对完善，其稳定性要比企业好得多，因此，小微企业主个人信用状况对小微企业信用评级至关重要。通过分析企业主个人的贷款记录、个人财务能力情况及个人行为可以评估小微企业的履约意愿及能力。Vassiliou（2013）通过对印度小微企业贷款案例分析发现，信用风险影响因素包括企业主经营理念、企业主经营水平、企业主有无违法记录、企业主经营思路、贷款利率、用途等。

以德国国际项目咨询公司（IPC）为例，IPC 是一家专门为以小微企业贷款业务为主的银行提供一体化咨询服务的公司。IPC 模式主要考察借款人偿还贷款的能力、借款人偿还贷款的意愿及内部操作风险的控制。关于客户的还款意愿，IPC 公司会首先评估客户个人的信用状况，具体衡量其包括个人声誉、信用历史、贷款申请的整体情况和所处的社会环境，随后要求贷款人提供严格的抵押品以降低客户的道德风险。该公司凭借 20 多年为小微企业提供金融服务的经验，在 10 多个国家运作小微贷款项目，平均不良贷款率低于 3%（张志勇和吴娇，2014）。

（五）交易记录信息

就支付信息征信贷款模式而言，小微企业的交易记录数据是影响企业信用评级的主要因素。交易数据主要来源于淘宝、京东等电商平台上形成的购销数据，包括网上商铺的交易流水数据和消费者的消费数据。商铺的在线交易流水能够反映其日常经营情况，可作为信贷风控的评价依据。国内主要电商平台通过获得金融业务资质开展中小微信贷业务，主要依据本平台交易数据，服务其网商生态圈内的小微企业。

以阿里巴巴小微信贷为例，阿里巴巴作为国内电商巨头，线上、线下拥有众多商户积累，旗下的蚂蚁金服为阿里巴巴生态圈内的小微企业提供各类贷款服务。从2010年开始，蚂蚁金服旗下的阿里小额贷款公司就为阿里系多个平台上的商户提供小额信用贷款，以帮助平台商户周转资金。在小额贷款公司成立的第二年，阿里巴巴开通了专线直联中国人民银行征信系统，最大限度地丰富了公司所掌握的数据（杨燕，2019）。之后，为了在获取企业生产、销存、销售、人员管理等数据方面拓展更多渠道，小额贷款业务还与以国内中小型企业为客户群的ERP企业管理软件——“管家婆”、全国统一的企业增值税发票开具软件——“航天金税”达成合作，以更好地把握企业的发展经营情况及信用等级（杨燕，2019）。2015年6月，蚂蚁金服将此类业务逐渐转向旗下网商银行的纯线上信用贷款“网商贷”，客户群以淘宝、天猫等电商平台的线上商户及口碑服务等线下码商为主，信用依据是商户在使用电商平台交易、线下扫码支付等进行交易结算时留存的交易数据（清华大学互联网产业研究院，2019）。通常在贷后阶段，传统信贷机构很难知悉贷款资金的使用情况。而在电商平台上，卖家的资金使用行为和运营行为能被部分监控，因此贷款后小微企业的交易行为也会对小微企业的信用评级造成影响。

五、改善宏观信用环境的建议

解决小微企业资金不足问题需要多方共同努力建立一个互惠互利的信用体系，包括资金的提供方（信贷机构）、资金的需求方（小微企业）、相关政府机构、行业协会及媒体机构。

第一，加快培育良好的诚信文化和信用环境。政府和媒体应加大宣传力度，提高社会对小微企业信用体系建设的认识，引导小微企业主动提高信用意识，完善内部信用制度建设。具体而言，可在全国范围内加大诚信经营的宣传力度，鼓励小微企业通过诚信经营、信息公开和规范财务操作，逐步提高和完善自身的信用记录；加大对非法集资危害的宣传力度，引导小微企业避免通过高利贷等非法渠道进行融资。针对当前小微企业普遍存在的财务制度不健全问题，国家相关部门可以出台统一的小微企业财务制度，规范小微企业的采购、付款、销售、资金回笼等财务操作，明确要求需要向金融机构融资的小微企业建立完善的财务制度，便于金融机构通过企业的财务信息准确评估其履约能力、偿债能力和未来的成长性。对长期保持良好信用记录的小微企业，政府应通过补贴等形式鼓励金融机构对其予以优惠。与此同时，为了从制度上遏制小微企业主转移资产、逃废银行债务等行为，应完善对小微企业银行信贷违约的追责机制。

第二，小微企业积极完善内部信用制度建设。信用是企业的无形资产，企业应争取树立良好的口碑，积极积累信用资本。小微企业内部应积极建立符合现代企业制度要求的财务制度和基本的信用制度。以市场交易信用、融资信用、电子商务信用为重点，积极开展企业内部的信用制度建设和普及工作，加强企业内部的合约管理、营销预警、应收账款管理等。同时，培养信用调查分析、评价和监督等方面的专业人才。通过建立企业信用档案、信用评级、信用制度等，不断提升企业自身的信用等级及融资能力。

第三，利用金融科技手段实现信用服务数字化。建立一套完整的征信系统需要工商、银行、商务、税务、人保、法院等各部门的共同努力。2013 年，国务院办公厅出台了《国务院办公厅关于金融支持经济结构调整和转型升级的指导意见》（国办发〔2013〕67 号），意在加速整合政府各部门拥有的信息资源，推动企业信用服务体系的优化和完善。2014 年，国务院出台了《国务院关于扶持小型微型企业健康发展的意见》（国发〔2014〕52 号），中国人民银行随后颁布了《中国人民银行关于加快小微企业和农村信用体系建设的意见》（银发〔2014〕37 号），两个意见明确了小型微型企业信用服务体系建设的具体思路和指导方针。具体而言，就是要充分利用大数据、人工智能和机器学习等金融科技技术，在政府主导下，构建开放的信息共享平台，强化政府部门、商业银行、保险机构、证券公司、担保公司、创业投资机构等专业机构的合作，将各类数据转化为信贷数据，还原小微企业信用水平与风险画像，快速计算出信审结果。

从普惠、共赢及社会信用体系建设的角度，以各类数据为核心，运用金融科技服务小微企业信贷服务，前景十分广阔，可以提升社会整体效能。小微企业最大的特点就是变化快、波动大、抗干扰能力弱。因此，在小微企业的征信过程中，需要通过参考更全面的信息对小微企业作出公平、公正的信用评级。大数据对软信息的提炼反映出更加动态的征信效果，使其更加契合小微金融的征信需求（贝多广和李焰，2015）。此外，大数据征信不受地域限制，可以形成广泛的征信覆盖面，对于小微金融客户众多、流动性强的特点来说，大数据征信可以充分发挥信息扩散度和影响面大的优势，通过提高声誉机制约束力，增加客户违约成本（贝多广和李焰，2015）。

第四，加速建立科学规范的信用服务指标体系。小微企业信用服务指标体系的构建是小微企业征信系统建设的关键环节，因此需要对现有的信用评级指标体系进行不断地改进、优化和完善，以适应小微企业的信用特征（张晓静，2017）。针对小微企业的具体情况，应根据企业规模、企业家素质、所在行业、财务状况、无形资产等方面的差异及信用评价和信贷需求的共同因子构建全面的信用服务指标体系。指标初步选定之后，还应选择有代表性的企业进行体系测试，根据测试结果优化和完善适合小微企业的评级指标体系，构建针对小微企业的科学规范的信用评估体系。

第五，加速构建小微企业担保服务体系及增信措施。小微企业自身资金实力差、抗风险能力低是各国小微企业普遍存在的问题。政府通常在小微企业融资体系中扮演着融资支持者、信用保障者和市场环境建设者的角色。鉴于小微企业在国民经济发展和就业中的重要地位，各国都普遍采取了专项基金、政府担保、政府采购等辅助的增新措施。针对小微企业轻资产、缺乏有效抵押物等问题，可设立国家层面和地方政府层面的信贷风险专项基金、成立专门为小微企业融资提供担保的政府性担保公司，统一相关政策和制度，扩大对小微企业的覆盖范围，帮助小微企业融资增信（吕逸楠，2013）。与此同时，在大力推进小微企业信用担保体系建设中，为鼓励担保机构提高对小微企业担保业务规模、降低对小微企业的担保收费，政府可对符合条件的信用担保机构实施免征营业税政策，加大各级财政资金的引导和支持力度，从而进一步解决银行业等金融机构在支持小微企业时面临的风险分担问题，调动金融机构支持小微企业发展的积极性，降低小微企业融资成本。

案例

商通贷：多渠道服务小微企业

一、服务定位

随着宜信多年在普惠金融领域的深耕细作，宜信的普惠金融服务也朝着规范化、专业化、数字化和规模化的方向发展。具体到普惠金融服务产品战略方面，宜信提出了“三步走”战略，分别是小额信贷、微金融和能力建设。商通贷同宜人贷、宜农贷、宜信租赁等产品共属于小额信贷战略的组成部分，但是不同的产品聚焦的客群不同。商通贷聚焦的客群是小微商户，为其提供在线实时信贷服务，高效快捷地解决小微企业的融资需求。

商通贷从 2015 年开始发展以来，产品的类型和业务思路与宜信普惠金融服务整体的战略思路相吻合，即利用金融科技释放客户的信用价值，让金融更加贴近客户，助力实体经济发展。商通贷通过与多种类型的合作商合作，综合利用小微商户的交易记录、税务、财务数据等信息，充分运用自身成熟的金融科技能力进行高效的风控，提供符合客户自身经营状况和需求的贷款。

二、产品特点分析

经过四年的发展，商通贷累计注册用户突破 60 万，共为来自 70 余个行业的几十万家小微企业提供了信贷服务，构建起商通贷、小微企业和合作伙伴三方的闭环合作关系。目前，商通贷累计交易金额超过57亿元。在用户体验方面，以纯线上信用贷款为主，申请与审批过程总共在10分钟内即可完成，借款期限最多为24个月，额度方面可选范围较大，从2万～100万元均可，综合最低月成本可低至0.67%，还款方式以等额本息与先息后本为主，目前整体产品不良率[①]控制在4%以内，整体资产质量表现良好，资金来源主要以宜信自身的P2P平台和互联网小额贷款公司为主。

商通贷目前针对不同的客群主要有两类产品，一类是电商贷，主要的客群为内贸与外贸的电商商户，通过与全球网店平台或服务机构合作，根据网店的实际经营数据进行大数据风控以提供信贷服务。目前电商平台的合作伙伴包括淘宝、天猫、京东、苏宁、Ebay、亚马逊、Wish、Lazada等，涉及内贸与外贸多种电商商家。

商通贷第二类产品为数据贷，即通过与小微企业主服务平台建立合作伙伴关系，根据小微企业主实际经营在线数据进行信贷。这类平台主要以小微企业的税务平台、ERP、餐饮类平台为主，包括畅捷通、管家婆、二维火、金蝶等，获取仓储管理、物流管理、财务管理及运营管理等多种数据类型。

综合两类产品，商通贷目前主要通过不同的合作方，依靠小微企业客户的财务数据、税务数据、企业主信用数据、交易记录等数据对小微企业进行信贷审批。按照各种合作平台划分的借贷余额如图所示：

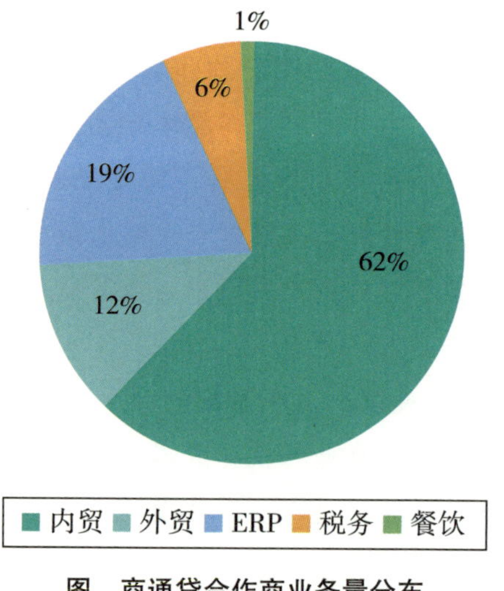

图　商通贷合作商业务量分布

① 此处的不良率是指超过180天的逾期的资产比例。

由此可见，在商通贷产品内，内贸类即国内的电商平台占据主导地位，这也与商通贷的发展过程相呼应，商通贷在初始阶段聚焦于国内各大电商平台的小微商户，后来逐渐推广到外贸电商和数据贷产品。由于不同合作方所从事商业活动的特征、数据的质量与特点均不同，商通贷所服务的客户群体更加广泛，在不断开拓新产品的同时，商通贷需要不断完善自身的数据分析能力和风控能力，以适应不同平台甚至不同行业特征的客户。

在额度方面，目前纯信用的信贷产品额度普遍偏低，这与大数据风控技术的数据积累相关。商通贷产品对于额度较大的信贷业务，也需要进行一定程度的人工干预以保证资产质量，这也与行业普遍的业务做法一致，线上线下相结合的方式更加适合额度稍大的小微企业信贷业务。

参考文献

[1] 中华人民共和国统计局．可支配收入差距变化情况［DB/OL］．http：//www. stats. gov. cn/ztjc/zdtjgz/yblh/zysj/201710/t20171010_1540710. html，2017.

[2] 中国普惠金融研究院．最后一公里到最后一厘米：金融聚合器在数字生态系统中的角色转变［R］．BFA，2018.

[3] 于转利，罗剑朝．小额信贷机构的全要素生产率——基于 30 家小额信贷机构的实证分析［J］．金融论坛，2011（6）.

[4] 何光辉，杨咸月．中国小微企业信用违约影响因素的实证检验 ——来自某国有银行地区分行的证据［J］．上海财经大学学报（哲学社会科学版），2015（6）：67－79.

[5] 何颖．日本金融消费者保护制度改革［J］．日本学刊，2011（1）.

[6] 刘彦谡．浅析我国金融消费纠纷解决机制存在的问题和改进［J］．成都理工大学学报（社会科学版），2011（1）.

[7] 刘思芹，陈威．金融消费纠纷多元化解决机制的层次体系［J］．财会月刊，2018（12）.

[8] 刘晓蓉．金融申诉专员制度对我国的启示［J］．中国商论，2018（27）.

[9] 何娅．基尼系数：城乡历史政策的解构［DB/OL］．http：//www. stats. gov. cn/tjzs/tjsj/tjcb/zggqgl/200704/t20070411_37555. html.

[10] 叶挺舟．国际视域下的中国金融消费者保护 ADR 路径探析［J］．西南金融，2013（11）.

[11] 周翀．金融消费纠纷多元化解决机制研究［J］．现代经济信息，2017（17）.

[12] 国家信息中心分享经济研究中心．中国共享经济发展年度报告［R］．2019.

[13] 国家市场监督管理总局．全国市场主体数量［R/OL］．http：//www. samr. gov. cn/xw/tp/201811/t20181106_289856. html.

[14] 国家法官学院案例开发研究中心．中国法院 2018 年度案例 · 金融纠纷

[M]. 北京：中国法制出版社，2018.

[15] 国家统计局 . 全国居民人均可支配收入基尼系数 .

[16] 国家统计局 . 2000—2017 年经济增长与进出口、就业的关系 .

[17] 国家统计局 . 城乡储蓄增长与城镇收入差距变化的关系 .

[18] 国家统计局 . 不同阶层的收入结构 .

[19] 国家统计局 . 农村居民不同收入水平家庭纯收入增长情况 .

[20] 国家统计局 . 进出口增长与收入增长的相关系数 .

[21] 国家统计局 . 从基尼系数看贫富差距 [DB/OL]. http://www.stats.gov.cn/tjzs/tjsj/tjcb/zggqgl/200210/t20021024_37364.html.

[22] 张志勇，吴姣 . 德国 IPC 微贷技术对大型商业银行的启示与借鉴 [J]. 河北金融，2014 (11) .

[23] 张晓静 . 小微企业信用服务体系发展的现状和对策研究 [J]. 中国集体经济，2017 (7)：86 - 87.

[24] 新华社 . 银保监会：2018 年末普惠型小微企业贷款余额 9.36 万亿元 [DB/OL]. 新华社，2019.

[25] 李庚南 . 差异化监管：小企业信贷商业化可持续的内在要求 [J]. 中国农村金融，2011 (8).

[26] 李敏 . 金融科技的监管模式选择与优化路径研究——兼对监管沙箱模式的反思 [J]. 金融监管研究，2017 (11).

[27] 杨东 . 我国金融消费者保护的统合立法体系的构建——以日本的立法经验借鉴为视角 [J]. 社会科学，2013 (81).

[28] 杨燕 . 蚂蚁小贷：普惠金融的社会价值 [N]. 中国经营报，2019 - 06 - 03.

[29] 杨虎峰，何广文 . 小额贷款公司经营有效率吗——基于 42 家小额贷款公司数据的分析 [J]. 财经科学，2011 (12).

[30] 洪玫 . 资信评级 [M]. 北京：中国人民大学出版社，2006.

[31] 清华大学互联网产业研究院 . 金融科技在小微企业信贷中的应用发展研究报告 [R/OL]. https://www.useit.com.cn/thread - 23276 - 1 - 1.html.

[32] 王华庆 . 完善金融消费权益保护机制 [J]. 中国金融，2012 (22).

[33] 王力为 . 金融监管改革应设立消费者保护机构 [DB/OL]. 财新网，2016 - 04 - 22.

[34] 王静，张文彬 . 小微企业银行信贷抑制：因素、程度与影响——基于浙江台州市的经验研究 [J]. 中国市场，2012 (50)：41 - 47.

[35] 皮特·斯帕布姆，艾瑞克·迪弗洛. 中华人民共和国的金融普惠状况——对

现有研究和公开数据的分析［R］．CGAP，2012.

［36］罗豪才，宋功德．软法亦法——公共治理呼唤软法之治［M］．北京：法律出版社，2019.

［37］艾瑞咨询．中国互联网消费金融行业报告［R］．2017.

［38］董晓琳，高瑾．小额贷款公司的运营效率及其影响因素——基于江苏227家农村小额贷款公司的实证分析［J］．审计与经济研究，2014（1）.

［39］贝多广，李焰．好金融　好社会——中国普惠金融发展报告（2015）［M］．北京：经济管理出版社，2016.

［40］贝多广，等．普惠金融能力建设［M］．北京：中国人民大学普惠金融研究院，2017.

［41］贝多广，莫秀根．超越普惠金融［M］．北京：中国金融出版社，2017.

［42］贝多广，顾雷．重塑我国金融消费者权益保护机构［N］．金融时报，2018-07-16.

［43］费孝通．乡土中国·生育制度［M］．北京：北京大学出版社，1998.

［44］贾晓雯．双峰监管：理论起源、演进及英国监管改革实践［J］．海南金融，2018（5）.

［45］赵峰．金融监管治理的指标体系：因应国际经验［J］．改革，2010（9）.

［46］邢会强．金融消费纠纷的多元化解决机制研究［M］．北京：中国金融出版社，2012.

［47］门植渊．如何运用大数据防控互联网金融犯罪［N］．检察日报，2016-10-25.

［48］顾雷．海龟派PK土鳖派：互金监管向左or向右？［DB/OL］．OBT商业科技观察，2019-01-10.

［49］黄宗智，李强．中国非正规经济（上）［J］．开放时代，2011（1）.

［50］国家统计局．历年城乡收入差距．

［51］王靖一．现金贷果如洪水猛兽？——来自断点回归设计的证据［J］．金融研究，2018（11）.

［52］叶文辉．互联网现金贷平台存在的风险和监管对策［J］．武汉金融，2017（10）.

［53］巴曙松，黄文礼，许南燕．现金贷的风险来源分析及其监督［J］．武汉金融，2018（4）.

［54］艾瑞咨询．2018年中国小微企业融资报告［R/OL］．https：//www.useit.com.cn/thread-21366-1-1.html，2018.

[55] 吕逸楠．小微企业信用体系建设若干问题的探讨 [J]. 对外经贸，2013（5)：137－138.

[56] 中国人民银行征信中心．征信系统建设运行报告（2004—2014）[R]. 2015.

[57] 黄宗智，李强，等．中国非正规经济（上）[J]. 开放时代，2011（1).

[58] Laura Brix，Kathatine Mckee. 低可得性环境下的金融消费者保护监管——发展负责任金融的契机 [J]. 西部金融，2011（11).

[59] 赖丹妮，张亦辰．P2P 网贷机构的问题、诱因与可持续发展对策 [J]. 中国经贸导刊（中)，2019（3).

[60] 单晗杰．网络交易中消费者隐私权保护问题研究 [D]. 宁波：宁波大学硕士学位论文，2017.

[61] 高锡荣，杨康．网络隐私保护行为：概念、分类及其影响因素 [J]. 重庆邮电大学学报（社会科学版)，2012（4)：18－24.

[62] 韩迎春．网购消费者个人信息保护研究——基于电商经营者义务的角度 [J]. 佳木斯大学学报（社会科学版)，2019（1).

[63] 陈剩勇．互联网平台企业的网络垄断与公民隐私权保护——兼论互联网时代公民隐私权的新发展与维权困境 [J]. 学术界，2018，242（7)：39－52.

[64] 刘成玉，徐丹．小额信贷利率市场化对农民金融服务的影响及保障政策探讨 [J]. 农村经济，2014（15).

[65] 中国人民银行赣州市中心支行课题组. 市场分割与信贷配给：利率市场化的体制及经济效应 [J]. 金融研究，2006（1).

[66] 催收已成小贷“主业”：全国三分之一小贷公司处于停业、半停业状态 [DB/OL]. http：//www. oeeee. com/mp/a/BAAFRD00002017022227917. html.

[67] 中国银行业监督管理委员会．中国人民银行关于小额贷款公司试点的指导意见（2018).

[68] 莫秀根．国际普惠金融前沿趋势与经验启示 [J]. 中国银行业，2018（6).

[69] 潘素梅，周立．格莱珉银行的反传统模式及金融普惠 [J]. 银行家，2016（1).

[70] 穆罕默德·努鲁·阿拉姆，迈克·葛图比，安德里亚·芬德利，等．格莱珉模式小额信贷项目创建和运营指南 [M]. 格莱珉基金会，2012.

[71] PITTIGLIO RABIN TODD，MCGRATH. 产品及生命周期优化法 [M]. PRTM 公司，1986.

[72] 腾讯 Fit Design，价值在定义——腾讯金融产品体验设计之作 [DB/OL]. https：//www. fitdesigh. com，2018.

［73］IPD 在华为成功的 6 个原因［DB/OL］. http：//baijiahao. baidu. com/s?id=1598685286567116016.

［74］陈晓俊 . 揭秘头部 P2P 平台借款人画像［DB/OL］. 网贷之家，https：//www. wdzj. com/news/yanjiu/4394774. html.

［75］李建勇，宋明莎 . 中国投资者教育现状调查报告（2018）［N］. 证券时报，2019-03-07.

［76］A. S. P. F. and P. ROBERT. Digital Labour Markets in the Platform Economy-Mapping the Political Challenges of Crowd Work and Gig Work［M］. The Friedrich-Ebert-Stiftung，2017.

［77］ARMSTRONG M. Competition in Two-Sided Markets［M］. University College London，2002.

［78］BAKER M. J. and S. HART. The Marketing Book［M］. Routledge，2016.

［79］BASSEM B. S. Efficiency of Microfinance Institutions in the Mediterranean：An Application of DEA［J］. Transition Studies Review，2008（15）：343-345.

［80］BECK T. and A. D. L. TORRE. The Basic Analytics of Access to Financial Services［R］. Working Papers，2006.

［81］BERNARD C. and J. BRUNO. Chicken & Egg：Competition among Intermediation Service Providers［R］. 2002.

［82］BERTAND M.，et al.. A Behavioral Economics View of Poverty［J］. American Economic Review，2004（94）：419-423.

［83］CGAP Implementing Consumer Protection in Emerging Markets and Developing Economies：A Technical Guide for Bank Supervisors［J］. Washington，DC，CGAP.

［84］CGAP. Costing Tool，CGAP，2004.

［85］CGAP. Customer Centric Guide Executive Summary［R］. Responsible Finance：Putting Principles to Work，2017.

［86］CHIEN J.，et al. Good Practices for Financial Consumer Protection 2017 Edition［R］. World Bank Group，2017.

［87］COLLINS D.，et al. Incorporating Consumer Research into Consumer Protection Policy Making.［R］. Focus Note 74，2011.

［88］COPESTAKE J. Mainstreaming Microfinance：Social Performance Management or Mission Drift［J］. World Development，2007，35（10）：1721-1738.

[89] CORDANA P. and M. MILAN. Two-stage DEA Use for Assessing Efficiency and Effectiveness of Micro-loan Programme [R]. The 7th Balkan Conference on Operational Research, 2005.

[90] CRACKNELL D. Electronic Banking for the Poor-Panacea, Potential and Pitfalls [R]. 2004.

[91] CRACKNELL D. and M. Hermann The Art and Science of Pricing Financial Services.

[92] DAVID B., et al. The Rise of the platform Economy [J]. Science and Technology, 2016.

[93] DEVELOPMENT C. O. G. A. The Growth Report-Strategies for Sustained Growth and Inclusive Development [R]. The World Bank, 2008.

[94] G20/OECD Update Report on the Work to Support the Implementation of the G20 High-Level Principles on Financial Consumer Protection G20/OECD.

[95] GUTIÉRREZ-NIETO B., et al. Social Efficiency in Microfinance Institutions [R]. 2006.

[96] HAQ M., et al. Efficiency of Microfinance Institutions: A Data Envelopment Analysis [R]. 2010.

[97] HELMS B. Access for All: Building Inclusive Financial Systems [R]. CGAP, 2006.

[98] HOLLIS A. and A. SWEETMAN . Microfinance and Famine: The Irish Loan Funds during the Great Famine [R]. 2006.

[99] Hong Kong Association of Banks and the DTC Association, H. K. M. A. Code of Banking Practice, Hong Kong Association of Banks and the DTC Association [R]. Hong Kong Monetary Authority.

[100] IANCHOVICHINA E. and S. LUNDSTORM. What is Inclusive Growth [R]. World Bank, 2009.

[101] INDUSTRY D. F. T. A. The Annual Percentage Rate and Total Charge for Credit Inconsumer Credit Regulations [DB/OL]. from www. dti. gov. uk.

[102] IRELAND C. B. Code of Conduct on the Switching of Current Accounts with Credit Institutions [R]. Central Bank of Ireland, 2016.

[103] ITU. Consumer Experience and Protection [R]. 2017.

[104] ITU. Guidelines Governing the Protection of Privacy and Transborder Flows of Personal Data ITU-T Focus Group Digital Financial Services, Consumer

Experience and Protection ITU [R]. 2017.

[105] KIM B. C. , et al. Two-Sided Platform Competition in the Online Daily Deals Promotion Market [R]. 2012.

[106] KING R. G. and R. LEVINE . Finance and Growth: Schumpeter Might be Right [J]. The Quarterly Journal of Economics, 1993: 717 - 737.

[107] KUZNETS S. Economic Growth and Income Inequality [J]. The American Economics Review, 1955: 1 - 28.

[108] LEDGERWOOD J. Microfinance Handbook: An Institutional and Financial Perspective World Bank [R]. The World Bank, 1999.

[109] LITTLEFIELD E. , et al. Is Microfinance as Effective Strategy to Reach the Millennium Development Goals [R]. Focus Note, 2003.

[110] MAZER R. , et al. Applying Behavioral Insights in Consumer Protection Policy [R]. Focus Note 95, 2014.

[111] NGHIEM H. S. , et al. The Efficiency of Microfinance in Vietnam: Evidence from NGO Schemes in the North and the Central Regions [R]. Centre for Efficiency and Productivity Analysis, 2006.

[112] OECD . G20 High-level Principles on Financial Consumer Protection [R]. OECD, 2011.

[113] PORTEOUS D. When Does Competiton Reduce Microcredit Interest Rates [R]. CGAP, 2011.

[114] QAYYUM A. and M. AHMED. Efficiency and Sustainability of Micro Finance Institutions in South Asia [R]. Islamabad, Pakistan Institute of Development Economics, 2006.

[115] RANIERI R. and R. A. RAMOS. Inclusive Growth: Building up a Concept [R]. 2013.

[116] ROCHET J. C. and J. TIROLE. Two-Sided Markets: An overview [M]. IDEI University of Toulouse Working Paper, 2004.

[117] ROCHET J. C. and J. TIROLE. Two-Sided Markets: A Progress Report [J]. Rand Journal of Economics, 2006, 37 (3): 645 - 667.

[118] SEIBEL H. D. History Matters in Microfinance [J]. Small Enterprise Development-An International Journal of Microfinance and Business Development, 2003, 14 (2): 10 - 12.

[119] SIMANOWITZ A. Microfinance, Poverty and Social Performance:

Overview [R]. 2003.

[120] STEIN P. S. , et al. Toward Universal Access: Addressing the Global Challenge of Financial Inclusion [R]. IFC, 2011.

[121] BECK T. , et al. Access to Financial Services: Measurement, Impact, and Policies [R]. 2009.

[122] BECK T. , et al. Finance, Inequality and the Poor [R]. 2007.

[123] Commision on Growth and Development. The Growth Report-Strategies for Sustained Growth and Incusive Development [R]. The World Bank, 2008.

[124] BRUCK, CONNIE. A Reporter at Large: Millions for Millions [J]. The New Yorker, 2006, 1 - 13.

[125] HUDON, MAREK. Fair Interest Rates When Lending to The Poor [J]. Ethics and Economics, 2007, 1 - 8.

[126] MCKINSEY, IIF. The Future of Risk Management in The Digital Era [R]. 2017.

[127] MCQUINN, ALAN, WEININGG GUO, DANIEL CASTRO. Policy Principles for Fintech [J]. Information Technology & Innovation Foundation, 2016.

[128] MIT. Digital Banking Manifesto: The End of Banks [R]. 2016.

[129] WORLD BANK. Crowdfunding's Potential for the Developing World [R]. 2013.

[130] WORLD BANK. Measuring Financial Inclusion and the Fintech Revolution [DB/OL]. The Global Findex Database, 2017.

[131] BANK W. Financial Capability in Low-and Middle-income Countries: Measurement and Evaluation [R]. 2013.

[132] DISNEY R. , GARHERGOOD J. Financial Literacy and Consumer Credit Portfolios [J]. Journal of Banking and Finance, 2013 (37): 2246 - 2254.

[133] NETEMEYER R. G. , WARMATH D. , FERNANDES D. , LYNCH J. J. How Am I Doing? Perceived Financial Well-Being, Its Potential Antecedents, and Its Relation to Overall Well-Being [J]. Journal of Consumer Finance, 2017 (11).

[134] VAN ROOJ M. , LUSARDI A. , ALESSIE R. Financial Literacy, Retirement Planning, and Households Wealth [J]. Economic Journal, 2012 (122): 449 - 472.

在本书编写过程中得到了以下单位的支持和协助

（排名不分先后）：

蚂蚁金服

度小满金融

美国大都会人寿基金会

美团金服

智惠乡村志愿服务中心

Bankable Frontier Associates（BFA）

国际农业发展基金